A History of
Transportation in
the Ohio Valley

River parade of Pittsburgh towboats of bygone days showing large storage of coal for shipment

A History of Transportation in the Ohio Valley

with special reference to its waterways, trade, and commerce from the earliest period to the present time

by

CHARLES HENRY AMBLER
Professor of History, West Virginia University

GREENWOOD PRESS, PUBLISHERS
WESTPORT, CONNECTICUT

Copyright © 1931 by The Arthur H. Clark Company

First Greenwood Reprinting 1970

SBN 8371-2905-2

PRINTED IN UNITED STATES OF AMERICA

Contents

Preface	13
The Ohio River	17
The Boatmen and their Craft	31
The Boatmen as Nation Builders	59
Shipbuilding on the Inland Waters	81
The First Steamboats west of the Alleghanies	107
The Day of Canals and Turnpikes	133
The Heyday of the Passenger Packet	161
Railroad *versus* River	185
Intermunicipal Rivalries	211
The Civil War Period	239
Post-bellum Days to 1900	265
The Coal Trade	295
Life and Customs	319
Commercial Decadence	347
Floods and Disasters	369
Internal Improvements	393
Recent Years on the Rivers	423
Index	451

Illustrations

RIVER PARADE OF PITTSBURGH TOWBOATS OF BYGONE DAYS	Frontispiece
THE FLATBOAT	39
THE KEELBOAT	facing 42
MIKE FINK, HERO OF THE KEELBOATMEN, AND COMPANIONS	55
WILLIAM MASON'S MAP OF PITTSBURGH, 1805	95
THE FIRST STEAMBOAT ON THE OHIO RIVER *	117
THE STAGE-COACH	135
THE CONESTOGA OR COVERED WAGON, THE "VEHICLE OF EMPIRE"	135
A PORTAGE BOAT *	145
VIADUCT AND TOWPATH ON THE PENNSYLVANIA CANAL *	145
THE "WASHINGTON," BUILT 1820, AT CINCINNATI	175
From an early woodcut in the possession of Frederick Way, Jr.	
THE "MESSENGER," FAVORITE OF THE FIRST PITTSBURGH AND CINCINNATI PACKET LINE	175
From a contemporary print. Courtesy of Henry Holt and Company.	
MAP SHOWING RAILROADS IN THE UNITED STATES, 1850-1860	187
THE CHESAPEAKE AND OHIO RAILROAD PACKET, "FLEETWOOD"	281
STEAMER "KATE ADAMS," THE "LOVIN KATE," BUILT AT JEFFERSONVILLE, IND., 1899	281
MAP SHOWING BOAT-LANDINGS ALONG THE OHIO, ABOUT 1900	289
TYPICAL ROUSTERS OF THE LOWER OHIO AND MISSISSIPPI	339
Courtesy of Waterways Journal.	

ILLUSTRATIONS

THE "CITY OF CINCINNATI" 383
    Wrecked by the ice gorge of January, 1918, at Cincinnati.

DAM NUMBER 1, MONONGAHELA RIVER, BUILT IN 1840 * . 419
    The now obsolete comb type of timber construction.

LOCKS AND FIXED DAM, EMSWORTH, PA. 419

THE "IOWA" OF 2000 HORSE-POWER * 431
    With three barges containing 6000 tons of iron pipe at Lock number 2, Ohio river.

THE "SAM CRAIG," APRIL 16, 1930 * 435
    With a tow of 10,000 tons of steel.

MAP SHOWING IMPORTANT WATERWAYS AND HIGHWAYS IN THE UNITED STATES ABOUT 1836 449

Preface

The purpose of this book is to give an historical account of transportation in the Ohio valley with special reference to its waterways, trade, and commerce. The early phases of this subject are somewhat hackneyed, and its later phases, except the spectacular, have been almost completely neglected. It is the hope of the author that these may be given their historical settings and their proper relations to other events and conditions. It is his belief that those who have helped in the more recent decades and generations in making our country what it is today are deserving of some attention along with the "pioneers." As will be seen, however, the fields of transportation were never without their pioneers, the transportation facilities of any age of American history being inadequate to its needs and thus serving as a constant stimulus to initiative and invention.

The sources used comprise practically all the available public documents bearing upon the subject of transportation in the Ohio valley, but chief reliance, particularly for local color and intimate accounts, was upon newspapers. Of these, Pittsburgh and Cincinnati papers proved most helpful, but newspaper files found in both Charleston and Wheeling, West Virginia, were storehouses of information for the decades before the Civil war. For the more recent decades extensive use was made of the *Waterways Journal*, published in St. Louis. Information gathered through interviews with scores of former rivermen, most of whom have passed on within the last ten years, at ages well in the eighties and the nineties, aided the author in the interpretation of data gathered otherwise, as well as in his efforts to lend life and color to his narrative. It is hoped that a liberal use of footnotes will make unnecessary an extended and critical bibliography.

For the most part, the subject matter of this book is presented more or less chronologically, but for the purpose of economizing space, some chapters, such as those on the coal trade, internal improvements, life and customs, and floods and disasters, are presented as separate topics. In this arrangement some duplication was unavoidable, but it is hoped that it will be helpful rather than confusing.

For many kindnesses and courtesies of librarians and for assistance from friends, given in the twelve years this work was in progress, the author makes grateful and general acknowledgments. Special mention is due Dr. L. D. Arnett, librarian of the West Virginia University, whose resourcefulness was a constant aid; to my wife who read each and every chapter and offered helpful suggestions; to my colleagues and associates in the faculty of the West Virginia University, Professor David Dale Johnson of the department of English, who read the entire manuscript and made constructive criticisms, and Professor J. M. Callahan of the department of history, who read most of the chapters and rendered like aid; to Assistant Professor Louis K. Koontz of the University of California at Los Angeles, Associate Professor Fred A. Shannon of Kansas State Agricultural College, Manhattan, Kansas, and Professor Carl Wittke of Ohio State University, Columbus, Ohio, each of whom read the entire manuscript and contributed to its form and substance; to the late Captain Edward P. Chancellor of Parkersburg, West Virginia, who aided in collecting and evaluating materials; to Captain Thomas M. Rees of James Rees and Sons Company, Pittsburgh, who made corrections contributing to a greater degree of accuracy; and to John W. Black, editor of *National Waterways*, Pittsburgh, for permission to use illustrative material, as well as helpful assistance in selecting it. To the score or more students in the West Virginia University, who aided him in so many ways, the author can extend only a general acknowledgment. For possible errors in statements of fact and in interpretations, as well as for important omissions, he alone assumes entire responsibility.

CHARLES HENRY AMBLER

West Virginia University
Morgantown, West Virginia
December 12, 1930

The Ohio River

There is a lingering glory about many of the streams of inland America, that is not easily forgotten. Some of them have unique and unsurpassed beauty; others are rich in association and tradition. It is doubtful whether any rivers of the world have a more romantic history than those that led Marquette and La Salle into the heart of an unexplored continent and those by which American pioneers crossed the Alleghanies into the Ohio valley to build homes and rear families. To the initiated the impressions and memories of these rivers are not unlike those that come from watching the flights and habits of native birds, from watching the sun and planets in their course and the flowers and grains in season. They are the essence of patriotism.

Of all these rivers the Ohio, known to French explorers as the "Beautiful River," is the most beautiful, as well as the most important. There are grander and more majestic streams, even in America, but there are few anywhere of such graceful loveliness. On a broad scale its banks suggest the soft and pastoral landscapes of the German Neckar and the Main, with their constant successions of curves and gently rounded hills, according in their natural state, with as true a harmony as that of music. More important still, the Ohio is the main thoroughfare between the Atlantic coast and the Mississippi valley. By way of its waters, more than any other route, a whole continent was peopled.

Some persons develop interest in and love for the

Ohio; others inherit them. One boy, born and reared near its banks in the last quarter of the nineteenth century, discovered them. It was a mid-summer afternoon, and he was on his way to a blacksmith's shop for the repair of a part belonging to a mowing machine. As he hastened along a winding dirt road, impelled by an urgent paternal request for haste and by the warning rays of the declining sun, he came up close behind a supposed tramp leisurely moving before him. At that time, possibly more than now, tramps were a bane to the life and happiness of country boys, and the thought of passing this one on the public highway struck terror into the heart of his unwilling follower, but there seemed to be no other alternative. Accordingly he pressed forward hoping that some favorable turn of fortune, such as comes to country boys, would save him from the frightful possibilities of the situation. Thus sustained he came within speaking distance of the forbidding stranger, whose gentle voice and kindly manner soon arrested his haste and quieted his suspicions. A short conversation disclosed the fact that the supposed tramp was in reality a professor in a noted German university and that he was then on a tour of America, having already seen much of Europe and Asia.

Forgetting the importance of his errand and the lateness of the day, the youth surrendered himself to the influence of the professor and continued the journey with him. As they walked on together, talking of the beauties of the Rhine and the comparative size and importance of certain European and American cities, they suddenly turned another curve in the road and came out upon a high point overlooking the Ohio, as it wound its course through the distant hills to the southwest, and gradually disappeared in the golden rays of the setting sun. The view was at that time only commonplace to the boy and aroused no emotions in him, but to the professor it was new and appealing. For a few minutes he stood motionless, silently gazing into space. Indeed, his manner was such as to revive a feeling of fear within his companion, who again thought only of a means of escape. Luckily the suspense was only momentary. Turning to him with a beaming and reassuring smile, the professor said: "This is the most beautiful river I have ever seen. It is more beautiful than the Rhine."

Increasing familiarity with geography gave this youth greater appreciation of the Ohio as a natural course of empire. To the eastward of the Alleghanies he found numerous rivers easily accessible to the Ohio by way of portages. To the west were a number of streams having their sources in these mountains and in the region immediately south of the Great Lakes. The latter streams the Ohio gathered into one and pointed a common course to the west. Indeed, it seemed that nature had conspired in this arrangement to aid the well known course of empire.

To those who lived on and near the Ohio forty years ago it was a wonderful stream. Information about it was general. Many got this from actual contact; others as they did folk songs and nursery rhymes; a few learned only from school-masters. The significant thing is that this information was general and approximately correct. For example, all knew that the Ohio was about one thousand miles long; that one-fourth of the water reaching the Gulf of Mexico through the mouth of the Mississippi came from it; that the total area drained by it and its tributaries was approximately two hundred thousand square miles; that its high water mark was more than sixty feet above its low water mark; that its source was more than four hundred feet higher than its mouth; that the Falls at Louisville were the greatest in its course; and that its total navigable waters, together with those of its tributaries, aggregated more than four thousand miles.

But it was the natural features of the Ohio that made abiding impressions. There were the precipitous banks rising from one hundred to four hundred feet in height and extending their cliffs and forests to the very margin of the stream. Opposite these, with almost unvarying regularity, were broad alluvial bottom lands, the sites of farms and even cities. Then there were beautiful islands and islets, more than a hundred in number, some of which are still the domain of the forest primeval. But more enticing still, were the silvery rapids, the low monotony of the sweeping current, the threatening white caps, and the splendid beauty of the river as a whole.

Before its improvement and the intrusions of industry the Ohio had moods all its own. In the winter season it sometimes retired from the world, clothing itself in a coat of ice and snow. When summer came it grew intimate, even coquettish. Bathers and picnikers frequented its banks, and at low water stages men and kine sometimes crossed its course over paths almost dry, so modest and gentle could this mighty stream become. In fact gentleness and serenity were the normal traits of the Ohio. But for occasional "freshets," it never lost its poise and dignity. When these came the rush of its waters was tremendous, the force of its currents irresistible. These outbursts depopulated lowlands, covered the bosom of the river itself with the wreckage of homes and industry, and temporarily spread fear and dismay in the hearts of every living creature within its environs. Fortunately ice floes and destructive floods were infrequent. As soon as they were gone, however great their damage to life and property, all was forgiven and almost forgotten. Nothing adverse to "the River" was ever long remembered; only the ice floes and floods were blamed.

Moodishness is not the only element of uncertainty about the Ohio. Its very name is hidden in obscurity, both as to its meaning and as to its origin. Most writers on the subject agree as to its Indian origin, but few are in accord as to the meaning of the word Ohio. Some adhere to the French interpretation which makes it mean "the Beautiful River," *La Belle Riviere.* To others Ohio means simply fine or fair. Still others adhere to the translation of the Moravian missionary, John G. Heckewelder, who, after an exhaustive study of the subject, made with a view to correcting the French translation, concluded that the word Ohio was derived from the Indian word "Ohi," a prefix meaning "very," and that it was also frequently used by the Indians in a combination of words meaning "the white foaming river," descriptive of the Ohio when covered with white caps. Among early geographers common names were applied to the Ohio and the Wabash, and also to the Ohio and the Allegheny.[1] It is possible that the original meaning of the word Ohio has not been and never will be determined.

For our purposes tributary streams are second only in importance to the Ohio itself. First of all are those that unite to form it, the Allegheny and the Monongahela, each with its particular characteristics, some of

---

[1] Hulbert, A. B. *The Ohio River, a course of empire* (New York, 1906), 2-4.

which are recognizable hundreds of miles distant from these rivers themselves. This is especially true when the ice runs. That from the Monongahela usually comes first and is coarse and cloudy; that from the Allegheny is clear as crystal and floats deep in the water. The latter of these tributaries reaches far into New York, while the former winds its way north through one of the richest coal fields of the world.

Most of the lateral tributaries of the Ohio flow from the south. Advancing from its source towards its mouth, the most important of these are the Little Kanawha, the Great Kanawha, and the Big Sandy, each extending eastward to, and in the case of the Great Kanawha beyond, the top of the Alleghanies and tapping some of the richest mineral lands of the continent; then come the Kentucky and Green rivers, natural outlets for the famous Kentucky blue-grass country, followed in turn by the Cumberland and the Tennessee, connecting it, as they do, with both the Old South and the Cotton states, and giving the Ohio valley a temperature varying all the way from the sub-tropical to the north temperate. To the north, proceeding in the same direction, there are the Muskingum, Scioto, Miami, and Wabash with accompanying minor streams, which reach well to the Great Lakes.

The area drained by the Ohio and its tributaries has been described as a "land of milk and honey." However faulty this characterization may be, the Ohio valley does embrace everything needed to make another England, together with the lumber of Norway, the wines and fruits of Germany, France, and Italy, and the cotton of India. In all his travels Henry Clay had never seen a "section for which God had done so much and man so little." It is significant that the great river at or near the center of this region is the only one of importance flowing from east to west in North America and that the mountains surrounding this area shelter natural resources sufficient in quantity and quality for an ideal workshop of the world.

Of such a river and its tributaries one naturally expects to find much in both history and literature, and much is to be found. But accounts, even the historical, are almost as evasive as is the river itself. Of the scores who have written about the Ohio few have found objects of common interest, and these objects have made separate and individual appeals. But they wrote of changing times and conditions. This was true even of proper names. But for the abiding quality of names, however, there is little in common between the writers of today and those of a hundred years ago, who took the Ohio and its environs for their themes.

But why expect uniformity or even consistency in the writings of those who have preserved the history of the Ohio river? They wrote of life and change without which there is no history and no description worth while; they dealt with the course of universal history epitomized within a few generations; they told the story of the transformation of a "long shining aisle through a fair green world" into a great thoroughfare of commerce surrounded with all that exalts and embellishes civilized life; they told of the growth of small societies into great and populous commonwealths, each, in turn, influenced more or less by that residuum of ideas and efforts left by a constant tide of immigrants moving to the task of founding still other commonwealths beyond the Mississippi.

There is not even certainty as to who first discovered the Ohio and when. French accounts attribute discovery to Robert Cavalier de la Salle. In his search for a stream thought to lead to the long-sought South Sea he is said to have reached the Ohio at or near what is now Louisville in 1669, two years before a party sent out by Abraham Wood from what is now Petersburg, Virginia, discovered the New river, an affluent of the Great Kanawha; but historians now agree in attributing priority of discovery to the English.[2]

It was, however, the geographer Franquelin, through maps made in 1688, who gave the first authentic information regarding the Ohio and its tributaries. Already it was known to English and French traders whose wares were soon descending its waters and laying the basis for an international feud that determined the destiny of empires and peoples.

Despite the glowing accounts of discoverers and the subsequent impressions made on those who lived near it, the Ohio has not appealed to everyone. To some, in fact, it has been quite repelling. To those who first saw it there was something in the problems involving its mastery to inspire awe and to challenge the genius of the most resourceful. Its whirling eddies, its treacherous shoals, its lurking logs and snags were veritable terrors to the boatmen. The havoc of its floods and ice gorges and its overhanging vines and trees bade defiance to the Indians. The absence of important native villages upon its banks, at the time of discovery, was significant.

Except for short reaches, the sites of Indian cornfields, the upper Ohio, at the time of the earliest white explorers, was lined on each side by one continuous forest, the branches of which dipped into its waters

---

[2] Alvord, C. W. and Lee Bidgood. *The First Explorations of the Trans-Alleghanies by the Virginians, 1650-1674* (Cleveland, 1919), 96.

THE OHIO RIVER

and at the narrowest places almost spanned its course. Its waters and forests teemed with life. There was the agile pike, the fat groveling cat-fish, and the silver scaled perch; bison and deer quenched their thirst in its waters; and, in his birch bark canoe, the Indian warrior pursued his enemy and wooed his dusky mate. Then, too, birds of many varieties, some permanent inhabitants, others coming only in the spring and the autumn, found homes or temporary resting places on its banks. Among these birds were the bald eagle and the turkey buzzard that soared in safe retreat above the hills that lined its course.

In its natural and most beautiful state the Ohio was a thoroughfare of traffic. The craft most used was the canoe, long since dedicated to savage warfare and romance. The period of its supremacy, which has been fittingly called the Canoe Age, was one of the longest and most interesting in the history of inland navigation. Although the rivers of the Ohio valley may have been secondary to trails in these days, they were, nevertheless, important thoroughfares. They had a part all their own in the fur trade, and, as has been said, over their balmy waters the Indian made war and love. The numerous mounds and battlefields that dot their banks seem to point to a day of even greater usefulness. Could they break their silence, it might be to tell stories of river activities rivaled only by those told of the Nile and the Euphrates in the dawning days of civilization.

Before the coming of the whites the craft of the Canoe Age had become standardized. First there was the two-place canoe, twelve to fourteen feet in length, carrying two passengers and three to four hundred pounds of freight. Next came the four-place canoe, twenty feet long, with a carrying capacity of four persons and one to two thousand pounds. Finally there was the master canoe, thirty-six feet long, four feet wide, and two and one-half feet deep, with a capacity of fourteen persons and several thousand pounds of freight.[3] When suitable barks could not be secured and more substantial craft were required, "dugouts" were made by hollowing a log, durability and lightness making that from the cypress tree a favorite. Sometimes canoes were also made by stretching hides of native animals over frameworks of wood. It was by the use of such a craft that John Howard and others, in 1742, descended the Ohio and the Mississippi all the way to New Orleans.[4]

The skill and dexterity of native artisans in the fabrication of canoes and kindred craft were, indeed, marvelous. In emergencies little more than a day sufficed to find a suitable tree, strip it of its bark, fit this to the desired shape, and patch, caulk, and pitch the whole in such a fashion as to make it serviceable for long journeys. It required longer to make a dugout but scarcely less skill. A tree was felled and fabricated to the desired state, fire and crude implements being used for both purposes.[5]

Like the craft of other periods in the history of inland transportation, canoes continued to be used beyond the period they dominated. They were admirably suited to the needs of the white explorer and the trader. With little care they could be used to float down stream in safety, and for light traffic they could be moved against currents with dispatch. Moreover, the end of navigation did not destroy their usefulness, for they could be

---

[3] Chambers, H. E. *Mississippi Valley Beginnings* (New York, 1922), 22.
[4] *Virginia Magazine of History and Biography* (Richmond, 1893-date), vol. xxx, 203.
[5] Dunbar, Seymour. *A History of Travel in America* (Indianapolis, 1915), vol. i, 21-25, 281.

carried across portages and used to continue expeditions that would otherwise have been impossible. It was with the aid of canoes that La Salle made his voyages of exploration; that Celeron, in 1749, descended the Ohio to take formal possession of the Ohio valley for the king of France; and that George Washington and others subsequently penetrated the Transalleghany to assert ownership for the English and to spy out new lands.

During the last years of this period the chief services of the canoe were to the fur-trader.[6] By its use English traders are thought to have reached the Ohio shortly after 1700. Years before that date La Salle found merchandise of English origin among Indians on the Mississippi. Twenty years later the French complained of the presence of English on the Ohio, and before another generation ended this primitive age of transportation witnessed a conflict between the English and the French to determine the ownership of the Ohio valley.

Despite the priority of English discovery, the French claims to this region were well founded. Very early in the eighteenth century they established themselves at Kaskaskia, Vincennes, and other points near the mouth of the Ohio. From this region they built up a trade to the lower Mississippi which is said to have begun as early as 1705, when a quantity of fur was sent thence to New Orleans. This trade continued to increase in volume until the French and Indian war, by which time the primitive craft formerly used on the Mississippi had been displaced by a more adequate one, the galley bateau,[7] which will be described in the next chapter.

When the English took possession of the upper Ohio

---

[6] Clark, C. M. *The Picturesque Ohio* (Cincinnati, 1887), 33-53.

[7] U. S. House. *Executive Documents*, 50 cong., 1 sess., vol. xx, no. 6, pt. ii,

valley in 1758 as a result of the surrender of Fort Duquesne, they renamed that fortress, calling it first Fort Pitt and finally Pittsburgh. A census taken two years later showed its total population to be one hundred forty-nine persons; eighty-eight men, twenty-nine women, and thirty-two children. All were sheltered and otherwise accommodated in one hundred forty-six houses and thirty-six huts. The following year the population almost doubled, and local taverns began to be frequented by trappers, traders, mule drivers, and pioneer farmers. Nearly everyone there drank heavily, and almost everyone was a fugitive, if not from justice, certainly from creditors. Drunken Indians staggered through the village and yelled as if on the war-path, and white traders were unabashed with temporary wives, some of them squaws. With few exceptions churches and schools were unthought of in this typical frontier outpost, as yet more barbarous than civilized.[8]

Nevertheless, the English were even then planning a great future for this strategic point, the "Forks of the Ohio." First of all it was to be made an emporium of trade surpassing in importance both Quebec and New Orleans. Already curious natives were seeking it in increasing numbers to learn the character and plans of their new masters. As usual, they expected presents and trade, and the exigencies of the situation seemed to dictate liberality on the part of the English in providing both. Already pack-horses and wagons were reaching the upper Ohio more or less regularly. They brought provisions for garrisons, presents for natives, and articles of merchandise.

---

179 of Wm. F. Switzler's "Report on the Inland Commerce of the United States."

[8] Volwiler, A. T. *George Croghan and the Westward Movement, 1741-1782* (Cleveland, 1926), 214.

As a result of these developments the volume of traffic on the Ohio increased, and its primitive craft no longer served adequately the needs of transportation. As with the French on the Mississippi, the galley bateau came into favor with the English on the Ohio, and the Canoe Age on that stream practically ended. Following the subsequent failure of the English to build up a great inland commercial center at Pittsburgh, French and Indian traders to the west, upon whom they were dependent, preferring to trade with former customers in Canada and in Louisiana and finding it easier to move with river currents than against them, primitive conditions gained a new lease on life in the region of the upper Ohio, and the canoe again came temporarily into use as the chief means of commercial intercourse. But homeseekers were already knocking at the gates of the West. Defying royal proclamations and imperial policies, they could not be denied admission. With their coming, in the years immediately following 1765, the Canoe Age on the Ohio passed forever, as did much of its primitive beauty.

The Boatmen and their Craft

The Revolutionary period in America marked the beginning of a new era in the transportation history of the Ohio valley. From the outstanding craft used it has been fittingly called the Flatboat Age. Had the naming been with reference to navigators rather than to craft, it would doubtless have been the Boatman Age. As already indicated the craft of the former period now almost completely disappeared. The dugout held on somewhat longer than did the canoe, particularly on the lower Ohio and with the French on the Mississippi, but it, too, soon entered the discard.

The first impetus to this change came with the termination of the French and Indian war and the subsequent collapse of the so-called Conspiracy of Pontiac. The English now took permanent possession of the Ohio valley, and traders, accompanied in some instances by actual settlers, began to reach the upper Ohio in considerable numbers, stationing themselves along the Monongahela and in the vicinity of Fort Pitt. Of these movements George Croghan wrote: "As soon as peace was made last year contrary to our arrangements to them a number of our people came over the Great mountain and settled near Redstone creek and upon the Monongahela before they [the Indians] had given the country to the King, their Father." [9] Referring again to the same movement a letter from Winchester, Virginia, dated April 30, 1765, said: "The

[9] *Western Pennsylvania Hist. Mag.* (Pittsburgh, 1918-date), vol. ii, 115.

frontier inhabitants of this colony and Maryland are moving fast over the Alleghany mountains in order to settle and live there." [10]

Meanwhile private individuals and firms were making active preparations to participate in the Indian trade on the Ohio. Two rival firms, Baynton, Wharton, and Morgan, predominantly Quaker, and David Franks and Company, predominantly Jewish, were especially active. In 1765 and before England had taken formal possession of the Ohio valley, the former of these firms tried to send merchandise to Fort Pitt under protection of a convoy carrying presents from George III to be used by that prince of pioneer diplomats, George Croghan, in an effort to win the friendship and trade of wavering Indian tribes. Fearing the consequences of reopening the Indian trade, especially that in arms and ammunition, frontiersmen in Cumberland county, Pennsylvania, fell upon this convoy, killing pack-horses, destroying merchandise, scattering drivers, and jeopardizing the prestige of Croghan who was personally interested in the success of Philadelphia traders. Nevertheless, he was permitted to continue his negotiations with the Indians, which resulted in opening up the entire Ohio valley to free and uninterrupted trade with the English.[11]

Thus it was that Fort Pitt first became a boat building center. The most profitable trade thence was with the Illinois country. To reach it from the upper Ohio it was necessary to traverse the whole course of that stream, and suitable craft therefore became imperative. As early as 1765, Baynton, Wharton, and Morgan established a boatyard at Pittsburgh for the fabrication of galley bateaux and other craft. Materials, except

[10] — *Idem*, 116.   [11] Volwiler, *op. cit.*, 180-190.

timber, were carried all the way from Philadelphia by packhorses and wagons, six hundred of the former being employed at one time by this one firm. In a short time sixty-five boats had been completed; three hundred rivermen were navigating the Ohio; and merchandise valued at £50,000 was finding a market in the interior.[12]

As already indicated, the Indian trade of the Ohio valley was a great disappointment to the English, but the Treaty of Fort Stanwix, 1768, paved the way for a new era. Scarcely had this treaty been concluded, before a tide of settlers began to pour across the Alleghanies. During the spring and summer of 1770 they were coming in continuous streams, the arrivals for the years immediately preceding aggregating between four and five thousand. While on a visit to the Trans-alleghany in 1770 George Washington found that all the best lands along the southern bank of the Ohio from its source to the Little Kanawha had already been taken, and he predicted that another year would suffice to carry the land grabbers to the Great Kanawha.[13] His prediction came true, the tide of westward-moving settlers growing larger during each of the years immediately following. The Revolution decreased this volume somewhat but did not turn it back. Thus, by 1780, the best lands in what is now northern West Virginia and southwestern Pennsylvania were taken, and the first English-speaking frontier west of the Alleghanies was tending to become a land of steady habits.

---
[12] — *Idem*, 203-204, 225-230.
[13] *Old South Leaflets* (Boston, 1883-1894), vol. ii, general ser., no. 41, p. 12; Washington, *Writings* (New York, 1889-1893. ed. Ford), vol. ii, 310; see also Alfred P. James's "The First English-speaking Appalachian Frontier," in *Miss. Valley Hist. Review* (Cedar Rapids, Iowa, 1919), vol. xvii, 55-71.

Independence and the treaty by which it was assured augmented the volume of immigrants passing into the Trans-alleghany. By the latter the United States acquired all the lands to the west between the Alleghanies and the Mississippi. Meanwhile, in some of the older sections to the east times were hard and discontent was general. Accordingly many persons sought an opportunity to begin life anew under more favorable conditions. As usual they went west, but the numbers now seeking that refuge were unprecedented. Failing to find suitable lands on the upper Ohio, they turned their course to Kentucky.

It was under these conditions that Pittsburgh again became a boat building center, although boats had been built along the Monongahela during the Revolutionary period.[14] Arrived at either Redstone (Brownsville) or Pittsburgh, the immigrant's chief concern was for a suitable boat, the primitive craft of the natives being inadequate for the transportation of large families, most of them with household goods, farming implements, and domestic animals. In fact, each family desired a craft suited to its particular needs. To supply these, boat building was undertaken on a large scale, skilled artisans from the East being employed to direct it. By 1783, Elizabeth, Pennsylvania, was advertising for sale "boats of every dimension,"[15] together with provisions of all kinds, particularly flour. Cargoes, both passenger and freight, were supplied from the East by the use of pack-horses and wagons and, after 1783, largely by the Conestoga wagon which, with the pack-horse, formed an important link in the transpor-

---

[14] Volwiler, *op. cit.*, 179 ff., 190-200; Thurston, George H. *Allegheny County's Hundred Years* (Pittsburgh, 1888), 99-101; Thwaites, R. G. editor. *Early Western Travels* (Cleveland, 1904-1907), vol. i, 53-173.

[15] *Western Pennsylvania Hist. Magazine*, vol. ii, 116.

tation system to and from the interior. This importance will justify more than passing mention of each of these means of transportation.

Pack-horses usually moved in trains which wound their way over former Indian trails and improvised roads that then crossed the Alleghanies. The most frequented of these were called "tote-roads," "pack-roads," or simply "horse-ways." Some idea of the volume of traffic passing over them may be had from the fact that many of them were worn into deep gullies, the banks of which brushed the sides of passing horses and sometimes dislodged their burdens.

The age of pack-horse travel to and from the headwaters of the Ohio extended from about 1760 to near 1790. Just before and after the Revolution thousands of horses and mules were employed in this service. Taverns and ferries, towns and villages, sprang up along the most popular routes, and some of these towns became popular centers of entertainment. Among these was Carlisle, Pennsylvania, on the Lancaster-Bedford route, where as many as five hundred horses, with drivers, were frequently cared for over night.[16]

In time the pack-horse business became systematized, taking the form of an organized and established service in the hands of a few persons who owned most of the animals used, employed drivers and packers at more or less fixed wages, and made contracts for the transportation of persons and goods. So well established did this business become that subsequent invasions of its

[16] Earle, Alice Morse. *Stage Coach and Tavern Days* (New York, 1900); Dunbar, *op. cit.*, vol. i, 192-200; Doddridge, Joseph. *Notes on the Settlement and Indian Wars of the Western Parts of Virginia and Pennsylvania from 1763 to 1783* (Wellsburgh, Va., 1824); Monette, John W. *History of the Discovery and Settlement of the Mississippi Valley* (New York, 1848), vol. ii.

field were looked upon as destructive of vested interests and were resented accordingly.

In his *Notes*[17] Joseph Doddridge left an excellent description of the organization and progress of a pack-horse train engaged in carrying salt over a part of what is now "U. S. 40."

In the fall of the year, after seeding time, every family formed an association with some of his neighbors for starting the little caravan. A master driver was selected from among them, who was to be assisted by one or more young men and sometimes a boy or two. The horses were fitted out with pack saddles, to the hinder part of which was fastened a pair of hobbles made of hickory withes, — a bell and collar ornamented their necks. The bags provided for the conveyance of the salt were filled with feed for the horses; on the journey a part of this feed was left at convenient stages on the way down, to support the return of the caravan; large wallets well filled with bread, jerk, boiled ham and cheese furnished provisions for the drivers. At night after feeding, the horses, whether put in pasture or turned out into the woods, were hobbled and the bells were opened.

The barter for salt and iron was made first at Baltimore; Fredrick, Hagerstown, Oldtown, and Fort Cumberland, in succession, became the place of exchange. Each horse carried two bushels of alum salt, weighing eighty four pounds to the bushel. This, to be sure, was not a heavy load for the horses but it was enough, considering the scanty subsistence allowed them on the journey. The common price of a bushel of alum salt, at an early date, was a good cow and a calf.

The Conestoga wagon first came into general use on the overland routes across the Alleghanies about 1783.[18] As soon as roads were laid out in the American frontier, it, in one form or another, followed the pack-horse until the Pacific coast was reached. The form used for transportation across the Alleghanies seems to have originated near Lancaster, Pennsylvania. It probably took its name from that of a tributary of the Susque-

---
[17] Ritenour and Lindsey edition (Pittsburgh, 1912), 12.
[18] U. S. Department of Agriculture. *Report* 1863, 178.

hanna. By 1790 it had practically superseded the packhorse as a popular means of communication between the East and the West.

In size and appearance the Conestoga wagon was a huge structure, heavily built, with broad wheels suited to dirt roads and a bed higher at either end than in the middle, so as to prevent its contents spilling out in going up or down hill. It was topped by a dull white cloth, curved so as to present a rather artistic appearance. All exposed wood work was painted, the under body blue and the upper parts red. Thus, when not covered with mud, the colors of this pioneer vehicle might have suggested those used for the national flag.

This "vehicle of empire" was drawn by four to six horses, the driver generally riding a wheel-horse. Sometimes it moved in solitary grandeur, at other times in immense caravans that stretched uninterruptedly for miles. Its slow but steady progress accompanied by the rumbling of wheels, the creaking of harness, and the weeping and singing of women and children told of an advance that knew no retrogression. The Conestoga wagon was, in fact, one of the most distinctively American devices of all our transportation history.

Its contributions, together with those of the packhorse, are numerous and varied. In the wake of the latter and the "pony express" this "frigate of the land" did the pioneering for the canal boat and the locomotive. Like the automobile it accelerated the construction of turnpikes, the Cumberland road and other highways being direct results of its use. The contributions of each to the manners and customs of the Appalachian mountain region are even more varied. To this day those residing there are good judges of horse flesh; the Pennsylvania Dutch and their Scotch-Irish neighbors "pack" articles of merchandise and other things, including babies, instead of carrying or "toting" them, as do people elsewhere; and entertainment, as practiced in the early taverns and hostelries of the Alleghany mountain region, took on a leveling and democratic form that has characterized it to this day, in the West.

For our immediate purposes the greatest contributions of the pack-horse and the Conestoga wagon were to the river traffic of the interior. As has been indicated, they supplied cargoes in such quantities as to make necessary a new age in inland river transportation. It must not be inferred, however, that the flatboat was the immediate result of their use or that it was used exclusively. Like most other craft used on the inland waters, the flatboat evolved and was used contemporaneously with numerous other boats.

Some of these craft were unique. One such was a semi-mechanical device suggesting the steamboat, built at Fort Pitt in 1761 by William Ramsey. As described by a Quaker trader, James Kenny, it consisted of two small boats joined together by a swivel in such a way as to make one. This boat was propelled by wheels attached to a treadle which was moved by the feet of the operator. Although devices of this kind proved impractical, it was claimed that this boat could turn in a shorter space than could smaller boats and that it could rise over falls with great safety.[19]

Most of the craft of this period were non-mechanical and of local origin, but ideas for others were borrowed from the East and even from Europe. A confusing local terminology and an overlapping in time and geography make it difficult for any present day writer to name accurately and describe even the important boats of this

---

[19] Thurston, *op. cit.*, 99-100.

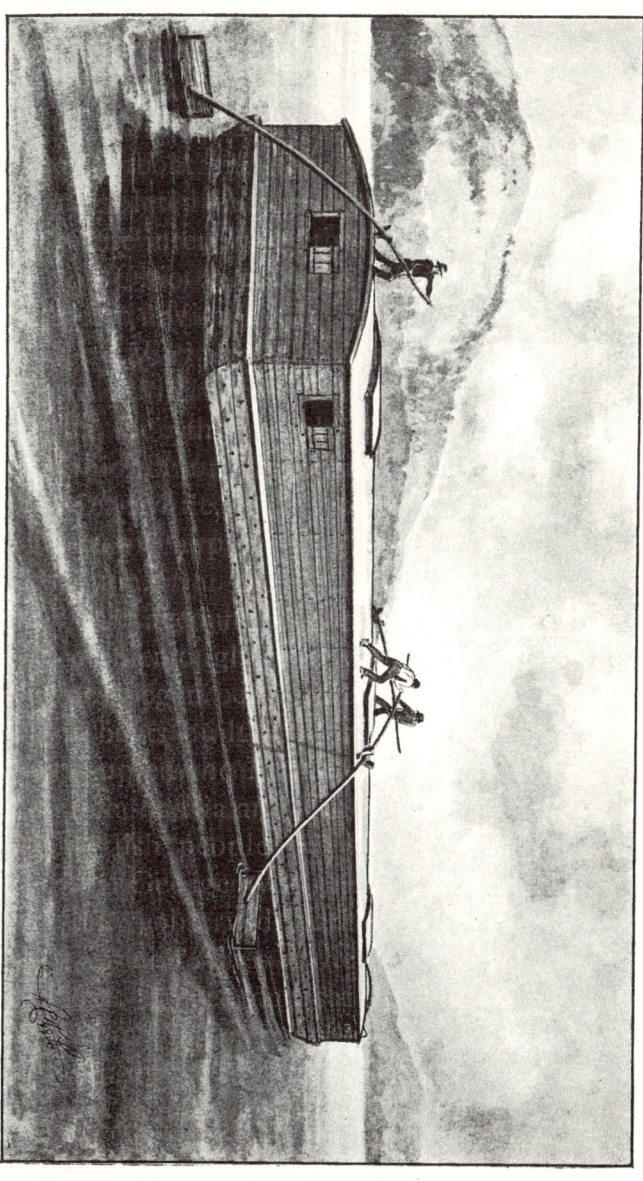

THE FLATBOAT

The boat that "never came back," being sold for lumber on reaching destination. An average of 3000 flatboats descended the Ohio river every year between 1810 and 1820

period. In this effort some have wished for aid from the antiquarian, in the hope that he might yet be able to find specimens of these pioneer craft. During the greater part of this period one could have built or bought, almost anywhere on the waters of the upper Ohio, any of the following craft of local origin: flatboat, ark, barge, broadhorn, Kentucky boat, and New Orleans boat. Among the importations or modifications were skiffs, bateaux, and, toward the middle of the period, packet-boats.[20]

Of all these craft the flatboat was easily the most popular and the most useful. It was a favorite with "moving families," hence its importance and preëminence. In size flatboats varied greatly, the earliest ones being built with reference to the particular needs of the numerous families using them. Generally speaking, they included anything that could float from the primitive raft to the mammoth barge. Those in most general use were rectangular structures boarded up at both sides to a height of from two to three feet. The poorer sort had no covering but were provided with a shed in the rear for horses and cattle and a cabin forward for the use of the owner and his family. Others, those used for short trips, were partly covered and were called Kentucky boats, or broadhorns. Those used for longer trips were known as New Orleans boats and were covered throughout their entire length. As a rule these were more substantial than those built for local uses.

All forms of flatboats were propelled by "sweeps"

---

[20] Dunbar, *op. cit.*, vol. i, 280-288; Flint, Timothy. *Recollections of the Last Ten Years* (Boston, 1826); U. S. House, *op. cit.*, 185; McKnight, Charles. *Our Western Border* (Philadelphia, 1876). See, also, Pittsburgh *Gazette Times*, November 24, 1924; *idem* (Sunday), September, October, and November, 1917, for a series of articles by George T. Fleming.

alongside, a long oar astern, which served as a rudder, and by a short oar in front known as the "gouger." Sails and oars were sometimes used, but main reliance was upon the current. Every flatboat was provided with a "hawser" which was used to "whip" it over sandbars and riffles. The "hawser" was simply a strong rope which was made fast to a tree or stump on shore and wound by a reel on board the boat after the manner of the "cordelle" used on the Mississippi.

In both popularity and usefulness the flatboat had a close second in the keelboat which, during a long period, was the only practicable craft on the inland waters for up-stream uses. Although not of local origin it was well suited to its purposes. It was built about a long heavy piece of timber called the keel which was so placed as to absorb the shock of collisions. The frame, or hull, was built of stout planks and was ribbed like a ship. It was from thirty to seventy-five feet long, the cost of construction being determined by the length of the boat, prices varying from two-fifty to three dollars per running foot. In width keelboats varied from seven to nine feet. Most of them carried masts and sails. The body of the boat was usually covered for the protection of passengers and cargoes. Its capacity varied from fifteen to forty tons.

Keelboats were steered from the stern by the use of a long swing oar, although their course was sometimes determined by the use of poles in the hands of those who supplied motive power. A walk, or running board, extended on either side the entire length of the boat. Each boat carried from six to eighteen "hands," as its size and the conditions of navigation determined, more power being required when waters were low and rapids swift. It required great power and patience to move a

THE KEELBOAT

Prior to the steamboat, the only practicable craft on inland waters for the transportation up-stream of both passengers and freight.

boat of any kind against the current of the Ohio. The favorite method was "poling." Advancing to the prow the crew, being divided equally on either side, "set" their long sharp poles on the bottom of the stream and pushing against them with shoulders to the "sockets," walked slowly from prow to stern. At the command "lift" they returned to the prow and repeated the operation in unison at the word "set." In very swift water pole-men did not work in unison but always in such a fashion as to hold every inch gained. It was only with the greatest care and physical exertion that the swiftest rapids could be passed. The slightest error on the part of any member of the crew might cause the boat to "swing," thus driving it upon the rocks. Any boatman responsible for such a mishap or one who had been compelled to "back water" in a "chute" usually lost caste among his fellows.

The barge was a cumbrous craft resembling an Atlantic schooner of its day. It was from thirty to seventy-five feet long, from seven to fifteen feet wide, and carried a mast, sails, and a rudder. Progress down stream was sometimes accelerated by an oar. For up-stream use motive power was supplied by numerous men, twenty-five to fifty, who used iron-tipped poles to push against the current. Barges were covered either wholly or in part, and sometimes carried cannon for defence. During troublous times they anchored at night and posted sentries, few landings being made by any craft at other than fortified places or permanent settlements before 1794. The barge was a pioneer craft and soon gave way almost completely to the more practicable and elegant keelboat.

After the termination of Indian hostilities the ark came into general use. It was from seventy-five to one hundred twenty feet long, from fifteen to twenty-five feet wide, and from three to five feet deep. It was built of heavy timbers covered by planks and was sometimes V-shaped at both bow and stern. Its size and unwieldiness restricted it to down stream uses, a long sweep sufficing to keep it in the channel. Like the flatboat it, too, sometimes supported two wooden houses, one at either end, that in front being for passengers, the other for animals.

Skiffs and bateaux were flat bottomed boats of the same general construction and propelled by oars, bateaux being much the larger. They were each built of strong planks and were ribbed. The former were used for ferries, for long distance trips requiring dispatch, and, in the earliest days, to attend larger craft in receiving and discharging freight. In its crudest form, no ribs being used, the skiff became a "Johnboat" and, as such, was used largely as a ferryboat on small streams. Bateaux accommodated whole families and were used for long and hazardous journeys. They were also used for the transportation of military parties.

From these craft there evolved, in time, the packet-boat which was used in 1794, when a regular packet service was first established on the Ohio. These boats were of the galley keelboat type and were from seventy-five to one hundred feet long. They were armed and covered so as to make them bullet proof, thus suggesting the modern cruiser. They were floated and rowed down stream, but progress against currents was made by the use of poles in the hands of pole-men after the manner of the keelboatmen. For passing riffles and shoals the "cordelle" or "hawser" was sometimes used. Despite the difficulties encountered, these packets maintained a regular schedule between Cincinnati and

Pittsburgh, the time for a round trip being one month.

"Having maturely considered the many inconveniences and dangers incident to the common method heretofore adopted of navigating the Ohio, and being influenced by a love of philanthrophy, and a desire of being serviceable to the public," the proprietors of the above mentioned packet line advertised the following accommodations: "A separate cabin from that designed for the men is partitioned off in each boat for accommodating the ladies on their passage. Conveniences are constructed on board each boat, so as to render landing unnecessary, as it might at times be attended with danger. Rules and regulations for maintaining order on board, and for the good management of the boats, and a table accurately calculated for the rates of freightage, for passengers, and carriage of letters to and from Cincinnati to Pittsburgh; also, a table of the exact time of the arrival and departure to and from the different places on the Ohio between Cincinnati and Pittsburgh may be seen on board each boat, and at the printing office in Cincinnati. Passengers will be supplied with provisions and liquors of all kinds, of the first quality, at the most reasonable rates possible. Persons desirous of working their passage will be admitted, on finding themselves subject, however, to the same order and directions from the master of the boats as the rest of the working hands of the boat's crew. An office of insurance will be kept at Cincinnati, Limestone, and Pittsburgh, where persons desiring to have their property insured may apply. The rates of insurance will be moderate." [21]

---

[21] Cincinnati *Centinel*, January 11, 1794; Dunbar, *op. cit.*, vol. i, 303; Hulbert, *op. cit.*, 230; Hall, James, *The West, its commerce and navigation* (Cincinnati, 1848), 117.

All boats of this period were subjected to numerous hazards such as would test the patience and alertness of any master. Worst of all probably were attacks by Indians and by river pirates. During the years immediately preceding Wayne's victory at Fallen Timbers, 1794, which broke the savage power in the Northwest, they took a toll in excess of fifteen hundred persons along the Ohio alone. Probably the most offensive feature of these losses was the fact that they were sometimes planned and abetted by renegade whites. It was in one of these attacks that Captain May, founder of Maysville, Kentucky, lost his life.

It was in this period that a group of notorious pirates composed of French, Spanish, Indian, American, and half-breed renegades infested the lower Ohio. Their rendezvous was Cave-in-Rock located about twenty-five miles below old Shawneetown, Illinois. Here they were sheltered by an overhanging cliff, from which they had a commanding view of the river both up and down stream. From this strategic point these pirates studied and systematized murder and robbery. The unusual conditions served to conceal the extent of their depredations, which terrorized the whole inland waters from Pittsburgh to New Orleans.[22]

Other perils were more natural and consequently less irritating, although equally destructive. Probably most serious of these were trunks and limbs of trees imbedded in river bottoms so firmly and at such angles as to inflict serious injury to the craft of nonsuspecting and uninformed navigators. An obstruction of this kind that moved slowly up and down with periodic action under the influence of waves, winds, and currents was

---

[22] Rothert, Otto A. *The Outlaws of Cave-in-Rock* (Cleveland, 1924) chap. 3; Dunbar, *op. cit.*, vol. i, 298-300.

called a "sawyer," whereas one so firmly planted as to be immovable under such influences was a "planter." Other perils were "falling banks," "floating islands," and stationary masses of trees and driftwood known as "wooden islands." In fact, every inland river had its own well-known danger spots, most of which received their names from previous accidents. The mere mention of such places to old boatmen sufficed to produce a reflective ejection of tobacco juice and to start a narrative of some harrowing incident in their history.[23]

The commercial hazards of this period were not, however, all in the field of navigation. Modern storage methods were unknown, the cellar and the smoke-house taking the place of modern cold-storage plants and refrigerated cars. Only surpluses were marketed, and the only practicable time for shipment was the spring. Then only could the quality and quantity of marketable goods be determined and "boating stages" be depended upon. These conditions combined to glut markets, lower prices, and foster uncertainty.

Thus caution became a characteristic of the boatmen. As a rule before departing from a port on the upper Ohio they purchased a guide, the *Navigator*, published at Pittsburgh by Zadok Cramer in the early years of the last century, being a favorite.[24] Such aids indicated navigable channels, the location of obstructions to navigation, and, in some cases, headquarters of brigands. As an additional means of safety, many early navigators on the Ohio moved in companies, some of which were convoyed. In the former manner the English descended the Ohio to take formal possession of the Northwest

---

[23] —*Idem*, vol. i, 296-301; Hulbert, *op. cit.*, 250.

[24] The *Western Navigator* (Philadelphia, 1822) and the *Western Pilot* (Cincinnati, 1832 and 1840) were amplifications and modifications of Cramer's *Navigator*, as were also other like publications.

Territory, and numerous parties later reached the Kentucky country. In 1790 Captain Denney saw eighteen boats, sixteen Kentucky boats and two keelboats, descending the Ohio in one company. The Kentucky boats were lashed together, three abreast, while the keelboats played the rôle of attendants and defenders. The women and the domestic animals of the party rode in the middle tier of boats, while the men not needed on the keelboats rode alongside. But many rivermen refused to make return trips by water even with the use of guides and in the company of others. Instead, they preferred the overland route through Mississippi, Tennessee, and Kentucky which was shorter and, although infested with robbers and wild beasts, safer.

The coming of the steamboat in 1811 did not at once destroy the supremacy of the boatmen and their craft. Five years after the first steamboat descended the Ohio, up-stream traffic, both passenger and freight, was carried largely in barges and keelboats. "Moving families," almost all of whom went down stream, continued, of course, to use the flatboat and the ark. For a longer time thereafter almost all down stream shipments, particularly of produce, were by flatboat. In 1826 three hundred of these craft descended annually from the Wabash alone.[25] A decade later four thousand keelboats reached the lower Mississippi annually, most of them from the Ohio. In 1826 Timothy Flint described the craft then in use on the Ohio in these words:

> There is the stately barge, of the size of an Atlantic schooner, with its raised and outlandish looking deck. This kind of craft, however, which requires twenty-five hands to work it up stream, is almost gone into disuse, and although so common ten years ago, is now scarcely seen. Next there is the keelboat, of a long, slender and elegant form, and generally carrying from fifteen to thirty tons.

[25] Hall, *The West*, 130.

THE BOATMEN AND THEIR CRAFT

This boat is formed to be easily propelled over shallow water in the summer season, and in low stages of water is still much used, and runs on waters not yet frequented by steamboats. Next in order are the Kentucky flats, or in the vernacular phrase, "broad-horns," a species of ark, very nearly resembling a New England pig-stye. They are fifteen feet wide, and from forty to one hundred feet in length, and carry from twenty to seventy tons. Some of them, that are called family-boats, and used by families in descending the river, are very large and roomy, and have comfortable and separate apartments, fitted up with chairs, beds, tables and stoves. It is no uncommon spectacle to see a large family, old and young, servants, cattle, hogs, horses, sheep, fowls, and animals of all kinds, bringing to recollection the cargo of the ancient ark, all embarked, and floating down on the same bottom. Then there are what the people call "covered sleds," or ferry-flats, and Alleghany-skiffs, carrying from eight to twelve tons.[26]

But, as already indicated, the Flatboat Age on the Ohio was near its close. By 1840 arks, broadhorns, and primitive barges were rarely seen. The flatboat remained, but its use had already been restricted almost completely to the transportation of agricultural products, passengers now preferring the steamboat. Meanwhile flat-bottomed, light draught steamboats, first used in the late thirties, had driven the keelboat to the upper reaches of tributary streams,[27] whence it returned only in periods of low water. Of such a reversion the Cincinnati *Commercial* for June 30, 1862, said: "The keelboatmen have it their own way on the Allegheny again, as it is entirely too low for steamboats."

The actual navigators of this period were commonly known as boatmen, and represented all classes and conditions of society. Along with the meanest renegades of their respective communities, Henry Clay, Abraham Lincoln, U. S. Grant, and others, scarcely less distin-

---
[26] Carnegie Library of Pittsburgh. *Pittsburgh in 1816* (Pittsburgh, 1916. Pamphlet), 31, quoting Flint's "Recollections," 13.
[27] Esarey, Logan. *A History of Indiana from its Exploration to 1850* (Indianapolis, 1918), vol. i, 306-308.

guished, did manual labor at the oar and the setting-pole. It was a hard but certain way to earn needed cash, while seeing the world which did not mean much to a frontiersman of inland America who had not been in New Orleans. Many farmers and merchants of the Ohio valley visited the lower Mississippi in their own boats and in company with their own wives who went along as cooks for the hands and as clerks for the great open-air markets conducted by the Yankees for the sale of their products in southern river cities. Preparations for such adventures were usually gala affairs. Whiskey flowed freely, and friends and relatives assembled in large numbers to wish departing companies good luck in a venture never free from vicissitudes.

Professional boatmen, those who followed the river for a living, were a distinct type, the self-styled "half-horse" and "half-alligators" of their day. Some of them actually bore the marks of the draft horse in large callouses on their arms and shoulders, products of the setting-pole and the socket of the keelboat. Their resemblance to alligators was less evident but not wholly lacking, certainly not when they ate. They were indeed a fearless and hardy set with no peers of their kind, except among professional frontiersmen and Indian fighters. Hatless, stripped to the waist, and tanned by the combined effects of water and sun, they resembled Indians more than whites. Accustomed to every species of exposure and privation, they despised luxury. Their chief indulgence was hero worship, their idols being those of their own number who had successfully undertaken the most thrilling adventures.

The boatman's restless spirit and fondness for excitement has been aptly described in these words:

In his normal state he was silently waiting for something to happen, knowing quite well that it certainly would. When the bomb of circumstance exploded the human creature was on that dot of time transformed into a combination of rubber ball, wildcat and shrieking maniac, all controlled by instantaneous perception and exact calculation. After the tumult he subsided again into his listless lethargy of waiting, the monotony being endured by chewing tobacco and illustrating the marvelous accuracy with which he could propel a stream of its juice for any distance up to fifteen feet.[28]

With the professional boatman, fighting was a pastime. Dressed in frontier style—flannel shirt, trowsers of linsey-woolsey, cap, moccasins, and a leather belt from which hung a hunting knife and a tobacco pouch—he was always ready for a fray. The bully who boasted that he had never been "licked" was in honor bound to fight whoever disputed his prowess. Encounters between rival bullies sometimes lasted for hours at a time, the contestants remaining clinched, meanwhile chewing each other's ears and fingers and gouging each other's eyes. Sometimes encounters were staged on a large scale. Keelboatmen and bargemen looked upon raftsmen and flatboatmen as natural enemies, and meetings between them were usually the prelude to a battle-royal. Assemblies of boatmen were often riotous and lawless to the extreme, city authorities being defied for days at a time in their efforts to maintain order. This was especially true when "licker" flowed, as it usually did, and when rival bullies and their retainers met. To creoles on the lower Mississippi boatmen from the Ohio were veritable terrors, yet quite American.

Another distinguishing characteristic of the professional boatman was his original vocabulary of metaphors and similes interspersed with more than the average amount of profanity. For example, acts performed with celerity happened "quicker nor an alligator can

---

[28] Dunbar, *op. cit.*, vol. i, 293.

chaw a puppy," whereas to be silent in speech was to be as "dumb as a dead nigger in a mud hole." Persons commanded to move were told to "shake yer skids" or "start yer trotters." Drowning persons "choked to death like a catfish on a sand-bar," and difficult tasks were "harder nor climin' a peeled saplin' heels uppard." [29] Imagination can possibly supply illustrations of accompanying profanity.

However hard and unnatural their life may have been, few professional boatman ever left it for another. The charm of their excesses, their frolics, and their fist-fights lured them ever onward. Fatigue of the running board was easily drowned in a "fillee," or ration of whiskey, and a night's repose in the open, under a heavy blanket and the canopy of heaven, prepared all to "stand to" their places and "set off" without complaint. In the call of the bugle with which every flatboat and keelboat was provided, in the recollection of difficulties met and conquered, and in the daily prospect of new adventures upon a broad thoroughfare of life there was something to charm the imagination of the most unromantic.

Something of this appeal may be had from General Wm. O. Butler's poem entitled *The Boatman's Horn*, lines of which follow:

> O, boatman! wind that horn again,
> For never did the listening air,
> Upon its lambent bosom bear
> So wild, so soft, so sweet a strain!
> What, though thy notes are sad and few,
> By every simple boatman blown,
> Yet is each pulse to nature true,
> And melody in every tone.
> How oft in boyhood's joyous days,

---

[29] — *Idem*, vol. i, 294.

Unmindful of the lapsing hours,
I've loitered on my homeward way
By wild Ohio's banks of flowers;
While some lone boatman from the deck
Poured his soft numbers to the tide,
As if to charm from storm and wreck
The boat where all his fortunes ride!
Delighted Nature drank the sound,
Enchanted echo bore it round
In whispers soft and softer still
From hill to plain and plain to hill
Till e'en the thoughtless, frolic boy,
Elate with hope and wild with joy,
Who gamboled by the river side,
And sported with the fretting tide,
Feels something new pervade his breast,
Change his light step, repress his jest,
Bends over the flood his eager ear
To catch the sounds far off, yet dear —
Drinks the sweet draft, but knows not why
The tear of rapture fills his eye.[30]

A hero of these days was the notorious, though somewhat mythical, "Mike" Fink. He is said to have been born in Allegheny county, Pennsylvania, about 1781. As a mere lad he played a prominent part in the Indian wars of his time, winning the enviable distinction of being the best shot in the Ohio valley. Early in life he answered the call of the river, where he soon became notorious as an adept in its most lawless and questionable practices. On the upper Ohio he was "Bang All," the superb marksman, and was consequently generally excluded from shooting contests for beef, receiving for his forbearance the "fifth quarter," the hide and tallow. His share was soon exchanged for whiskey which he

---

[30] *Western Pennsylvania Hist. Magazine*, vol. i, 26; *Western Review* (Lexington, Ky., 1821).

caused to flow freely, as long as it lasted, always managing to consume a large quantity himself.

On the lower Ohio and the Mississippi Fink was a rough and tumble fighter and a daring and successful pillager of chicken roosts and barnyards. In this rôle he won fitting epithets. On the Ohio he was the "Snapping Turtle," while on the Mississippi he was simply the "Snag." To all he was a veritable Rob Roy without a peer for deviltry and meanness, unless it was in "Colonel Flug" (Colonel Fluger), a bad man of that part of the Ohio below Louisville. Good people stood in awe of Fink; officers avoided him; the bad idolized him.

To all, accounts of Fink's exploits were good reading. Accordingly, local and most of the more cosmopolitan newspapers of the day, and even of a later period, published his biography, first given to the world, with some embellishments, by the fertile pen of Morgan Neville. Fink, however, probably gave the best epitome of himself in these words: "I can out run, out hop, out jump, throw down, drag out, and lick any man in the country. I am Salt river roarer. I love the wimin, and am cock full of fight."

"Mike's" closest friends were Carpenter and Talbott, two kindred spirits whom he had schooled in the arts of his own prowess. They were each close seconds to him in pilfering, fighting, and shooting. Carpenter and Fink were particular friends and at one time had great confidence in each other. As proof of this they are said to have shot from each others' heads cups of whiskey at a distance of seventy yards. No injury to either ever occurred so long as their prowess rested upon the score of friendship.

About 1823 Fink and his companions are said to have

MIKE FINK, HERO OF THE KEELBOATMEN, AND COMPANIONS
"Keep your noddle steady, Carpenter, and don't spill the whiskey."

answered the call of the Far West, thus leading the way for boatmen of a later period, who were among the first of the frontiersmen on the upper Missouri. Engaging themselves to fur traders they ascended the Missouri in the double capacity of boatmen and trappers. After a successful season on the headwaters of that stream, they took up their abode for the winter in a "dug-out" near the mouth of the Yellowstone. Here followed a bitter quarrel between Fink and Carpenter, supposed to have had its origin in their rivalry for the affections of an Indian squaw. Despite the efforts of friends at reconciliation and their temporary truces, they had broken forever.

When spring came and fancy of outlaws, as well as of young men, turned to love, their quarrel was renewed, but a reconciliation was again effected and was to have been solemnized by the usual ceremony of shooting cups of whiskey from each others' heads. As usual the first shot was determined by "skying a copper," and as usual, Fink won. Doubtful of his sincerity, yet scorning to save his own life by refusing to keep a contract, Carpenter prepared for death. His gun, shot-pouch, powder-horn, belt, pistol, and wages he bequeathed to his friend Talbott who was present. Then, without changing features, he filled a cup to the brim, took his distance, and placed it on his head. Fink loaded his gun, picked the flint, leveled and fired, and Carpenter fell dead.

Fink at once disavowed the deed declaring it an accident and cursing his gun, powder, and himself. Thus a cold blooded murder passed unpunished. But Talbott knew the truth and secretly determined to be revenged for his friend's death. For months no opportunity offered, but one day, in a fit of gasconade, Fink declared that he had intentionally killed Carpenter and that he rejoiced in the deed. Talbott immediately drew the pistol which Carpenter had bequeathed him and shot Fink through the heart. He died without a word, and his bones repose on the banks of the upper Missouri in an unmarked grave with those of others of the boatmen who later answered the call of the Far West.

However fantastic the stories of "Mike" Fink may be, they illustrate a type all too plentiful in the Ohio valley in his day. Moreover, this type was not confined to the rivers. Conditions on land were almost as bad as on the waters, tough times making tough men everywhere. Every town and village boasted its bully. Drinking, gambling, and horse-racing were favorite pastimes; churches and schools were few and far between; the sacrifices of human life, of human effort, and of the accumulated culture of the ages were appalling; and meanwhile vice and disease made their inroads. It was a period of extreme individualism, of tremendous physical and mental efforts, and of supreme sacrifices. The marks of the struggle are visible to this day. From those who survived uninjured and uncontaminated came some of the greatest leaders of the nation; from those who fell came some of the worst leaders in crime and vice. It would be useless to specify. "Mike" Fink was only a somewhat exaggerated prototype of the worst of the boatmen of his day, as well as the worst of those who lived on land – of the worst of all classes of a great society in its beginnings.

The Boatmen as Nation Builders

The immigration movement into the Trans-alleghany, beginning about 1765, is without a parallel in American history. Unlike most other immigrations it was natural and went on doubling and trebling for decades. The only other movement that can compare with it, that into California, was due to unusual and exceptional causes. Unlike the former, the latter grew marvelously for a time, then almost stopped, only to proceed more rapidly and normally in recent years.[31]

Each of these movements played a distinct part in the national development of the United States. In a very real way that into the Trans-alleghany made the United States a nation, while that into California tested its strength. It was in the Ohio valley that northerners and southerners first met and mingled, on a large scale, under conditions that made for toleration on the part of each. Here they intermarried and developed common interests and purposes. Moreover, by 1820 the new society thus formed was assimilating foreigners in such numbers and under such conditions as to cause it to be spoken of as "the melting-pot of the world."[32] Where sectional rivalries and jealousies persisted, they were intense, but most of these were finally forgotten in the conflict precipitated by the immigration movement into California, a movement that demonstrated Abra-

---

[31] Monette, *op. cit.*, vol. ii, 143; McMaster, J. B. *History of the People of the United States* (New York, 1883), vol. i, 149.

[32] Adams, Henry. *History of the United States* (New York, 1889), vol. i, chaps. 1 and 2.

ham Lincoln's contention that the United States is an indestructible union of indestructible states.

To some observers the first of these movements, in its earliest stages, was anything but assuring. Eastern capitalists and conservatives generally regarded it as a good riddance of worthless debtors, incurable demagogues, and insufferable malcontents. Others saw in it germs of fratricidal strife and possible dismemberment. They could not forget those lessons of history that seemed to indicate the inability of peoples to overcome the barriers of nature in their efforts at international comity. Most of the mountains of Europe then formed international boundaries, separating in some instances peoples of the same race, religion, and politics, into rival, even hostile, nations.

To those participating in the movement its objects were mainly economic betterment.[33] Matters political were important but secondary and always a means to an economic end. On one point all were agreed, and that was that the western movement into the Trans-alleghany was irresistible, for said a representative participant: "You may as well endeavour to prevent the fishes gathering on a bank in the sea, which offers them plenty of nourishment."

To those who saw the movement through the pages of history Dr. Ferrero, a famous Italian historian, may speak. "It were," said he, "as if the whole American Nation unconsciously or almost unconsciously was being driven forward by a superior, not to say mystic force, to reach in pain and travail the goal of its destiny." [34]

---

[33] McMaster, *op. cit.*, vol. i, 518.

[34] Chambers, H. E., *op. cit.*, 7; see also "The Ohio Valley in American History," in Turner, F. J. *The Frontier in American History* (New York, 1920), 157-177.

THE BOATMEN AS NATION BUILDERS 61

The boatmen of the Ohio and their craft were important factors in this movement. Without them the Ohio valley might have become a "melting-pot of the world," but certainly not when it did and as it did. Chief credit for this consummation has been given the steamboat and the locomotive, but it was practically completed before either became a determining factor in the interior. Although the first steamboat descended the Ohio as early as 1811-1812, the practicability of steam navigation for up-stream uses was not determined until 1817 and the steamboat did not become a real factor in the western world for almost two decades later. On the other hand, the locomotive did not reach the Ohio before the middle of the nineteenth century. Meanwhile, every foot of territory drained by it had become a part of a great and populous state in the Union.

An account, however brief, of the services of the boatmen ought to be worth while. As already indicated, they began before the Revolution. It was with the aid of boats built at Fort Pitt that the English, in 1765, occupied the Northwest Territory, planting their flag at Kaskaskia and Vincennes, where the authority of the English people has been recognized ever since.[35] In 1770 George Washington, while on a visit to the Ohio valley, observed that the Ohio was navigable, even over dams and riffles at the heads of its numerous islands, by boats "rowed and set up with poles" and with canoes "which made twenty miles daily against the current and with it a good deal more."

Washington might also have told of contemporary plans for the development of the Ohio valley with re-

---

[35] Alvord, C. W. *Mississippi Valley in British Politics* (Cleveland, 1917), vol. i, 299-301; *idem*, vol. ii, 113; Volwiler, *op. cit.*, 188; Alvord, C. W. *The Illinois Country, 1673-1818* (Springfield, 1920), 274.

ference to its natural thoroughfares. Outstanding among these was that for a colony to be called Vandalia with boundaries suggesting those of the present state of West Virginia.[36] More significant still, certainly for our purposes, were incidental suggestions looking to the development of the resources of the same region and to the transportation of products thence directly to the markets of the world. As set forth in answers to Lord Hillsborough, president of the Board of Trade for the Colonies, who objected to granting a charter for the proposed colony of Vandalia, the difficulties in the way of such undertakings were insignificant. The data for these answers were collected and compiled by Samuel Wharton, a merchant prince of Philadelphia, but they were presented by Benjamin Franklin who, in doing so, pointed out the possibility of drawing from the Ohio valley naval stores and raw materials for the "manufactories" of Europe, as well as the possibility of supplying the West Indies, the Floridas, and Mexico with lumber and provisions, particularly flour and corn from the same source.

Furthermore, continued Franklin: "The Ohio is, at all seasons of the year, navigable with large boats, like the western country barges, rowed only by four or five men; and from February to April, large ships may be built on the Ohio and sent to sea laden with hemp, iron, flax, silk, tobacco, cotton, potash, etc." It was, also, asserted that shipments could then be made direct by way of the Ohio to the West Indies safer and cheaper than from either Philadelphia or New York, and a

---

[36] See "Journal of a Tour to the Ohio River in 1770," in Washington, *Writings* (ed. Ford), vol. ii, 310; Alvord, *op. cit.*, 212; Turner's "Western State Making in the Revolutionary Era," in *Amer. Hist. Review* (New York, 1895-date), vol. i, 70-87, 251-269; Alden's "New Governments West of the Alleghanies before 1780," in *Bulletin of the University of Wisconsin* (Madison, 1897), hist. ser., vol. ii, no. 1, 1-74.

THE BOATMEN AS NATION BUILDERS

prediction was made that "Whenever the farmers and merchants of the Ohio shall properly understand the business of transportation, they will build schooners, sloops, etc. . . . suitable for the West Indian and European markets."

Finally these proposals were urged as practicable.[37] Already counties in western Pennsylvania had surpluses of agricultural products, and the French in the Illinois country had demonstrated that use could be made of such supplies. As early as 1746 they had transported several thousand pounds of flour thence to New Orleans.

Although none of the plans for participation in world commerce on the part of the residents of the Ohio valley bore fruit immediately, immigrants in increasing numbers continued to settle there. In 1775 approximately thirty thousand persons resided west of the Alleghany mountains, most of them along the Ohio and its upper tributaries. Moreover, they continued to arrive during the entire Revolutionary period, the region thus populated being sometimes spoken of as the "child of the Revolution."[38] Although these settlers seem to have been interested primarily in their own economic welfare, they were not, however, lacking in patriotism, a fact attested by Washington when he expressed a determination to "retreat beyond the Susquehanna river, and thence, if necessary, to the Alleghany mountains," in the event of continued British successes in the East.[39]

---

[37] — *Idem*; Craig, Neville B. *The Olden Time* (Pittsburgh, 1846-1848), vol. ii, 6; Cramer, Zadok. *Navigator* (Pittsburgh, ed. 1818); Gould, E. W. *Fifty Years on the Mississippi* (St. Louis, 1889), 175; Franklin, *Works* (Boston, 1856. ed. Sparks), vol. iv, 348.

[38] Volwiler, *George Croghan and the Westward Movement*, 210-232.

[39] Sparks, Jared. *Life of George Washington* (New York, 1902. ed. Adam), 196.

Meanwhile rivermen of the interior were making distinct contributions to the cause of independence. From the banks of the Ohio went privateers who inflicted losses on English commerce during the Revolutionary war.[40] It was with the aid of craft built at Redstone (Brownsville) on the Monongahela that George Rogers Clark moved to the conquest of the Northwest Territory. With the aid of boats built at or near Pittsburgh – regular communication between the East and the West having been interrupted – patriots of the interior supplied themselves with gun powder from New Orleans. But the most outstanding service of the inland river craft of this period was that of the galley bateau "Willing." With its aid George Rogers Clark was able to recapture Vincennes, thus breaking the British power in the Northwest and sending their commander, General Hamilton, to Richmond, Virginia, a prisoner of war.

Nevertheless, the year 1780 found the immediate valley of the Ohio little more than a wilderness. At its head under the guns of Fort Pitt, nestled the hundred or more cabins called Pittsburgh. The site of what is now Wheeling was occupied by a fort and a few log cabins. Farther down, on a flat that spread out at the foot of a low range of hills, were some squalid huts that marked the site of what is now Cincinnati; still farther down, at "the Falls," were the three streets and a cluster of cabins that already bore the name of Louisville, the only place on the lower Ohio that could boast a store; a fort had been built at the mouth of the Great Miami; some rude dwellings marked the present site of Clarksville; and the location of Limestone, now

---

[40] Ambler, C. H. *Life and Diary of John Floyd* (Richmond, 1918), 23-24.

Maysville, had been determined. In 1778 the Kentucky district contained less than two hundred residents.[41]

Along the southern bank of the Ohio this condition was soon altered. Heretofore immigrants had confined their settlements largely to the Monongahela valley and the vicinity of Pittsburgh, but, in 1779, Virginia opened an office for the sale of lands in the Transalleghany. Soon the volume of immigrants passing thither increased tremendously. Forts along the upper Ohio became villages, and intervening spaces were filled with an industrious population. In a short time all the remaining good lands were taken, and the immigrant tide turned its face toward Kentucky, hitherto known as the "Dark and Bloody Land." By 1783 the population of that region reached twelve thousand and continued to double and treble during the decades immediately following.[42]

Although many of those settling in Kentucky came direct by way of the Wilderness road and the Cumberland and Tennessee rivers, most of them came by way of the upper Ohio and its tributaries. Fortunately data regarding their movements are abundant. For example, during a part of the autumn of 1785 an average of eight boats passed Fort Harmar weekly, all bound for Kentucky. By 1787 this average had increased to ten, "still others passing in the night uncounted." By the following year efforts to keep accurate accounts of passing boats were abandoned for estimates of their passenger contents, the number of persons for that year alone being placed at twelve thousand.

But the boats then descending the Ohio carried other

---

[41] McMaster, *op. cit.*, vol. i. 148.
[42] Monette, *op. cit.*, vol. ii, 143; Bodley, Temple. *The History of Kentucky before the Louisiana Purchase in 1803* (Louisville, 1928), 199-214.

cargo than passengers, most moving families being accompanied by horses, cattle, sheep, hogs, farming implements, and household and kitchen goods – by everything, in fact, necessary to begin life anew in the wilderness. For instance during a seven months period including a part of 1786 and extending into 1787, one hundred seventy-seven boats passed Fort Harmar carrying cargoes estimated to contain 2,679 persons, 1,333 horses, 766 cattle, and 102 wagons, to say nothing of other particulars.[43]

For a time the possibilities of this movement were disconcerting. It had originated in discontent, and, in its earlier stages, it seemed to encounter only snares and disappointments. Lands were plentiful and cheap, and crops were abundant; but in the absence of markets all were valueless beyond the means of a mere subsistence. Access to the only available market, New Orleans, had been denied, as had, also, the right to deposit goods there, even temporarily. Moreover, John Jay and the wily Gardoqui, who represented Spain, had considered a treaty by the terms of which the United States was to forego the use of the Mississippi river for a period of twenty-five years, receiving instead certain commercial concessions of primary benefit to New England. British and Spanish agents were, also, abroad in the interior with bribes of land and gold, and James Wilkinson and others were planning the alienation of at least a part of the West. Under such conditions it was feared that the improvised boats of the Ohio had carried their cargoes beyond the control of established governments,

---

[43] Schouler, James. *History of the United States* (Washington, 1887), vol. ii, 242-248; Roosevelt, T. *Winning of the West* (New York, 1889); *Miss. Valley Hist. Review*, vol. vii, 26; Winsor, Justin. *The Westward Movement* (Boston, 1897); Phillips, U. B. *American Negro Slavery* (New York, 1918), 169.

even beyond the reach and influence of home and kin. Letters and petitions from those recently settled in Kentucky spoke of a possible war with Spain, of proposed independent states in the Ohio valley, and of possible foreign alliances, provided the right to navigate the Mississippi freely was not otherwise assured.[44]

Fortunately counter influences were at work, foremost of these being that of George Washington who had just relinquished command of the Revolutionary army. In 1784 he again visited the Ohio valley, this time to examine lands and study conditions. From his studies he concluded that the only way to bind the interior to the older sections of the country was by ties of commerce. He was struck, also, with the diffusion and the importance of the inland navigation of the United States and before returning to the East made surveys with a view to its improvement. Immediately upon his return he wrote Governor Harrison and other Virginians of the transportation needs and possibilities of the interior. Shortly thereafter he visited Richmond to lay before the general assembly of Virginia plans and proposals for connecting the eastern and western waters by means of canals.[45]

Meanwhile, other Virginians had sensed the transportation needs and possibilities of the interior. With one accord they seem to have thought of the state's many navigable rivers in which Patrick Henry recognized the "finger of heaven" marking out a course of empire, inviting new settlers to enterprise, and pointing them to wealth and power.[46]

---

[44] McLaughlin, A. C. *The Confederation and the Constitution* (New York, 1905), Amer. Nation ser., vol. x, 94-101; Hulbert, *op. cit.*

[45] Winsor, *op. cit.*, 250-256; see also *Filson Club Publications* (Louisville, 1884-date. irreg.), no. 27, p. 18.

[46] Winsor, *op. cit.*, 248.

As a result Washington's suggestion for binding the East and the West by ties of commerce met with favor. In 1785 the Virginia assembly authorized the formation of local canal companies for this purpose, Washington becoming their first president. At the same time James Rumsey was promised an adequate reward for any invention he might make to propel boats against river currents, and a number of new roads were authorized in the Trans-alleghany. Among these was a road to connect the navigable waters of the James and Kanawha rivers, also, a road to connect Winchester and Romney with a possible extension to Morgantown and beyond, that would divert traffic from roads then being built and planned in Pennsylvania.[47]

The political results of Virginia's interest in internal commerce greatly accelerated the contemporaneous movement for a stronger central government. First, difficulties between Virginia and Maryland over the navigation of the Potomac river and Chesapeake bay were adjusted. This led to an attempt to adjust similar difficulties involving neighboring states and finally to the Philadelphia Convention, where the federal constitution was drafted.

The paternity of this document has been generally attributed to Virginia, but few have appreciated her interest in its commercial provisions. This is probably due to the fact that Virginia's interests were chiefly in agriculture, those in commerce being largely potential and centering in the interior rather than on the high seas. They were, nevertheless, real, as was attested in the writings of her leaders, and by none more forcibly than by Washington. In a letter to Madison, dated

---

[47] — *Idem*, 257; Callahan, J. M. *Semi-Centennial History of West Virginia* (Charleston, 1913), 90-110.

November 30, 1785, in reference to the movement that led directly to the making of a stronger national government, he said: "It appears that no country in the universe is better calculated to derive benefit from inland navigation than this [Virginia]." [48]

Appreciation of commercial opportunities under the proposed new government was a deciding factor with the delegates from Trans-alleghany Virginia in their vote for the ratification of the federal constitution. An outlet to market, either to the East or to the South, seemed more certain under the proposed stronger government than under that of the Articles of Confederation. But for the eloquence of Patrick Henry who spoke largely for the non-commercial sections of his state, the affirmative vote of the interior would have been all but unanimous. As it was, it included all the delegates, except one, from what is now West Virginia north of the Great Kanawha river, together with those of the Louisville district of what is now Kentucky.[49]

Meanwhile another westward movement into the Ohio valley had got under way, that was to continue, with slight interruptions but always with similar impulses and purposes, until the oceans were united by a continuous settlement. The choicest lands south of the Ohio having been taken, Congress opened to settlement the "Indian Country," as the lands north thereof were then called. Armed with a constitution, the famous Ordinance of 1787 for the government of the Northwest Territory, which pointed the way to separate state-

---

[48] Winsor, *op. cit.*, 256.

[49] Libby, O. G., "The Geographical Distribution of the Vote of the Thirteen States on the Federal Constitution, 1787-1788," in *Bulletin of the University of Wisconsin* (Madison, 1894), economics, political science, and history ser., vol. i, no. 1; Ambler, C. H. *Sectionalism in Virginia, 1776-1861* (Chicago, 1910), 58.

hood for frontier peoples and guaranteed certain fundamental rights and liberties, Rufus Putnam, Manasseh Cutler, and others of another Ohio Company, launched this movement. Their settlement at Marietta, April 7, 1788, was the first in what is now the state of Ohio. Moreover, in the same year, John Cleves Symmes made a settlement at Cincinnati, thus opening to permanent occupation a stretch of country several hundred miles long. Washington thought that no colony in America had been settled under more favorable auspices.[50]

Like those that had preceded, the unprecedented immigration movement that followed was made possible by the boats and boatmen of the Ohio. The founders of Marietta reached their destination in the "Mayflower," a namesake of the ship that bore their fathers to the bleak New England shores one hundred and sixty-eight years before. In the course of the first eleven months of 1788 more than nine hundred other boats descended the Ohio, most of them bound for Kentucky. They carried cargoes estimated to contain, among other things, eighteen thousand persons, almost eight thousand horses, about two thousand five hundred cattle, more than one thousand sheep, and almost as many hogs. In the older sections fear was expressed that the "fools going west would drain the East of its best blood."[51]

To avert this and other possible catastrophies to the country at large, Congress, like the general assembly of Virginia, tried to keep the interior attached to the East by ties of interest. To this end one of its first acts, under

---

[50] Washington, *Writings* (ed. Ford), vol. xi, 282; Winsor, *op. cit.*, 289-315.
[51] McMaster, *op. cit.*, vol. i, 518; Schouler, *op. cit.*, vol. ii, 242; *Miss. Valley Hist. Review*, vol. vii, 26.

THE BOATMEN AS NATION BUILDERS

the constitution, was that making Louisville a port of entry. In the course of the twelve years immediately following, this act was followed by others giving Palmyra on the Cumberland, Cincinnati, Fort Massac, and Marietta similar designations.[52] Numerous efforts were also made to adjust differences between the United States and both England and Spain regarding the interior, treaties of 1794 and 1795 resulting in the withdrawal of the former from the Northwest Territory and in permission from the latter allowing Americans the right, temporarily, to deposit goods at New Orleans. Subsequently, and in anticipation of war, Congress provided for the construction of naval vessels on the Ohio and, during the Indian wars of the nineties, maintained a regular mail service between Pittsburgh and Cincinnati.[53] The boats used by the government for this service were of the galley-keelboat type. They were armed and were operated in relays, changes being made at Limestone, Gallipolis, Marietta, and Wheeling, whence the service was continued overland by horses and wagons. The time for the round trip between Wheeling and Cincinnati was eighteen days, twelve up and six down.[54]

Despite these and other services the inhabitants of the Ohio valley did not hesitate to ask other things of the central government. This was particularly true when their right to use the Mississippi freely was questioned, as it frequently was. Their requests were set

---

[52] Hulbert, A. B., "Western Ship-building," in *Amer. Hist. Review*, vol. xxi, 721.

[53] U. S. House. *Executive Documents*, 50 cong., 1 sess., vol. xx, no. 6, pt. ii, 185; Thurston, George H. *Allegheny County's Hundred Years*, 103.

[54] *Magazine of Western History* (New York, 1884-1888), vol. ii, 60; *Ohio Arch. and Hist. Quarterly* (Columbus, 1906-date), vol. xxii, 60; Thurston, *op. cit.*, 103.

forth in numerous letters and petitions but in none more comprehensively than in one of 1798 which said, in part:

> The Mississippi is ours by the law of nature; it belongs to us by our numbers and by the labor which we have bestowed upon these spots, which before our arrival were desert and barren. Our innumerable rivers swell it and flow with it into the Gulf of Mexico. Its mouth is the only issue which nature has given to our waters, and we wish to use it for our vessels. We do not prevent the Spanish and French from ascending the river to our towns and villages. We wish, in our turn, to descend it without any interruption to its mouth, to ascend it again, and to exercise our privilege of trading on it and navigating it at our pleasure. If our most entire liberty in this matter is disputed, nothing will prevent our taking possession of the capital [of Louisiana], and when we are once master of it, we will know how to maintain ourselves there. If Congress refuses us effectual protection, if it forsakes us, we will adopt the measures which our safety requires, even if they endanger the peace of the Union and our connection with the other states. No protection, no allegiance.[55]

Such demands as the above had a direct bearing upon the purchase of Louisiana. It might not be putting it too strongly to say that they made it imperative, even in the supposed absence of constitutional authority therefor. Months before it was made parties on the upper Ohio estimated the price that should be paid. More significant still, they calculated the ultimate loss to the Union in the event that Louisiana were allowed to pass to the permanent possession of either England or France, the amount being fixed at twenty times the price paid.[56]

Meanwhile the boatmen of the Ohio continued to advance the material development of the interior. In 1798 they were transporting thence down the Mississippi,

---

[55] U. S. House, *op. cit.*, 182.
[56] Pittsburgh *Gazette*, March 25, 1803; Hulbert, "Western Ship-building," in *Amer. Hist. Review*, vol. xxi, 720.

THE BOATMEN AS NATION BUILDERS

annually, goods valued at almost one million dollars which amount increased by more than three hundred thousand dollars during each of the years immediately following. By 1802 river shipments from Kentucky alone amounted to almost one million two hundred thousand dollars annually.[57] Descending the Mississippi in 1801 Moses Austin was surprised at the number of boats he saw from the Ohio.[58] In 1807 almost two thousand flatboats and keelboats arrived in New Orleans annually from that stream. They carried goods valued in excess of five million dollars.[59]

Thus, through the aid of its boats and rivermen, the Ohio valley, by 1800, was practically transformed. A population of a few thousand twenty years before had grown to more than half a million. Kentucky and Tennessee were states in the Union, the former being ninth in population, having outgrown New Hampshire, Vermont, Rhode Island, New Jersey, and Georgia; Ohio, with a population of forty-five thousand, was planning for statehood; former treasonable plottings had been submerged in visions of loyalty to a greater Union; and a tongue of settlement paralleling both sides of the Ohio and its tributaries reached the Mississippi and pointed to regions beyond.

Six years later, Thomas Ashe, an English traveler descending the Ohio, found there many evidences of a well-developed and vigorous society. On the sites of the Indian camps of Washington's day were thriving villages and cities: Pittsburgh, Steubenville, Wheeling, Marietta, Gallipolis, Limestone (Maysville), Cincinnati, Louisville, and others, each with such composite

---
[57] U. S. House, *op. cit.*, 182-183 of Switzler's "Report."
[58] Barker, E. C., "Austin Papers," in Amer. Hist. Assoc. *Report* (Washington, 1919), vol. ii, pt. 1, 69-74.
[59] U. S. House, *op. cit.*, 185.

populations of English, Irish, and German peoples and such varied interests, as almost to defy description. Forests were rapidly giving way to cornfields; fruits and vegetables of many varieties were contributing to the revenues and sustenance of the inhabitants; from a thousand hills the voice of domestic animals broke the monotony of woodland and wave; and horse-racing, drinking, and gambling were favorite pastimes.[60] In fact a rough and ready society, resourceful beyond precedent, crude beyond description, and independent beyond comparison, yet typically American, had planted itself in the Ohio valley.

In the development of this society the river craft of the period supplied more than mere transportation. The flatboat has been rightly proclaimed "the all important craft that made the Ohio a power in the world." Its services to early settlers alone would have entitled it to this distinction, but there were other achievements to its credit. Upon reaching its destination it and kindred craft, barges and arks, were "knocked down" and transformed into homes, barns, and even furniture and street paving materials. Thousands of homes along the Ohio, some of them of the better sort, were made from lumber taken from boats that bore their owners thither. This was certainly an unique service. Rarely have immigrants to a new land come floating in their own homes, towing school houses and stores in their wake.[61]

But the boats of this period rendered still other services. Having supplied the needs of "moving families" for transportation, they were, as previously stated, next used to market surplus agricultural products. Meanwhile, they were used as retail, or "boat stores." As

---

[60] Ashe, Thomas. *Travels in America* (London, 1808).

[61] Flint, *Recollections*; Hulbert, *The Ohio River*, 230; Dunbar, *op. cit.,* vol. i, 305-306.

such, their more or less regular arrivals at river towns were heralded as community affairs. As a rule, contemplated landings were announced from the boat itself by the use of a bugle. Such a call summoned the women of the favored landing to their shopping. It was in this way only that many persons secured groceries, dry goods, crockery, china, paints, cutlery, boots and shoes, in fact all that merchandise most needed in a pioneer society. Fascinated by the aroma of store goods and by reports from the outside world, shoppers, both men and women, sometimes abandoned their regular routine and took a holiday, when the "boat store" came to town. It was a familiar sight along the Ohio until after the Civil war and was used until quite recently for the distribution of china, glass ware, crockery, and other breakable merchandise.

The contributions of Ohio boatmen were not, however, confined to the material. The non-professional among them were real home builders. In fact, the continuity of their home life was rarely broken, the daily routine of life on a flatboat not differing much from that on land, except for the actual work of navigation. At one end of the boat was a large room, often called a parlor or sitting room, where passengers ate their meals and children romped between times. Such boats were furnished with chairs, a table, a looking-glass, and such other articles as the women needed for their work. The kitchen was adjoining. A stove was set up there with its pipe projecting through the roof. A narrow passage way extended down the center of the boat for a considerable part of its length. In front the hall opened into the parlor, and on either side of it were several small bed-rooms. At the rear of the boat was another large compartment for the storage of provisions, furniture, and agricultural implements, and still further astern was the abode of the live stock.

The common experiences and privations of the boatmen tended to weld societies founded by them into one large family with an ever increasing bent toward nationalism. A boat in distress, and hundreds of them got into that plight, was a call for aid to all who saw it. Not to answer was to proclaim the offender a brigand, for the iron clad rule of the inland waters was help for all who needed it. It was this spirit that carried the boatmen to their future homes, collectively warding off Indians, escaping natural perils, bringing children into the world, and burying their dead. Their descendants are today regulating railroads, suppressing competition in restraint of trade, reducing infant and maternity mortality, and trying to subsidize agriculture, each by legislative enactments.

Boatmen also had a part in developing those more personal traits, resourcefulness, patience, and hope, American characteristics that have ever since manifest themselves on trying occasions. Of these traits in the making James Hall, a noted English traveler, saw:

> Two large rafts lashed together, by which simple conveyance several families from New England were transporting themselves and their property to the land of promise in the western woods. Each raft was eighty or ninety feet long, with a small house erected on it; and on each was a stack of hay, round which several horses and cows were feeding, while the paraphernalia of the farm yard, the ploughs, waggons, pigs, children, and poultry, carelessly distributed, gave to the whole more the appearance of a permanent residence, than of a caravan of adventurers seeking a home. A respectable looking old lady, with *spectacles on nose*, was seated on a chair at the door of one of the cabins, employed in knitting; another female was at the washtub; the men were chewing their tobacco, with as much complacency as if they had been in the "land of steady habits," and the various family avocations seemed to go on like clock work.

THE BOATMEN AS NATION BUILDERS

Furthermore, said he,

> In this manner these people travel at slight expense. They bring their own provisions; their raft floats with the current; and honest Jonathan, surrounded with his scolding, grunting, squalling, and neighing dependents, floats to the *point proposed* without leaving his own fireside.[62]

Possibly the greatest service of the boatmen in the development of American nationality was that of keeping young America attached to old America. Without this service the fears, and in some instances the hopes, of those who had predicted dismemberment as a result of the early westward movement, would have come true. This service was the special contribution of the keelboat. If the flatboat made the Ohio "a power in the world," the keelboat made that power national, for, as has been aptly said by another, writing of the calamity howlers of the time, "they never heard a boatman's horn or read aright its simple and powerfully patriotic message."[63] Many of those who fought in the armies of the Revolution did so to preserve America as a land of opportunity, and to them opportunity meant largely new homes. Under such conditions the hardships encountered in reaching the interior were only sequels to independence. The tears and sufferings of pioneer women *en route*, the deprivations endured by boys and girls, and the sacrifices and adventures of men only enhanced the love of all for their common country. All that was needed to maintain common interests, hopes, and aspirations was an adequate means of intercommunication.

Proofs of these generalizations are numerous, but no one of them is more significant than the failure of Aaron Burr to rehabilitate himself in the West follow-

---
[62] Hall, James. *Letters from the West* (London, 1828), 87.
[63] Hulbert, *op. cit.*, 6-7.

ing his unsuccessful effort of 1804 to become governor of New York and his subsequent killing of his chief political rival, Alexander Hamilton, in a duel. When Burr visited the West in 1805 conditions there were ripe for the successful consummation of almost any adventure. Politics were unsettled; Spain was not yet reconciled to the necessity of giving up her long cherished plans for territorial expansion in the Mississippi valley; and everywhere settlers were dissatisfied with existing conditions, transportation being inadequate, markets poor, and protection against the savage foe ineffective. Moreover, Burr was popular in the West, where his killing of Hamilton was generally regarded as a patriotic service. He was able, also, to find there kindred spirits in the person of James Wilkinson and others, and the existing means of transportation, although inadequate for other purposes, were suited to the ends of destruction. With boats hastily constructed on the Ohio and the Cumberland, Burr and his accomplices finally reached the lower Mississippi, where they were arrested. Their plans, whatever they may have involved, had, meanwhile, aroused the patriotic opposition of the West which swept them to pitiful failure.[64]

A tragic incident of this adventure was as significant as was its failure. This was the ruin of Harman Blennerhassett, an eccentric and gullible Irishman who, a few years before, had acquired a part of Backus island (now Blennerhassett island) in the Ohio just below what is now Parkersburg (then Newport), where he had built a palatial residence. This Burr visited in the absence of its owner and interested its hospitable mistress in the possibility of still finer homes to be built on

---

[64] — *Idem*, chap. 12; Gibbens, Alvaro F. *Historic Blennerhassett Island Home* (Parkersburg, W. Va., 1899); *Lippincott's Magazine* (Philadelphia, 1868-1916), February, 1879.

THE BOATMEN AS NATION BUILDERS 79

lands still farther to the westward. In turn she interested her husband, already dissatisfied, and as a consequence he decided to cast his lot with Burr, with results already indicated. Ever since, the latter has been described as

> The despoiler of a tempting eden
> That knew no impulse to demur.

The Burr incident was, however, only a flurry. It was soon spent, and the inhabitants of the Ohio valley went on planting crops, accumulating surpluses of farm products, fostering infant industry, and perfecting their inadequate transportation. To all these activities the War of 1812 gave new impetus but to none more than to commerce. Travelers commented upon the increased number of boats ascending and descending the Ohio. The hazards of ocean travel had increased the interdependence of inland communities. From the "up country" the lower Mississippi now received annually increasing quantities of fruits, flour, whiskey, lard, pork, bale-rope, bagging yarn, venison, fowls, and feathers, giving in exchange cotton, wine, sugar, hides, coffee, indigo, copper, salt, and salt-peter. Products from the lower Mississippi were, also, now temporarily finding markets in the East by way of the Ohio and Pittsburgh, a keelboat reaching that port almost daily from the south during a large part of the period of hostilities.[65]

The results are well expressed by Judge Hall who made a second tour of America in 1820. Everywhere in the Ohio valley he then found numerous evidences of future national greatness. For example, the number of children there was surpassed only by the squirrels of the surrounding forests. Although most of these chil-

---
[65] Cramer, Zadok. *Navigator* (Pittsburgh, 1818).

dren lived in log huts, they were, nevertheless, as "plump and active as health, hard fare, and exercise could make them." Moreover, their environment was one of the most wholesome in the world, for here Thomas Ashe, another traveler, had already witnessed "the novel spectacle of the coming together of the nations of the world, each bringing its own language, politics, and religion, and all sitting quietly down together to erect states, make institutions, and enact laws without bloodshed and disorder." In it all he recognized the workings of some mysterious force attracting peoples to a common center and welding them into a great and powerful nation.

Shipbuilding on the Inland Waters[66]

For more than half a century following 1760 the transportation facilities of inland America, always poor, were discouragingly inadequate. Worse still, most persons directly interested were wedded to old-time methods, pack-horses, wagons, and non-mechanical river craft. A few only were determined to solve the difficulties of the situation, with them necessity being the mother of invention. Moreover, the future of America seemed to depend upon their success, and fabulous fortunes were in store for those who achieved it, to say nothing of consequent benefits.

In the solution of this problem many plans were proposed, and others were cogitated. Accustomed to the use of sea-going vessels for navigating the high seas and the rivers of tidewater America there were, from the first, those who thought of using them on the "Father of Waters" and its chief tributary, the Ohio. It is probably significant that most proposals to this end emanated from Philadelphia. As early as 1761 *Father Abraham's Almanac*, published in that city, predicted that Fort Pitt, then only a frontier outpost, would become a shipbuilding center, sending thence "every spring" sailing vessels of from one to two hundred tons burden. Already mention has been made of

---

[66] For data used in this chapter the author acknowledges indebtedness to Professor A. B. Hulbert's "Western Ship-building," in *Amer. Hist. Review*, vol. xxi, 720-733, also to R. T. Wiley's "Ship and Brig Building on the Ohio and its Tributaries," in *Ohio Arch. and Hist. Quarterly*, vol. xxii, 54-64.

an "Address" of 1770 from Benjamin Franklin and others to Lord Hillsborough suggesting the practicability of building sloops and schooners on the Ohio to be used for carrying food supplies thence to the West Indies and raw materials to the "manufactories" of Europe. The independence of the American colonies did not terminate these suggestions. As already indicated, they gave rise to a new immigration movement into the Ohio valley, that made access to markets on the part of its inhabitants imperative. Meanwhile leaders in the immigrant movement continued to place great store on the possibilities of the Ohio and the Mississippi. Manasseh Cutler, one of the founders of Marietta, Ohio, expected to see these streams "more laden than any . . . on earth" with "heavy articles suited to the Florida and West India markets." Nor did he expect this traffic to be entirely down stream, for said he: "It has been found by experiments that sails are used to great advantage against the current of the Ohio."[67]

The example of American sea-board sailors of the time was inspiring to the would-be salts of the interior. Denied coveted and expected commercial relations with the mother country, New England shipbuilders directed their barques to the Spanish West Indies and to South America; their whalers reached the mouth of the Columbia; their heavier craft even found a way to China and Japan; and by 1800 they had practically succeeded in driving foreign merchantmen from our waters, leaving to them only eleven per cent of our total exports and imports as compared with seventy-six per cent carried by foreigners only ten years before. These activities of American merchantmen, together with the current rumors of war, contributed, also, to give us a

[67] *Magazine of Western History*, vol. ii, 258.

SHIPBUILDING ON THE INLAND WATERS 83

navy and a broadened outlook regarding our interests and rights upon the high seas.[68]

At this time the Ohio valley contained shipbuilders and shipbuilding materials in abundance. The former came largely from New England, whereas the latter were produced locally. A subsequent writer described them in these words:

> Along the Muskingum and the Monongahela towered large forests of black walnut, a wood so lasting that farmers, plowing deep, to this day encounter roots of black walnut trees felled a century ago. Timbers of this wood could be had of great length; they had nearly the strength of white oak and the durability of the live oak of the South but without its weight. Vessels with frames of this timber planked with seasoned oak would have, it was believed, preference over ships of any other material in any port where there were competent judges. The necessary iron for ships at first had to be obtained from the East, as it was a year or two before the bar-iron works near Pittsburgh were, to quote their proprietor, sufficiently "upheld by the hand of the Almighty" to operate with regularity. Cordage ... was being made in greater quantities than even the large local demand required; numerous rope-walks existed at Pittsburgh, Marietta, and Cincinnati, being supplied with hemp from adjacent territory, where it had been found growing wild by the first comers.[69]

It is not known when or where the first sea-going vessel was built in the Ohio valley. Elizabeth, Pennsylvania, had a ship-yard before the government under the federal constitution was established. In 1793 a schooner built there descended the Ohio and the Mississippi rivers by "that extraordinary inland navigation" and subsequently arrived safely in Philadelphia.[70] That this feat was repeated shortly thereafter seems probable. The private papers of John Brisbane Walker, a noted

---

[68] Marvin, W. L. *The American Merchant Marine* (New York, 1910), chaps. 3-6; *Amer. Hist. Review*, vol. xxi, 721-722.

[69] Hulbert, *op. cit.*, 722.

[70] Gallatin's "Report," in Inland Waterways Commission. *Preliminary Report* (Washington, 1908), 553.

editor and a grandson of John Walker, owner of the Elizabeth ship-yard, contains a passport in these words: "I grant free and sure passport to John Walker in order that on the schooner Polly, her captain, Mr. John Bain, he may go to New York, showing his baggage at the office of the royal duty. Given in New Orleans on the 17th of July, 1795. Baron de Carondalet."[71]

There is a bare possibility that this "Polly" was the same vessel that descended the Ohio in 1793. It will be recalled that that vessel reached Philadelphia. In any event, at least one sea-going craft was built on the Ohio before the opening of the last century. It also descended to New Orleans and passed thence to the high seas.[72]

The contemporary troubles with Spain, still pending at that time, over the free navigation of the Mississippi, seem to have checked, temporarily, shipbuilding on the Ohio. Although that power, in 1795, granted Americans permission to deposit goods at New Orleans, the concession was temporary and was followed by repeated threats of revocation. Under such conditions commercial ventures, on a large scale by the use of ships, were too hazardous to be attempted. When the period of the Spanish concession finally expired in 1798 and a request for renewal was denied, American frontiersmen demanded war and induced Congress to prepare for that contingency. To this end two armed sea-going vessels, the "President Adams" and the "Senator Ross," were built at Pittsburgh. Although little is known of the subsequent use of these vessels, their qualities for sea service can not be doubted. According to Major Isaac Craig the former was "as fine a vessel of

---

[71] *Ohio Arch. and Hist. Quarterly*, vol. xxii, 61.

[72] Hulbert, A. B. *The Paths of Inland Commerce* (New Haven, 1921), Chronicles of Amer. series, vol. xxi, 95; *Ohio Arch. and Hist. Quarterly*, vol. xxii, 56-60.

her burden and construction, as the United States possesses," and he pronounced the latter "a fine piece of naval architecture, and one which will far exceed anything the Spanish can show on the Mississippi." [73]

Subsequent concessions on the part of Spain diverted American activities into the paths of peace. Fortunately conditions on the frontier and in the world at large made such a shift possible and profitable. Both Spain and England had ceased to occupy territory belonging to the United States; the savage power in the Northwest was broken, thanks to the prowess of General Wayne; leading settlements on the lower Ohio were already ports of entry; throughout the Ohio valley surpluses of agricultural products were increasing annually; and, best of all, European wars insured high prices for any farm products that could be got to market, either in the West Indies or in Europe. Already seaboard sections of the United States, particularly the Potomac valley and Piedmont Virginia, were supplying England with large quantities of wheat at good prices.[74] Meanwhile, the annually increasing surpluses of the interior could not be sold at all for lack of access to market. Hence it was that farmers of western Pennsylvania were compelled to feed their wheat to cattle, and their "rye, corn, and barley had almost no value for man or beast." [75]

It was under these conditions that shipbuilding first became an important and, for a time, a leading industry on the Ohio and its tributaries. Influenced doubtless by the plans and purposes of her founders, Marietta seems to have led the way. In 1800 Stephen Devol built there

---
[73] Thurston, *op. cit.*, 103.

[74] See W. F. Galpin's "The Grain Trade of New Orleans," in *Miss. Valley Hist. Review*, vol. xiv, 496.

[75] *Western Pennsylvania Hist. Magazine*, vol. vi, 182.

the brig "St. Clair" of one hundred ten tons burden. In May of that year this vessel cleared the Port of Marietta for Havana, Cuba, under the command of Commodore Abraham Whipple of Revolutionary fame. She carried flour and pork and was manned by an inexperienced crew, her commander being the only person on board who could determine latitude and longitude. To avoid the payment of duties and other possibile recognitions of Spanish authority, she did not land at New Orleans, anchoring instead mid-stream in the Mississippi. In August, 1800, she reached Havana, whence she cleared with a cargo of salt for Philadelphia. Here she was sold, her commander returning home by land.

The return of Commodore Whipple to the sea after an absence of almost a generation was an event so spectacular and unusual as to set the poetic muse working in the mind of his fellow townsman, Captain Jonathan Devol, who commemorated the event in the following lines in which Neptune and the Tritons joined in welcoming the old hero to their dominions:

> The Triton crieth:
> 'Who comes now from shore?'
> Neptune replieth
> ' 'Tis old Commodore,
> Long has it been since I saw him before.
> In the year seventy-five from Columbia he came,
> The pride of the Briton on ocean to tame;
> And often, too, with the gallant crew
> Hath he crossed the belt of the ocean blue
> On the Gallic coast
> I have seen him post,
> While his thundering cannon lulled my waves
> And roused my nymphs from their coral caves,
> When he fought for freedom with all his braves
> In the war of the Revolution.

But now he comes from the western woods,
Descending slow with gentle floods,
The pioneer of a mighty train,
Which commerce brings to my domain.'
Up, sons of the wave,
Greet the noble and the brave —
Present your arms unto him.
His gray hair shows
Life's near its close;
Let's pay the honors due him.
Sea maids attend with lute and lyre,
And bring your conchs, my triton sons;
A chorus blow to the aged sire,
A welcome to my dominions.[76]

About the same time the "Monongahela Farmer" of two hundred fifty tons was built at Elizabeth, on the Monongahela, by the Walkers. She was the property of twenty local farmers, each owning an equal share. With a cargo containing, among other things, 721 barrels of flour, 500 barrels of whiskey, 4000 deer skins, 2000 bear skins, large quantities of hemp, flax, firearms, ammunition, and provisions for a crew of eight, she left the upper Ohio in May, 1800. In her descent of that stream she was attacked by Indians, lost one of her crew by drowning, and was delayed at the Falls three months by low water. She finally reached New Orleans where her cargo was disposed of to advantage, despite the fact that much of the flour had soured in the hold of the vessel. Thence, full rigged, and with a new captain, the "Monongahela Farmer" entered the regular trade between New Orleans and the West Indies. Captain Walker returned home to superintend the construction of the brig "Ann Jane" of four hundred fifty tons,

---

[76] Howe, Henry. *Historical Collections of Ohio* (Cincinnati, 1888), vol. ii, 790; Lyford, W. G. *Western Address Director*, 1837 (Baltimore, 1837); Hulbert, *The Ohio River*, 241.

which departed, in due time, from the upper Ohio for New York with a cargo of flour and whiskey.[77]

Meanwhile the Tarascons and others were establishing shipbuilding in Pittsburgh. Influenced doubtless by conditions already indicated, possibly also by a desire to aid the French Directorate, Louis Anastacius Tarascon, a French merchant of Philadelphia, in 1799, sent two clerks "to examine the course of the Ohio and Mississippi from Pittsburgh to New Orleans, and ascertain the practicability of sending ships, and clearing them ready rigged, from Pittsburgh to Europe and the West Indies." The report of his agents was favorable, and soon thereafter he and his associates under the firm name of "John A. Tarascon Brothers, James Berthoud & Co.," established, at Pittsburgh, "a large wholesale and retail store and warehouse, a shipyard, a rigging and sail loft, an anchor smithshop, a block manufactory, and all other things necessary to complete seagoing vessels." [78]

As shipbuilders the Tarascons and associates gave a good account of themselves. The first year of operations, 1801, they built the schooner "Amity" of one hundred twenty tons, also, the ship "Pittsburgh" of two hundred fifty tons. Both vessels went to sea at once, the former loaded with flour, to St. Thomas, the latter, also loaded with flour, to Philadelphia. In time they both reached Bordeaux, France, and returned thence to America with a cargo of wine, brandy, and other goods, some of which came to Pittsburgh by the overland route from Philadelphia. These vessels were followed in turn by the brig "Nanina" of two hundred fifty tons, 1802; the

---
[77] Elizabeth (Pa.) *Herald*, June 7, 1900.
[78] Thurston, *op. cit.*, 103.

ship "Louisiana" of three hundred tons, 1803, and, in 1804, by the ship "Western Trader" of four hundred tons; and by still others.

Because of her somewhat typical experience the career of the "Louisiana" is here given in some detail. Sailing in ballast from Pittsburgh she stopped first at Marietta, the home of her owner, E. W. Tupper, where she was re-christened, becoming the "Louisiana of Marietta." Her next stop was at the mouth of the Cumberland river where she took aboard a cargo of cotton, staves, and hides. After grounding in the Ohio and becalming in the Gulf of Mexico, and subsequently protesting the cause of each delay, that her master and crew might escape responsibility for damages to ship and cargo from causes beyond their control, the "Louisiana of Marietta" reached the Gulf Stream and finally arrived at Norfolk, Virginia, weeks behind her expected time. Here she shifted her crew and again protested, "blaming the calms and weather, the sickness of the crew and all other events and occurrences aforesaid for all the losses, costs, charges, damages, and expenses." Reaching Liverpool, England, at an unknown date, she took on a cargo of merchandise for Trieste, Italy. At Messina, Sicily, a stop was made to protest "not against Scylla and Charybdis" but against "repeated gales and bad weather." Here her cargo was "surveyed" and found to be damaged "through the laboring of the vessel." After some delay at Trieste due to difficulty in establishing her identity, the Italians insisting that there was no such port in the world as Marietta, the "Louisiana of Marietta," in the "Year of Human Salvation 1805," was given legal permission to return to Liverpool. Thence in time, she again reached Philadelphia bringing, among other things, more than four thousand bushels of white salt. With Philadelphia as a home port, she continued to ply the high seas for years.[79]

Following these initial successes shipbuilding became a popular and profitable industry on the Ohio and some of its tributaries, particularly the Monongahela. Of the possibilities the *Tree of Liberty* (Pittsburgh) for May 30, 1801, said:

> The spirit of enterprise which exists now is really worthy of a free and industrious people. Traders need not be confined to one market, but may carry the products of the western country to any port in their own vessels.

Travelers commented upon the industry. For example Michaux, 1802, said:

> What many, perhaps, are ignorant of in Europe is, that they build large vessels on the Ohio, and at the town of Pittsburgh. One of the principal shipyards is upon the Monongahela, about two hundred fathoms beyond the last houses of the town. The timber they make use of is white oak, the red oak, the black oak, a kind of nut wood [walnut], the Virginia cherry, and a kind of pine which they use for masting, as well as for the sides of the vessels, which require a slighter wood. . . . The cordage is manufactured at Redstone and Lexington, where there are two extensive rope-walks, which also supply ships with rigging that are built at Marietta and Louisville.[79a]

In spite of advantages, difficulties encountered by the builders and operators of these vessels were numerous, discouraging, sometimes fatal. First of all these craft were built to sail *in* the high seas and not *on* inland rivers. Although the possibilities of craft of the latter construction were realized at an early date,[80] 1803, the

---

[79] For a somewhat different version of this account see Lloyd, James T. *Steamboat Directory and Disasters on the Western Waters* (Cincinnati, 1856), 41.

[79a] See Michaux's "Travels" in Thwaites, *Early Western Travels*, vol. iii, 160.

[80] Pittsburgh *Gazette*, May 20, 1802.

SHIPBUILDING ON THE INLAND WATERS 91

tendency was to follow the conventions of maritime construction. Thus some of the first ships built on the Ohio drew ten feet of water; still others had holds twelve feet deep. The use of such vessels restricted sailings to the freshet season, spring, and increased the hazards of navigation. It will be recalled that the "Monongahela Farmer" was delayed three months at the Falls of the Ohio because of low water. Such possibilities restricted cargoes to non-perishable articles, glutted markets, and made for low prices generally, even in the West Indies. It was partly because of such conditions, in the spring of 1803, that the price of flour in New Orleans fell from nine to five dollars per barrel, which was little more than the price then paid in Pittsburgh.[81] From such conditions the commercial loss of that city alone, for 1802, reached sixty thousand dollars.[82]

But the greatest difficulty encountered by inland commerce was lack of credit. Banks existed, but they were few and far between and could not meet the demands made upon them even by unhazardous investments. Chief reliance was upon the East, particularly Philadelphia, which was an exacting creditor, the proverbial shrewdness of her lawyers, as displayed in adjusting accounts and guarding contracts, lingering to this day among the unpleasant traditions of the Ohio valley. Many moons passed between the time of planting a crop and that of selling its surplus product. Meanwhile tonnage was required to market the latter, and a new crop had to be planted. Frequently those who supplied the necessary credit to finance the operations did so on faith; others simply took a chance.

---
[81] — *Idem*, May 27, 1803.
[82] Pittsburgh *Tree of Liberty*, October 9, 1802.

The wide leeway given John Walker, master of the "Monongahela Farmer," in the instructions given him for the disposal of that ship and its cargo, was not only a tribute to him personally but, also, emphasized some of the uncertainties involved in such commercial enterprises. First of all, he was to proceed to New Orleans without delay. Should "the flour markets for flour be low" there and "the vessel appear to sell to disadvantage," he was to dispose of a part of the cargo and use the proceeds to rig and man the ship so that he might carry it to any islands that he, in his judgment and information, might elect. Thus this particular adventure was self-sustaining, certainly in emergencies. Walker's ability to sell sour flour direct to the cracker makers of New Orleans, thus thwarting the exacting commission merchants of that place,[83] was a bit of good fortune which could not be depended upon to finance future undertakings.

Nevertheless, profits from such ventures as the above were sometimes fabulous and always appealed to pioneer ingenuity. Devices for sharing possible losses as well as possible gains were all that was needed to inspire ventures. To this end, in 1802, residents of Pittsburgh and vicinity, under the leadership of the venerable Ebenezer Zane, founder of Wheeling, formed an association of exporters known as the Ohio Company. Although an alliance with eastern merchants and bankers was contemplated, membership in this association was restricted to residents of southwestern Pennsylvania and northwestern Virginia. The capital stock was one hundred thousand dollars divided into shares of one hundred dollars each. Somewhat later the

---

[83] Elizabeth *Herald*, June 7, 1900; Hulbert, *The Ohio River*, 243.

Miami Exporting Company was authorized with resources restricted exclusively to commercial uses.[84]

Just as the shipbuilding and exporting interests of the Ohio valley were getting on their feet financially they received a shock that was felt around the world. On October 16, 1802, the Spanish intendant at New Orleans formally refused to continue to permit Americans to deposit goods there and gave them forty days to leave Spanish territory, pending its transfer to France. Already American frontiersmen had speculated upon the possibilities of such a contingency. Some had even estimated the ensuing loss to the United States, one placing it at three hundred thousand dollars, a fabulous sum for that day.[85] The results of the above announcement were, therefore, immediate and paralyzing. Silence reigned in the boatyards; agriculture came to a standstill; and credit again became demoralized, goods valued at almost two million dollars having gone into the interior during the previous year, most of them on promises to pay. Again westerners expressed a desire to "arm ourselves, descend the river, and take New Orleans," regardless of who owned it. Napoleon and Jefferson were condemned alike in the same breath.

Luckily the outcome was again favorable to the interior. Instead of Louisiana being transferred permanently to France, it was transferred to the United States, France acting only as an intermediary. The attitude of inland America, as expressed above, had doubtless helped to soften Jefferson's scruples regarding the constitutionality of the proposed purchase and

---

[84] Pittsburgh *Gazette*, October 8, 1802.
[85] — *Idem*, October 22, 1802; *idem*, February 18, 1803; *idem*, March 25, 1803.

to make it possible. In any event local interests in the Ohio valley now prepared to make the most of a great opportunity. It was at this time that the Ohio Company effected a banking alliance with the Bank of Pennsylvania, located in Philadelphia, in what may have been the first of such arrangements between the Ohio valley and the Atlantic coast. The fact that this arrangement grew out of the exigencies of the shipbuilders and exporters of the former section is significant. Moreover, about the same time, more local banks came into existence, one in Kentucky and another in New Orleans, and shortly thereafter shipbuilding in the Ohio valley attained its greatest importance. Of the commercial possibilities of the interior Jefferson, in a letter to the first governor of Louisiana, said: "New Orleans will be forever, as it is now, the mighty mart of the merchandise brought from more than a thousand rivers, unless prevented by some accident in human affairs. This rapidly increasing city will, in no distant time, leave the emporia of the Eastern World far behind." [86]

The commercial results of the purchase were immediate. Among other things a commercial chain, long in process of formation, was completed, connecting the East, the West, and the South by way of Philadelphia, Pittsburgh, and New Orleans. The strongest links in this chain were the merchants and exporters of the Ohio valley. They purchased goods in the East on credit, and sold them to inland farmers at a profit, receiving in payment farm products which formed cargoes for ships and schooners locally built. In turn both cargoes, ships and schooners were sold either in southern or Atlantic markets; if in the former, local prod-

---

[86] *Amer. Hist. Review*, vol. xxi, 731; U. S. House. *Executive Documents*, 50 cong., 1 sess., vol. xx, no. 6, pt. ii, 185.

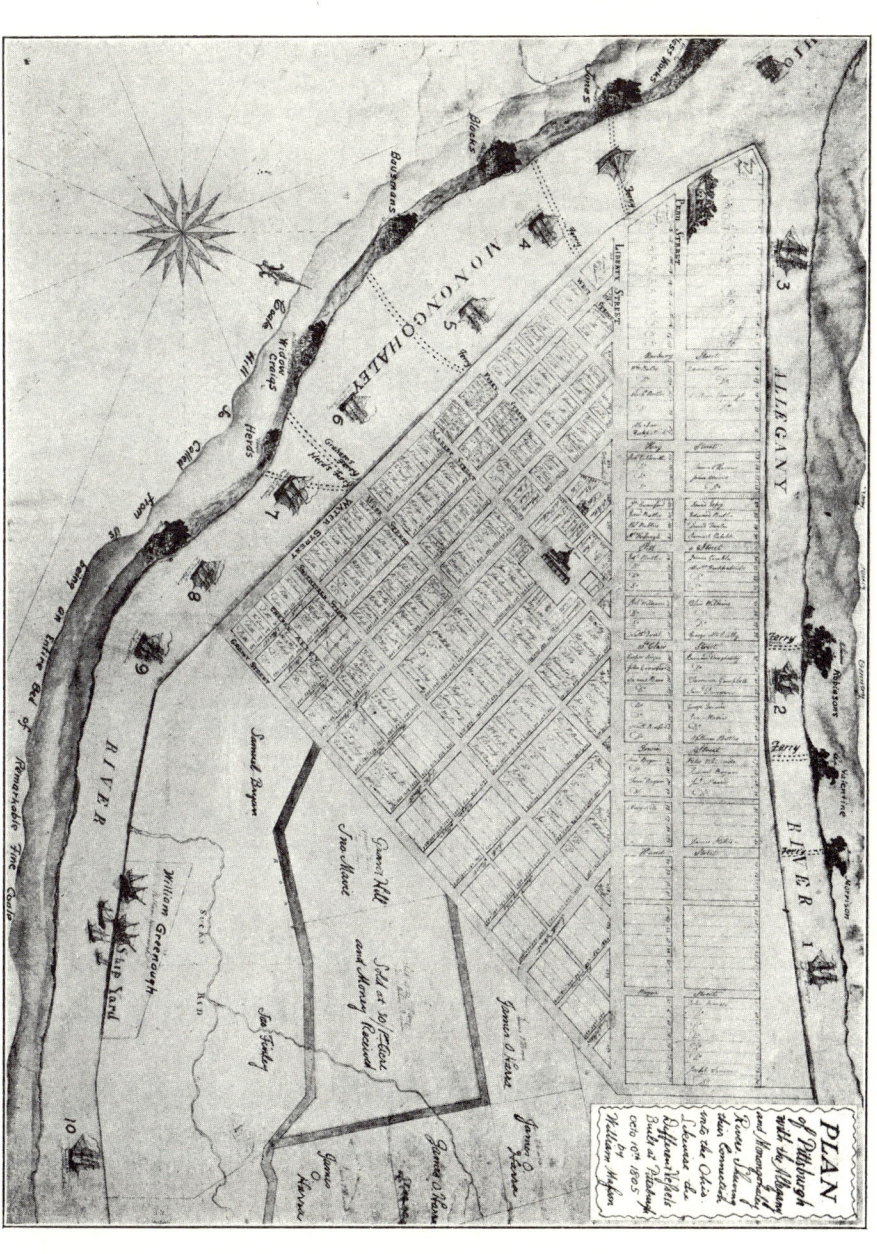

William Mason's Map of Pittsburgh, 1805

Names of vessels: (1) Brig Bison, (2) Schooner Allegany, (3) Brig Fayett, (4) Ship Customs Trader,

SHIPBUILDING ON THE INLAND WATERS

ucts, cotton, sugar, tobacco, etc., were accepted in payment and re-sold in the latter, where the vessels themselves found their best market. For instance, the "Ohio," which sailed from Marietta in 1804, was sold the same year in Philadelphia for ten thousand dollars exclusive of her cargo.[87]

The volume of traffic descending the Ohio in sea-going vessels during the early years of the last century can not be ascertained, the incomplete port records of the time making no distinction between it and that carried by other craft. It is certain that dozens of such craft descended to New Orleans and beyond, many of them with capacity cargoes. During the period at least twenty-five sailing craft were built about the mouth of the Muskingum and descended thence to the high seas. Contemporary accounts mention shipbuilding in Allentown, Freeport, Wheeling, Cincinnati, Louisville, and other places in addition to those already mentioned elsewhere.[88] Mason's map of Pittsburgh for 1805 shows twelve sailing vessels and an extensive shipyard.[89] The shipbuilding possibilities of the Ohio valley now attracted agents of eastern firms, who built there sea-going vessels for use on the Atlantic. For example, the "Francis" and the "Robert Hall" of New York and the "Dean" of Philadelphia were built on the Ohio, the first two at Marietta and the last at Pittsburgh. According to the Liverpool *Saturday Advertiser* for July 9, 1803, the "Dean" was the first vessel "which ever came to Europe from the western waters

---

[87] Ashe, *Travels in America*, 20; *Amer. Hist. Review*, vol. xxi, 728-729; Thwaites, *op. cit.*, vol. iii, 158-159.

[88] *Ohio Arch. and Hist. Quarterly*, vol. xxii, 62.

[89] Cramer, Zadok. *Navigator* (Pittsburgh, 1818), 60; Pittsburgh *Gazette Times*, July 2, 1922; *idem*, July 9, 1922.

of the United States." [90] A conservative estimate placed a value of one million dollars on the sailing craft built on the Ohio during the first eight years of the last century.

It is doubtful, however, whether the material results of this industry were the most important. Along with these came a broadened outlook that led inland America to participate in world commerce and aroused its interest in international affairs. Henceforth New Orleans was more than a convenient market for the cargoes of flatboats and barges. It was a window from which, for the first time, interior America could view the world to advantage. That is why Jackson's subsequent victory over the British at New Orleans meant more to inland America than did the victory of Washington and Lafayette at Yorktown. Ever since the former event there were those who have commented upon the anomaly of a war launched and waged by an inland people to establish their right to use the high seas.

Unfortunately the events leading to this war worked irreparable injury to the shipbuilding industry on the Ohio. Misled by the poetic license of a local bard of Marietta, who celebrated Independence Day, 1808, and incidentally took a fling at the administration, some persons have concluded that this industry was ruined "forever." [91] The language of the local bard was indeed deceptive. He said:

> Our ships all in motion
> Once whitened the Ocean
> They sailed and returned with a cargo;
> Now doomed to decay
> They have fallen a prey
> To Jefferson, worms, and Embargo.

---

[90] *Amer. Hist. Review*, vol. xxi, 729-730.
[91] —*Idem*, 732.

SHIPBUILDING ON THE INLAND WATERS

Records seem to indicate, however, that sea-going craft continued to be built on the Ohio in the years immediately following 1808. Gallatin's report of that year on internal improvements, prepared in obedience to a resolution of the Senate of March 2, 1807, says:

> Numerous vessels, from one hundred to three hundred and fifty tons burden, are now annually built at several shipyards on the Ohio, even as high up as Pittsburgh, and bringing down to New Orleans the produce of the upper country consumed there, carry to Europe and the Atlantic ports of the United States the cotton, the sugar, and the tobacco of Louisiana and of the states of Tennessee and Kentucky.[92]

It may be recalled incidentally that Gallatin resided on the Monongahela not far from Pittsburgh. Furthermore, continued his report:

> That branch of national industry gives value to the immense forests of the Ohio and of its numerous branches, and will soon make a considerable, and perhaps necessary, accession to the shipping of the United States, and has a tendency to diminish the price of freights from New Orleans to the other American and to foreign ports. The importance of this last consideration will be duly felt, if the magnitude of the exports of which New Orleans is destined to be the emporium, be contrasted with the probable amount of its importations; for such are the labor, time and expense necessary to ascend the rapid stream of the Mississippi . . . that, whilst the greater part of the produce of the immense country, watered by that river and its tributary streams must, necessarily be exported through its channel, the importations of a considerable portion of that country will continue to be supplied from the Atlantic seaports, by water and land communications, susceptible of considerable improvement; and thus, unless another outlet be found for a portion of the exports, or unless the upper country can supply vessels, those exports must necessarily pay a double freight.

Thus, in 1808, it seemed necessary to the best interest of the Ohio valley, as well as of the country at large,

---
[92] Inland Waterways Commission. *Preliminary Report*, 553.

that inland shipbuilding be continued. Moreover, the subsequent writings of travelers described ships in process of construction and in action on the Ohio. In the last days of 1810 a brig of one hundred sixty tons burden descended that stream from the Allegheny,[93] and for years thereafter Pittsburgh and neighboring ports maintained "ship-yards." It was not until 1811 that Zadok Cramer, editor and publisher of the *Navigator* and a careful observer of local events, bade adieu to the "white sail of commerce" of the interior. In announcing the completion of the "New Orleans," the first steamboat on the Ohio, he said: "Now the white sail of commerce is to give place to vessels propelled by steam." It is true that flatboats, barges, arks, and keelboats sometimes used sails; but their main reliance for motive power was upon currents and brawn, and they continued to be used for decades. Moreover, Cramer himself later attributed the decline of shipbuilding on the Ohio to the "misfortunes and accidents" in getting ships thence to the ocean.[94]

Some may ask, what did kill early shipbuilding on the Ohio, if it was not the Embargo? To this question one might answer that it was not killed, it died; and as usual under such conditions a number of things contributed to its passing. Among the most important of these was the absence of credit facilities. Despite the stabilizing influences of the Louisiana Purchase, money could not be had at any price in inland America, certainly not for hazardous undertakings. Furthermore, no attempt was made to improve the navigation of the inland rivers until well into the nineteenth century, the consequent delays at the Falls of the Ohio being de-

---

[93] Cramer, *op. cit.*, 20; *Ohio Arch. and Hist. Quarterly*, vol. xxii, 64.
[94] Cramer, *op. cit.*, 60.

structive of more than patience. Inland-built sailing craft continued to be designed, also, for use on the high seas and not for navigating the inland rivers, years being required before artisans learned to design steamboats for the latter use. Finally, possibly the decisive factor in the passing of the shipbuilding industry of the Ohio valley of this period was the coming of the steamboat, as indicated by Cramer.

But, like later steamboat building on the Ohio, shipbuilding there had a "come-back," made possible by the developments of the years immediately following our second war with Great Britain. On the high seas the American clipper ship became a formidable competitor for all commerce; repeal of the English Corn Laws created a foreign demand for American food products; and the annexation of Texas stimulated the African slave trade, regardless of the fact that England and other countries then condemned it as piracy. Moreover, at home the corporate method had simplified financing; the inhabitants of the Ohio valley had learned needed lessons in business coöperation, as was attested by the numerous banks that had been established there; and initial steps had been taken to improve the navigation both of the Ohio and the Mississippi.

It was under these changed conditions that citizens of Marietta, in 1844, organized the Marietta Ship Company, a joint-stock concern. Although the incorporators had forgotten the art of shipbuilding, they had not forgotten the land of shipbuilders in America. Accordingly they turned to New England, the home of their fathers, where they found a master builder, Captain Ira Ellis. Under his directions a ship-yard that bore his name was established in Marietta.

The first sea-faring craft built at Marietta in this period of construction was the "Muskingum." She was launched in 1844, full rigged, except for her sails which were made in Boston and set in New Orleans. She left Marietta in March, 1844, being towed by a steamboat thence to Cincinnati, where she received her cargo. Thence she was towed to New Orleans whence she sailed under the command of Captain Wm. R. Wells direct to Liverpool, England. Of her safe arrival there the *Times* of that city, January 30, 1845, in a statement at some variance with facts, said:

> We have received a file of Cincinnati news papers, brought by the first vessel that ever cleared out of that city for Europe. The building of a vessel of 350 tons on a river 1700 miles from the sea, in itself, is a remarkable circumstance, both as a proof of the magnificence of the American rivers and the spirit of the American people. The navigation of such a vessel down the Ohio and the Mississippi and thence across the Atlantic would, a few years ago, have been thought impossible. She brings a cargo of provisions, and we trust that the success of this first venture will be such as to encourage its frequent repetition.[95]

Later the "Marietta," an exact counterpart of the "Muskingum," was built at Marietta and sent thence to the sea, also under command of Captain Wells. From New Orleans she sailed to Boston, where an effort was made to sell her. Failing in this her captain turned to the high seas and made many voyages, one of which carried her to Montevideo, South America. It was there that the "Marietta" met her sister ship, the "Muskingum," the two lying side by side in that port for some time. To those familiar with the anti-slavery traditions of Marietta the hankerings of her sailing craft of the forties for the environs of Africa would

---

[95] Cist, Charles. *Cincinnati in 1851* (Cincinnati, 1851), 322.

indicate that not all her inhabitants were interested in underground railroads.

The second period of shipbuilding on the Ohio reached its height about 1847 but extended beyond the Civil war. Throughout, Marietta was an important building center, sending thence many ocean-going vessels. Among others there was the "Walhoning" of two hundred forty tons, built in 1847. Then followed the "America," "Grace Darling," "Ohio," and others, but the most popular of all was the "John Farnum" of two hundred forty tons. She was built in 1847 and went out as a relief ship to sufferers of the Irish famine. She was towed from Marietta to Portsmouth, Ohio, where she took on a load of corn. Her subsequent safe arrival at Cork, Ireland, was announced by the English and American press which alike predicted the building of many other such ships, provided only that the European demand for American food products continued.[96]

Meanwhile, other Ohio river ports established shipyards and launched sea-going vessels, the number and character of which almost defy determination and description. Among other builders were English capitalists who now purchased large tracts of land on and near the Ohio for their timber alone; Cincinnati, Pittsburgh, which now built sailing craft of iron, and Point Pleasant became outstanding building centers, rivaling Marietta; and subsidiary industries, notably brickmaking, the products of which were used for ballast, sprang up. The possibilities seemed to call for unusual preparations. Accordingly, the Illinois river was surveyed with a view to connecting the Great Lakes and the Mississippi river by a canal suited to the use of sea-

[96] *Cist's Weekly Advertiser* (Cincinnati), May 17, 1847; *idem*, July 27, 1847.

going vessels. In various ways Americans manifested pride in the situation. Among other things, representations of inland-built ships were considered suitable decorations for the glass cup-plates then in use in the homes of the most fastidious, and, commenting upon the fact that five hundred steamboats were then navigating the inland waters of the United States, *Cist's Weekly Advertiser* (Cincinnati) for May 17, 1847, said: "But this does not satisfy us: we must build ships of iron and wood to float on the ocean waves and carry our commerce as we carry our flag around the world." More significant still, John C. Calhoun took the place of Thomas Jefferson in predicting a great future for the Mississippi and for New Orleans in particular under the changed conditions.[97]

Writing in 1851, John Swasey, a shipbuilder of Cincinnati, expressed the belief that sea-going vessels could then be built on the Ohio to as good advantage and "at less cost" than in any eastern city. He had already built and launched there three such craft, namely: the "Louisa" of 200 tons; the "John Swasey" of 300 tons; and the "Salem" of 350 tons. His account of their and other activities throws light upon contemporaneous shipbuilding as well as upon the use made of the products. He said:

> The "Louisa" and the "John Swasey" took in full cargoes at this point for Salem and Boston, proceeding down the river in tow of steamers to New Orleans and putting right out to sea, stopping at New Orleans only long enough to bend sails and ship a crew. These craft have proved themselves fine vessels and fast sailers. The "Louisa" lately returned to Salem from a six months' trading voyage to the west coasts of Africa, and the captain reported her sailing and weather qualities to be of the highest order. The "Salem" which was

[97] — *Idem*, May 9, 1848; *Waterways Journal* (St. Louis, 1891-date), May 20, 1910.

SHIPBUILDING ON THE INLAND WATERS 105

launched about two months ago, left this place light in the expectation of being able to procure at New Orleans a profitable cargo for California, eastern ports, or Europe.

Three years ago we built at Marietta on the Muskingum, two schooners – the "Grace Darling" and the "Ohio" of 150 tons burden. Both of these vessels we loaded at this spot with provisions and other produce for Salem. These vessels have ever since been engaged in the African trade and are in no respect behind any vessels in their class. About three years ago the "Minnesota," a ship of 350 tons, was built at this place for Captain Deshon of New Orleans. She was entered for the cotton carrying trade but has since made several voyages to several parts of the world and proved herself a good ship. We are now getting out the timbers for another ship of 350 tons, to be built at Covington, and ready to launch in the early part of next fall. The timbers for this vessel we procured from the neighborhood of Point Pleasant on the Kanawha.[98]

As already indicated ships continued to be built and to descend the Ohio until after the Civil war. There are those yet living who saw some of the last ones built, in frames, and on their way to the high seas. Probably the last of these craft was the barque, "Mary Belle Roberts," built near the mouth of the Little Hockhocking, where she stood in frames during the greater part of the early sixties. Of her final completion and the preparations for her sailing the Cincinnati *Commercial* for March 2, 1865, said:

The new A1 copper barque, "Mary Belle Roberts," of 600 tons capacity, Captain Chas. E. Ware, will soon arrive and load here going directly to New York by way of New Orleans. Several vessels in the past years have been built here and loaded for Liverpool direct, yet it is a novel spectacle to see an ocean vessel at our levee giving through receipts for New York.

In conclusion it may be worth while to compare the outstanding facts in the two periods of shipbuilding on the Ohio described in this chapter. Possible contrasts,

[98] Cist, *Cincinnati in 1851*, 323.

pass in review important facts in our national development. First of all, it will be recalled that the ships of the earlier period were the handiwork of local owners and builders operating as partners, whereas those of the later mid-century were the products of imported artisans who built for joint-stock companies and as a business. More significant still, the earlier craft drifted to the sea with the current, whereas those of the later period were towed to New Orleans by steamboats. Throughout, rigging and all, the inland-built ships of the early century were the products of the Ohio valley. Those of the later period depended upon the East, Salem, and Boston, for ropes, sails, and other rigging supplies. The ships of each period descended the Ohio with cargoes of surplus agricultural products, but the demand for such goods was stimulated in the earlier period by international wars, in the later by international free trade. As a rule ships of the earlier period were sold immediately after reaching New Orleans and discharging their cargoes, while on the other hand those of the later period were built to order for permanent owners who used them for participation in world commerce, even the African slave-trade. Finally, the first period ended amid a group of unfavorable conditions — lack of credit facilities, difficult navigation, embargoes, wars, and the coming of the steamboat; whereas the second period closed in the midst of civil war and after the advent of the locomotive and the steamship.

The First Steamboats west of the Alleghanies

Many things combined to make 1811 the *annus mirabilis* of the West. Among others the waters of its principal rivers overflowed their banks; unprecedented sickness followed; numberless gray squirrels left the North and pressed forward in deep and solid phalanx toward the South; for short periods countless numbers of passenger pigeons blackened the skies by day and mutilated forests by night; the splendid comet of the year long shed its twilight over the forests; toward the end thereof the whole Mississippi valley, from the Missouri to the Gulf of Mexico, was shaken by an earthquake; in political circles "war-hawks," having turned their backs upon the Old World, talked of an appeal to arms in defence of free trade and sailors' rights; and finally the first steamboat began its descent of the Ohio and Mississippi rivers.

Had it marked only the coming of the steamboat, the year 1811 would have been memorable in the annals of inland America. It was a high point in a long period of endeavor and sacrifice to solve its transportation needs by the use of steam.[99] Prominent among local characters who worked and sacrificed to this end were John

---

[99] For general summaries of the transportation history of the Ohio valley see U. S. *Census*, 1880, vol. iv, 659-666; Preble, George H. *History of Steam Navigation* (Philadelphia, 1883), 1-97; Sweeney, John M. *The Construction of Steamboats navigating the Western Waters of the United States* (Wheeling, 1893. Pamphlet. Paper read before the World's Columbian Exposition Engineering Congress, Chicago, 1893); Winsor, *The Westward*

Fitch of Connecticut, Pennsylvania, and Kentucky, James Rumsey of Virginia, and Edward West of Kentucky. For more than a decade prior to 1811 many persons throughout the whole country were more or less familiar with the particulars of a "war of pamphlets" between Fitch and Rumsey over the merits of their respective inventions and their claims to priority. Fitch contended that Rumsey's boat of 1784, built at Bath, Virginia, propelled by a series of "setting-poles," and approved by General Washington, was not adapted to the use of steam as a motive power. The subsequent application of steam to navigation by Fitch, 1786, attracted much attention and resulted, the following year, in acts of the legislatures of Pennsylvania, Delaware, New York, and Virginia giving him exclusive rights to navigate the waters within their boundaries. This was very discouraging to Rumsey who had meanwhile perfected a boat that could move against river currents, steam being employed to pump water into tubes and discharge it in such a way as to move the boat forward. Encouraged by his exclusive privileges, Fitch constructed at least two other steamboats before the end of the century, one of which was operated for some time on the Delaware river.

Both Fitch and Rumsey were, however, overtaken by disappointment and consequent despair and left the scenes of their early achievements, the latter going to England where he died in 1792, and the former to Kentucky, where he is said to have terminated his own life, in 1798, at Bardstown, leaving a request that his remains be buried on the banks of the Ohio, "where the

Movement, 620-625; Gould, *Fifty Years on the Mississippi*, chaps. 2-4; Thurston, *Allegheny County's Hundred Years*; U. S. *Congressional Record*, March 2, 1915; Kettell, Thomas P. *Eighty Years Progress* (Hartford, 1869).

songs of the boatmen would enliven the stillness of his resting place, and the music of the steam engine soothe his spirit." [100]

Little is known of the achievements of West other than that in 1802 he was granted a patent for a steamboat which he is said to have built in Kentucky.

Elsewhere other Americans were trying to solve the mysteries of the proposed steamboat. Prominent among them were: Jehosaphat Starr and Captain Samuel Mowry of Connecticut; Nathan Reed of Massachusetts; Wm. Longstreet of Georgia; Elijah Ormsbee of Rhode Island; John Stevens of New Jersey; Oliver Evans and Robert Fulton, both of Pennsylvania; and John French, Robert Livingston, and Nicholas J. Roosevelt, all of New York. Although none of the devices first constructed by these would-be inventors proved practicable, some attracted wide attention. Among them was the "Eruktor Amphibolis," a steamboat built by Oliver Evans, in 1804, on the Delaware river, which is said to have made sixteen miles on a trial trip, "leaving all the vessels that were under sail full half way behind." In the same year John Stevens perfected machinery which was installed on a boat and operated successfully. In 1844 this same machinery was reinstalled on a barge which it moved at the rate of six miles an hour.[101]

From the practical standpoint Robert Fulton was certainly the most successful of these experimenters.

---

[100] Gould, *op. cit.*, 18.

[101] Almost simultaneously with the completion of the "Clermont" by Fulton, John Stevens launched the "Phoenix" at Hoboken, New Jersey. As the "Phoenix" could not be used on the Hudson because of the alleged exclusive rights of the Livingstons and others, she was taken to the Delaware river. The trip was made by sea, the "Phoenix" thus being the first steam vessel to navigate the ocean. See U. S. *Census*, 1880, vol. iv, 662; also *Waterways Journal*, January 17, 1914.

More favored with this world's goods than some of his rivals, he was able to study abroad, where he made helpful and influential friends. Among these were Benjamin West, the great English artist; James Watt, perfector of the steam engine; Robert R. Livingston, ambassador of the United States to France, inventor of experimental steamboats, and owner of the exclusive rights formerly granted to John Fitch for the navigation of the rivers of New York by steam appliances; and the Emperor Napoleon who was interested in Fulton's experiments and under more favorable circumstances might have become a real benefactor. These and other friends were able to put at Fulton's command the accumulated knowledge of the ages upon the subject of steam. The results were the "Clermont," the first practicable steamboat. She ran on the Hudson river between New York and Albany, her first successful trip beginning August 17, 1807. Other boats followed, and soon the practicability of steam navigation in the Tidewater was established.[102]

It must not be inferred that Americans were the sole contributors to the invention of the steamboat. Centuries before they wrought, the possibilities of such a device had challenged the genius of other lands. From Blasco de Garay who, in 1543, is said to have exhibited before the Emperor Charles V. a vessel the motive power of which came from "a caldron of boiling water and a movable wheel suspended on either side," to the numerous foreign contemporary rivals of Fitch, Rumsey, and Fulton, there were scores of persons, most of whom resided in Europe, who cogitated the various possibilities of steam. The invention of the steam engine by the Marquis of Worcester, 1597, gave new impetus

---

[102] U. S. *Census*, 1880, vol. iv, 659-670.

to their endeavors, and new suggestions followed with each succeeding generation. The most practical of these seems to have been that by Jonathan Hulls who was granted a patent by George II. of England for the perfection of a steam invention designed to carry boats against wind and tide. In 1737 Hulls published a treatise, a drawing of which shows a picture of a steamboat not unlike those "invented" fifty years later. Hence, public information of steam navigation must have circulated before the experiments of the later eighteenth century, and, while similarity of ideas is possible, absolute originality is difficult to establish.[103]

Fortunately Robert Fulton's chief concern was not with honors and credits. Otherwise he might have devoted his time to pamphlet writing in defence of his claims as an inventor.[104] Instead, the practicability of steam navigation having been demonstrated in the Tidewater, he turned to the West, where boatmen and shipbuilders were then wrestling with a difficult navigation. Luckily, the commercial possibilities of this region had long occupied a place in Fulton's plans. In 1803 he had written to James Monroe, then ambassador to Great Britain: "You have perhaps heard of the success of my experiments for navigating boats by steam engines and you will feel the importance of establishing such boats on the Mississippi and other rivers of the United States as soon as possible."

Meanwhile Fulton had associated with himself in business Robert R. Livingston whose brother, Edward Livingston, was already prominent in Louisiana; De Witt Clinton who, as governor of New York, later built

---

[103] U. S. *Congressional Record*, March 2, 1915; *Waterways Journal*, January 17, 1914.

[104] Sutcliffe, Alice Crary. *Robert Fulton and the Clermont* (New York, 1909).

the Erie canal; Daniel D. Tompkins, then governor of New York and later vice-president of the United States; Nicholas J. Roosevelt, a practical engineer; and others who numbered among their friends persons in high financial and official positions. Resources were matters of minor concern to this association, their first and chief interest being to determine the practicability of steam navigation on the western waters and to secure exclusive privileges to navigate them.[105] Un-American as the latter purpose may now seem, it was not generally so regarded in that waning day of special privilege.

Accordingly Nicholas J. Roosevelt was sent to the West to make surveys of physical, as well as political conditions, the latter being almost as important as the former. "If everything was favorable," Fulton and his associates planned to build steamboats on the inland waters and to operate them on the Ohio and the Mississippi rivers, boats being designed in each case for the use of trades later to be established. As then planned there were to be three separate trades: first, that between New Orleans and Natchez; second, that between Natchez and Louisville; and finally, in the event the first two proved practicable and profitable, that between Louisville and Pittsburgh. From the beginning it was understood that Roosevelt was to make surveys and supervise construction, Fulton and his other associates supplying the necessary capital.

Encouraged by the greatness of the undertaking and by the presence of his young wife, a sister of the celebrated attorney and writer, J. H. B. Latrobe of Baltimore, Roosevelt arrived in Pittsburgh in May, 1809. A flatboat designed for convenience and comfort was secured, and the happy pair were soon on their way to

[105] *Ohio Arch. and Hist. Quarterly*, vol. xxii, 17.

New Orleans. *En route* they gauged river currents to determine, as far as possible, their velocity for different seasons of the year, and collected stores of statistical information concerning every phase of life in the interior. In true Roosevelt fashion plans and purposes were not shrouded in mystery. From the outset everybody was told to expect his speedy return, and that too in a steamboat! As proof of his earnestness Roosevelt caused coal mines to be opened on the Ohio and collected a quantity of fuel near Pomeroy. The survey ended at New Orleans in December, 1809, and soon thereafter Roosevelt's associates were in possession of an exhaustive and impressive report endorsing and urging the practicability of steam navigation on the western waters.

Immediate action was delayed, however, waiting decisions of inland legislatures upon requests for exclusive privileges to navigate local rivers which the states and territories were then supposed to control. Following the initial successes of the "Clermont" the Fulton interests found themselves opposed by those who would have destroyed their monopolies. In addition to formidable business rivals there were those who questioned both the legality of their patents and their concessions. From the free and liberty-loving West came rumors of an intention to recognize neither. Nevertheless, the Fulton interests pressed their claims and plans with vigor, powerful forces being set to work throughout the entire Union in their behalf.

As a result a territorial legislature granted them the exclusive rights of steam navigation on the Mississippi within the Territory of Orleans.[106] Unfortunately for them but fortunately for the interior and the whole

---

[106] Claiborne, W. C. C. *Official Letter Books*, 1801-1816 (Jackson, Miss., 1917), vol. v, 220; *idem*, vol. vi, 2-4.

country as well, this concession placed its recipients in a position not unlike that occupied by Spain in the days before the purchase of Louisiana and revived the long-drawn-out fight for the freedom of the western waters. Influenced by natural antipathies and wise counsel other inland legislatures refused to make similar concessions.

Confident of further success in the political game and encouraged by Roosevelt's report, the Fulton interests prepared for the next feature of their program, that of building and operating steamboats on the Ohio and the Mississippi. First the Ohio Steam Navigation Company was organized, and Roosevelt was again sent to the West, this time to supervise the construction of a steamboat and to initiate steam navigation. Accompanied by his loyal wife he reached Pittsburgh in the spring of 1810 and in characteristic fashion proceeded to the undertaking before him. It took only a short time to lay the keel of the proposed steamboat that was to do much to revolutionize the life and industry of the West. The scene of this momentous event was on the Allegheny side of Pittsburgh immediately under a bluff called Boyd's hill.

Construction proceeded slowly, however. Unforeseen difficulties delayed the work and at times threatened the success of the enterprise. Strange as it may seem, suitable timbers could not be had within reasonable distances, the earlier boat builders having wrought a destruction not unlike that of a modern lumber camp; the saw-pit, then the only means for manufacturing lumber in the interior, was inadequate; and despite the fact that hundreds of workmen were then employed in the boatyards of the upper Ohio, skilled workmen, such as were needed for the fabrication of steamboats,

FIRST STEAMBOATS WEST OF ALLEGHANIES 115

were scarcely to be had at any price. Then, too, the elements seemed to conspire to defeat success. Storms descended and floods came carrying away timbers and threatening the destruction of the boat itself.[107]

Nevertheless, the very fact that a steamboat was being built on the waters of the Ohio aroused strange reflections in the minds of many, so momentous were the possibilities. The following from Zadok Cramer, as recorded in his *Navigator*,[107a] is probably typical:

> There is now on foot a new mode of navigating our western waters, particularly the Ohio and the Mississippi rivers. This is with boats propelled by the power of steam. This plan has been carried into successful operation on the Hudson river at New York, and on the Delaware between New Castle and Burlington. It has been stated that the one on the Hudson goes at the rate of four miles an hour against wind and tide on her route between New York and Albany, and frequently with five hundred passengers on board. From these successful experiments there can be but little doubt of the plan succeeding on our western waters, and proving of immense advantage to the commerce of our country . . . It will be a novel sight, and as pleasing as novel to see a huge boat working her way up the windings of the Ohio, without the appearance of sail, oar, pole, or any manual labor about her – moving within the secrets of her own wonderful mechanism, and propelled by power undiscoverable! – This plan, if it succeeds, must open to view flattering prospects to an immense country, an interior of not less than two thousand miles of as fine a soil and climate as the world can produce, and to a people worthy of all the advantages that nature and art can give them, a people the more meritorious, because they know how to sustain peace and live independent among the crushing of empires, the falling of kings, the slaughter and bloodshed of millions, and the tumult, corruption and tyranny of all the world beside. The immensity of country we have yet to settle, the vast riches of the bowels of the earth, the unexampled advantage of our water courses, which wind without interruption for thousands of miles, the numerous sources of trade and

---

[107] Gould, *op. cit.*; Maryland Hist. Society, *Fund Publication* (Baltimore, 1867), vol. viii, 32.

[107a] Edition 1818, p. 30, quoting an earlier edition.

wealth opening to the enterprising and industrious citizens, are reflections that must rouse the most dull and stupid.

Roosevelt's boat was launched in March, 1811, and was later christened the "New Orleans" in honor of her future home port. She was one hundred thirty-eight feet long, twenty-six and one-half feet beam, and cost approximately forty thousand dollars. Her capacity is not definitely known but is variously estimated at from three hundred to four hundred tons. In general design she was not unlike the sailing craft of her day, having port-holes, a bowsprit eight feet in length, and was painted sky-blue. Both cabin and machinery were in the hold.[108]

Important facts about the "New Orleans" being veiled in obscurity, descriptions are hazardous. At the time of her construction independent promoters were trying to copy her design and to get suggestions from it. Accordingly, authoritative statements about her are few and meager, and other statements are conflicting. Some even deny that she was the first steamboat built on the Ohio; some picture her as a stately side-wheeler with a cabin extending almost the entire length of her deck; and still others say she was a stern-wheeler with two cabins, one fore and the other aft, each mounted by a mast.

The Centennial Anniversary of the introduction of steam navigation on the western waters, 1911, gave rise to numerous conjectures and contentions regarding the essential features of the "New Orleans." From information from Latrobe, Habermehl, Thurston, and others, some continued to maintain that she was a stern-wheeler. On the other hand others were equally certain

---

[108] U. S. *Census*, 1880, vol. iv, 662; U. S. House. *Executive Documents*, 50 cong., 1 sess., vol. xx, no. 6, pt. ii, 187.

The First Steamboat on the Ohio River

There exists a controversy as to whether this was a stern-wheeler or a side-wheeler. The two plates above give the two prevailing ideas. *See* text pages 114-120.

FIRST STEAMBOATS WEST OF ALLEGHANIES 119

that she was a side-wheeler. Among the latter was Captain James A. Henderson of Pittsburgh, who supervised the construction of a replica of the "New Orleans," which, under his command, descended the Ohio and the Mississippi in commemoration of the earlier event. His conclusions were based upon studies of the machinery used, or thought to have been used, on the first "New Orleans," results of researches made in the federal Patent Office, and upon information regarding the general character and purpose of the early Fulton steamboats used in the interior.[109]

The present writer is unable to decide this controversy. There is a possibility of the correctness of either side. It is certain that both stern-wheel and side-wheel steamboats were in use in 1811 and that Fulton was familiar with all the facts. It is not improbable, also, that builders and prospective builders were more or less agreed upon the superior advantages of the side-wheeler for lower river courses and upon those of the stern-wheeler for the upper and swifter currents. The uniformity of early writers as to the stern-wheel for the "New Orleans" is significant, as is also the fact, on the other side, that she was intended for use on the lower Mississippi. In the light of recent contentions the accompanying illustrations, each of the first steamboat built on the Ohio, are more interesting than informing.[109a]

As the "New Orleans" approached completion, interest in her grew apace. A trial trip on the Mononga-

---

[109] Pittsburgh *Gazette Times*, November 11, 1917; *Waterways Journal*, September 28, 1907; idem, October 28, 1911; idem, December 2, 1911; idem, June 8, 1912; *Ohio Arch. and Hist. Quarterly*, vol. xxii; Hulbert, *Paths of Inland Commerce*, 78.

[109a] Several other illustrations might have been used. For example see Dunbar, *op. cit.*, vol. i, 337, and Habermehl, John. *Life on the Western Rivers* (Pittsburgh, 1901), 14.

hela quieted misgivings about her ability to move against a current. Local interest then shifted to Mrs. Roosevelt who, it was rumored, intended to accompany her husband on his proposed voyage. To the surprise of many, particularly the women folk, the rumor was confirmed, whereupon Mr. Roosevelt was entreated not to place his wife's life in peril, however reckless he might be with his own. But Mrs. Roosevelt believed in her husband and in the ultimate success of his undertaking and was immovable in her purpose to accompany him. Moreover, the muse of history beckoned her to a choice place in its annals, and the new steamboat was palatial in comparison with the flatboat in which she, as a bride, had journeyed from Pittsburgh to New Orleans only two years before.

On her descent of the Ohio the "New Orleans" was manned by the following: Roosevelt, who acted as captain; an engineer named Baker; Andrew Jack, the pilot; six hands; two female servants; a man waiter; and a cook. Except for Mrs. Roosevelt, there were no passengers, immigrants to the West doubtless preferring passage on the tried barge and the flatboat. Accompanying the solitary passenger was an immense Newfoundland dog named Tiger.

The departure of the "New Orleans" was an important event in the history of Pittsburgh.[110] It was late in October, 1811, low water having prevented a contemplated earlier start. As she "rounded off" before an enthusiastic crowd of wellwishers, cheers rent the air; flags floated in the breezes; and hats were tossed on high. Neither bells nor whistles disturbed the applause, the trumpet being the sole mechanical device then in use for giving commands both upon the high seas and

---

[110] Pittsburgh *Gazette Times*, November 11, 1917.

upon the inland waters. Moving at the rate of eight to ten miles an hour she disappeared behind the headlands "leaving infant Pittsburgh behind forever." In the minds of those who witnessed this event there were doubtless strange interminglings of hope and fear. Probably only a few realized the importance of the event in the history of the Ohio valley, one of the most important before the coming of the locomotive.

Without mishap the "New Orleans" reached Cincinnati, where for lack of a levee, she anchored in midstream. Her presence was soon known, however, and practically the whole city assembled to celebrate the event. By the aid of skiffs persons came aboard to remind the Roosevelts of their promise to revisit Cincinnati in a steamboat. Though surprised, all were delighted that the promise had been kept, but there were yet some who doubted the practicability of steam navigation. They could not deny what they saw, but they were certain that they would never witness it again. They admitted that the new boat might descend the Ohio and the Mississippi but insisted that it could never ascend them in a regular river traffic. Meanwhile keelboatmen and bargemen surveyed the inland wonder but with little apprehension for their vocations.

The visit to Cincinnati was brief, only long enough to take on a supply of wood for the voyage to Louisville, where the "New Orleans" cast anchor at midnight on the eighth day out. It was a glorious scene that greeted the boat at this strategic point of her venture. On this occasion the moon shone brightly, embellishing in golden hues the waves of the river, and a large crowd had already assembled at the landing. Aroused by the noise of escaping steam, some came to see the comet, then in the heavens, which they thought had fallen into the river. Instead, there were their old friends, the Roosevelts, and the promised steamboat! In true southern fashion Louisville responded with a dinner in honor of her distinguished guests.

Not to be outdone by the hospitality of strangers the Roosevelts gave a return dinner. At the appointed time many of the leading residents of Louisville sat down to the first of the later famous steamboat dinners on the Ohio. In the midst of their repast guests were suddenly aroused by a strange rumbling of the boat accompanied by its perceptible motion. One thought possessed all — "Our boat has escaped her anchor and is drifting toward the Falls to certain destruction." There was a sudden rush to the deck, where it was discovered that instead of drifting the boat was actually making headway up-stream. After an excursion of a few hours all were returned in safety and in a hopeful frame of mind regarding the future of steam navigation on the inland waters.

Finding the Falls impassable, the "New Orleans" returned to Cincinnati, whether with a view to things political or to dispelling the pessimism of that city regarding the future of the steamboat would be difficult to determine. The fact that the Fulton interests expected to secure exclusive rights to navigate the Ohio and that requests to that end were then pending before inland legislatures is significant. It is not improbable, also, that Roosevelt planned to overawe independent builders and inventors who were then said to be interested in rival boats. Some said he was only awaiting the arrival of an expected heir. In any event he made good use of his time.

Toward the end of November, conditions being favorable, the "New Orleans" hastened back to Louisville and made ready to pass the Falls. Again crowds assembled to witness her departure. When all was ready, Mrs. Roosevelt with her new-born babe remaining aboard, Captain Roosevelt gave the command, and each one on board grasped the nearest object and with bated breath awaited the results. Black ledges of rock appeared only to disappear, as the "New Orleans" dashed by them in her more or less precipitous descent. The waters whirled and eddied and threw their spray as the more rapid places in the Falls caused the vessel to pitch forward to what at times seemed certain destruction. Not a word was spoken, the pilots directing the men at the helm by motion of their hands. Even the great Newfoundland dog, companion of Mrs. Roosevelt, is said to have been affected by apprehensions of fear and to have crouched close to the feet of his mistress. Fortunately the passage was made safely.

Contrary to expectations the passage of the Falls was only the prelude to "days of horror." This supposed greatest danger passed, nature seemed to go into travail. It was the time of the great Madrid earthquake, the vibrations of which shook the beds of the Mississippi and the lower Ohio. More than once the ground rose and fell and burst into great fissures which emitted clouds of water and sand. Trees and islands disappeared between days, the former filling the river with new and terrible dangers; the air was filled with gaseous vapors; the sun assumed an ominous hue; the natives were unfriendly; and, on at least one occasion, the vessel was in danger of being destroyed by fire.[111]

In due time the romance ended in safety and the

---

[111] Maryland Hist. Society, *op. cit.*, vol. viii, 84-89; Preble, *op. cit.*, 66-70; Claiborne, John F. H. *Mississippi as a Province, Territory, and State* (Jackson, 1880), vol. i, appendix, 537-545.

"New Orleans" entered the trade for which she was intended. For almost two years she was a financial success, making thirteen regular trips annually between New Orleans and Natchez, an average of ten days being required for each. There were also many side excursions. Down stream she carried from ten to twenty passengers at eighteen dollars each and up-stream from thirty to forty at twenty-five dollars each. Allowing for interest on the investment, her first year's business is said to have netted her owners twenty thousand dollars, a handsome sum for a day of small enterprises.[112]

Encouraged by their initial successes the Fulton interests hastened to complete their original plans for connecting Pittsburgh and New Orleans by steam navigation. To this end they next built the "Vesuvius" of three hundred forty tons. Like her sister boat she too was built at Pittsburgh and only two years later. Meanwhile Roosevelt had yielded his place as superintendent of construction to Benj. H. Latrobe, the distinguished architect of the capital at Washington. Under his direction the "Vesuvius" was launched and sailed in command of Captain Ogden who was succeeded in turn by two other famous pioneer masters, Captains Clement and De Hart. In keeping with original plans she was intended for the trade between Natchez and Louisville, but following the destruction of her famous predecessor which hit a snag and foundered on the lower Mississippi in the summer of 1814, the "Vesuvius" entered the trade between New Orleans and Natchez. Here she aided Jackson against the British and became a source of profit to her owners until destroyed by fire two years later. Subsequently the Fulton interests entered the "Aetna" of three hundred

---

[112] Cramer, *op. cit.*, 3.

forty tons in the Natchez-Louisville trade and the "Buffalo," a lighter boat of special design, in that between Louisville and Pittsburgh.[113]

Influential friends, patent rights, initial successes, and legal monopolies could not win for the Fulton interests the exclusive right to navigate the western waters. In less than one year after the launching of the "New Orleans" Samuel Smith, an independent, built, on the Monongahela, the "Comet" of twenty-five tons. She was a stern-wheeler and was constructed under direction of Daniel French who had been given a patent on light draught steamboats of the stern-wheel type. Moreover, the next year this act of defiance was followed by another, when the same interests built the "Enterprise" of forty-five tons at Brownsville, Pennsylvania. Other independent steamboats followed in rapid succession, so eager were their owners to maintain the freedom of the western waters and to share the profits from their successful navigation.

Of all these independent boats the "Enterprise" already mentioned, gave the best account of herself. After two trips from Pittsburgh to Louisville and return, she entered the employ of the federal government, sailing from Pittsburgh to New Orleans under the command of Captain Henry M. Shreve. After aiding Jackson to defeat the British, Captain Shreve decided to use the "Enterprise" to demonstrate the practicability of steam navigation up-stream between Natchez and Louisville, the swollen condition of the Mississippi and the Ohio lending interest to the undertaking. Fortunately this was to the advantage of his boat, enabling her to use "cut-offs" and "slack-water," thus dodging the most

---

[113] Preble, *op. cit.*, 69; *Ohio Arch. and Hist. Quarterly*, vol. xxii, 22; Gould, *op. cit.*, 138.

dangerous currents. In this way the "Enterprise" was able to reach Louisville in twenty-five days out from New Orleans, being the first steamboat to accomplish that feat. Although her strategy detracted from her credit, her accomplishment was significant.[114] Commenting upon it, the Pittsburgh *Gazette* for June 15, 1815, remarked: "The celerity and safety with which this boat descends and ascends the current of these waters ... must be equally interesting to the farmer and the merchant."

Meanwhile the captain of the "Enterprise" had challenged the claims of the Fulton interests to exclusive rights to navigate the lower Mississippi. Fresh from his services against the British, Shreve thought the conditions favorable for such an undertaking which he doubtlessly regarded as a continuation of his services in the interest of his country. As was expected, he was arrested and his boat detained. Luckily a local court ordered the release of both on the ground that the act of 1812 admitting the state of Louisiana had guaranteed the free navigation of the Mississippi and thus suspended all rights previously granted by the Territory of Orleans. An unqualified victory was denied Shreve, however, pending the decision of a higher tribunal to which the case was appealed.[115]

Meanwhile other independent steamboats continued to appear on the western waters and to demonstrate further the practicability of steam navigation. One of these, the "Zebulon M. Pike," was built in Henderson, Kentucky, by David Prentiss, a distinguished engineer. The "Pike," as she was called, was a sort of cross be-

---

[114] — *Idem*, 94, 101 ; Wheeling *Times*, September 9, 1847.
[115] *Waterways Journal*, August 6, 1921 ; *Ohio Arch. and Hist. Quarterly*, vol. xxii, 17-27.

tween the keelboat and the steamboat, being propelled by both oars and steam, thus betraying some misgivings about the practicability of the latter. She was able, however, to ascend the Ohio to Pittsburgh and the Mississippi to St. Louis, being the first steamboat to reach the latter port. The date of her arrival was August 2, 1817, two months before that of the "Constitution," another independent.[116]

Already Captain Shreve and associates had built the "Dispatch" which was followed in 1816 by the "G. Washington," the largest and most pretentious craft that had yet appeared on the western waters. She was built at Wheeling, Virginia (now West Virginia), by George White, but under the direction of Captain Shreve himself, and was a marked advance in the art of steamboat construction. First of all she floated on the water and not in it. Then, too, she was a double decker, the first on the western waters. Her machinery, boiler and all, was on the first deck, almost entirely out of the hold. Her elegant rooms for the accommodation of passengers are said to have been named for states of the Union, a fact that may have contributed to the perpetuation of the term "state-room." There was also marked improvement in her machinery, high pressure engines of stationary horizontal cylinders being used instead of the low pressure engines of upright cylinders such as were then in use on the Fulton boats.

With this splendid boat Captain Shreve determined to make another test of the legality of the Fulton claims to exclusive privileges to navigate the lower Mississippi. Accordingly she was purposely taken into their alleged domain. The expected happened: he was again

---

[116] *Waterways Journal*, August 6, 1921; Missouri *Gazette* (St. Louis), May 9, 1819; Gould, *op. cit.*, 95-110.

arrested and his boat detained, but again the local courts came to his rescue by requiring his prosecutors to file an indemnifying bond to cover all losses in the event the litigation went against them. Instead, they attempted to bribe the intrepid captain by offering to share with him their alleged monopoly, provided, of course, he would arrange to lose his suit at law. The offer was declined, and the subsequent decision of the court of a lack of jurisdiction pending the outcome of similar litigation in the case of the "Enterprise," left the rights of independents on the lower Mississippi temporarily undetermined but in such a status as to permit them to operate.[117]

Other independent steamboats followed the "G. Washington" even to the lower Mississippi. Some were detained, but none were prosecuted. The required indemnifying bonds were not forthcoming, and public sentiment was decidedly opposed to monopolies of any kind, particularly those suggesting the days and methods of the Spaniards. Indeed, it is doubtful whether court decisions sustaining the Fulton monopolies could have been executed on the lower Mississippi without resort to force. In that event there were then thousands of persons residing along the Ohio who would have joined in reviving the old slogan, "Let's arm ourselves, descend the river, and take New Orleans." Thus the principles in the celebrated case, Gibbons *vs.* Ogden, were effective on the inland waters before they were legally affirmed by John Marshall and his associates and thus became the law of the land.

Still another triumph was in store for Captain Shreve and the "G. Washington." The success of the

---

[117] Chambers, H. E. *History of Louisiana* (Chicago, 1925), vol. i, 525; *Ohio Arch. and Hist. Quarterly*, vol. xxii, 16-27.

"Enterprise," operating against the current of the Mississippi and the Ohio at flood stage and by near cuts over cornfields and meadows, had not convinced the skeptical of the practicability of steam navigation on the upper Mississippi and the Ohio. Accordingly, Captain Shreve determined to remove all doubt about this mooted question. In fact, his new boat, the "G. Washington," had been designed for use in the upper river trades and possibly for further demonstrating the practicability of steam navigation. Hence, it was decided to make another trial trip from New Orleans to Louisville, this time under normal conditions. To the great delight of her owners and others the "G. Washington" accomplished the feat in twenty-five days out. Everywhere in the interior independents rejoiced, and the city of Louisville celebrated the event with a public dinner to Captain Shreve who took advantage of the occasion to predict that the time of steamboats from New Orleans to Louisville would be reduced to ten days. He lived to see it reduced to five.[118]

Locally the effects of the application of steam to navigation were numerous and far reaching. Prospective purchasers of lands along the Ohio are said to have been thrilled by accounts of the "Clermont" and her successful feats on the Hudson. Some of them had already visited the West, only to turn back in despair at the sight of keelboatmen slowly and laboriously "poling" their way up-stream against the currents of the western rivers. Following the success of the "New Orleans" and the "G. Washington," however, the future of the West seemed assured, and settlers again turned their faces towards it in increasing numbers.

---

[118] Gould, *op. cit.*, 105-143; Thurston, *op. cit.*, 106. For a biography of Captain Shreve see *Democratic Review* (New York, 1848), 159-171, 241-251.

The manorial estates which they established along the Ohio and its chief tributaries in the decade immediately following 1817 were testimonials of their hopes and ambitions. It will be recalled that this was the period when negro slavery made its most rapid and extensive growth in what is now West Virginia and when many of its prominent families first established themselves there.

Of the larger and more general effects of the advent of the steamboat on the western waters much has been written and more spoken. Naturally one finds some exaggerations, but there is no denying the fact that this event brought the "Father of Waters" under control. Henceforth its extreme distances and tortuous shiftings ceased to be insuperable barriers to trade and commerce. Immigration on a large scale was stimulated; transportation became a business apart from farming and merchandising; and the volume of traffic, particularly that down stream, was stimulated tremendously, the steamboat providing a safe and quick return for boatmen who had disposed of their craft and cargoes on the lower Mississippi. In 1818-1819, the first year after the practicability of steam navigation on the inland waters was assured, the freight receipts at New Orleans rose to approximately 136,300 tons, valued at almost $17,000,000.[119] and the volume of domestic produce exported thence was greater than that from any other port in the country.

In the Ohio valley at large the coming of the steamboat made possible the dawn of an industrial age that is now the marvel of the world. At once Cincinnati became the "Porkopolis" of the West, hogs being slaugh-

---

[119] U. S. House. *Executive Documents*, 50 cong., 1 sess., vol. xx, no. 6, pt. ii, 191 of Switzler's "Report."

tered and packed at home instead of being driven to eastern markets; Pittsburgh became more closely identified with the iron producing industry; Wheeling increased its production of flour, glass, and paper; and still other cities enlarged their boatyards and established engine and boiler works. In fact, there were then persons in the Ohio valley and elsewhere in the interior who began to think of and to plan for a self-sufficing America. It was to meet their demands that Henry Clay formulated the principles of the "American System." [120]

---

[120] See W. T. Van Metre's "Internal Commerce of the United States," in Johnson, Emory R., et al. *History of Domestic and Foreign Commerce of the United States* (Washington, 1922. Carnegie Institution), vol. i, 213-214; U. S. Bureau of Statistics, 1887. *Report on Internal Commerce*, 199; *Hunt's Merchants' Magazine* (New York, 1839-1870), vol. xxix, 661; U. S. *Census*, 1880, vol. iv, 671.

The Day of Canals and Turnpikes

Steamboating did not enter its heyday on the Ohio until almost two decades after Captain Shreve demonstrated the practicability of steam navigation on the inland waters of America and made them free. The years between marked an interlude in which many things contributed to delay the fullest use of the steamboat. First of all, the panic of 1819 was a depressing influence, and for years thereafter credit was unstable and insufficient. Steamboat architecture was in an experimental stage; annually increasing surpluses of agricultural products, although large, were insufficient to sustain commerce on a grand scale; and lateral feeders, such as roads, canals, and improved rivers, without which few channels of commerce have ever maintained large volumes of traffic, were only in process of construction. Toward the end of the period pestilence in the form of cholera, sectional rivalries over the tariff and internal improvements, continued and recurrent low waters, and impending panic were disturbing and depressing factors. As late as 1816, five years after its introduction in the interior, the steamboat was a "losing concern," the keelboat being the safest and most expeditious method of navigating the Ohio when waters were low, and rivermen were still awaiting "some more happy century of invention" for the solution of their transportation difficulties.[121]

This period was, however, one of preparation for a

---
[121] Carnegie Library of Pittsburgh, *Pittsburgh in 1816*; Cramer, *op. cit.*

great, even a glorious, era in the history of inland river transportation. Toward its close credit became more stable and adequate; steamboat architecture improved; and immigrants continued to reach the interior in increasing numbers, foreigners, many of whom had seen service in the armies of Europe during the Napoleonic wars, now joining natives as they moved from the East to the West. After all it was the spirit and purpose of its people that made inland America a power in the world. Their formative influence was always present but nowhere more so than in a band of immigrants that came under the observation of Henry Rowe Schoolcraft, an American ethnologist. Of them he left this vivid description:

> I mingled in this crowd, and, while listening to the anticipations indulged in, it seemed to me that the war [of 1812] had not, in reality, been fought for "free trade and sailors' rights" where it commenced, but to gain a knowledge of the world beyond the Alleghanies ... The children of Israel could scarcely have presented a more motley array of men and women, with their "kneading troughs" on their backs and their "little ones," than were there assembled, on their way to the land of promise. To judge by the tone of general conversation, they meant, in their generation, to plough the Mississippi valley from its head to its foot. There was not an idea short of it. What a world of golden dreams was there.[122]

It was in the midst of such a movement, 1818, that the Cumberland, or National, road reached the Ohio river. First authorized in 1806 in fulfillment of a promise made four years before to the new born state of Ohio, and begun in 1811, this, our first national highway, had pressed its way west through the beautiful Cumberland gateway leading from the Potomac over Savage mountain to Pine run, Red hill, and the top of Negro mountain, at an elevation of 2,328 feet, the highest point,

---

[122] Carnegie Library of Pittsburgh, *op. cit.*

The Stage-coach
The usual means of overland travel in the days before the railroad.

The Conestoga or covered wagon, the "Vehicle of Empire"

thence across the Youghiogheny river at Somerfield, through Great Meadows, by Braddock's grave, and by Laurel Ridge summit to Uniontown, thence almost due west to Brownsville on the Monongahela, and finally to Wheeling on the Ohio by way of Washington, Pennsylvania. For a generation thereafter this route was the great Appian Way over which passed the life-giving and sustaining forces of the nation. It was selected as a compromise between the long-standing rival claims of Pennsylvania, Maryland, and Virginia to the trade of the West. When completed it was at once tapped by numerous lateral roads, notably that from Baltimore to Cumberland. Stage-coach and freight lines were established thereon, more primitive vehicles giving way first to those of Conestoga and finally to those of Concord type; its overland transportation companies became known far and wide, chief among them being the National, the Good Intent, the Pioneer, and the June Bug; and its local drivers, "Red" Bunting, "Devil Bill" Patterson, and others became better and, in some instances, more favorably known, than their passengers, Henry Clay, Andrew Jackson, William Henry Harrison, Thomas Hart Benton, and other scarcely less distinguished westerners who used this road in going to and from the national capital and the eastern markets. Searight, a local historian, has described the traffic over it in these words:

> As many as twenty-four-horse coaches have been counted in line at one time on the road, and large, broad-wheeled wagons, covered with white canvass stretched over bows, laden with merchandise and drawn by six Conestoga horses, were visible all day long at every point, and many times until late in the evening, besides innumerable caravans of horses, mules, cattle, hogs, and sheep. It looked more like the leading avenue of a great city than a road through rural districts.[123]

[123] Searight, Thomas B. *The Old Pike* (Uniontown, Pa., 1894), 16, 107-116.

Going east, practically all this traffic came from the Ohio and the Monongahela, while that westbound went to augment the river burdens, in 1822 only one wagon in ten passing directly beyond Wheeling into Ohio. Before the end of this period the Monongahela river maintained regular packet lines between Brownsville and Pittsburgh, the steamers "Consul" and "McLane" being among the first thus used there. In a short time these were joined by others, among them the "Baltic," "Atlantic," "Luzerne," "Redstone," "Jefferson," "Franklin," "Telegraph," "Gallatin," "Elisha Bennett," and "John Snowden," each of which played a rôle in one of the most profitable steamboat trades in America.[124]

About the same time Wheeling became a popular river center, steamboats passing thence both up and down stream for the transportation of passengers and freight. Most of the mail passing west over the Cumberland road was redistributed at either Brownsville or Wheeling, and almost every town in the neighborhood of the latter had its own regular packet. Some idea of the volume of freight handled there in 1822, may be had from the fact that local commission merchants unloaded five thousand wagons, each wagon, being reloaded for a return trip to the East.[125]

About the same time other roads from the east tapped the Ohio. Most important of these were the James river and Kanawha turnpike, completed to Guyandot in 1831; the Northwestern turnpike connecting Winchester and Parkersburg, first opened to the Ohio in 1838 and intended from its inception as a rival route to the Cumberland road to the north; and those passing

---

[124] Elizabeth *Herald*, June 7, 1900.
[125] Searight, *op. cit.*, 107.

THE DAY OF CANALS AND TURNPIKES 139

west from Cumberland gap through the blue grass regions of Kentucky to Maysville and the "Mouth of Sandy." Each of these routes contributed to the volume of traffic on the Ohio, which now became so large as to justify the Mail line, operating packets between Louisville and Cincinnati, in extending a regular service of the same kind to Guyandot just above the mouth of the Big Sandy.[126]

Of these lesser routes that by way of the Great Kanawha was by far the most popular. First of all it was the most important post-road between Richmond, Virginia, and the West, a fact that now made necessary a regular steamboat connection with its western terminus. Then, too, it was a favorite with travelers, members of Congress, business men, and cattle and hog drivers. Probably more live stock passed over this one route than over any other connecting the East and the West, the number of hogs in the autumn of 1826 being in excess of sixty thousand. Taverns and hostelries spring up along it, and one of the former, White Sulphur springs, became a famous health resort and social and political center.[127] The following from the pen of a contempora-

[126] See Wayland F. Dunnaway's "History of the James River and Kanawha Canal," in *Columbia University Studies in History, Economics, and Public Law* (New York, 1891-date. irreg.), vol. civ., no. 2; Verhoeff, Mary. *The Kentucky Mountain Transportation and Commerce* (Louisville, 1911); *Waterways Journal*, March 27, 1926; Callahan, *Semi-Centennial History of West Virginia*, 93-110.

[127] The beginnings of the Hotel Ruffner, Charleston, West Virginia, were announced in these words: "Daniel Ruffner has opened a place of private entertainment at his commodious residence one and one-half miles from Charleston on the road leading thence to Lewisburg. His pastures are extensive and corn abundant. For travelers on horseback or in carriages he will be able to furnish good stables well equipped with all kinds of provender for horses." See *Kanawha Western Virginian and Kanawha County Gazette*, November 1, 1826; *Western Virginian*, July 2, 1828; idem, October 29, 1828; MacCorkle, W. A. *The White Sulphur Springs* (Charleston, W. Va., 1924).

neous writer tells something of the cosmopolitan character of the traffic passing that way. He wrote:

> During the past year the roads passing through Charleston have been crowded with travel of every sort. There was the seeker for health passing from the mountains; the adventurer, who after years of absence, was returning to the home of his infancy; the immigrant from the sand hills and red clay of eastern Virginia wending his way to the land of promise far toward the setting sun, gladly changing the country of herrings and chinquopins for one not flowing with milk and honey but producing abundantly of the more substanial enjoyments of "hog and hominy;" the farmer and speculator with their herds of swine, horses and mules, in defiance of the tariff phobia and anti-hog resolutions of Georgia and South Carolina, pressing onward to the gold region, wisely calculating that their brethren of the South will exchange their "yellow dirt" for the good cheer which they bring them and find it more comfortable to live upon bacon than hasty resolutions and *paper manifestoes* – the demon in human form, the dealer in bones and sinew, driving hundreds of his "fellow worms," clanking the chains of their servitude, through the free air of our valley, and destined to send back to us from the banks of the Mississippi the sugar and the cotton of that soil moistened with sweat and blood – all these and more we have seen passing in review before us in the course of a few months.[128]

Meanwhile roads terminating in and about Pittsburgh, from the east, continued to bear annually increasing volumes of traffic. Most of the traffic east by these routes came from the Ohio and its tributaries, while that going west was reshipped by river. This was particularly true of the traffic passing over the Bedford-Lancaster pike which accommodated almost twelve thousand wagons in the year 1817. As on the Cumberland road at a later date, these conveyances were of Conestoga type drawn by four to six horses. From the East the traffic, thus borne, consisted largely of immigrants, general merchandise, and products of

[128] *Kanawha Register* (Charleston, Va.), February 5, 1830.

eastern industry, merchandise and industrial products being exchanged for the agricultural and other raw products of the interior. On his way from Chambersburg to Pittsburgh on this route, in 1818, Henry Bradshaw Fearon, a traveler, saw one hundred three wagons together with sixty-three others with families "from the several places following: – twenty from Massachusetts, – ten from the district of Maine, – fourteen from [New] Jersey, – thirteen from Connecticut, – two from Maryland, – one from Pennsylvania, – one from England, – one from Holland,– and one from Ireland." He also saw about two hundred persons on horseback, twenty on foot, and "one family, with their wagon, returning from Cincinnati, entirely disappointed – a circumstance which, though rare, is by no means, as some might suppose, miraculous." [129]

At the same time the Ohio was being tapped from the north by towpath canals over one of which a future president of the United States, James A. Garfield, was aiding to divert more traffic from that stream than to it. In 1825 New York succeeded in joining the waters of the Hudson and those of Lake Erie by a canal popularly called "Clinton's Big Ditch," for De Witt Clinton who had done most to make it possible. Fearful of the consequences to their commercial prestige and to the river traffic of the Ohio, in which each was interested, both Ohio and Pennsylvania now embarked upon canal building on a large scale. A pet enterprise with each was that of connecting the Ohio and Lake Erie by an artificial waterway, first suggested by George Washington more than a generation before.

Ohio was the first to launch her canal building program, the day selected therefor being a red letter one

---
[129] Carnegie Library of Pittsburgh, *op. cit.*, 26-28.

in her history. The place was Licking summit, a high point between Portsmouth and Cleveland on one of the proposed routes; the guest of honor, who threw the first shovel of dirt, was De Witt Clinton, fresh from triumph in his native state; the local orator was Thomas Ewing, a young man, who later filled many public trusts; and the date was July 4, 1825, just three years to the day before Charles Carroll of Carrollton, last surviving signer of the Declaration of Independence, and John Quincy Adams, president of the United States, in a similar way, began the construction of the Baltimore and Ohio railroad and of the Chesapeake and Ohio canal, respectively. The whole state of Ohio is said to have echoed and reëchoed with the internal improvement plans of the earlier date, fraught as they were with political as well as commercial possibilities.[130]

Backed by a driving local enthusiasm and, in some cases, by federal aid, these enterprises were soon carried to successful completion. The first opened to traffic, 1832, was the Ohio canal, extending from Portsmouth on the Ohio up the Scioto by Columbus and down the Cuyahoga to Cleveland on Lake Erie, a distance of more than three hundred miles. Later, 1840, a branch, the Muskingum canal, was opened to Zanesville on the Muskingum river, which was navigable thence to the Ohio at Marietta. Farther west was the Miami canal which was opened in 1828, and extended from Cincinnati to Toledo with a branch reaching westward well into the heart of Indiana. To the east, almost wholly within the state of Pennsylvania, was the Pennsylvania and Erie canal, opened in 1834 to connect the Ohio and Lake Erie by way of the

[130] *Ohio Arch. and Hist. Quarterly*, vol. xiii, 460.

Beaver and Shenango rivers. Later, lateral feeders were built, one by way of French creek to the Allegheny river, the other, the famous "Cross Cut" canal, to intersect with the Ohio canal at Akron.[131]

It must not be inferred that these canals destroyed or even lessened the volume of traffic on the Ohio. Advantages were comparative, and traffic on that stream tended to increase, although it did not keep pace with that passing over its rival, the Erie canal. Both Pittsburgh and Cincinnati grew in importance as river centers, the chief trade of the latter, until well into the fifties, being with the South and in steamboats. It is true that local interests then deplored the tendency of the canals leading north from the Ohio to divert traffic thence, but others appreciated their benefits. These rejoiced in a wider and more stable market for local and southern products. For example, New Orleans molasses became as cheap in Cleveland as in New York, and better prices were paid for Virginia and Kentucky wheat in Montreal than in either New York or New Orleans.[132] In central Ohio wheat prices were better than in central Pennsylvania, where transportation facilities were inadequate. The results are best seen, probably, in the population figures for the states lying immediately north of the Ohio river. From 1820 to 1840 they showed a total increase of 1,897,693, that for

---

[131] Tanner, Henry S. *Brief Description of the Canals and Railroads in the United States, 1834* (Philadelphia, 1834); Van Metre, et al., *op. cit.*, vol. i, 228.

[132] *Kanawha Register* (Charleston, Va.), February 5, 1830; idem, September 4, 1832; Kilbourn, John. *Ohio Canals* (Columbus, 1832), 21; *Kanawha Banner*, January 28, 1831; idem, May 5, 1831; idem, August 12, 1831; idem, September 14, 1832; Van Metre, et al., *op. cit.*, vol. i, 245; Turner F. J. *Rise of the New West* (New York, 1906), Amer. Nation ser., vol. xiv, 133; Huntington, Charles C. and C. P. McClelland. *History of Ohio Canals* (Ohio State Arch. and Hist. Society, Columbus).

Ohio being 938,033, Indiana 538,688, and Illinois 420,972. Such an increase, accompanied as it was by a corresponding growth in wealth and enterprise, was among the forces that paved the way for the heyday of the passenger packet on the Ohio.

Gleanings from experiences of a family that found a home on the upper Ohio in this period tell a typical story. In 1832 Andrew Muhleman, eldest son of a family of cheese makers residing in the mountains of Switzerland, came to America in search of lands. After an extended journey through the West, he finally chose a tract of several hundred acres on the Ohio river near Sun Fish, now Clarington, the home site of which is still known as "Buck hill." Shortly thereafter, sometime in 1833, his father and brothers, John, Jacob, and Rudolph, with their wives, followed him to America, pushing their effects in a cart before them all the way from Berne to Havre. Thence they sailed to New York City. From this point they proceeded by steamboat to Albany on the Hudson, and thence to Buffalo by canal boat. Here they sailed for Cleveland, whence they journeyed by canal to Canal Dover in central Ohio, where they purchased a horse and wagon with the aid of which they were able to reach Wheeling on the Ohio river. Unwilling to part with their horse and wagon which were needed for prospective farming operations, they continued overland down the Virginia side of that stream to their destination.

Their arrival was unexpected, and the consequent delay of one night in crossing into their promised land permitted an event of future consequence to the upper Ohio to occur on the soil of Virginia. This was the birth of Charles Muhleman, who first saw the light of day under the pawpaw bushes that grew on the river

A PORTAGE BOAT

Operated by stationary engines over a series of inclined planes connecting Hollidaysburg and Johnstown, Pa., 1835-1854.

VIADUCT AND TOWPATH ON THE PENNSYLVANIA CANAL

THE DAY OF CANALS AND TURNPIKES   147

bank opposite the palatial home he later built at "Buck hill." Whatever the circumstances of his beginnings, Charles Muhleman later became a popular and successful riverman. Throughout the course of the Ohio he was known for his cultured manners, gentlemanly bearing, and punctilious business methods. During the Civil war and for almost two decades thereafter he did much to shape transportation activities on the Ohio and to aid friends and relatives to become successful rivermen. It was largely through his efforts that Clarington, Ohio, became an important river center, a distinction retained to this day.

Canals extending west from the Atlantic coast toward the Ohio, also, served as feeders to that river. Stimulated by the example of New York, construction of the Chesapeake and Ohio and the James river and Kanawha canals was resumed. In 1850 the former reached Cumberland, and one year later the latter reached Buchanan in the valley of Virginia. But neither the western terminals of these belated waterways nor the time of completion thereto determined their usefulness. Construction had meanwhile proceeded in a piecemeal fashion, long stretches to the east, such as that between Richmond and Lynchburg, first opened to navigation in 1840, being available for use long before the western terminals were reached or definitely determined. Thus, even before their completion, these artificial waterways were increasing the volume of traffic passing to and from the navigable waters beyond the Alleghanies.[133]

The Pennsylvania canal was, however, by far the most important tributary of its kind to the Ohio. Beginning at Columbia, Pennsylvania, it followed the Susquehanna and Juniata rivers to Holidaysburg. By

---
[133] U. S. *Census*, 1880, vol. iv, 731-762.

a portage railroad of inclined planes and stationary engines it crossed the Alleghanies to Johnstown, a distance of thirty-two miles, thence by way of the Conemaugh, Kiskiminitas, and Allegheny rivers it continued to Pittsburgh. A branch connected the Susquehanna and the Schuylkill, extending along the latter to Philadelphia which was connected by rail with Columbia, the place of beginning. Launched in 1825 and completed in 1835, sections having meanwhile been opened to earlier use, this system was, from its inception, planned and maintained as a rival to the Erie canal.[134] In the volume of traffic carried it never approached its rival, but it was, nevertheless, an important thoroughfare between the East and the West. Until the completion of through railroads connecting Pittsburgh and Philadelphia, this canal was the most important outlet of the upper Ohio valley to the east. Total receipts are a barometer of its usefulness. These increased gradually from $250,000 in 1834 to almost $1,500,000 in 1852, after which the decline was rapid to 1856, when it became precipitous, the railroad having become a formidable competitor.[135]

Excluding the canal connecting the Susquehanna and the Schuylkill, this enterprise cost almost sixteen and one-half million dollars and was financed largely by foreign capital, conservative Pennsylvanians hesitating to invest in anything fraught with possibilities for reducing the price of horse flesh and grazing lands and with disturbing influences to established businesses such as stage driving, tavern keeping, and the local trade in grain and hay. But for their conservatism, other things

---

[134] Pittsburgh *Gazette*, November 2, 1832; *Magazine of Western History*, vol. viii, 42.
[135] U. S. *Census*, 1880, vol. iv, 738; Tanner, *op. cit.*

THE DAY OF CANALS AND TURNPIKES 149

being equal, as they were not, Philadelphia and Pittsburgh might have fared better in their rivalry with New York and Buffalo for a share of the commerce and trade of the American hinterland. However, in 1829, the "General Abner Leacock," a canal boat bearing the name of a popular local leader of western Pennsylvania, inaugurated canal boat service between Johnstown and Pittsburgh, and in the same year the "Hit and Miss," a keelboat, passed all the way from the Susquehanna river to St. Louis without breaking cargo.[136]

The results of these developments were immediate. Among other things Pittsburgh, the "sin and sea-coal cursed emporium of the West," in 1826 described as in the death throes of an arrested development, took on new life, and local commission merchants and transfer men, among them the Clarks and the Thaws, laid the basis of fortunes that are intact to this day. Wagons operating between Pittsburgh and Philadelphia now gave way, almost completely, to canal boats with their distinctive names and luxurious cabins lined with berths.[137] The volume of flour, pork, lard, beef, wool, tobacco, hemp, and other local products passing east from Pittsburgh to Philadelphia doubled, as did also the volume of cotton, woolen and leather goods, porcelain, earthen ware, coffee, tea, spices, dried fruits, drugs and liquor going west from the latter city, most of it to augment the steamboat traffic on the Ohio and its tributaries.

A recent writer has summarized the strategic com-

---
[136] Pittsburgh *Post*, July 1, 1921. See also Hulbert, A. B. *Historic Highways* (Cleveland, 1902-1905), vol. xiii, chap. 4.

[137] Pittsburgh *Gazette*, April 22, 1837; Pittsburgh *Gazette-Times*, October 28, 1917; Harris, Isaac. *Pittsburgh Business Directory, 1837* (Pittsburgh, 1837).

mercial advantages of Pittsburgh at that time, in these words:

> Nearly all the traffic between the central states and Philadelphia passed through Pittsburgh, which was situated in an advantageous position at the western terminus of the Main Line canal and occupied the same relation with regard to the trade over that waterway that Buffalo occupied with regard to the trade over the Erie canal. From Pittsburgh the merchandise coming from Philadelphia and Baltimore was distributed by means of the Ohio river and the canals and railroads of the central states among the towns of Ohio, Kentucky, Indiana, Illinois, Missouri, and Tennessee, and even to Mississippi and Arkansas. In addition, Pittsburgh sold large quantities of iron, glass, and bituminous coal to the various cities down the river, and received flour, provisions, and tobacco for local trade and for transportation to Philadelphia and Baltimore.[138]

These advantages aroused the opposition of neighboring cities, particularly Wheeling which, since the completion of the Cumberland road, had questioned the right of Pittsburgh to be regarded as the chief port on the upper Ohio. The story of this rivalry will be told in another chapter, but the effects of the completion of the Pennsylvania canal upon steamboating on the Ohio may be briefly noted here. They were, probably, best set forth in a Wheeling print quoted in the Pittsburgh *Gazette* for June 24, 1835, which said:

> Since the completion of the Pennsylvania canal much of the produce of the West, which before sought the New Orleans and Baltimore markets, has been drawn to Philadelphia. We have heretofore mentioned that two steamboats have commenced running the present season between Bridgeport, opposite Wheeling, and Pittsburgh, to carry produce to the canal spoken of; and we have now to add that one will in a few days commence its regular trips between Warren and Pittsburgh. ... We hope to see, in two or three years, this western trade which Philadelphia is thus diverting, restored by the completion of the Baltimore and Ohio railroad, to its natural channel.

---

[138] Van Metre, *op. cit.*, vol. i, 236.

THE DAY OF CANALS AND TURNPIKES 151

But for the opposition of local interests, among others, stage drivers, tavern keepers, and grazers, who feared that horses would become valueless in such an event, this hope would have been realized before it was.

Simultaneously with the building of tributary roads and canals to the Ohio, navigable affluents thereto were being brought into the domain of the steamboat. Some of these, notably the Monongahela, Muskingum, Kentucky, and Green rivers, were being improved by the use of locks and dams in such a way as to make their conquest permanent. Shortly after the end of this period the Monongahela Navigation Company, first incorporated in 1836, provided slackwater in the lower course of the Monongahela, and the other streams named above were being similarly improved.[139] The conquest of the comparatively unimproved tributaries was, however, more spectacular, if not so complete, but the whole story can not be told here. Fortunately examples may suffice.

Except the Monongahela, the Great Kanawha was, at this time, probably the most important natural tributary of the Ohio. It was an important link in Virginia's pet scheme for connecting the East and the West, and as the James River and Kanawha improvement, then in progress, advanced, the strategic importance of the Great Kanawha became more and more evident. The Kanawha valley was the repository of vast natural resources of timber, coal, and salt, large shipments of the last named article having been made from Malden above Charleston annually since the early days of the century. Accordingly the Great Kanawha was a

---

[139] U. S. Senate. Document 325, 60 cong., 1 sess.; Inland Waterways Commission, *Preliminary Report*.

tempting field for rivermen, and in 1823 the "Eliza" was built expressly for that trade. She was successful and was followed, in turn, by the "Fairy Queen," 1824, "Paul Pry," 1826, "Kanawha," 1828, "O. H. Perry," and "Enterprise," both in 1830, and the "Tiskelwah" in 1832. Others came in rapid succession, so that by the end of this period a large steamboat trade was maintained between Great Kanawha and Ohio river ports.[140]

The conquest of the Allegheny was more spectacular because more difficult than that of most tributaries to the Ohio. To many it seemed that nature had reserved the former stream as a final and safe retreat for keelboatmen and raftsmen. Nevertheless, Sunday, February 24, 1828, saw the "Wm. D. Duncan" at Franklin. A cannon shot announced her arrival and heralded the dawn of a new era in this land of primeval forests and native red men. The following day she proceeded to the future site of Oil City, and two years later the "Allegheny" extended the domain of the steamboat to Olean, New York. Many stories were told of these strange boats that "spat fire." They were said to have provoked many inquiries and conjectures. To Cornplanter, a half breed Indian chieftain then residing on the Allegheny with a remnant of the Seneca tribe, they were, doubtless, marvelous assertions of the prowess of the white man.[141] However that may be, this river soon became one of the important feeders of the Ohio.

---

[140] Hale, John P. *Trans-Allegheny Pioneers* (Cincinnati, 1886), 310; *Kanawha Western Virginian*, September 24, 1828; *Western Register* (Charleston, Va.), August 7, 1829; *Kanawha Register*, January 16, 1830; *Kanawha Banner*, July 1, 1831; Isaac Lippincott's "Early Salt Trade in the Ohio Valley," in *Journal of Political Economy* (Chicago, 1892-date), vol. xx, 1029; *Waterways Journal*, August 7, 1909.

[141] At an earlier date the "Albion" ascended the Allegheny for a distance of fifty miles. See Pittsburgh *Gazette*, April 26, 1827; *Niles Weekly Register* (Baltimore, 1812-1849), April 28, 1827.

THE DAY OF CANALS AND TURNPIKES 153

For the extension of steam navigation to the larger tributary streams to the south the story of the conquest of the Cumberland alone must suffice. In 1832 the "Pennsylvania" was built at Pittsburgh to ply the waters between that city and Nashville, where she arrived late in December, breaking into a large and profitable keelboat trade to and from both the upper Ohio and the lower Mississippi. Other steamboats followed in rapid succession, among them the "Pittsburgh," "Rambler," "Superior," and "President." By 1835 more than a dozen such craft served this trade more or less regularly, while a smaller number were in that between Nashville and New Orleans, where single packets were carrying individual cargoes of thirty-six hundred bales of cotton, together with other freight and passengers. Net receipts for the cotton carried on such trips are said to have been in excess of ten thousand dollars, which explains the insatiable demand of the period for new steamboats for use on the western waters.

Traffic between Pittsburgh and Cumberland river ports was varied. Passengers, both deck and cabin in almost equal proportions, were carried each way in large numbers, totals for single trips one way ranging all the way from one hundred to one hundred fifty persons. Freight to Nashville consisted largely of iron, nails, glass, whiskey, paper, castings, and cotton and woolen goods, return trips being made up largely of cotton, tobacco, hemp, and other agricultural products. Toward the end of the twenties iron ore began to reach Pittsburgh from the Cumberland river. Commenting upon the beginnings of this epoch-making traffic the Pittsburgh *Gazette* for January 1, 1830, said:

> Some time ago we noticed the arrival of a quantity of pig metal from Tennessee. Since then another boat has brought to our wharves

a considerable quantity of blooms from the same works. A more forceful exemplification of the advantages conferred upon the Western Country by the introduction of steam power could not be given than is afforded by this single circumstance. Fifteen years ago, thousands of tons might have lain at the works on the Cumberland, and foundries and steam engine factories might have remained idle for months for want of materials. Indeed, if the metal had been delivered gratuitously on board keelboats and barges at the mouth of the Cumberland, the price here would not have paid the freight.

In a similar manner other navigable affluents of the Ohio and their tributaries were explored and used, the steamboats of that day accomplishing what seemed almost impossible feats. But their triumphs were not local. They extended to the upper Mississippi, the upper Missouri, and elsewhere. In May, 1823, the "Virginia," a few days out from Cincinnati, reached Fort Snelling near the head waters of the former stream. This accomplishment was heralded throughout the entire Ohio valley.[142] A short time sufficed to justify this enthusiasm. Five years later at least ten steamboats were making regular annual trips between this frontier outpost and Louisville, bringing the lead mines of Illinois and the rich farm lands of the upper Mississippi into touch with their future source of supply for merchandise, railroad iron, and farm machinery.

Of more importance still was the conquest of the Missouri which went forward more haltingly, always following the lure of the fur trade. In 1819 the "Independence" reached Franklin in Boone's settlement, more than two hundred miles from the Mississippi. Later in the same year the "Western Engineer," one of six boats built at Pittsburgh for a proposed expedition

---

[142] *Saturday Evening Post* (Burlington, Iowa), July 8, 1922; *idem*, July 15, 1922; *Western Virginian*, July 2, 1828; Gould, *Fifty Years on the Mississippi*, 116; see also W. J. Petersen's "The Lead Traffic on the Upper Mississippi," in *Miss. Valley Hist. Review*, vol. xvii, 72-98.

THE DAY OF CANALS AND TURNPIKES

to the Yellowstone under Major S. H. Long, reached Council Bluffs, at least four hundred miles farther by river. Here the conquest ended until competition from British rivals drove agents of the American Fur Company to the use of a more adequate transportation than the keelboat. To this end the "Yellowstone" was built at Louisville. The following year, 1832, she succeeded in reaching Fort Union on the Missouri and, a few months later, the mouth of the Yellowstone river.[143]

Unlike many other epoch-making events this was recognized as of consequence, even by contemporaries. Ramsey Crook, Kenneth McKenzie, and other interested parties commended Pierre Chouteau, in charge of the undertaking, in the highest terms. From Bellevue, France, John Jacob Astor, founder of the American Fur Company, wrote: "Your voyage in the 'Yellowstone' attracted much attention in Europe, and has been noted in all the papers here." Reflecting upon the incident, Indians who saw it are said to have advised the British to turn out their dogs and burn their sledges, as they would no longer be of use "while the *Fire-boat* walked in the waters."[144] Commenting upon its results at a later date Chittenden, the masterful historian of the American fur trade, said: "St. Louis became a great trade center, and soon her large levees had not space enough to accommodate the boats which assembled there from every direction — from New Orleans at the south and from the Falls of St. Anthony to the north; from the Alleghanies in the east and the Rockies to the west, and even from the distant cities of the Atlantic coast."[145]

---

[143] Chittenden, Hiram M. *History of the American Fur Trade of the Far West* (New York, 1902), vol. i, 111; *idem*, vol. i, 337-341; *Waterways Journal*, June 29, 1907; *idem*, January 14, 1922.

[144] Chittenden, *op. cit.*, vol. i, 337-341.   [145] — *Idem*, vol. i, 106.

Meanwhile Ohio river navigation was being improved, as if in contemplation of a new era. In the face of state rivalries and persistent opposition from local draymen and inn keepers the Portland and Louisville canal, locally known as the Portland canal, paralleling the Falls at Louisville, was opened in 1831. Tolls charged for its use were objectionable, the more so because the federal government was a large stockholder in the enterprise, but benefits were immediate and substantial, although defiant captains did continue to use the natural channel. To the surprise of many who thought her location the only reason for her existence, Louisville began to grow, her population of twenty-one thousand in 1840 being double that of 1830 which represented a half century's growth. Throughout the whole course of the Ohio "planters" and "sawyers" were removed by the use of the snagboat, whose inventor, Captain Henry M. Shreve, had become superintendent of western river improvements.[146]

This period also witnessed marked progress in the art and utility of steamboat construction. Before it ended practically every new boat built on the Ohio tended to adhere to the type of Captain Shreve's "G. Washington" rather than that of the "New Orleans" and her sister boats. High pressure engines were in general use, having demonstrated their superiority over the low pressure Fulton boats and others built at New York and Philadelphia and sent thence, under their own power, to the Mississippi; boilers and engines were completely out of the hold; paddle wheels were boxed; commodious upper cabins were equipped with state-rooms instead of long narrow aisles between cur-

---
[146] Lyford, W. G. *Western Address Directory*, 356; Wheeling *Times*, February 13, 1848.

tained bunks after the manner of canal boats; and boats everywhere were being adapted to their trades, the stern-wheeler tending to grow in favor on the upper Ohio and tributary streams and the side-wheeler holding its own on the lower courses of the Ohio and on the Mississippi. An important tendency was that to lengthen and lighten all newly built steam craft, thus adding both to their beauty and to their utility.[147] Toward the end of this period, 1836, local river prints were commenting upon the exit of the clumsy bobtailed steamboat of the earlier period and upon the increasing use of those of elegant design. Rugged tributary streams were being navigated by the use of "mountain boats" of light construction and shallow draught, and "low water boats" of similar design were used to maintain an uninterrupted service on the Ohio for the regular delivery of the mail.[148]

With these achievements came an important economy in the handling of steamboats. Previously, landings had been effected only after boats had come to anchor in mid-stream. Thence they were hauled to the bank by the use of a rope, a reverse operation being necessary to start them on their way. This took time and restricted landings to improved levees. Fortunately it was discovered that a steamboat could be "landed" almost anywhere. To do this, in most cases, all that was needed was to head to the bank, reverse machinery, and permit an accumulated momentum, under the direction of a good pilot, to do the rest. This simple discovery added greatly to the usefulness of all steamboats, permitting them to land at wayside points and increasing their possibilities for service generally.

[147] Sweeney, John M., *op. cit.* See also, articles by Mrs. S. Kussart, *Waterways Journal*, 1926, 1928, passim.   [148] Sweeney, *op. cit.*

Other economies of this period advanced inland steam navigation. For example, the time from New Orleans to Louisville was reduced from twenty-five days to seven days and eighteen hours, the latter record being that of the "Tuscarora" made in April, 1834, the cost of transportation for passengers and freight declining proportionately. In fact, except for an occasional accident, it was, when compared with earlier years, as safe to live on a steamboat as at home, and persons took advantage of this fact to spend a part of their time in travel.

These changes and conditions were reflected in the personnel of rivermen everywhere, but nowhere more noticeably than on the inland waters. Lawless and incompetent boatmen retired either to the upper reaches of tributary streams, there to continue their chosen calling, or to the woodyards that then lined the banks of the inland rivers and supplied passing boats with cordwood, the fuel in general use. The most competent of the boatmen meanwhile became captains, pilots, and engineers. Thus, in the days of Jacksonian Democracy, law and order began to prevail in the river circles of the interior, and gentlemen of means and culture took over the river business as professional steamboatmen. Many of these found their chief joy in life in the superior quality of their boats, particularly their speed. Even at that early day steamboats were beginning to reflect the tastes and qualities of their owners.

Other devices and inventions of this period, first applied elsewhere, ultimately affected steam navigation on the Ohio. Probably most important of these was the use of iron as a building material. The first steamboat of this construction was built in England in 1822

THE DAY OF CANALS AND TURNPIKES 159

and made successful voyages from London to Paris.[149] Before the end of this period several such craft were afloat on European waters; an unsuccessful attempt had been made to operate them on the Susquehanna in America; and suggestions were being made here and there looking to the possible use of floating ironclad arsenals as instruments of warfare. Furthermore, Ericsson and others had perfected the screw propeller, launching a century-old controversy between its advocates on one side and those of the paddle-wheel steamer on the other, and making possible the application of steam to ocean navigation.[150]

Material proofs of the progress of this period of inland navigation are abundant. Among other things the oldest steamboat line in the world, the Louisville and Cincinnati Packet line, first organized in 1818 and popularly known as the "Mail Line," was operating regular packets between Cincinnati and Louisville. One of its boats, the "Ben Franklin," carried passengers and mail only.[151] An auxiliary line connected Cincinnati and Guyandot, and both Cincinnati and Louisville had through shipping facilities to Pittsburgh and points east, as well as to all important ports in the West and the South. In 1835 fifty steamboats were launched from Ohio river ports, and two hundred thirty were employed on the western waters.[152] The total capacity of all steamboats in use on the former reached almost 40,000 tons, the operation of which entailed an expense of almost $4,650,000, about $1,675,000 of which was for wages, $1,395,000 for cordwood, $835,000 for provi-

---
[149] Preble, *History of Steam Navigation*, chap. 3; *Niles Weekly Register*, vol. xxiii, 19.   [150] Preble, *op. cit.*, chap. 3.
[151] Gould, *op. cit.*, 370; *Waterways Journal*, March 27, 1926.
[152] U. S. *Census*, 1880, vol. iv, 671.

sions, and $745,000 for contingencies.[153] Under such conditions the keelboat and kindred craft almost disappeared from the navigable rivers. But possibly more significant still was the increasing value of the river port receipts of New Orleans. These rose from less than $9,000,000 in 1816-1817 to almost $50,000,000 in 1840, when the "Crescent City" was the largest exporting center in the United States.[154]

---

[153] *Journal of the Franklin Institute* (Phila., 1826-date), new ser., vol. xiv, 353.

[154] U. S. House. *Executive Documents*, 50 cong., 1 sess., vol. xx, no. 6, pt. ii, 191; Van Metre, et al., *op. cit.*, vol. i, 243.

The Heyday of the Passenger Packet

The late thirties of the last century witnessed important events in the history of steam navigation. On the inland waters of the United States the construction of steamboats more than doubled, a total of fifty-one new boats built in 1835 increasing to one hundred seven in the following year. On the Atlantic coast new construction, for the same year, increased from eleven to thirty-nine, the total capacity from twenty-three hundred forty to sixty-six hundred thirty-six tons, respectively.[155] Two years later, on April 22, 1838, the "Sirius" and the "Great Western," under steam power alone, reached New York almost simultaneously, the former from Ireland, the latter from England, thus inaugurating a new era in ocean transportation.[156]

On the Ohio the Steamboat Age now entered a heyday that is yet referred to as the "good old days." This period extended to about 1856, when local railroads, formerly tributary to rivers, first effected through connections between the East and the West. In its beginnings chief interest of this age centered in tonnage construction, the Ohio as usual being the chief center of operations.[157] All of the one hundred seven steamboats built on the western waters in 1836 were launched from

---

[155] U. S. *Census*, 1880, vol. iv, 672-678.

[156] See A. D. Tasker's "Our Merchant Flag on the Seas," in *Current History Magazine* (New York, 1915-date), vol. xvii; Preble, *History of Steam Navigation*, 162-166; Day, Clive. *A History of Commerce* (New York, 1922), 305.

[157] Pittsburgh *Gazette*, April 22, 1837; *idem*, May 23, 1837; *Niles Weekly Register*, vol. xlix, 228; *idem*, 289.

its ports: sixty-eight from Pittsburgh; twenty-nine from Cincinnati; and ten from Louisville; the total value of those built in Pittsburgh in that year aggregating almost two million dollars. At the same time Cincinnati had five boatyards: Gordon's, Hartshorn's, Huger's, Leatherwood and Littleberry's, and Week's, and she was launching steamboats that varied in size from one hundred to four hundred tons burden. In 1837 fifteen hundred steamboat passages were made through the Portland canal, which represented an increase of one thousand in five years, keelboats and kindred craft using the same course having meanwhile declined from about four hundred to approximately two hundred, and Pittsburgh was announcing packet arrivals from Louisville, St. Louis, Florence, St. Anthony, Nashville, New Orleans, and other distant ports.[158]

Already steamboat owners and operators on the Ohio were tending to pool their interests to the extent that "lines" were being formed. These were gentlemen's agreements regarding time schedules and apportionments of cargoes. In the Pittsburgh-Louisville trade there were four such arrangements, viz: the United States Mail with twelve boats; the Express with eight; the Ohio Pilot with twelve; and the Good Intent with nineteen. In the Pittsburgh-St. Louis trade seven boats operated more or less regularly and coöperatively, as did three boats in a local trade between Pittsburgh and Wellsville.[159]

On the lower Ohio and the Mississippi steamboat

---
[158] — *Idem*, vol. xlix, 98; Wheeling *Times*, February 13, 1846; Wheeling *Tri-Weekly Gazette*, September 18, 1835; Pittsburgh *Gazette*, April 22, 1837; idem, May 23, 1837; Lyford, W. G., *Western Address Directory*, 1837, 165; Thurston, *Allegheny County's Hundred Years*, 108-110.

[159] U. S. *Census*, 1880, vol. iv, 662; Gould, *Fifty Years*, chap. 61.

THE HEYDAY OF THE PASSENGER PACKET 163

owners formed similar arrangements. The Louisville and Cincinnati Packet line, already mentioned, continued to operate and to grow in favor and in importance, and it was now joined by others. Important among these was the Ohio and Mississippi Mail line which was a sort of joint-stock company, probably the first of its kind on the inland waters. It was organized primarily to carry the mail between Cincinnati and New Orleans, the promoters being Levi James and Samuel Perry of Cincinnati and Chas. M. Strader and Henry Forsythe of Louisville. The boats used were sidewheelers, the largest then afloat on the inland waters, and the wheel-house of each bore the inscription, in large letter, "The Ohio and Mississippi Mail Line." [160]

Relying upon the prestige that came to them because of the fact that they carried the federal mail, a boon to any steamboat operator at that time, the owners of this line defied all competitors in the hope ultimately of monopolizing their trade. To this end they engaged their own forwarding and commission agents, ignoring completely such popular, influential, and well established agencies as that of Wm. D. James of Cincinnati and that of J. C. Buckles of Louisville. They even selected crews and officers from among their own friends and relatives.

This departure was opposed to the spirit of the West of that day, and soon the cry "monopoly" was directed against this new and haughty combine. As a result all those not in its favor united, as in the days of the fight against Fulton and Livingston, to "keep the river free." Cut rates were used, the freight charge on pork from Cincinnati to New Orleans falling from one dollar and fifty cents per barrel to thirty-seven and one-half cents,

[160] —*Idem*, chap. 54.

and other charges declined in proportion. One season of this sort of competition sufficed to bring the embryonic monster down, the individual owners dissolving their corporate relationship but continuing to operate as individuals and in a manner more in keeping with western ideas of democracy and equality.[161]

Meanwhile conditions on the upper Ohio continued to favor steamboating on a grand scale.[162] Light draught steamers, some of which, it was claimed, could make regular trips on nothing more than a heavy dew, increased in number there and on tributary streams. These, together with roads and canals, carried freight in large quantities, that passing over the Pennsylvania canal in 1844 being in excess of seventy-five thousand tons. At the same time a varied industry was developing in Pittsburgh, Cincinnati, and intermediate points. For example, almost two thousand residents of Cincinnati then found employment on or in connection with the river. Wheeling and vicinity had one hundred thirty-four flour mills that manufactured annually two hundred eighty thousand barrels of flour, one hundred eighty thousand barrels of which found a market in New Orleans by way of the Ohio. As already indicated, these were golden days for Pittsburgh commission merchants and transfer men.

Additional details regarding traffic then moving over tributaries to the Ohio may be interesting as well as informing. About 1840 eight lines of canal boats operated over the Pennsylvania canal to and from Pittsburgh. Some of these owned and used as many as twenty boats among which were express packets, freighters,

---

[161] — *Idem*, 376.

[162] U. S. *Census*, 1880, vol. iv, 736; *Western Virginia Times* (Wheeling, Va.), November 7, 1840.

THE HEYDAY OF THE PASSENGER PACKET

and boats carrying both passengers and freight. In name, design, and accommodations many of these were worthy rivals of inland river packets. Among such were the "John Hancock," "Lady Washington," "James Madison," "Lehigh," "Baltic," and others, each with its uniformed officers and regular schedule.[163]

The traffic developing on tributary streams was even more important. Although not as large as that on either the Monongahela or the Cumberland, the volume of traffic on the Allegheny was large and increasing. A brief outline of its development will suffice to show how traffic on the Ohio was augmented. In the early days persons living on and near the Allegheny received practically all their supplies from Pittsburgh, flatboats, keelboats, and Indian canoes sufficing for all the needs of transportation. By the use of this stream and its primitive craft Pittsburgh had even supplied a large part of the imports of Michigan territory and the army posts of the Northwest. To reach these distant parts keelboats and canoes ascended the Allegheny to Franklin, Pennsylvania, going thence by way of French creek to Waterford, New York. From this point wagons were used to Erie which had direct connections with western outposts, first by sailing craft and later by steam-propelled vessels. Returning lake craft brought furs and salt, the latter finding a ready market along the Allegheny and even in Pittsburgh.

By 1840 conditions on the Allegheny had changed. While continuing to draw merchandise and articles of general manufacture from Pittsburgh, the Allegheny valley was exporting large quantities of raw materials, most of which went to the lower Ohio and the Missis-

---

[163] Pittsburgh *Gazette*, May 1, 1840; Van Metre, et al., *op. cit.*, vol. i, 236; Hulbert, *Historic Highways*, vol. xiii, 169.

sippi. Important among these were lumber, shingles, hoop poles, staves, pot and pearl ashes, whiskey, and farm products. Six steamboats, the "Eliza," "Pulaski," "Forrest," "Beaver," "Pauline," and "Orphan Boy," plied the Allegheny regularly during the boating season. In low water stages flatboats, keelboats, and barges continued in use, more than four hundred flatboats reaching Pittsburgh from this stream in 1840. Their cargoes were either sold or reshipped, their containers then being sold to coal merchants who knocked them down and rebuilt them into coalboats which were sent to Cincinnati, Louisville, and other lower river markets. Moreover, hundreds of log and lumber rafts then descended the Allegheny annually to Pittsburgh and beyond,[164] its raftsmen rivaling the keelboatmen of an earlier day in their enterprise, as well as in their capacity for rowdyism and corn whiskey.

The passenger traffic was the greatest factor in making possible this heyday of the passenger packet. In the thirties immigrants began to reach the interior in ever increasing numbers, foreigners then joining natives in common efforts to find homes in the West. As the steamboat improved in design and security it found increasing favor with the traveling public. Of the immigrant movements of the earlier part of this period a contemporary writer left this vivid description:

> The amount of travel, east and west, over the Alleghany range is so great as almost to surpass belief. Notwithstanding the numerous routes, all are covered; notwithstanding the yearly additions to the number of stages and canalboats, all are crowded, crammed, packed, with the migratory public. The enormous and thickly wedged flocks of pigeons which yearly pass the Ohio in the upper element hardly exceed the human multitude who are floated, dragged, driven, and

---

[164] Harris, Isaac. *Directory of Pittsburgh*, 1841 (Pittsburgh, 1841), 129; Pittsburgh *Gazette*, April 10, 1852.

THE HEYDAY OF THE PASSENGER PACKET 167

steamed on below, and their forest resting-places, stripped of foliage and beech nuts, and broken down by their innumerable company, afford a happy analogy to the hotels and inns, whose dining tables are swept clean, and whose dormitories are crammed full with the ever-swelling torrent from the traveling caravans.[165]

During the years immediately following 1837 the immigrant tide, both foreign and domestic, increased with each succeeding year, a large part of it going to the West by way of the Ohio. The Baltimore and Ohio railroad, completed to Cumberland in 1843, added another important tributary, and the steamboat converted New Orleans into a port of entry rivaling New York City. Local newspapers continued to tell of immigrant movements, and almost any number of the Pittsburgh *Advocate and Advertiser* for 1840 and 1841 carried advertisements of the Tapscotts of England announcing weekly sailings of immigrant ships to America. Special mention was made of their New Orleans service which consisted of twenty-four "elegant first class ships," fitted out in superior style. By 1840 Cincinnati newspapers were announcing local arrivals of German immigrants by way of New Orleans, some of whom were born on the way and named for the steamboat on which they traveled. As yet river traffic in railroad iron inland from New Orleans was insignificant.

Toward the end of this period the passenger travel on the inland rivers, particularly the Ohio, increased in volume, as the foreign immigrant tide swelled to flood proportions. It was especially large during the years 1846-1848 which were marked by famine in Ireland and revolution on the continent of Europe. Most of the Irish settled in eastern cities where they found employment in construction work, industry, and practical pol-

---
[165] *Western Messenger* (Cincinnati, 1835-1841), August, 1836; Vanable, Wm. H. *Footprints of Pioneers in the Ohio Valley* (Cincinnati, 1888), 46.

itics. For the most part the Germans went west to found new commonwealths. About the same time, also, the movement into California began, and thousands of persons left the Ohio valley for the "gold regions," where they introduced the art of steamboat construction and operation.[166]

Some further idea of traffic on the Ohio, both freight and passenger, in the early part of this period, may be gained from a survey of the Port of Pittsburgh as of 1840. From August, 1839, to July, 1841, its steamboat arrivals and departures amounted to fifty-three hundred and seventy-nine, and the capacity of the eighty-nine boats owned there, wholly or in part, exceeded twelve thousand five hundred tons. Keelboats to the number of four hundred fifteen arrived in 1840, while the arrivals of "flats" and similar craft for the same year amounted to nineteen hundred sixty-three. During twelve days immediately preceding April 30, 1840, ninety steamboats arrived and ninety-one departed; at any time during the boating season there were thirty or more steamboats at the Monongahela wharf; and eight to ten canal boats arrived daily from the East by way of the Pennsylvania canal. Warehouses were stuffed to bursting with farm products, general merchandise, and articles of local and eastern manufacture. At the same time sailings were being announced for St. Anthony's falls, the upper Missouri, the lower Mississippi, and intermediate points.[167]

It was in the midst of these dynamic conditions that Charles Dickens, esquire, and lady descended the Ohio. Although they made the trip in March, 1842, an unattractive season of the year, Dickens wrote in his usual

---
[166] Pittsburgh *Gazette*, May 3, 1852.
[167] Harris, *Directory of Pittsburgh*, 1841.

THE HEYDAY OF THE PASSENGER PACKET 169

pessimistic strain of things American. The following from his pen is an excellent portrayal of life and conditions along the Ohio, removed from centers of traffic, at that time:

> The banks are for the most part solitudes, overgrown with trees which, hereabouts are already in leaf and very green. For miles, and miles, and miles, these solitudes are unbroken by any sign of human life or trace of human footstep; or is anything seen to move about them but the bluejay, whose color is so bright, and yet so delicate, that it looks like a flying flower. At lengthened intervals a log cabin, with its little space of cleared land about it, nestles under a rising ground and sends its thread of blue smoke curling up into the sky. It stands in the corner of the poor field of wheat, which is full of great unsightly stumps like earthy butchers' blocks. Sometimes the ground is only just now cleared: the felled trees lying yet upon the soil; and the log house only this morning begun. As we pass this clearing, the settler leans upon his axe or hammer, and looks wistfully at the people from the world. The children creep out of the temporary hut, which is like a Gypsy tent upon the ground, and clap their hands and shout. The dog only glances round at us; and then looks up into his master's face again, as if he were rendered uneasy by any suspicion of the common business, and had nothing more to do with pleasure. And still there is the same eternal forward. The river has washed away its banks, and stately trees have fallen down into the stream. Some have been there so long that they are mere dry drizzly skeletons. Some have just toppled over, and, having earth yet about their roots, are bathing their green heads in the river, and putting forth new shoots and branches. Some are almost sliding down as you look at them. And some were drowned so long ago, that their bleached arms start out from the middle of the current, and seem to try to grasp the boat and drag it into the water.[168]

Despite this unpromising picture, the year 1843 witnessed the organization of what was probably the most important steamboat line that ever coursed the waters of the upper Ohio. This was the Pittsburgh and Cincin-

---

[168] Dickens, Charles. *Miscellanies, American Notes* (Boston, n.d. Illustrated Cabinet ed. Dana, Estes and company), 232.

nati Packet line, later prefixed "First" to distinguish it from a line that bore the same name. The earlier line seems to have had its origin in the demands of a heavy passenger traffic, mostly immigrants, and in the unexpected success of the "United States Mail," an independent packet that had served this trade since 1840. In 1841 the "Mail" was joined by the "Swiftsure no. 2," and the two made "barrels of money" for their owners, Lineas Logan and P. Wilson Strader, who were joined by others in 1843 to supply what seemed to be a demand for a regular daily packet service between Pittsburgh and Cincinnati.

The venture was a success, and, from the first, consisted of seven boats, one daily, ten A.M., from each terminus. Each boat was adapted to its trade and, although not the largest or the swiftest on the upper Ohio, was of the best type then in use on the inland waters. The original boats, with their captains, were the "Monongahela," Captain Charles Stone; the "Allegheny," Captain Wm. Dean; the "Lehigh," Captain H. Price; the "Swiftsure," Captain J. J. Collins; the "Montgomery," Captain Elisha Bennett; the "Express," Captain James Parkinson; and the "Clipper," Captain N. Crooks. Five were owned in Pittsburgh and two, the "Clipper" and "Swiftsure," in Cincinnati. In a short time each of the original boats was succeeded by a larger and finer packet which, in turn, gave way to still another, the last boats of the line being more than twice the size of the first.[169]

At all times this line was a sort of "regulated company," neither partnership nor corporation, to serve the

---

[169] The capacity of these boats varied from one hundred sixty-three tons for the "Montgomery" to two hundred forty tons for the "Monongahela." See Pittsburgh *Dispatch*, October 14, 1876; Wheeling *Register*, October 6, 1875; Gould, *op. cit.*, chap. 54.

THE HEYDAY OF THE PASSENGER PACKET 171

convenience and advantage of the boats of which it was composed. Except as to the times of sailing and divisions of cargoes, each boat operated independently. For low water seasons "low water boats" were used, and the regulations applying at other times were somewhat disregarded. But the boating seasons of this period were unusually long and favorable. The years 1838 and 1854 excepted, they averaged more than ten and one half months annually.

Shortly after the organization of the Pittsburgh and Cincinnati and other packet lines the possibilities of steam navigation in the interior began to command the attention of statesmen and others. Outstanding among the many conventions called to consider the matter was that which met at Memphis in 1845. Practically every state of the South and the Southwest was represented, and the improved navigation of the Ohio and the Mississippi was urged as a national enterprise, necessary for the commercial growth and defense of the country. At the contemporaneous rate of advance John C. Calhoun, a delegate, estimated that by 1886 it would require forty-four thousand steamboats and flatboats to carry the produce of the Mississippi valley to New Orleans and that sixteen thousand six hundred eighty sea-going vessels would be needed to carry them thence to coast and foreign ports. Accordingly he and others urged the deepening of the mouth of the Mississippi at whatever cost, the unification of the Great Lakes and the Mississippi by means of an artificial waterway, and the reclamation of the alluvial lands along the Mississippi by the construction of levees.[170] Moreover, these occasional strict constructionists urged that these things be done at the expense of the federal government.

---

[170] U. S. House. *Executive Documents*, 50 cong., 1 sess., vol. xx, no. 6, pt. ii, 203.

The increased volume and variety of traffic on the Ohio during the decade immediately following 1845 would have justified the serious consideration of the proposals of the Memphis Convention. A survey of the commercial activities of Pittsburgh and Cincinnati for the years immediately following will suffice for illustration.[171] Pittsburgh then had at least one daily packet to and from each of the important ports of the upper Ohio and its tributaries. From these it received farm products, express packages, and articles of local manufacture such as plows, wagons, fire brick, bar iron, nails, paper, and furniture; from Cincinnati, Louisville, and the Cumberland and the Wabash rivers came meats of all kinds, whiskey, soap, candles, cotton, tobacco, feathers, cattle, and pig iron; from St. Louis direct – few packets then turning back at Louisville – came lead, pig iron, hides, furs, hair, and farm products; and New Orleans contributed, sometimes direct, cotton, molasses, sugar, rice, coffee, and wine. From January 1 to July 1, 1850, the total imports of Pittsburgh by river alone amounted to four hundred and ninety thousand tons. Exports were even greater, and immigrants continued to pass thence to the West by thousands. Most of these went to the Missouri and upper Mississippi valleys, but many continued to California. Among the travelers east bound the local press made occasional mention of Indians going to visit their "Father," the President of the United States.

Meanwhile Cincinnati continued to grow in prosperity. She was now the "Queen City," a title that was not often permitted to degenerate to "Porkopolis," and that, too, despite the fact that four hundred thousand

---

[171] Fahnestock, Samuel. *Pittsburgh Directory*, 1850 (Pittsburgh, 1850); Wheeling *Times*, December 20, 1848; Pittsburgh *Gazette*, May 3, 1852.

THE HEYDAY OF THE PASSENGER PACKET 173

hogs were slaughtered there in 1849. Her enterprises were, however, by no means restricted to pork packing. In 1852 steamboats going thence to the South and the Southwest carried plows, wagons, and numerous other implements of husbandry. Commenting upon these facts the Cincinnati *Commercial* for April 2, 1852, said: "Several sugar mills were shipped to the South yesterday, as well as cotton apparatus. Everything from a pitchfork to a sawmill is now going South." At the same time large quantities of Virginia tobacco and its less patrician sister, "Old Kentuck," were being shipped from Cincinnati southward to be returned and redistributed in the luxurious guise of "pure Havana."

The passenger and freight traffic to Cincinnati from New Orleans and other points on the lower Mississippi had meanwhile increased tremendously. Items gathered here and there from local prints tell the story. On January 19, 1852, the "Telegraph" arrived direct from New Orleans with five hundred passenger immigrants, only one-half of whom came in the cabin. On March 27, the "Ben Franklin" brought another five hundred about equally distributed between deck and cabin passengers. June 8 the "Midas" arrived with railroad iron and passengers, a large number having died en route from cholera. On June 9 the arrival of one thousand German and Irish immigrants was announced, two hundred of whom had come as deck passengers on the "Georgetown," which had escaped all sickness, except that of a woman who had given birth to a son. On June 22 the "G. W. Kendall" reached Louisville from New Orleans with a number of immigrants and a large cargo of railroad iron for use in Indiana. Similar items might be multiplied to great length.

Thus practically the whole economic life of the Ohio

valley in the forties of the last century centered in the river, where rivalries were intense and successes phenomenal. For example, for years after its organization, opposition packets tried to put those of the Pittsburgh and Cincinnati Packet line out of business. But the ever increasing volume of traffic insured cargoes for all, even for the scores of additional packets that joined the competition. Rivalry sometimes extended to packets of the same line and to those of friendly lines, that between the "Messenger" and the "Buckeye State" of the Pittsburgh and Cincinnati Packet line being the talk of the way-side in the early fifties. It is said that it was to show the "Messenger" a thing or two, she being a favorite with traveling celebrities and on this occasion carrying Jenny Lind, that the "Buckeye State," in April, 1851, made her famous run from Cincinnati to Pittsburgh.[172]

Conscious of their power and importance Ohio river steamboatmen assumed an air not unlike that of some modern railroad executives and near executives. To things political they were extremely sensitive. The rumor, studiously launched and circulated by the Whigs, to the effect that Stephen A. Douglas, a Democratic aspirant for the presidency, favored a tax on river tonnage, detracted from his popularity in river circles.[173] Moreover, through packets, after the manner of modern express trains, catered only to through traffic, passing large intermediate points without so much as a salute. This attitude fostered resentments which found expression in many ways. For example, one Gurley, writing for the Cleveland *Plain Dealer* and for rival commercial interests, said of them: "The cusses put on

---
[172] — *Idem*, April 25, 1851; Pittsburgh *Gazette*, November 7, 1920.
[173] Wheeling *Intelligencer*, September 29, 1852.

THE "WASHINGTON," BUILT 1820, AT CINCINNATI BY
GENERAL PAUL ANDERSON AND OTHERS

From an early woodcut in the possession of Frederick Way, Jr. Features:
Bob tail, crude paddle wheels, and absence of pilot house.

THE "MESSENGER," FAVORITE OF THE FIRST PITTSBURGH AND
CINCINNATI PACKET LINE

From a contemporary print. Charles Dickens, Jenny Lind, and Ole Bull
traveled on this steamer about 1850.

THE HEYDAY OF THE PASSENGER PACKET

as much airs as the New York ocean captains, yet 'nary one of 'em ever tasted salt water since they were infants, when they took it for worms." To which the reply came that Gurley had probably been denied a free pass on a coalboat, hence his "indiscriminate indignation." [174]

These conditions stimulated enterprise, competition, even genius. As a result steamboat construction made marvelous strides. One of the creations of this period, the "Eclipse," built in 1852 at New Albany, Indiana, by Hipple and Evans, was designed to merit her name. She was three hundred sixty-three feet long, thirty-six feet beam, and nine feet hold. She carried two engines of thirty-six inch cylinders and eleven feet stroke, fed by eight boilers, each of which was thirty-two and one-half feet long and forty-two inches in diameter. Her wheels were forty-one feet in diameter and carried buckets fourteen feet long and twenty-six inches wide. Her cabin glared with paintings and tapestries suggestive of an oriental palace. At the men's end of the long hall through the cabin was a gilt statuette of General Jackson, and at the women's end a similar figure of Henry Clay. There were forty-eight bridal chambers, state-rooms for scores of passengers, and sleeping quarters for servants. At the time of her extraordinary run from New Orleans to Louisville, 1853, when she beat all previous records, making the distance in four days, nine hours, and thirty-one minutes, there were few sea-going vessels of her size and elegance in the world.[175]

Most of the largest and finest of the boats of this period were built for Mississippi trades. Among the most talked of, after the "Eclipse," were the "Illinois"

---
[174] — *Idem*, May 16, 1860.
[175] *Waterways Journal*, April 9, 1927; Preble, *op. cit.*, 71; Thurston, *op. cit.* For steamboats built on the Ohio, 1811-1880, see U. S. *Census*, 1880, vol. iv, 671-672.

and the "John Simonds." Both of these boats were built at Pittsburgh in 1852 and were for the New Orleans-St. Louis trade, which had become the most important on the western rivers. The "Simonds" was the larger, being of eleven hundred tons burden. She had two upper cabins extending her entire length, seventy state-rooms, and a steerage cabin below for the accommodation of deck passengers. Cincinnatians, then as good judges of steamboats as their neighbors in Kentucky were of horse flesh, pronounced her the largest and the finest boat that had ever stopped at their levee.

Although not the largest, the "J. M. White" was the most unique and original steamboat of this period.[176] She was built at the Walker boatyard in Elizabeth, Pennsylvania, and was only two hundred fifty feet long, thirty-one feet beam, and eight and one-half feet hold. She carried seven boilers which fed engines with cylinders thirty-one inches in diameter and of ten feet stroke. Her famous run from New Orleans to St. Louis, 1844, in three days, twenty-three hours, and nine minutes was not beaten before 1870. She was a side-wheeler, and her speed came from placing her wheels farther aft than usual, so as to bite the swells created by her motion in such a way as to push her forward. This design also added to her grace and beauty.

The "White" was the handiwork of William (Billy) King and was built for Pierre Chouteau of St. Louis but under the direction of J. M. Converse. Her design is said to have met with the disfavor of Converse who, upon seeing it, shook his head and said: "It won't do, Billy." Whereupon King is said to have replied: "Then

---

[176] Elizabeth *Herald*, June 7, 1900; *Waterways Journal*, June 8, 1910; *idem*, February 17, 1917; Gould, *op. cit.*, 628.

I'm damned if I make the boat." Converse then appealed to Samuel Walker who made him understand that King's plans could not be interfered with by those who would retain his services. In desperation Converse then appealed to Chouteau who, after some reflection, is reported to have said: "Let Billy King go ahead. He knows his business."

The "White" made her designer famous. He received dozens of requests for similar craft, but to all he is said to have replied: "If there is ever a boat built that will walk away from the 'White,' I'll make another to beat her, but not until then." He was never called upon to fulfill his promise. For years thereafter the "White" was his love. Fearing that someone might copy her design, a beautiful creation of white pine and black walnut, he is said to have broken the model into fragments.

The annually increasing steamboat tonnage of this period kept transportation costs at a minimum never reached before or since and led to a degree of perfection in the art of construction little surpassed to this day.[177] By 1843 the steam whistle, of eastern origin, was in use on the Ohio along with double compound engines known as "clipper engines." The "cordelle" had developed into the "capstan," a sort of windlass first used to aid in moving boats by hand. In 1855 steam was applied to this device through the use of a small engine called the "nigger" that did the work of many deckhands. About the same time the "doctor," a boiler feed pump, was first used to doctor the ills of the engineer,

[177] James Rees and Sons Company. *Illustrated Catalogue* (Pittsburgh, n.d.); Preble, *op. cit.*, chap. 3. Authorities are not in accord regarding the first use of the calliope on the western waters. See *Waterways Journal*, March 12, 1910; *idem*, April 23, 1910; *idem*, December 24, 1910; *idem*, February 12, 1921.

making it no longer necessary for him to hitch and unhitch heavy machinery to feed the boilers on his boat. There were then in use valves of all sorts, such as cut-offs, slides, balances, pistons, poppets, etc. Boats with rudders at bow and stern and propelled by stern-wheel, side-wheel, Catamaran with wheel in the center, or stern-wheel working in recesses in the hull were all in use on the inland waters before 1856. More than ten years before, the "Texas," a lone star state-room for officers and owners, had been installed on top the upper cabin and beneath the pilot-house, and toward the end of this period Johnson's generating gas light and the steam calliope converted life on Ohio river packets into one continuous day of light and song.

The general principles of steamboat design now fairly settled, with utility, comfort, and safety as the determining factors, owners and captains gave free range to their individual vagaries in the use of gingerbread finishings and furnishings, each striving for something distinctive. To this end some used paintings on the wheel-house or the pilot-house, while others used emblems carried between the chimneys, or smokestacks. On the "Natchez" boats, of which their were seven, this emblem was a bale of cotton. Others carried stars, anchors, and globes, while still others decorated only the chimney using a white, red, or yellow collar, the famous "White Collar" lines of both the Ohio and the Mississippi being known far and near. Receipts alone determined the character and quality of cabin and state-room furnishings and decorations. When profits ranged all the way from ten to twenty thousand dollars for single trips, these approached the gorgeous, carpets alone costing as much as five thousand dollars for one boat, and only those of oriental make were acceptable.

Chandeliers were of sparkling glass, and tables and furnishings were of highly finished walnut and mahogany.

Such demands contributed generally to make boat building a business for capitalists, artists, and architects. When a boat was lost or junked, its owners sought to replace it at once regardless of cost. Profits were immense, and delays were expensive. As a result successful builders were always in demand, some of them attaining great popularity and accumulating fortunes. In the palmy days of this period some building centers, such as Elizabeth, Pennsylvania, had as many as fifteen boats in process of construction at one time, and Samuel Walker, a capable and successful builder of that place, was one of the most important personages in the Ohio valley.[178]

Thus it was that steamboating in its various phases dominated the economic life of the Ohio valley during this period. Machine shops, engine and boiler works, and sawmills existed, in the last analysis, to supply the needs of transportation, as did commission merchants, transfer men, and inn keepers. Except for four years, 1838, 1840, 1841, and 1843, when a large overproduction was being absorbed, the total number of boats launched annually was well over one hundred, which represented an aggregate capacity of about twenty-five thousand tons. In 1851 freight shipments were in excess of eight million tons transported in three hundred thirty boats. These represented an aggregate capacity of two hundred thousand tons valued at thirty-three million dollars. During a three year period, 1852-1854, Pittsburgh and vicinity alone launched new steamboats representing a total value in excess of four and a quarter million dollars, and thence to the city of Cairo, in every

---

[178] Elizabeth *Herald*, June 7, 1900; Gould, *op. cit.*; Thurston, *op. cit.*

important port, mammoth steamers nosed one another about for landing space at local levees which presented scenes not unlike those of modern ocean ports.[179]

A significant local development of this period was the use of iron in the construction of steamboat hulls.[180] Although iron had been used for this purpose in England for almost two decades, its earlier use in inland America had been retarded by an abundant and suitable timber supply; but, as settlement advanced into the interior from the Ohio, timber became scarce. Moreover river navigation remained somewhat hazardous, and rumors of war were abroad in the land. Accordingly, in 1839, the Washington Iron Works of Pittsburgh experimented by launching the "Valley Forge," the first iron steamboat to navigate the western waters. This boat cost sixty thousand dollars and was one hundred eighty feet long, thirty-nine feet beam, and five and one-half feet hold. After a short service she was dismantled, but not before two other boats of similar construction, the "Jefferson" and the "George M. Bibb," had taken her place. Each of these boats remained in continuous use for more than fifty years, the former on the Great Lakes and the latter on the high seas. Other boats of similar construction followed, among them the "Michigan," which was only recently dismantled after a long and creditable career.

The services of Ohio river steamboats were not restricted to transportation and defense. They supplied an effective means of political education, Henry Clay, Andrew Jackson, Abraham Lincoln, and others using them in going to and from the national capital. There

[179] *Cist's Weekly Advertiser*, June 29, 1847; Cincinnati *Commercial*, April 22, 1852; Wheeling *Intelligencer*, February 27, 1855; *Hunt's Merchants' Magazine*, vol. xxix, 749; Pittsburgh *Gazette*, June 10, 1852.

[180] Baltimore *Sun*, July 19, 1928; *Waterways Journal*, September 17, 1927.

were few persons living on the Ohio in the decades before the Civil war who had not seen these men and heard them discuss the issues of the day, their arrival at any port, however small, being the occasion for an address.

The educational benefits of the steamboat were not, however, wholly political. By the end of this period there were thousands of persons living on and near the Ohio, who had learned practical lessons in economics from the commercial needs and practices of their environment. This was particularly true of those having business relations with non-residents, for example those from the upper and the lower Mississippi and the far off Missouri. All such had difficulty in inducing local venders of cordwood to accept state banknotes in payment for this necessary article, refusals sometimes resulting in free for all fist fights. In 1896 many local Democrats, educated in this school of experience, refused to vote for W. J. Bryan for the presidency and voted instead either for William McKinley or J. M. Palmer who ran on gold standard platforms.

Moreover the Ohio and its steamboats made possible a common entertainment. By 1856 there were thousands of persons living on and near that river who had seen Charles Dickens and heard Ole Bull and Jenny Lind. "Dan" Rice and his elephants were popular in river ports, and P. T. Barnum was exhibiting "Tom Thumb" and a menagerie which even local church elders endorsed as affording a needed education for their children. Indeed, interest in the Ohio and its boats was nation wide and extended even to Europe. Scores of foreigners came to see them, and for those who could not come, Banvard, a celebrated landscape painter, depicted them in a panorama which was exhibited in Egyptian Hall, London.[181] The scene used was almost twelve hundred yards long and was displayed by the use of a revolving cylinder somewhat after the manner of the moving pictures of our own day.

Finally, the steamboats of this period offered the best and to some the only means of social intercourse. Besides the thousands who used them on missions of business, other thousands used them as a means of travel. During the first three years of its existence the Pittsburgh and Cincinnati Packet line carried almost two million passengers, and by 1855 the total annual passenger traffic on the Ohio reached the three million mark. The conditions under which they were transported made for wide acquaintances and for warm and intimate friendships. Officials acted as hosts; passengers were rarely selfish and exclusive; and, in the upper cabins at least, affability and freedom were chastened by decorum and good breeding. Music and dancing were the chief amusements; and at night one of these large boats, filled with well dressed men and women, was more like a floating palace than a mere conveyance of wayfarers.

---

[181] *Cist's Weekly Advertiser,* May 8, 1850.

Railroad *versus* River

On a chilly night, November 29, 1852, the first railroad train from the East reached Pittsburgh. It had started from Philadelphia the night before and spent most of the intervening day crossing the heavy mountain grades of the Alleghanies, the route being by the Portage Railroad connecting Hollidaysburg and Johnstown.[182] Although the trip was not made over a through line, inclined planes being used to cross the mountains, this "long distance triumph of the iron horse" was recognized as a marvelous feat. All those interested, even the tired and hungry passengers who rode in boxlike cars without dining and other accommodations, recognized that a new epoch in inland transportation was at hand. Already they were talking about the probable exit of the steamboat, and fears of national disintegration were vanishing, the West having at last been bound to the East by a tie that was thought to be permanent and effective.

Of even greater significance, possibly, was the celebration six weeks later, January 12, 1853, of the completion of the Baltimore and Ohio railroad to Wheeling, the Pennsylvania legislature of 1847 having refused permission to extend it from Cumberland to Pittsburgh. The first train had arrived January 10 over a continuous track, thus completing the "marriage of the East and the West," which was fittingly solemnized. To this

---

[182] Craig, Neville B. *History of Pittsburgh* (Pittsburgh, 1851); Pittsburgh *Gazette Times*, April 1, 1923; Van Metre, et al., *op. cit.*, vol. i, 238.

end local orators contributed a part, as did the Steubenville Grays, the Bridgeport artillery, and a dozen or more steamboats whose musical bells and newly devised whistles at times drowned the oratory of the occasion and even the roar of artillery. In attendance from the East, coming by way of the railroad, was a distinguished company which included, among others, the governors of Maryland and Virginia, Lowe and Johnson; members of the Maryland and Virginia legislatures, those of the former state having adjourned for the occasion; Benjamin H. Latrobe, engineer of the road; and Thomas Swann, its president.[183]

Locally the enthusiasm of this occasion exceeded all precedents. Practically everybody over a radius of several miles participated and rejoiced in the thought that at last Wheeling had come into her own. The injurious effects of the Pennsylvania and Erie canals had at last been repaired by a "through railroad" which was relied upon again to divert traffic in the direction of the Cumberland road, where it was thought to belong. Under the changed conditions the improvised railroad connecting Pittsburgh and Philadelphia was little feared. It was claimed that Wheeling was destined to become the emporium of the upper Ohio valley.

Meanwhile, a "railroad mania" had attacked the lower Ohio and the regions beyond to the west, a center of infection being at Cincinnati. A new westward movement fostered by the lure of gold, the invention of the reaper, and the possibility of federal land subsidies for prospective railroads kept the craze alive and stimulated local endeavor. Bent upon retaining for Cincinnati all the advantages that had already accrued from her location on the Ohio river and that were ex-

[183] Wheeling *Intelligencer*, January 1, 1853; *idem*, January 12, 1853.

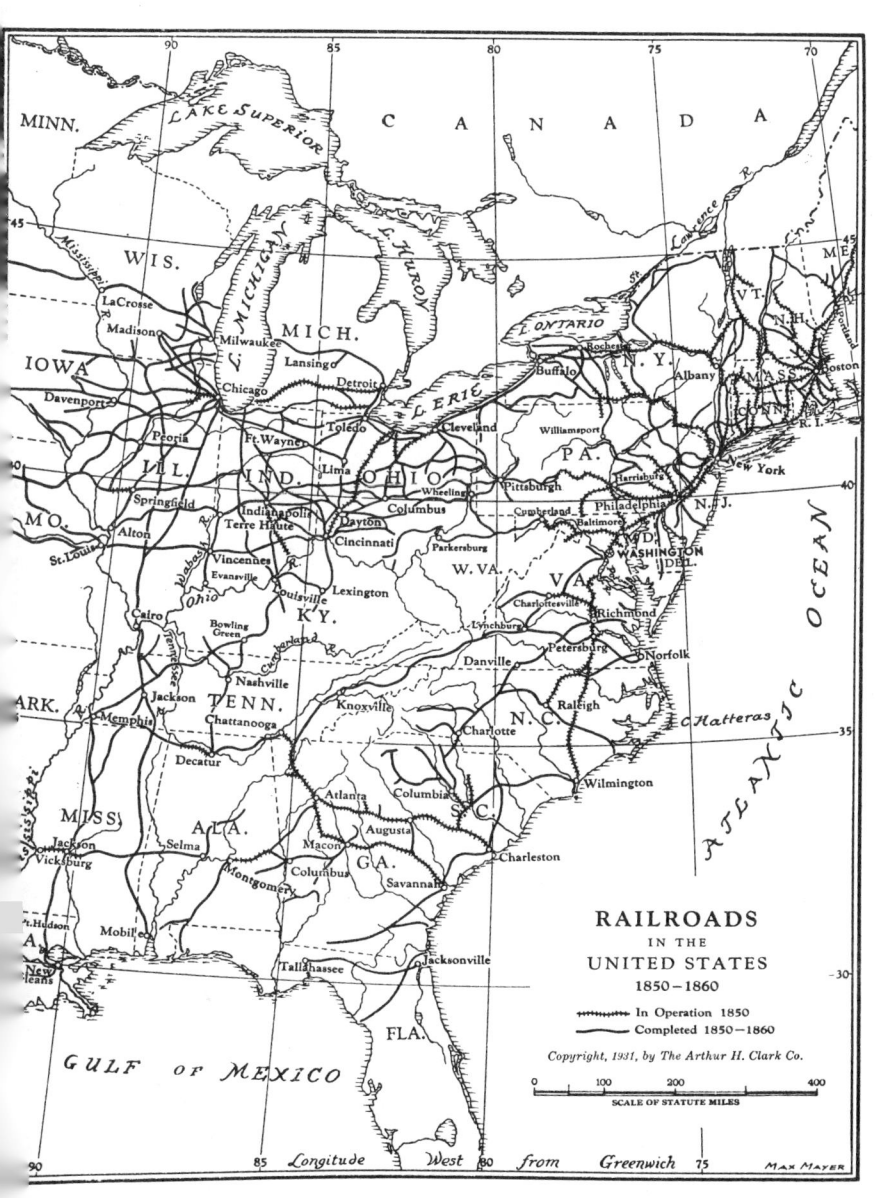

pected to flow from her strategic position on a through railroad line connecting Baltimore and San Francisco, Alphonso Taft and the venerable riverman, Jacob Strader, urged the necessity for railroads.

Taft was especially aggressive. In an address entitled "The Railroads of Cincinnati," delivered before the Mercantile Library Association in 1850, he presented at length the possible benefits of railroads to that city and suggested proposed lines. Following a summary of the internal improvement history of Ohio he urged immediate consideration of three railroad projects, the completion of which he claimed would make Cincinnati the great city of the West that was bound to arise in the near future, and to which New York and other Atlantic ports would bear a relation no higher "than that of ports of entry to a mart of commerce, such as Havre and some other seaports of France bear to Paris; and such as Joppa anciently bore to Jerusalem." [184]

The railroad projects proposed by Taft are of more than passing interest. First and most urgent of all was an additional line to connect Cincinnati and Lake Erie to divert thence the increasing volume of traffic passing through Indiana. Already "the pioneer of western railroads," the Little Miami, completed in 1846, afforded a direct connection between Cincinnati and the Lakes, but this was not considered sufficient for the purpose in view. Accordingly, Taft urged the completion of an additional line by way of the Great Miami to Dayton, thence to Sandusky. Strange as it may seem, none of the arguments urged in behalf of this enterprise suggested the possibility of future rivalry between Cincinnati and Chicago.

[184] Leonard, L. A. *Life of Alphonso Taft* (New York, 1920), 71, 60-92; *Cist's Weekly Advertiser*, March 27, 1850.

Of more importance was the proposed "great line, east and west" to connect Baltimore, Cincinnati, and St. Louis, and eventually San Francisco. This enterprise was urged as a "sublime plan," one that would intersect the commerce of the Mississippi at St. Louis and that of the Ohio at Cincinnati. Furthermore, Taft said, "It will unite the mines of the Sacramento with the golden harvests of the Mississippi valley. It will be direct; and yet will pass through all important commercial cities of the Union, except New Orleans. For it will be seen by a glance at the map that Philadelphia, New York and Boston are on the same line, extended, with but a small deviation."

The immediate completion of that part of the proposed line lying between St. Louis and the Atlantic coast was urged as imperative. Fortunately many former difficulties had been reduced to a minimum. To the east, as already indicated, the Baltimore and Ohio railroad was then extending its lines to the Ohio river at Wheeling, with a projected line to Parkersburg. Thus, all that was needed to give Cincinnati a through railroad to the Atlantic was the completion of a two hundred mile stretch to connect with the Baltimore and Ohio lines. To the west the difficulties were greater, the legislature of Illinois refusing to charter any railroad that might divert the commerce of St. Louis from Chicago to Cincinnati. Indiana had, however, approved such an enterprise, and Taft urged its immediate completion to the Wabash. By that time he hoped for a shift in the attitude of the Illinois legislature. In case it remained immovable, he suggested the possibility of extending the proposed road west from Cincinnati to the Mississippi at Alton, twenty miles above St. Louis, or to Chester, sixty miles below.

The third project contemplated a direct railroad from Cincinnati to the lower South. It was pointed out that this could be effected by a line to Lexington, where connections could be made with the Nashville and South Atlantic railroad and also with the Louisville and Frankfort line. The possible advantages were numerous. First of all Cincinnati "would form a profitable acquaintance with the rich interior of Kentucky, a country of whose vast wealth we have heard, but from which we have been effectively severed by bad roads, and a total want of improvements." Moreover, this connection was needed to counteract the possible effects of rival transportation enterprises to the southward, for, as Taft said, "Cincinnati cannot regard with indifference the fact that some of the southern cities are now pushing their improvements resolutely toward the Ohio. Charleston and Savannah have already advanced their railways, north and west, five hundred miles across the mountains to the Tennessee river at Chattanooga, on their way to Knoxville and to Nashville; to which latter place the whole line is already under contract and in process of construction."

Unfortunately these plans and suggestions encountered insuperable obstacles.[185] Ohio and other states of the Union were bonded for millions to pay for canals that were now to be abandoned, and states were on the point of repudiating debts incurred for internal improvements. As a result their credit was destroyed, and new state constitutions forbade states to incur additional indebtedness. Ohio's constitution of 1850 went even further and denied this power to counties and munici-

---

[185] Wheeling *Intelligencer*, April 22, 1853; Pittsburgh *Gazette*, July 9, 1853; *idem*, August 13, 1853; *Hunt's Merchants' Magazine*, vol. xxiv, 432; *Cist's Weekly Advertiser*, March 27, 1850.

palities. The result was a severe blow to the numerous railroad projects of that state, which were thus made almost wholly dependent upon private enterprise. Meanwhile, Illinois and states to the west went on with their railroad building programs, some of them through the aid of federal land grants. The first of these grants was made in 1850 to the Illinois Central railroad.[185a] The *Railroad Record* of Cincinnati thundered against the situation but was helpless, and Cincinnati remained a steamboat center despite the plans and wishes of her leading citizens.

Pittsburgh was more successful in her efforts to secure railroad accommodations, but she accepted this new mode of transportation with some misgivings. Her comparative inaccessibility may have contributed to this attitude. However that may be, her press continued to ridicule the "railroad mania" that had captured other parts of the interior and to invite those affected therewith to pause before it was too late. With foreign capital estranged because of losses in canals, Pittsburghers could not see where the money was coming from to build the scores of railroads then being projected in the interior. They conceded the advantages of railroads for the transportation of passengers and small freight shipments but would not admit even the possibility of their ever superseding rivers and canals as carriers of heavy and bulky articles. The possibility of junking a total inland river tonnage five times greater than the capacity of all the railroads then reaching the interior was unthinkable. Locally, railroads were wel-

---

[185a] Bronson, Howard G. *History of the Illinois Central Railroad to 1870* (Urbana, Ill., 1915), University of Illinois Studies in Social Sciences, vol. iv, nos. 3 and 4, September and December, 1915.

comed, but they were expected to remain tributary to rivers after the fashion of canals and turnpikes.[186]

These conditions brought the passenger packet on the Ohio into its zenith. Individual packets now attained an undreamed degree of perfection and elegance and local lines reached their greatest popularity and usefulness. New lines also came into existence. Gleanings from contemporaneous accounts to be found in the local press tell something of the story for Pittsburgh and vicinity. During the first three months of 1854 almost three million dollars in gold and silver bullion reached the mint at Philadelphia by way of the Ohio. Up-stream packets were carrying record-breaking cargoes of pig-iron, lead, agricultural products, horses, mules, and cattle, return shipments consisting largely of railroad iron, farming implements, merchandise, and passengers. For example, the "Granite State" left Pittsburgh January 21, 1854, "with almost every inch of her space covered with carts, wagons, wheelbarrows, plows, and empty molasses barrels." Later in the same year immigrants passed through Pittsburgh at the rate of fifteen hundred daily, "a half dozen or more steamboats being required for their transportation to St. Louis."[187] Meanwhile, boat building had taken on new life. The new boats built in 1854 were in excess of eighty, and many of them were of unprecedented size, power, and capacity. Summarizing the situation, a writer in *Hunt's Merchants' Magazine* for June, 1854, said: "Contrary to expectation and owing to the great demand for river shipment at points on the western waters, freights are

---
[186] Pittsburgh *Gazette*, August 3, 1853; *idem*, August 13, 1853.

[187] — *Idem*, January 16, 1854; *idem*, February 2, 1854; *idem*, February 17, 1854; *idem*, April 7, 1854.

high, steamboats are selling at a greatly advanced price, and the numerous boat builders are driven to the wall with work, and are hotly pressed to fill their orders."

It was under these conditions that the "First" Pittsburgh and Cincinnati Packet line attained its greatest success. This was the period of its finest boats and most popular captains, its older and smaller boats giving way to so-called "floating palaces." Among these, together with their captains, were the "Keystone State," Captain Charles Stone; "Allegheny," Captain Charles Batchelor; "Crystal Palace," Captain W. J. Kountz; "Philadelphia," Captain R. J. Grace; and the "Pennsylvania," Captain John Klinefelter. Although the smallest of these, the "Pennsylvania" may be taken as typical. She was two hundred seventy-five feet long, thirty-seven feet beam, and seven feet hold. She carried engines of thirty-five-inch cylinder and eight feet stroke and five boilers each forty-two inches in diameter. Her wheels were thirty-five feet in diameter. In comparison with the first boats of her line, those of 1843, she was a marvel. Her launching was the occasion for a celebration lasting from one day far into the next and calling forth the elite of Pittsburgh society.[188]

The first effects of the coming of the Baltimore and Ohio railroad were to stimulate traffic on the Ohio river. In anticipation of the event John McLure, Sr., Wm. List, and others, some of them southern sympathizers, incorporated the Union line of packets for the purpose of giving daily communications between Wheeling and Louisville. The boats used were "the finest that ever plied the waters of the upper Ohio in the line arrangement," their average capacity being in

---

[188] The "Pennsylvania" was of four hundred eighty-six tons burden, the "Crystal Palace," the largest of the line, of five hundred forty-one tons. See Pittsburgh *Gazette*, February 11, 1854; *idem*, February 18, 1854.

excess of eight hundred tons. They were the "Thomas Swann," named for the president of the Baltimore and Ohio railroad; the "Alvin Adams," bearing the name of the founder of the Adams Express Company; the "David White," named for a prominent resident of Madison, Indiana; and the "Falls City," the "Baltimore," the "Virginia," and the "Forest City," each of which bore a name that appealed to the South from which they expected to draw their chief patronage.[189]

Of these steamers the "Falls City" was typical. She was three hundred eight feet long, thirty-six feet beam, and less than seven feet hold. She carried five boilers each twenty-eight feet long and forty-six inches in diameter and two engines of thirty inch cylinders and nine feet stroke. Her upper cabin could be thrown into one room two hundred sixty-five feet long, one end of which was adorned by an elaborate painting of Louisville, and the other by an equally elaborate painting of Wheeling. In comparison with other upper Ohio river steamboats, her greater length and narrower beam were significant, as was also her shallow hold. In a comment widely copied the Louisville *Courier* described her luxurious state-rooms, her gold-etched ceilings and pillars, her skylights of stained glass, her imported queensware, and other things in keeping, all combining to produce an effect suggestive of oriental splendor.

As was anticipated the Union line of packets made its strongest appeal to the South. Many looked upon it as a possible link in the long-desired line of communication between that section and the West. Agents of underground railroads were making the transportation

---

[189] Wheeling *Intelligencer*, April 23, 1853; *idem*, April 27, 1853; *idem*, May 3, 1853; *idem*, May 14, 1853; *idem*, May 21, 1853; *idem*, August 11, 1853; *idem*, January 20, 1853; *idem*, January 24, 1853; *idem*, January 10, 1883.

of slave property on the Ohio dangerous, at times next to impossible. The pending controversy over the rights of slaveholders in the territories made such a service more imperative than ever. Accordingly the boats of the Union line were officered and manned, as far as possible, by persons of southern sympathies, some of the employees coming all the way from Richmond, Virginia. Thus the editor of the Richmond *Enquirer* was pleased to find aboard these packets an atmosphere "delightfully Southern." [190]

On the lower Ohio the steamboat more than held its own. Of its activities there, in the mid-fifties, statistics tell an otherwise voluminous story. In the year ending August 31, 1854, more than three hundred different packets touched at the port of Cincinnati, some of them daily. They brought imports representing a total value of almost sixty-five million dollars and took away exports scarcely less valuable. Total arrivals and departures reached almost eight thousand, or more than twenty daily including Sunday. Thus Cincinnati remained a river center. The profits of the trade between her port and that of Louisville were so large that the Lightning line entered it in competition with the Mail line whose packets had been without regular opposition for more than a generation.[191]

But the "good old days" of the passenger packet on the Ohio were numbered. Like some other days they were brightest and most promising just before the end. During the years immediately following 1855, those of Horace Bixby and Mark Twain, steamboating on the

---

[190] — *Idem*, May 2, 1853; *idem*, March 26, 1855; Reizenstein, Milton, "Economic History of the Baltimore and Ohio Railroad, 1827-1853," in *J. H. U. Studies* (Baltimore, 1882-date), vol. xv; Hungerford, Edward, *Story of the Baltimore and Ohio Railroad, 1827-1927* (New York, 1928).

[191] *Hunt's Merchants' Magazine*, vol. xiii, 544; *idem*, vol. xxxix, 605.

Mississippi was in its glory, but on the Ohio the local press told another, even a forlorn, story of river conditions. "River News" was almost completely superseded by "Railroad News" which grew daily in length and popularity. The following from the Wheeling *Intelligencer* for November 12, 1854, is typical of comments to be found regarding the river until the Civil war: "There does not appear that activity on our wharf that was wont to glad our eyes in the days gone by. Merchants and manufacturers look to speedy shipments and prefer the rail to water. Travelers do not generally care for expenses and want the quickest route, preferring the jolting car to the elegantly fitted-out steamer."

Incidents in this transition are tragic and not without strains of romance. This is certainly true of the proud packets that plied the waters of the upper Ohio. Unable to make profits there and hearing of possible business to be had elsewhere, their owners took them to the Mississippi and its western tributaries, there to begin life anew after the fashion of the pioneers. By 1856 not a packet of the Union line remained on the Ohio, all having answered the call of the West. With them had gone, also, the boats of the Pittsburgh and Cincinnati Packet line and scores of others. The following year a river item of the local press told of the dismantling of the "Buckeye State" on the lower Mississippi and added, incidentally, that she was the last survivor of her formerly famous line. Similar items had, meanwhile, announced the passing of all the packets of the Union line.[192]

On the lower Ohio the transition was equally complete. Immediately following 1854 Cincinnati reported

---

[192] Pittsburgh *Gazette*, February 2, 1854; Wheeling *Intelligencer*, February 9, 1854; *idem*, June 3, 1856; *idem*, June 19, 1859.

annual decreases in the number of steamboat arrivals and departures; by 1855 she was exporting almost as much to the East as to the South, most of it going by rail; and in 1857 she exported five times as much wheat and corn to the North and the East as she sent to the South. The change was at once reflected in her local packing industry, the number of hogs slaughtered there in 1857 being one hundred thousand less than in 1854, the banner year for the fifties. Thus, by 1860, "Cincinnati had ceased to be strictly a river city, and the commerce of the Mississippi had received a blow from which it was never to recover." [193]

These changes were reflected in the whole economic life of the Ohio valley, which now began to suffer from an arrested development that continued until the advent of modern industry, when the area became a "workshop of the world." There are thousands yet living who could testify to the former condition. Some of these themselves used the scythe and the grain cradle and cured meat in smoke-houses, long after the mowing machine and the reaper came into general use in the West, and after the slaughtering of hogs and cattle and the preservation of meat, on a large scale and by modern methods, became a profitable business in both the West and the East. Indeed, some of these persons continued to ride on horseback to country grist mills astride bags of wheat, corn, and buckwheat, long after a large part of the world was using flour made by the roller process. Reluctant to yield the contest with modern progress there are some of these folk who would now return to the "good old days" in the belief that their health would be improved, many modern maladies being locally attributed to the foods now used.

---

[193] *Hunt's Merchants' Magazine*, vol. xxxvi, 617; Van Metre, et al., *op. cit.*, vol. i, 246.

In a larger field the changes were even more marked. For instance, by 1860 the flour producing area of the interior had shifted to the Northwest; Tennessee had given place to Illinois as the largest corn producing state in the Union; and two-thirds of the corn and wheat produced in the interior for the eastern markets was transported by rail. Cattle, hogs, and sheep now rode to market alive in cars that had only a short time before been good enough for passenger traffic, and both Chicago and New York surpassed Cincinnati as distributing centers for their products.[194]

Of the effects upon rivermen excerpts from the diary of Captain W. L. Holmes, a successful riverman of Ravenswood, Virginia (now West Virginia), tell a story.[195] After a period of reverses on the Ohio, "carrying light trips at ruinous rates," January 1, 1858 found Captain Holmes and his boat, the "Crescent," in New Orleans. Thence they made a few trips to Bayou Sara on the lower Mississippi and other nearby points, "sometimes sustaining losses." On February 14, 1858, Captain Holmes left New Orleans for Cincinnati with a "good trip," a part of which was carried through to Wheeling to save the expense of reshipment, there being no business at Cincinnati. While on the way back from Wheeling it was decided to try Cincinnati for a trip to the Missouri river, "that seeming to offer the best chance." However, it took more than a month to assemble a paying cargo which, when completed, consisted of four hundred tons of freight and two hundred

---

[194] — *Idem*, vol. i, 244-248. In 1851 De Bow, editor of *De Bow's Review* (New Orleans), declared that northern enterprise had "rolled back the mighty tide of the Mississippi . . . until its mouth, practically and commercially, is more at New York and Boston than at New Orleans." See Van Metre, et al., *op. cit.*, vol. i, 246.

[195] Manuscript. In possession of descendents of Captain Holmes, Point Pleasant, West Virginia.

ten passengers, one hundred eighty of whom rode on deck. On April 26 the "Crescent" reached St. Joseph, to find business prostrate. May 8 found her back in Cincinnati planning for a trip that was never made. The reason may be inferred from items from the diary of her captain which ran as follows:

> There is greater complaint here now among rivermen than I have ever before known. Nearly all of them declare that they are virtually broke. Most any of them would be willing to sell their boats for about a third of their real value. I would be willing to sell the "Crescent" for $10,000, and I think, if business was brisk, I could sell her for $30,000 easier than I could now for $10,000.

The record for May 13 was:

> Today we got one dray load! This is certainly very encouraging. I think the City Fathers had better rent out the wharf to some good farmer and let him plow it up and plant potatoes on it. There never was, I think, so little done on the wharf at this season of the year as now. The wharf is crowded with boats, and all of them are not getting freight enough to load any one of them in ten days time.

Failing to get a second trip for the Missouri, Captain Holmes took his boat to St. Louis, carrying a light trip at a low rate because of competition from the Ohio and Mississippi railroad. In St. Louis he found business no better than in Cincinnati, and the "Crescent" was tied up for repairs and a return of better times. In the course of three months she was painted and put into "shipshape," at the end of which word came of possible profits for steamboats on the lower Mississippi, provided they could escape the ravages of the yellow fever which was then claiming victims there at the rate of scores daily. Although he experienced a "good deal of difficulty in shipping a crew," Captain Holmes, in the spirit of a true riverman, was off for the South. He took aboard a light trip at the mouth of the Ohio, but before it was unloaded his demise was noted in these words: "Captain Holmes, the author of this diary, died this day in the city of New Orleans, Louisiana, with yellow fever." Of all his effects only his diary reached his family which was never informed of the disposition made of his boat or of his remains.

Thus it was with many another riverman and steamboat of this period: they simply dropped out of sight. In most cases the passing was not as tragic as that of Captain Holmes and the "Crescent," but the results were the same. With some exceptions to be mentioned later, their exit from the Ohio would have been complete.

Outstanding among causes producing these results were great national and even international movements. Among the latter was the decline in European immigration that followed 1855, accompanied as it was by a temporary lull in the westward movement within the United States. It will be recalled that the passenger traffic was an important element in the success of the passenger packet which attained its greatest elegance and grandeur from the desire of boat owners to please the traveling public. After 1855 immigrants seemed to stand by, as if to await the outcome of an impending sectional conflict that was to test the strength of the American Union and disturb the repose of the world.

This conflict was not confined to the North and the South. In some phases it was a contest between the Ohio valley on the one side, with its comparatively rapid rivers, poor soil, and rugged hills, and the upper Mississippi valley on the other, with its more gentle rivers, rich soil, and level lands. The outstanding result was the triumph of St. Louis and Chicago over Cincinnati and Pittsburgh. By 1855 St. Louis was the greatest steamboat center on the western waters, and Chicago had outdistanced both Cincinnati and Pittsburgh as a railroad center.[196]

Among the more tangible factors in this transition, the railroads were certainly the most important. For a short time after they reached the Ohio it is true that the volume of river traffic increased annually, but when railroads effected through connections thence to the East and the West by the use of bridges spanning the Ohio, by the use of standard and through tracks, some of which paralleled inland rivers for long distances, and by the use of common terminals, the volume of river traffic at once fell off. These events synchronize too closely to be devoid of causal relations. For example, the locomotive made its trial trip between Pittsburgh and Cincinnati May 16, 1853,[197] and one year later, by the use of a tunnel under the Alleghanies, the Pennsylvania railroad made possible a through and direct connection between Philadelphia and Pittsburgh, which was extended to Chicago four years later by the use of a bridge over the Allegheny. Meanwhile most of the packets that had frequented Pittsburgh, in line and other arrangement, had ceased to run, and the steamboat business on the upper Ohio had become demoralized.

Elsewhere similar developments brought like results. For example, the Baltimore and Ohio railroad, which had been conceived with the purpose, among other things, of "restoring to the city of Baltimore, that portion of the western trade which has been lately diverted from it by the introduction of steam navigation, and by other causes," refused to subsidize the packets of the

---
[196] Van Metre, et al., *op. cit.*, vol. i, 244-248.
[197] Pittsburgh *Gazette*, May 18, 1853.

Union line, and in 1855 crossed the Ohio at Bogg's run (Benwood) and Bellaire, where its lines joined those of the Central Ohio railroad to form a through rail connection between Baltimore and Columbus and points beyond. Fearing that she would become a "mere wooding station for steamboats," Wheeling opposed the move, charging a breach of faith, but she was helpless to prevent it. As has been indicated her packets deserted her at this time, seeking employment elsewhere. In the same year and despite the opposition of the Illinois legislature, the Ohio and Mississippi railroad was put into operation between Cincinnati and St. Louis, reducing the distance between these important cities from seven hundred twenty miles by river to three hundred twenty-seven by rail.[198] The effects on the river traffic between these points has already been indicated by the experience of Captain Holmes.

A recent authority has described the effects of the railroads of the interior upon the river commerce of the Ohio valley and elsewhere in these words:

> In addition to the freight taken from the canal, the railroads easily secured the traffic that was accustomed to go from the north central states to the eastern coast and to Europe by way of New Orleans. . . . The speed of the railroads and the superiority of New York as an importing point gave the direct rail routes to the East a decided advantage over the long roundabout route by way of New Orleans. In 1852 the Galena lead trade, which had long formed an important item of the river and coasting commerce of New Orleans, was captured by the railroads. Flour and provisions of Illinois, Indiana, and Kentucky that had formerly been sent to Philadelphia, Washington, Baltimore, and other cities by way of New Orleans and New York were taken directly over the mountains to the points of consumption. Shipments downstream from Cincinnati and other important centers on the Ohio shrunk rapidly in volume and, even

[198] Van Metre, et al., *op. cit.*, vol. i, 237-241.

before the war broke out, the direct commerce of Cincinnati with the East was much larger than its trade with the South.[199]

Despite evidence, even admissions, to the contrary, the conditions just described cannot be attributed wholly to a temporary shift in the immigration movement, to sectional conflicts, or to the railroads. Low water, ice, pestilence, panic, accidents, politics, extravagance, and other factors contributed their parts, the decade 1850-1860 being as unfavorable to river activities on and along the Ohio, from the above named causes, as the preceding decade had been favorable. During the fifties nature seemed to vie with the railroad in the undoing of the steamboat.

Of these natural forces ice was, probably, most destructive. In the fifties, when competition with railroads was keenest, the Ohio was closed to navigation for long periods at a time, each "freeze-up" being preceded, as usual, by a dry spell that suspended navigation, except with low water boats. For example, one of these periods extended from December 6, 1854, to March 6, 1855, and another from January 2, to March 8, 1856.[200] The fact that the Ohio would not float a coal-boat during a period of more than two hundred days in 1856 was destructive of more than patience. Commenting on the effects of an earlier "freeze-up," the Cincinnati *Commercial* for January 20, 1852, said: "Many boats have changed hands, but nearly all have maintained themselves." The conditions revived the memory of John Randolph who, at an earlier date, opposed the improvement of the Ohio on the ground that

---
[199] — *Idem*, vol. i, 238-239.

[200] Wheeling *Intelligencer*, March 23, 1859; *idem*, January 17, 1860; *idem*, March 19, 1860; *idem*, April 24, 1860.

it was frozen over one half the year and dry the other half.[201]

Details regarding the operation of other destructive influences may be worth while. Among other things fuel was becoming scarce and expensive, prices of cordwood tending to advance as the native forests receded from the banks of the rivers. The contracted dimensions of the canal paralleling the Falls at Louisville prevented the passage of large boats that had come into use, thus diverting through traffic to the railroads and driving boat building to the lower Ohio.[202] Moreover, cholera and yellow fever continued, meanwhile, to make more or less regular visits to Ohio river ports, defying medical skill and driving homeseekers to the high lands in the interior, made accessible by the railroads.

As a rule periods of decline and adversity, in river circles, as elsewhere, are attended by more than a proportionate share of accidents and disasters. This period was no exception to this rule. It was an age of extreme individualism, when river captains and others were allowed to do about as they pleased regardless of their responsibilities. Racing continued to be the bane of the rivers, few captains being able to withstand the ever-recurring temptation to show the speed of their "nags." Many of the numerous accidents of this period were attributed to this practice. Accordingly Congress, in 1852, was forced to enact the Davis bill which provided for the licensing of pilots and engineers and for a more rigid inspection of steamboat boilers and hulls than that required under an earlier act, that of 1838.[203]

---

[201] — *Idem*, February 16, 1856; *idem*, November 11, 1854; *idem*, December 27, 1854; *Hunt's Merchants' Magazine*, vol. xl, 508.

[202] — *Idem*, vol. xxix, 749; Cincinnati *Commercial*, April 12, 1852.

[203] Rhodes, James Ford. *History of the United States from the Compro-*

Wholesome and necessary as the Davis act was, its benefits were neutralized somewhat by the unfavorable advertising which rivers received in the course of its enactment. The press of important railroad centers kept the public well informed regarding low waters and other uncertainties of river navigation. Accidents and other disasters were reported religiously, attention being called to the fact that whereas more accidents occurred on the railroads, they were attended by fewer casualties. In 1856 Lloyd's *Steamboat Directory and Disasters on the Western Waters* came from the press with all its gruesome illustrations of exploding boats and dying passengers, some of whom were tossed to the four winds of heaven. Even the *Congressional Globe*, and that too at a time when that publication was read and taken somewhat seriously and when there was some talk of the improved navigation of the inland waters at national expense, either consciously or unconsciously joined the list of publications that were then poisoning the minds of the traveling public and others on the subject of river transportation. The following from Senator T. J. Rusk of Texas is a sample of what appeared there:

> The perils accompanying steamboat navigation, under the present system, are so great, and the chances of encountering an instant and horrible death are so numerous, that, for my part, I would rather encounter almost any risk than that with which I am threatened on the journey of some three or four thousand miles from this place to my home. . . . Sir, I will candidly avow, that I would rather take part in an Indian fight; ay, or enter on a long Indian campaign, than venture on undertaking this voyage.[204]

mise of 1850 (New York, 1896), vol. ii, 25; *Hunt's Merchants' Magazine*, vol. xxx, 636; *idem*, vol. xxxiv, 369; *idem*, vol. xliv, 236, 752.

[204] The sinking of the "Henry Clay" on the Hudson River and the "Atlantic" on Lake Erie, about this time, with a total loss of more than four hundred lives made action on the part of Congress necessary. See *Congressional Globe*, 32 cong., 1 sess., vol. xxiv, pt. 3, 2426.

In the midst of the above adversities the river interests of the whole country were overtaken by the panic of 1857 which was of unprecedented severity, as far as rivermen were concerned. The competition that followed led to ruinous extremes but fortunately to better organization and coöperation among rivermen. These benefits did not come in time, however, to save many individual owners from bankruptcy. Many of the boats that remained afloat on the Ohio continued to carry both passengers and freight at low rates and in small quantities. Except for occasional trips to the Missouri, passengers had practically deserted steamboats, and bad times, accompanied by the usual cut-throat competition of such periods, played greater havoc with steamboat profits than did competition from railroads, and this despite the fact that their charges were tending to decrease generally.

But for certain local and exceptional conditions the commercial decadence of the Ohio, in this period, would have been complete. Most important of these, probably, was the strategic position of Cincinnati and Louisville, the latter the doorway of the Middle West to the South, while the former was the portal of the South to the Middle West. Despite the fact that the Ohio and Mississippi railroad paralleled the Ohio somewhat closely for a considerable distance between these two points, they maintained uninterrupted steamboat connections and a large river traffic with points in both the West and the South.

On the upper Ohio following the completion of the Baltimore and Ohio railroad to her gates in 1857, Parkersburg became an important river center. Packets plied the river thence both up and down stream, some of them in line arrangements, and barges came into use for the transportation of freight to and from

Baltimore and Ohio river termini.[205] The iron horse continuing to shy at the rugged hills of western Virginia, to the southward, Great Kanawha river ports, particularly Charleston, continued to maintain important river relations with both Cincinnati and Louisville to the south and Pittsburgh to the north. The discovery of oil (petroleum), about 1859, at several points near Parkersburg, and the contemporaneous interest in the development of other natural resources, coal, salt, and timber, stimulated enterprise and tended to keep steamboating alive. Moreover, demands from the Mississippi and its other tributaries preserved the boat building industry on the Ohio, in 1860 Wheeling alone launching as many as twelve steamboats, most of them for the cotton trade of the Red river.[206]

During the entire period large through steamboats from both the lower and the upper Mississippi and their respective tributaries, continued to reach Ohio river ports, even Pittsburgh. From the latter they brought large quantities of iron ore, pig iron, farm products, and other raw materials, while from the former came the usual sub-tropical products. Returning, these boats continued to carry merchandise, railroad iron and equipment, and agricultural implements which consisted of "everything from a wheelbarrow up." [207] In fact river shipments of railroad iron and raw materials were now so large as to necessitate the use of "model" and other barges which were towed to and

[205] Wheeling *Intelligencer*, March 22, 1848; *idem*, May 15, 1857; *idem*, July 3, 1857; *idem*, July 10, 1857; *idem*, January 8, 1858; *idem*, March 9, 1858.

[206] *Hunt's Merchants' Magazine*, vol. xl, 508; Wheeling *Intelligencer*, December 7, 1854; *idem*, January 28, 1856; Lippincott's "Early Salt Trade in the Ohio Valley," in *Journal of Political Economy*, vol. xx, 1029.

[207] Wheeling *Intelligencer*, March 23, 1859; *idem*, January 17, 1860; *idem*, March 19, 1860; *idem*, March 21, 1860; *idem*, April 24, 1860.

from their destinations. Packets carrying agricultural implements had practically every foot of their available space taken and, unlike the cotton boats which were solid masses of white, presented a grand spectacle of varied colors.

But in the absence of the "floating palaces" that had formerly served the river trades between Pittsburgh and Cincinnati and between Wheeling and Louisville, to say nothing of other evidences, the commercial decadence of the Ohio in the late fifties was a fact. This condition has generally been attributed to the railroad. It can not, however, be termed a victory, all the breaks of the short contest that preceded being against the river, which seemed to owe its undoing to the cumulative force of a number of factors.

Intermunicipal Rivalries

From early times to the present a spirit of rivalry has permeated the life of Ohio river towns and cities. Today it has extended to the field of sports, among the trophies fought for being those of the diamond and the gridiron. A century ago, however, the advantages sought involved more largely the future of industry, trade, and commerce. Our present concern is with the earlier period which lies near the beginnings of things decisive in the material welfare of the Ohio valley. Industry was then in its beginnings; commerce was seeking new routes; and trade was becoming definnitely established. For all these purposes most Ohio river ports possessed natural advantages. Nevertheless, all realized that God helps most those who help themselves. Consequently every loyal resident of a port town became a booster, efforts in behalf of "my town" being not confined to its limits. They extended to the courts, both local and national, to state legislatures, and even to the halls of Congress.

Toward mid-century chief rivalry among these local units was largely for commercial advantages. The contemporaneous shift from roads to canals and later from canals to railroads, together with the accompanying uncertainties of steam navigation, kept all alive to their particular interests. It was a period when cities were made or ruined by individual plans and legislative enactments. For instance, as long as the Ohio river terminus of the Baltimore and Ohio railroad remained unsettled, Wheeling questioned every move to locate it to the advantage of Pittsburgh or of towns and cities within the bounds of Virginia, such as Wellsburg, Moundsville, Sistersville, St. Marys, Parkersburg, and even Point Pleasant. Plans to make Madison, Indiana, a railroad center for a vast hinterland also ran counter to similar plans of the neighboring cities, Jeffersonville and Lawrenceburgh, and led to an accumulation of grievances against both Cincinnati and Louisville.

Lack of space forbids detailed accounts of these rivalries. Only outlines of those between Pittsburgh and Wheeling on the upper Ohio and Cincinnati and Louisville on its lower course will be attempted. Each epitomizes the conflicting interests between slave and free areas of the Ohio valley, as well as phases of the larger sectional contest between the North and the South.

The struggle between Pittsburgh and Wheeling began early in the century and became acute about a decade before the Civil war.[208] From the beginning the advantages were with the former. She is the industrial and commercial outpost of the Keystone State which rests eastward upon the Atlantic, northward on the Great Lakes, and westward on the Ohio river which connects her with the Gulf of Mexico and the vast regions of the South and the West. The commercial advantages of Pennsylvania have long been recognized. Moreover, they were improved at an early period, Pittsburgh being the chief western beneficiary with her tributary state-built roads and canals. As a result of these factors, together with her location at the junction of the Monongahela and Allegheny rivers and her rich

---

[208] For much of the data used in this chapter acknowledgements are made Professor J. M. Callahan. See his "Rivalry for Headship of the Ohio," in Callahan, *Semi-Centennial History of West Virginia*, appendix.

natural resources, she early became the most important industrial and commercial center of the upper Ohio valley. At times an ultra conservatism and an over self-sufficiency have threatened her ascendancy, but she has always been sensitive to designs of would-be rivals.

Despite her oft-asserted claims to insuperable natural advantages, the Ohio thence to the north being rapid, tortuous, and obstructed, and thence to the south comparatively gentle, straight, and open, Wheeling is less advantageously situated than Pittsburgh. Except for the Ohio, the former has few physical advantages. No large tributary streams empty there and her natural resources are comparatively limited. Situated in a narrow panhandle between Pennsylvania and Ohio, she has received favors from neither and was too far removed from the center of Virginia to come within the scope of the state's feeble efforts to conserve her commercial interests. Her hopes for greatness in the commercial and trade world were first aroused in 1818, when the Cumberland road entered her gates. After a period of disappointment the arrival of the Baltimore and Ohio railroad, in 1853, gave new impetus to her ambitions, which were again to be thwarted. Her advantages from the railroad were only temporary, Pittsburgh being preferred as a western terminus even by the Baltimore and Ohio Company. The selfish interests of Virginia in keeping any railroad tributary to Baltimore as far north as possible were, also, well understood. She was determined to permit no plan to interfere with her pet scheme, a central line of internal improvements by way of the James and Kanawha rivers terminating to the eastward at Richmond and Norfolk.[209]

---

[209] Ambler, *Sectionalism in Virginia, 1776-1861*, 125-126.

Nevertheless, Wheeling made a plucky fight for permanent trade and commercial advantages. To this end, in the early period, one of the things most desired was a local bridge across the Ohio. Thus it was planned to make the area to the north tributary to the Cumberland road and incidentally to Wheeling. In anticipation of the latter improvement Noah Zane and others, in 1816, induced the legislatures of Ohio and Virginia to incorporate the Wheeling Bridge Company for the purpose of erecting the proposed bridge. The only condition imposed was that it should be so built as not to interfere with navigation. As steamboating was then in its infancy, most traffic on the Ohio still being by flatboats, barges, and keelboats, this requirement was not exacting. Moreover, the prospects of returns in tolls for the use of a bridge located at this crossroad of the interior seemed to invite private initiative and to insure immediate returns.

Despite these favorable conditions the Wheeling bridge did not materialize. Private capital was not forthcoming, and for some time after 1818 traffic over the Cumberland road to Wheeling continued thence by way of the Ohio. With the completion of the Erie and Pennsylvania canals and the consequent diversion of traffic from the overland routes between the Atlantic coast and the Ohio valley, Wheeling became alarmed. Accordingly, in 1830, she appealed to Congress for an appropriation to aid in the construction of her proposed bridge.

Although possessed of superior advantages, Pittsburgh did not ignore these efforts of her rival. Already the completion of the Cumberland road was a matter of importance to most Pennsylvanians. When it was nearing completion Zadok Cramer, speaking for Pittsburgh interests, said of it: "The United States' [Cumberland] road, when completed, will naturally draw a great deal of trade of the northern states to the states of Ohio, Kentucky, Tennessee, and to Louisiana, through that channel, thereby abridging very much the trade from those states through Pennsylvania." To offset the possible disadvantages to his state Cramer joined others in urging the completion of the turnpike then in process of construction between Harrisburg and Pittsburgh and the improved navigation of the Ohio river.[210]

Subsequently steamboat navigation on the western waters became practicable, and Pittsburgh developed into an important boat building center. She also became the western terminus of a system of state-built canals that gave her direct water communications with the East and the Great Lakes. Accordingly she memorialized Congress against the "obstruction to navigation" at Wheeling. Her influence prevailed, and this phase of the contest ended in the defeat of the latter. But local enterprise had meanwhile succeeded in financing and erecting a bridge over the lesser channel of the Ohio at Wheeling, that separating its Ohio bank from Zane's island.[211]

Undaunted Wheeling refused to accept defeat, local conditions seeming to make victory over Pittsburgh in the matter of the bridge controversy imperative. The Baltimore and Ohio Company was then planning to extend its railroad lines to the interior, provided a means of crossing the Ohio could be assured. As local farmers and others who had hitherto opposed railroads, fearing that they would lower the price of horses, were now less insistent, Wheeling again appealed to Con-

[210] Cramer, *Navigator* (ed. 1818), 26.
[211] Wheeling *Tri-Weekly Gazette*, September 16, 1835.

gress, this time with the request that her local bridge be built at national expense. This request was urged in fulfillment of a contract under which Congress in 1802, had agreed to build a road "to the state of Ohio," which, in lieu thereof, was to relinquish all claims to the proceeds from public lands sold or to be sold within her borders. Furthermore, it was set forth that this request had the endorsement of Ohio through a resolution of her legislature and that numerous bodies of a more local character had approved it.[212]

It was under these conditions that the Wheeling bridge became a national issue, members of Congress and others favoring or opposing it as their sectional interests seemed to determine. At times, conditions seemed to indicate that it would be undertaken as a national enterprise. In 1836 it received the approval of a congressional committee on roads, and about the same time a corps of government engineers pronounced it both desirable and practicable. They also submitted a plan for a structure with a movable floor by the use of which it was claimed that the Ohio could be navigated at any time, even at flood stages. In 1840 the Postmaster General endorsed the proposal as necessary for the safe and prompt dispatch of the mails which were then being delayed at Wheeling by ice, floods, and low water, for weeks at a time.[213]

Nevertheless, work on the proposed bridge was again delayed, thanks, among other things, to the political influence of Pennsylvania in the Jacksonian period, to traditional notions of inland America regarding the freedom of its rivers, and to current controversies over the powers of Congress in the matter of internal im-

---

[212] Wheeling *Daily Times*, November 16, 1844; Pittsburgh *Gazette*, July 24, 1846. [213] Wheeling *Daily Times*, September 14, 1846.

provements. Despairing of aid from other sources Wheeling again appealed to the national government. In support of her request the conditions of Ohio's admission to the Union, previously mentioned, were revived, and attention was called to the fact that Virginia had, meanwhile, endorsed the Wheeling bridge as a national enterprise within the constitutional powers of Congress, and that the bridge had the unqualified approval of federal officialdom. Since the objections thereto came only from parties who had not raised a voice against a bridge over the Ohio at Louisville, from parties who had themselves built several bridges over the Monongahela and the Allegheny at and near Pittsburgh, the former river being the only natural outlet for a large part of Virginia, it was maintained that the objections to the Wheeling bridge had their origin in fears less public and commendable than concern for free navigation. Finally, the construction of the proposed bridge was urged as a national enterprise, a connecting link in a thoroughfare between the East and the West, that would, in time, follow the "immigrant trail to the Rocky mountains and the Pacific," providing a direct route to the national capital and a necessary means of transportation for soldiers and military supplies.

Realizing that the decision on this request would be final, every effort was made to convince Congress of its merits. To this end a plan was submitted. It was the work of Charles Ellett, a famous engineer, and received the approval of a congressional committee on roads. To meet a frequent objection Lewis Steenrod, the local member of Congress, proposed the use of hinges on steamboat smoke-stacks, attached in such a way as to permit of lowering them in cases of emergency.

Meanwhile, Pittsburgh was becoming more and more interested in preserving the free and uninterrupted navigation of the Ohio. A tributary system of canals was bringing and taking thousands of tons of freight and hundreds of passengers daily. The Monongahela had been locked and dammed all the way thence to Brownsville and the Youghiogheny from its mouth to West Newton, thus increasing the volume of traffic on the Monogahela, as well as that on the Ohio. As already indicated elsewhere, scores of packets were plying the upper Ohio, some of them in line arrangements, and the famous Pittsburgh and Cincinnati Packet line was being organized. Some of the packets of this and other lines were already palatial, and in the mania for speed, they had extended their smoke-stacks to unprecedented heights. Accordingly Pittsburgh resolved upon a fight to the finish. In her behalf the Pennsylvania legislature of 1844 made another formal protest against any "obstruction" over the Ohio at or near Wheeling in the form of a bridge. Every possible resource, both local and national, was resorted to in order to make this protest effective. As in the past Pittsburgh won, and Wheeling abandoned hope of getting her proposed bridge through aid from Congress.

Persistent in her purpose to bridge the Ohio, Wheeling next sought authority therefor by the state's right route which led to Richmond, where the remonstrating voice of Pennsylvania was less potent than in Washington. Fortunately the times and conditions were opportune for such a move. Leading southern statesmen were then planning for a united South that would include all slaveholding territory. To this end political and other concessions were being made those sections that were comparatively free, such as the Trans-alleghany, and the newly organized southern churches were making a vigorous fight to hold that section within their jurisdiction. For these and other reasons the Wheeling and Belmont Bridge Company was re-incorporated by the state of Virginia with authority to construct a bridge across the Ohio at Wheeling. Inasmuch as Virginia's jurisdiction extended to low water mark on the Ohio side, her power and rights in the matter were not seriously questioned, so long as their exercise did not interfere with navigation. To avoid any controversy on this point the act of incorporation provided that the proposed bridge might be abated as a nuisance, in the event that it proved an obstruction to steamboats and other craft using the Ohio in the "usual manner."[214]

As no aid had been expected from the state of Virginia, the proposed bridge was financed as a private enterprise of the joint-stock variety. Progress was rapid, former failures serving to allay opposition and the suspicions of Pittsburgh. Plans were made for a suspension bridge, and in September, 1847, Charles Ellett was employed to supervise its construction. In little more than two years the masonry was in place, and local enthusiasm began to exult over the prospect of an approaching triumph. Moreover, the Baltimore and Ohio railroad, the first through line between the Atlantic coast and the Ohio river, was nearing completion to Wheeling which again seemed in sight of her long cherished ambition to become the chief commercial city of the upper Ohio.

It was under these conditions that Pittsburgh renewed her efforts to prevent the construction of a bridge across the Ohio at Wheeling. The state of Pennsylvania had made large expenditures for internal im-

---
[214] — *Idem*, July 30, 1846.

provements in her western counties, and the steamboats plying the upper Ohio had grown in height. As the proposed bridge would be only thirty feet above high water mark, it was claimed that it would be an obstruction that would practically suspend navigation for long periods at a time, thus rendering valueless Pennsylvania's internal improvements. In June, 1849, a mass meeting of Pittsburgh rivermen and their friends set forth these contentions and demanded action to protect their interests. In response Pennsylvania, in July, 1849, appealed to a local resident, Judge Grier of the federal Supreme Court, for an injunction to stop the progress of work on the Wheeling bridge. The request was granted, but before the writ embodying it could be served, a wire cable for the objectionable structure had been placed in position. Outgeneraled, Pennsylvania next asked the Supreme Court to abate the "obstruction" as a nuisance in violation of the spirit and the letter of the act of Virginia incorporating the Wheeling Bridge Company.[215]

As immediate action on this request could not be had, work on the bridge went forward to completion, October 20, 1849. Through the local press and otherwise the event was heralded as one "joining Virginia and Ohio in perpetual union" by the "longest and the most powerful single span ever projected in the world." To awaiting crowds that had visited the scene for days, hoping to see the last spike driven, two flags, one bearing the insignia of Virginia, the other that of Ohio, announced this triumph from their respective towers on the bridge. This demonstration called forth a shout that was echoed and reëchoed by the surrounding hills. A few minutes later a cannon shot announced the safe

---

[215] — *Idem*, August 24, 1849.

passage of the first traffic, the builders in a one horse carriage. Later in the day the fairy equipage of "General Tom Thumb," in a carriage drawn by Shetland ponies, gifts of Queen Victoria, crossed and re-crossed the bridge, bringing to a fitting close its spontaneous and informal dedication.[216]

The formal dedication of the Wheeling bridge, November 15, 1849, was an event of national interest and importance. Thousands of persons heard the speaker of the day, B. W. Thompson of Indiana, as well as letters from Benjamin Ruggles of Ohio, Governor John B. Floyd of Virginia, Thomas Swann, president of the Baltimore and Ohio railroad, Henry Clay, and others. As a part of the ceremony women of Wheeling and vicinity crossed and re-crossed the bridge in solemn procession. The ceremony ended in a blaze of light, the product of one thousand lamps so arranged as to bring out the grace and elegance of the proud structure. To every suggestion of removing it under an order from the Supreme Court the reply was that of Henry Clay: "You might as well try to take down the rainbow."

The following lines from "Dick Doleful," sung on the above occasion to the air of "Carry Me Back to Old Virginia" tell something of its spirit: [217]

> Our wants are many here below,
> But do not want them long;
> We ask one thousand and ten feet —
> Of bridge that's high and strong.
> We want steamboats to pass beneath,
> And stages to pass o'er;
> And stout enough to bear the train
> That comes from Baltimore.
>   Then give us the track, the railroad track,

---
[216] Wheeling *Gazette*, October 22, 1849.
[217] — *Idem*, August 10, 1849; *idem*, November 17, 1849.

>   From here to the eastern shore;
>   O give us the track to carry us back
>   From Wheeling to Baltimore.
>
> 'Tis wrong to build your steamboat pipes
> To reach up to the moon,
> For when you look down at our bridge,
> Your feathers drop too soon.
> Since you in vain oppose our bridge
> To reach from shore to shore,
> Be generous now, and give the road
> To us from Baltimore.
>   Then give us the track, etc.
>
> You'll find in law your great mistake,
> And this will be a pity,
> Too late alas, a light will break
> Upon your Smoky City.
> Then don't hold out about the route,
> Ere eighteen fifty-four,
> You will see stars when you hear cars
> Come in from Baltimore!
>   Then give us the track, etc.

While Wheeling celebrated Pittsburgh planned to destroy the source of her rival's joy by pressing her appeals to the Supreme Court. In fact every effort was made to establish a winning case. To this end, among other things, packets approached the "Bridge of Size" cautiously, sometimes "lying by" for hours and even transferring passengers and freight without trying to pass under. The masters thus deporting themselves proclaimed their injuries far and wide. Some were accused of subsidizing the press, even that in the East, and the state treasurer of Pennsylvania attempted to fortify the case by statistics showing how an obstructed river at Wheeling would injure the industrial growth of Pittsburgh, thus tending to destroy the value of public improvements in western Pennsylvania. Finally Robert

J. Walker and Edward M. Stanton, each as well versed in things political as in things legal, were retained as counsel.

Mindful of her experiences with Congress, Wheeling was not disposed to allow actual possession to decide her case. Fortified with a resolution of the legislature of Virginia approving her bridge as in keeping with the intent of the act under which it was authorized, she determined to fight for the retention of every advantage already gained. To this end much was said about the rights of sovereign states, and two able attorneys, each of the Whig variety of politics, Alex. H. H. Stuart of Virginia and Reverdy Johnson of Maryland, were retained to present her case to the Supreme Court.[218]

At this stage the Wheeling bridge called forth many and varied comments.[219] For example, David Embree, a famous engineer, thought the Supreme Court should deny to any one, who did not have the permission of Congress, the right to use a single foot of land within the banks of a navigable stream; the Cincinnati *Commercial* hoped that the bridge would be permitted to stand as a bond of union between the North and the South; Governor Floyd of Virginia believed that the efforts to destroy it could be traced to morbid and jealous rivalry, rather than to any serious apprehension regarding the freedom of navigation; and the governor of Pennsylvania urged its abatement as a nuisance destructive of the public improvements of his state and injurious to the commerce of the whole country.

In presenting their case, counsel for Pennsylvania

---

[218] — *Idem*, August 29, 1849; *idem*, November 20, 1849; *idem*, March 1, 1850; Callahan, *op. cit.*

[219] Wheeling *Gazette*, Jaunary 10, 1850; *idem*, January 16, 1850; *idem*, February 19, 1850.

maintained that the Wheeling bridge was built with a view to the malicious injury of Pittsburgh, whose boats, it was claimed, carried thence three-fourths of all the traffic passing over the Pennsylvania canal. Of the general effects upon the public works of Pennsylvania Mr. Stanton said:

> The injury occasioned by this obstruction is deep and lasting. The products of the South and the West, and the Pacific coast are brought in steamboats along the Ohio to the western end of her canals at Pittsburgh, thence to be transported through them to Philadelphia, for an eastern and foreign market. Foreign merchandise and eastern manufactures, received at Philadelphia, are transported by the same channel to Pittsburgh, thence to be carried south and west, to their destination, in steamboats along the Ohio. If these vessels and their commerce are liable to be stopped within a short distance, as they approach the canals, and subjected to expense, delay, and danger to reach them, the same consequence to ensue on their journey departing, the value of these works must be destroyed.[220]

Admitting some of the contentions of Pennsylvania, particularly the fact that she had made large expenditures for internal improvements in her western counties, counsel for the Wheeling Bridge Company would not concede that the bridge was an obstruction to steamboats and other craft navigating the Ohio in the "usual manner," as contemplated in the charter under which it was constructed. As proof thereof they submitted a resolution of the legislature of Virginia approving the structure. Furthermore, they denied the corporate capacity of Pennsylvania to bring the pending suit, and justified the bridge as within the sovereign power of Virginia and as a necessary connecting link in a great highway second in importance only to the Ohio itself.

With Associate Justice Daniel of Virginia dissenting, the Court accepted jurisdiction and appointed R.

---

[220]—*Idem*, February 23, 1850.

H. Woolworth of New York a special commissioner to take testimony and report his findings. After months of investigation, during which the local press kept the matter before the public, he reported that the Wheeling bridge had a tendency to divert traffic from the public improvements of Pennsylvania and, also, that boats of the Pittsburgh and Cincinnati Packet line had been delayed and otherwise inconvenienced by it. For example, the "Hibernia," in November, 1849, had been delayed for thirty-two hours and had been forced to re-ship a part of her cargo, including passengers, in a smaller boat. Later she had twice been compelled to abandon trips. Although the commissioner recognized the beneficial results of fair competition between river and railroad transit and, to this end, the necessity of bridging rivers, when it could be done without obstructing navigation, he reported the Wheeling bridge an obstruction to navigation resulting in injury to packets plying waters leading to and from Pittsburgh.[221]

The opinion of the Court was based upon this report and was given in May, 1852. It was written by Associate Justice McLean of Cincinnati, Ohio, who held that the Wheeling bridge, in so far as it interfered with navigation, was inconsistent with and in violation of acts of Congress and that it could not therefore be authorized and protected by Virginia. Furthermore, he volunteered the opinion that, however numerous and important railroads might become in the future, they would never supersede waterways as arteries of commerce. The Court had, therefore, ruled for the unobstructed use of the latter. It was willing, however, to permit the bridge at Wheeling to remain, provided it could be raised to an elevation of one hundred eleven

---
[221] — *Idem*, June 5, 1850; *Waterways Journal*, March 25, 1922.

feet above low water and maintained at that elevation for a distance of three hundred feet over the main channel, or provided it were altered in any other way so that it would not interfere with navigation. The Company was given until February 1, 1853, to comply with this order.

The dissenting opinions of Chief Justice Taney and Associate Justice Daniel are both interesting and informing. The former held that Congress could not subsequently intervene to decide the Wheeling bridge unlawful having once acquiesced in its authorization by a sovereign state. He also thought that the location and regulation of bridges were legislative rather than judicial matters. On the other hand, Associate Justice Daniel resolved the case to state and local rivalry and concluded that "if mere rivalry of works of internal improvement in other states, by holding out the temptation of greater dispatch, greater safety, or any other inducement to preference to those works over the Pennsylvania canals, be wrong and a ground for jurisdiction here, the argument and the rule sought to be deduced therefrom should operate equally." Reasoning thus Pennsylvania would have recourse against Virginia for damages, should the latter succeed in her plan to construct a railroad from the seaboard to the Ohio river at Point Pleasant, thereby diverting traffic from Pittsburgh. Thus Daniel concluded that it was folly and injustice to attempt to regulate commerce to particular interests.

Meanwhile Wheeling had appealed to Congress to save her pet enterprise. This body was asked to declare the Wheeling bridge a post-road and to require steamboats using the waters under it to adjust their smokestacks to existing conditions. The immediate object was to secure such action before the order of the Supreme Court directing its removal or alteration became effective. This move had the approval of the legislatures of Virginia and Indiana, the conflicting railroad interests of Ohio alone preventing it from receiving the approval of that state. However, a large minority of the Ohio legislature favored it, as did thirty-six members of that of Pennsylvania and numerous local organizations.

Through the influence of aggressive friends Congress acted at once. In July, 1852, a committee on roads endorsed the request, and on the last day of the session, August 31, 1852, it became a law, as a rider to the Post Office Appropriation bill. Among the members favoring it were: (1) those who believed that the entire proceeding originated in Pittsburgh's jealousy of Wheeling; (2) those who felt that the decision of the Supreme Court in the Wheeling bridge case was a blow at state sovereignty; and (3) those who believed in the superior advantages of railroads over rivers as a future means of transportation. Those opposing the measure condemned it as a malicious device to injure Pittsburgh and pointed out the possibility of bridging the Ohio near Wheeling but at a point where navigation would not be obstructed.[222] The vote on the passage of the rider was, however, decisive, that of the Senate being thirty for to ten against and that of the House being ninety-two for to forty-two against.

Many saw in the results of this act a crisis not unlike that involved in nullification. With the support of Virginia, Ohio, and Indiana the Bridge Company relied upon the action of Congress to supersede the order of the Supreme Court. On the other hand Pennsylvania

---
[222] Wheeling *Intelligencer*, September 8, 1852.

insisted that the action of Congress was unconstitutional and that the order of the Court could and would be enforced. Meanwhile Pittsburgh's river captains were needlessly "lying by" and lowering chimneys upon approaching the Wheeling bridge, and showing other signs of detention and oppression. As a consequence the New York *Courier* feared "that all the most grave and important issues which had ever arisen under our form of government might occur at any time." But the Wheeling *Intelligencer* was more optimistic, expressing the belief that Pittsburgh would in time see the error of her way and repent and not be like Demetrius of old who showed greater concern for the craftsmen of Ephesus than for the salvation of his own soul.[223]

With the advent of the locomotive in the Ohio valley the rivalry between Pittsburgh and Wheeling took on a new aspect. When the first Wheeling bridge was destroyed during a storm, May, 1854, Pittsburgh made an unsuccessful effort to prevent its restoration, again carrying her petition to the federal Supreme Court.[224] In aid of her efforts there, her steamboatmen again approached the "Bridge of Size" at Wheeling with lowered smoke-stacks and would have persisted in such offences but for the dissuading power of stones and other physical arguments in the hands of an indignant local populace. Despite her manifestation of concern in river transportation, Pittsburgh's chief interest had shifted to railroads. On the point of attaining through and direct rail connections with Philadelphia, she was planning to extend them to the West by way of Steubenville, Ohio. Moreover, she was interested in a proposed extension of the Baltimore and Ohio railroad

---

[223] — *Idem*, August 24, 1852; *idem*, January 11, 1853.
[224] — *Idem*, July 4, 1854; *idem*, July 17, 1854; Callahan, *op. cit.*

from Cumberland to her gates. Among the numerous proofs of this shifting interest was the fact that Pennsylvania was not even represented when the original Wheeling bridge case was called for final hearing in the federal Supreme Court in December, 1853, her legislature having failed to appropriate funds to continue the suit.

Meanwhile Wheeling was not indifferent to the growing importance of railroad transportation and to the efforts of her rival. As a consequence her interest shifted from the river to the railroad. Among other things she desired rail connections with Marietta, Columbus, and Cleveland by way of her bridge. A proposed treaty of reciprocity with Canada was relied upon to bring great benefits to Cleveland and incidentally to Wheeling. Wheeling also planned for direct rail connection with Philadelphia by way of Little Washington and Brownsville over the proposed Hempfield line, with not so much as a branch to Pittsburgh. But the proposed railroad between Pittsburgh and Steubenville, thence to the West with the possibility of a line paralleling the west bank of the upper Ohio, gave Wheeling greatest concern. She regarded it as a "malicious plan" to cripple her commerce and tried to prevent it. As any such road would of necessity have to cross Virginia, Wheeling appealed to the legislature of that state asking that a charter be refused. Her petition was granted, whereupon the promoters of the proposed road adopted the novel plan of purchasing a right of way from local owners in Virginia, rushing the road to completion, and then asking Congress to make it a post-road, as had been done in the case of the Wheeling bridge. The local situation led to threats of secession on the part of the two northernmost counties of Virginia and to a vigorous assertion of the doctrines of state sovereignty on the part of the Wheeling *Intelligencer*, soon to become a self-appointed organ of nationalism. As a last resort Wheeling was willing to prevent the construction of the proposed road by opposing the building of a bridge across the Ohio at Steubenville.[225]

Despite their plans for a greater future the years immediately following 1854 brought reverses to both Pittsburgh and Wheeling. Of the two, Wheeling suffered most. Her projected railroads did not materialize, and the Baltimore and Ohio Company extended its lines into Ohio by a bridge at Benwood, four miles below Wheeling which remained for some time a "wooding station for steamboats." Charges of bad faith fell upon deaf ears and only served to place her in a class with Erie, Pennsylvania, then engaged in the "Erie War" to prevent railroads from effecting through connections thence to the East and the West. Before the end of the fifties the steamboat center of inland America shifted to St. Louis, the railroad center to Chicago. Meanwhile, as previously indicated, the "floating palaces" that had claimed Pittsburgh and Wheeling as home ports sought other ports, some of them going to the lower Ohio, others to the Mississippi. Thus common adversities and, in more recent times, common industrial interests tended to allay the differences between these rival cities. Shortly after the Civil war they were engaged in a common effort to prevent the construction of bridges across the Ohio, one at Steubenville, the other at Parkersburg.

The rivalry between Cincinnati and Louisville was not unlike that between Pittsburgh and Wheeling and

---

[225] Pittsburgh *Gazette*, February 9, 1854.

is almost as old as the cities themselves.[226] With her initial start in trade, commerce, and population and her superior location at the point of a bend in the Ohio reaching far into the Old Northwest, Cincinnati had the advantage and, like Pittsburgh in her contest with Wheeling, played the major rôle. Unlike Wheeling, however, Louisville had many natural advantages. From an early date her location at the Falls of the Ohio was relied upon to make her the leading commercial center of the interior, and she occupied a natural gateway to the South.

The first announcements of plans for local railroads called forth the conflicting interests of these two cities. The prize fought for was favor in the southern markets, Louisville making the most of her natural advantages, Cincinnati of her traditions and influence. Cut off from her coveted goal by "lands highly unfavorable to railroad construction – wild, unsettled, difficult of access, of extremely irregular geological formation, intersected by a wide mountainous region, and cut off by three great rivers and numerous smaller streams," Cincinnati desired a direct route, however bad, to the South. Of course Louisville did every thing in her power to prevent the realization of this ambition. Thus, when the legislature of Kentucky, in 1836, chartered a proposed Cincinnati, Louisville, and Charleston railroad, Cincinnati went wild with joy, staging a celebration in the midst of a snow storm, that was long remembered because of its brilliant illuminations. Soon

---
[226] For fuller data see Hollander's "The Cincinnati and Southern Railway: a study in municipal activity," in *J. H. U. Studies in History and Political Science*, vol. xii, 7-96; U. S. *Congressional Globe*, 42 cong., 1 sess., pt i, 22, 73, 74; E. M. Coulter's "Commercial Intercourse with the Southern Confederacy in the Mississippi Valley," in *Miss. Valley Hist. Review*, vol. v, 377-395.

thereafter, in a southern railroad convention meeting at Knoxville and presided over by Governor Hayne of South Carolina, Cincinnati was designated, also, as the northern terminus of a proposed railroad to connect Charleston and the Ohio river by way of the French Broad river and the Cumberland gap, so that her commercial future seemed assured.[227] But Louisville demanded a branch line in exchange for a franchise to cross the state of Kentucky and insisted upon other conditions that defeated the project. Had it been carried to completion, the results might have changed the course of American history by the fact that railroads would have run north and south as well as east and west.

During the next fifteen years or more Cincinnati enjoyed great preëminence as a river city. Toward the end of this period agitation for a railroad connection with the South was revived, but nothing to that end was accomplished. Finally she awoke to find that the river center of the interior had shifted to St. Louis and that most of her commerce was being carried by rail to the North and the East. Three railroad lines between the Middle West and the Atlantic coast competed with the Ohio river, and St. Louis was extending tributary railroads into Illinois, Indiana, and Missouri, having increased her connecting mileage from three hundred thirty-nine in 1850, to forty-one hundred eighty-six in 1856. Meanwhile, with the approaching completion of the Louisville and Nashville railroad, Louisville was being placed in direct communication with almost every important point in the South. Comparatively, Cincinnati was helpless due largely to the debt-restricting provision of the Ohio constitution of

---

[227] Amer. Hist. Assoc., *Annual Report* (1899), vol. ii, 411.

1850. As late as 1859 the total railroad mileage of the state of Ohio was eighteen hundred sixty-nine miles, and this in spite of the fact that a pioneer line of the West was within her borders. It mattered not that much of this mileage was tributary to Cincinnati. Her transportation situation was, nevertheless, grave. But for the necessity of crossing the state of Ohio in effecting through rail connections between the East and the region of the upper Mississippi, it would have been worse.

It was under these conditions that Cincinnati again gave her transportation problems serious attention. Among other things efforts were made to construct a direct railroad to the South by public subscriptions. Failing in this, an effort was made to stimulate such initiative by offers of cash bonuses to be raised by private subscriptions. The Kentucky Central railroad was already in operation between Cincinnati and Lexington, Kentucky, and the Cincinnati, Lexington, and East Tennessee railroad was in operation between Lexington and Nicholasville. The plan was to extend the latter to Knoxville, thus giving Cincinnati an independent and somewhat direct line into the heart of the South. With one-half of the necessary one million dollars subscribed for putting this enterprise through, the approach of civil war put an end to further efforts.

During the Civil war the relations between Cincinnati and Louisville were anything but amicable. Immediately following the opening of hostilities the former city suddenly lost much of her predilection for things southern and became surprisingly loyal. The Mississippi was soon closed to transportation, and Louisville became an important source of supplies for the Confederacy, traffic going thence directly south through the neutral state of Kentucky by way of the Louisville and Nashville railroad. For a time she was the busiest city on the Ohio. Freight shipments thence by rail were held up for weeks at a time, so great was the congestion.[228]

It was to prevent this species of "neutral rascality" that Cincinnati prepared to use force against Louisville. Meanwhile every effort was made by the former to cut off the latter's source of supplies from the Wabash and other points north of the Ohio, some of them near Cincinnati herself. Despairing of Lincoln's leniency toward Kentucky neutrals, she finally accused the national government of criminal negligence for permitting traffic between the North and the South by way of Louisville.[229]

At one time it seemed that Civil war conditions would solve Cincinnati's transportation problems. In his annual message of December, 1861, President Lincoln asked Congress to open direct rail communications thence to the South at government expense and as a war measure. Under direction of General Burnside, surveys were made to determine the most practicable route for this purpose, and plans were made for grading a road bed. Congress took no action, however, and with the abandonment of the proposed Union advance by way of Cumberland gap, the enterprise was dropped, to the great disappointment of interests on the Ohio.

Cincinnati came out of the Civil war more completely isolated than ever. The traffic of the Ohio valley had continued to shift to St. Louis, Chicago, Cleveland, and Buffalo. Trade with the southern states was almost completely cut off, Cincinnati's only communication

---

[228] *Miss. Valley Hist. Review*, vol. ii, 275-300.
[229] — *Idem*, vol. v, 377-395.

with the lower South, aside from the all-water route, being by way of the Ohio to Louisville, thence by the Louisville and Nashville railroad. As a means of transportation, in competitive trade and commerce, this latter route was both indirect and inadequate. Moreover, the Louisville and Nashville railroad was then a "Louisville Road," controlled by and operated in the interest of its merchants. Rates were determined arbitrarily and sometimes with a view to injury to Cincinnati. Through freights from that point were delayed to the extent that her board of trade found it necessary to station agents at Louisville to expedite shipments, particularly those to the South. Relief from this situation seemed imperative, if Cincinnati were to regain any of her former trade and commercial prestige.

The situation has been ably summarized in these words:

> Cincinnati and Louisville were active competitors for southern trade. This trade was definitely established upon the basis of railroad transportation. Cincinnati possessed no direct railroad to the South; Louisville did. The advantages enjoyed by the former city in the era of water transportation were now held by the latter. Southern merchants dealing directly with the North were diverted from Cincinnati by the closer proximity of Louisville. The advantages of commercial travel were minimized by inadequate transportation facilities, unreasonable delays, and arbitrary freight charges upon southern consignments shipped *via* Louisville. Louisville, in a word, threatened to displace Cincinnati as the chief distributing point of northern manufacturers to southern consumers.[230]

The situation challenged the best resources of Cincinnati. Many plans and suggestions were made, but all encountered opposition. Finally, Edward A. Ferguson, an able constitutional lawyer of Cincinnati, suggested a municipally constructed and operated railroad.

---
[230] Hollander, *op .cit.*, 18.

He believed that the constitutional prohibition preventing a city from lending its credit to such an enterprise would not prevent a city from building and operating it as a municipal undertaking. This plan received the endorsement of the local council, board of trade, and chamber of commerce, and was finally embodied in a bill which received the approval of the Ohio legislature, May 4, 1869, but not before it had been so amended as to limit the capital stock of the proposed railroad to ten million dollars, none of which was to be sold below par. In a short time thereafter Cincinnati accepted the terms of the act by a popular referendum, and Chattanooga, Tennessee, was designated as the southern terminus of the proposed railroad which was christened the "Cincinnati Southern," later being popularly known as the "Queen and Crescent." Under the terms of the act of incorporation the construction and operation of this road were intrusted to a board of trustees appointed by the Supreme Court of Cincinnati.

While preliminary plans and surveys went forward, this board attacked the most difficult feature of the entire undertaking, that of securing a right of way through Kentucky and Tennessee. Under conditions favorable to all parties, Tennessee readily gave her consent, but Louisville was able to prevent favorable action on the part of Kentucky. Thus baffled Cincinnati resolved to appeal directly to the people of that state in its next legislative election. Fortified by a decision of the Supreme Court of Ohio confirming the legality of the proposed railroad, even the much-mooted question of the right of a city to spend public funds beyond its limits or vicinity, Cincinnati made a vigorous and thorough appeal in behalf of her pet enterprise. Her best argument was its possible benefits to Kentucky. For example, it was shown that all the coal then used in central Kentucky was floated down the Ohio from Pennsylvania and Ohio to Covington and sent thence by rail throughout the state, and that residents of the eastern counties were thus obliged to pay from thirty to fifty cents per bushel for fuel, while great fields of coal lay within a few hours ride of them in their own state. Moreover, it was asserted that the proposed road would be of advantage to the stock raisers of Kentucky, who would thus be able to reach the South directly and avoid long and expensive delays. Louisville again prevailed, however, alleging undue "meddlesomeness" on the part of certain "influential citizens of Cincinnati," and the desired right of way was denied.

Following the example of Wheeling in her contest with Pittsburgh, Cincinnati now turned to the federal government for relief. She asked that her proposed municipally owned railroad be made a post-road, in the belief that Congress could thus legalize it and make it possible. A local delegation went to Washington in support of this request, which received the approval of the House by a two-thirds vote but failed in the Senate, seemingly only for lack of time to consider it.

Following this failure, local conditions seeming to admit of no delay, Cincinnati again appealed to Kentucky, directing her efforts to those sections that had been the most effective in refusing her previous request. During the summer and autumn of the year 1871 an active canvass won many new friends for the proposed railroad. These now asked to be given complete charge of its future before the Kentucky legislature, a request readily granted in view of the alleged cause of the previous failure. For weeks the fate of the bill granting the desired right of way hung in the balance, but, after "the most determined and positive opposition that was ever inaugurated against any bill before any legislature," it became a law but with conditions that made it impossible. Among other things the proposed road was to pay to the state of Kentucky, in addition to ordinary taxes, fifty cents for every passenger carried across that state, twenty-five cents for every passenger traveling a distance of one hundred miles within it, and one cent for every hundred pounds of through freight carried.

As these conditions were prohibitive, Cincinnati now turned to other alternatives. Most promising was the proposed purchase of the Kentucky Central railroad and its subsequent extention to some point further south under concessions already granted. The possibilities of this course, together with its serious consideration by the legislature of Ohio and the city of Cincinnati, caused Kentucky to relent and make possible conditions under which the proposed Cincinnati Southern railroad could go forward. Following these concessions Cincinnati soon carried to successful completion one of the most interesting enterprises in municipal railroad construction and operation in America. The resulting benefits to Kentucky helped Cincinnati and made Louisville comparatively impotent as a rival. Ever since, the conflicting interests of these two cities have tended to keep in the background.

The Civil War Period

When Jefferson purchased Louisiana from France most exports from the Ohio valley went to market by way of New Orleans. Less than sixty years later, however, almost nine-tenths of this total found an outlet east, chiefly by way of New York, Philadelphia, and Baltimore, so completely had canals and railroads revolutionized transportation in the United States.

In the opening days of the Civil war the result of this transformation was a source of gratification and assurance to friends of the Union, who referred with pride and security to the economic sufficiency of the North.[231] Abolitionist Cleveland, blustering Chicago and "smoke and sin-cursed" Pittsburgh, each formerly despised in many river circles along the Ohio, thus suddenly became allies and havens of security for cities to the southward, even those in slaveholding territory.

Nevertheless, the secession movement was of vital concern to Ohio valley rivermen. Among other things, it meant the possible dissolution of the Union and the consequent loss of the free navigation of the Mississippi river, long cherished locally as a natural right. To the Northwest, with its railroads extending in every direction, the Mississippi was a potential regulator of railroad rates and services. For those living on the Ohio, the Mississippi and its tributaries were still arteries for a large and important domestic commerce that might

---

[231] Cincinnati *Commercial*, May 27, 1861; *Hunt's Merchants' Magazine*, vol. xlv, 541; *idem*, vol. xlvi, 363.

have gone far towards uniting permanently the North and the South, but for the aggressiveness of the abolitionists in the former and the cotton planters in the latter section. As in the days of the hated Spaniard, the mere suggestion of closing the Mississippi or of restricting its free use was sufficient to arouse threats of a resort to arms throughout the whole Ohio valley.

Following the panic of 1857 and the first effects of the completion of through rail communications between the East and the West, river traffic between the Ohio valley and the lower South showed signs of returning vitality, thanks largely to the comparative absence of competing railroads. Some idea of the commercial relations between these sections may be had from a brief survey of the river traffic between them. The former was still pouring its food and industrial products into the cotton South. In return it continued to receive sugar, cotton, molasses, oranges, coffee, and, what was more important, millions of dollars annually for the services of its rivermen and their craft, the steamboats of the Ohio being to inland America, at that time, what the British merchantmen are to the world today. Meanwhile, most of the commerce of the Cumberland and Tennessee valleys continued to be by river, and Cincinnati, St. Louis, Memphis, and New Orleans were important centers of a large intra-valley river trade. Prosperous steamboat lines operated daily packets out of Cincinnati for Madison, Louisville, Nashville, Pittsburgh, St. Louis, Memphis, and New Orleans.[232]

These intra-trade and commercial relations were not without results. Among other things, as late as 1861 Cincinnati displayed many aspects of a southern city.

[232] — *Idem*, vol. xliv, 752.

She did not yet tolerate abolitionists, and, even after the formation of the Southern Confederacy, her local press was strong in its southern leanings. The Cincinnati *Daily Enquirer* was for peace at any price; the *Daily Gazette* would say nothing to injure the commercial interests of the Ohio valley in the South; and the forward-looking *Daily Commercial*, under the direction of Murat Halstead, was only mildly anti-southern. Indeed, there were those who feared lest Cincinnati would "follow the lead of her purse strings" and cast her lot with the South.[233] In April, 1861, in the midst of a period of business depression, she elected a mayor, George Hatch, who was a strong state's rights Democrat favorable to concessions to the South. About the same time her authorities permitted cannon consigned to parties in Jackson, Mississippi, for use of the Confederacy, to pass her port without question. Of course, cities like Wheeling and Louisville, situated in slave territory and dependent upon southern markets, were even more pro-southern. On the other hand, ties of interest had much to do with determining Kentucky's position of neutrality and the divided sentiment to be found in western Virginia, Missouri, and southern Ohio, Indiana, and Illinois.

Secession leaders were fully aware of the pro-southern interests and sympathies in the Ohio valley and were hopeful of making them even more favorable to their cause. Some are thought to have entertained the possibility of an alliance between the South and the grain-producing Northwest. Many of the early settlers of the latter section were pro-southern, and, as has been shown, there were many possibilities for that section

---

[233] Cincinnati *Commercial*, December 11, 1860; Goss, Charles F. *Cincinnati, the Queen City, 1788-1912* (Cincinnati, 1912), vol. i, 206-207; *Miss. Valley Hist. Review*, vol. vi, 470.

in the Mississippi as a thoroughfare of commerce. All things considered, the ultimate success of the secession movement seemed to depend most upon its ability to use and control inland transportation.[234]

To this end both the traditions and the immediate interests of the Confederacy seemed to dictate a policy of free trade. Accordingly the Confederate Congress, in one of its first acts, declared for free trade in the intra-Mississippi valley commerce. Moreover, and of even greater importance, it provided "that the peaceful navigation of the Mississippi is hereby declared free to the citizens of any of the states upon its borders and upon the borders of its navigable tributaries." [235] The opening of hostilities did not change this policy which was re-affirmed in the general tariff act of the Confederacy passed in May, 1861, with the exception that a tariff was placed on the manufactures of New England entering the seceding states by way of the inland rivers.

Meanwhile other zealous seceders, as a rule of the less responsible type, were straining the friendly relations of the inland sections. In both New Orleans and Memphis, rivermen from the up-country were detained and asked to prove their loyalty to southern institutions; their boats were searched; and some persons were forced to leave southern waters. In January, 1861, the "A. O. Taylor" was stopped near Memphis by a six-pound shot fired across her deck, possibly the first shot of the Civil war, and the press of the Ohio valley began to express doubts as to the sincerity of the South regarding its promises of free trade and free naviga-

---

[234] Cincinnati *Commercial*, December 13, 1860; Columbus (Ohio) *Crisis*, January 31, 1861; *idem*, February 28, 1861.

[235] Confederate States of America, *Statutes at Large*, chap. 3: 28, January 8, 1861; *idem*, chap. 14: 36, February 25, 1861.

tion.²³⁶ But satisfactory explanations were forthcoming, and the river press along the Ohio was, for a time, able to keep public sentiment in line with traditional economic interests. That of Cincinnati delighted in the obeisance of "King Cotton" to the "Queen City." The *Daily Commercial* was certain that "His Royal Highness" would continue to seek markets where he could find pork, flour, and whiskey, and that, in any event, he would not sink steamboats carrying these cargoes.²³⁷ Meanwhile the quantity of food products going south and of cotton going north increased daily.

This condition was changed completely by the bombardment of Fort Sumter and the events that followed. As a result civil war became inevitable, and majorities in the Ohio valley generally remained loyal to the Union and determined to fight for the retention of the advantages which they enjoyed under it, including the free navigation of the inland rivers. Trade advantages were not to stand in the way of settling moral and political questions involving human rights. Those who did not care for this side of the issue, and they were undoubtedly in the majority, could not ignore the unfavorable economic effects of negro slavery then evident in most all parts of the border.

Cincinnati remained surprisingly loyal. Promised shipments of pork thence to Charleston, South Carolina, were cut off, and her residents joined others from Ohio and Indiana in an effort to prevent the neutrality of Kentucky from becoming a menace to the Union, through the tempting opportunity thus afforded for

---

[236] Cincinnati *Commercial*, January 15, 1861; *idem*, January 18, 1861; *idem*, January 23, 1861; *idem*, February 20, 1861; *idem*, February 27, 1861; Wheeling *Intelligencer*, January 19, 1861.

[237] Cincinnati *Commercial*, January 25, 1861.

getting arms and supplies to the Confederacy by way of the Cumberland and Tennessee rivers and the Louisville and Nashville railroad, only recently completed.[238]

Following the outbreak of hostilities loyal leaders of the Ohio valley manifested an active concern in the future of inland navigation. Their sentiments found best expression in a widely quoted extract from an oration by Edward Everett delivered July 4, 1861, in which he claimed that the Mississippi belonged to the Union "by the Law of Nature and of God." With them he thought it absurd "that ten million of the free people of the Union will allow her [Louisiana] and her seceding brethren to open and shut the portals of this mighty region at their will."[239] In messages to their respective legislatures both Governor Dennison of Ohio and Governor Morton of Indiana expressed grave fear lest the mouth of the Mississippi might be obstructed by the seceders. At the same time the *Illinois State Journal*, May 8, 1861, announced that "The great Northwest will wage war with the slave states bordering on that river [the Mississippi] as long as she has a man or a dollar but what she will enjoy the free and unobstructed navigation of her natural southern outlet," and a contemporaneous writer in *Hunt's Merchants' Magazine* declared that "With God's help the North will keep the Mississippi."[240] Moreover, many persons in both Kentucky and Tennessee now showed signs of apprehension and began to waver in their allegiance to the Confederacy, when confronted with the economic exigencies of the situation.

---

[238] — *Idem*, April 15, 1861; Smith, E. C. *The Borderland in the Civil War* (New York, 1927), 169; *Miss. Valley Hist. Review*, vol. vi, 285.

[239] *The Rebellion Record*, editor, Frank Moore (New York, 1861), vol. i, 41-42. [240] Vol. xlviii, 277.

Most rivermen had anticipated the beginning of hostilities. Influenced by the dull times of February and March, 1861, and by the shouts for "Jeff" Davis and the Southern Confederacy on the one side and those for "Abe" Lincoln and the Union on the other, they had sought home ports, there to await developments and the desires of their respective governments which, it was rumored, would have profitable employment for all boats and rivermen. Attracted by the possibility of large profits to be drawn from this hazardous situation, a few rivermen, both in the North and in the South, lingered in the land of the enemy. Some of these saw their boats confiscated, while others made their escape by "French leave" and through a veritable gauntlet of lawless bands to whom a steamboat and its cargo were coveted prizes. For two generations persons have told of thrilling experiences on "the last boat through," of which there seems to have been more than one in each direction.

Thus by June, 1861, except for local packets, the Mississippi below Cairo was closed to navigation for the first time in more than sixty years. With the same exception, traffic on the Ohio and most of its tributaries was also practically suspended. Insurance companies refused to assume risks; the Union maintained a blockade at the mouth of both the Mississippi and the Ohio; and the Confederacy had blockades at both Memphis and Vicksburg. Boats permitted to pass the lines of the former were, of course, not permitted to pass those of the latter.[241] For a time a few rivermen tried to operate their craft by the *ruse de guerre* of two flags, but most rivermen accepted the situation and settled down to watch the outcome of a struggle, the termination of

---

[241] Cincinnati *Commercial*, May 27, 1861.

which depended largely upon the control of the inland waters.[242]

Until invading armies blocked the way, the Louisville and Nashville railroad took the place of the river route to the lower South.[243] As a part of a plan for winning the border states Lincoln respected the neutrality of Kentucky, thus effectively removing her from the operation of all non-intercourse orders applying to the seceding states. Under the circumstances it took a higher sense of patriotism than that possessed by many farmers along the Ohio to prevent them from shipping produce across the river and doubling profits, even if the transactions were known to benefit the enemy.

Accordingly, Louisville became the busiest city in the Ohio valley. All roads, particularly river roads, led to her gates, and the Louisville and Nashville railroad leading thence to the South was in a short time taxed to its utmost capacity.[244] Commenting upon the situation the Cincinnati *Daily Gazette* said: "Day and night for weeks past, every avenue of approach to its depot has been blocked with vehicles waiting to discharge their loads, while almost fabulous prices have been paid for hauling."

A miniature civil war between Louisville on one side and her neighboring river cities to the north on the other soon followed. In the course of this contest Cincinnati threatened to use force; that local products might not reach Kentucky some proposed a blockade of the Wabash river; and the citizens of New Albany and Jeffersonville were urged not to send "one dime's

---

[242] *Waterways Journal*, August 24, 1918; *idem*, September 11, 1920; Cincinnati *Commercial*, May 6, 1861; Pittsburgh *Gazette*, May 10, 1861.

[243] *Miss. Valley Hist. Review*, vol. vi, 275.

[244] Cincinnati *Commercial*, August 23, 1861; *idem*, June 15, 1861.

worth of any supplies – not even a pound of butter or a dozen eggs" across the river, "till this species of neutral rascality is at an end." In desperation Cincinnati appealed to the central government which she accused of criminal negligence and predicted a popular uprising in the West to suppress this "villainous traffic." [245]

As a result the federal government was forced to act. A new collector was appointed for the port of Louisville, and more stringent shipping regulations for traffic on the lower Ohio were adopted. But the smugglers were not to be outdone. Small river towns on the lower course of that stream now became starting points for wagon trains which either discharged their loads at railroad stations south of Louisville or continued their way completely across the state of Kentucky.[246] In many instances these overland caravans received their tonnage from local steamboats, the "Masonic Gem" for a long time, being active in this traffic which continued until the Union army was ready to take the offensive.

In all this sparring for advantages, preparations for active warfare were not neglected, each side relying somewhat upon its boats and rivermen. A survey, made for the Union by Colonel Joseph G. Totten, showed that there were then 250 passenger steamers, "rather more than less," on the Ohio, that could be called into service. It was estimated that these, together with 150 other available steamboats at St. Louis, could transport 120,000 men. Besides, there were 100 freight barges on the Ohio with a total capacity of 250,000 barrels and 200 coal barges with a total capacity of 2,000,000 bush-

---

[245] — *Idem*, April 19, 1861; Cincinnati *Gazette*, May 29, 1861; *idem*, June 12, 1861; *idem*, June 15, 1861.

[246] *Illinois State Journal* (Springfield), June 12, 1861; *idem*, July 17, 1861.

els, all of which, it was claimed, could be made ready for military service in a short time.[247]

Regarding the river resources of the Confederacy, General Leonidas Polk could conceive of no men more able to cope with the enemy "than the boatmen of the Mississippi." On December 27, 1861, he wrote President Davis as follows: "With your knowledge of the daring and bravery of the captains, pilots, and men that live on this river, I think you will sustain me in this opinion." [248]

From the very first there were those on the Ohio who insisted upon the practicability of a fleet of gunboats, not only as a means of defense, but also as an indispensable auxiliary in the aggressive warfare which was to be waged. It mattered not that gunboats had been unsuccessful in the Crimean war and that they would be exposed to plunging fires from shore batteries. The Cincinnati *Commercial* insisted that they could, nevertheless, be specially designed for protection against shore batteries and that they would, in any event, be indispensable as convoys.[249] They would also afford an opportunity to the rivermen of the Ohio to try their prowess, nothing being too hazardous for them.

Accordingly, early in the spring of 1861, Commander John Rogers was authorized by Secretary of War Stanton to purchase three strong towboats and to convert them into war vessels, without iron plating. Under this authority Commander Rogers purchased the "Conestoga," "A. O. Taylor," and "Lexington," each of which was equipped for service at New Albany, Indiana. The Louisville *Journal*, August 8, 1861, an-

---

[247] U. S. War Department. War of the Rebellion, *Official Records* (Washington, 1880-1901), ser. I, vol. lii, pt. 1, 164.

[248] — *Idem*, ser. 1, vol. vii, 798.

[249] Cincinnati *Commercial*, May 8, 1861.

nounced their completion and departure in these words: "The gunboats ... left for Cairo yesterday morning, fully equipped. The three boats have on board sixteen guns, ten of which are 32-pounders, and the balance 64-pounders. The boats will run only during the day." These three wooden boats formed the advance guard of a western flotilla that rendered gallant service to the end of the war. Of their subsequent use Admiral David D. Porter said: "These were the first gunboats that fired a shot in support of the Union, and became well known for their many encounters with the enemy." [250]

Meanwhile James B. Eads had been actively engaged at St. Louis in the construction of ironclad gunboats for the use of the national government. The first of these vessels, the "St. Louis," subsequently renamed the "Baron De Kalb," was launched October 12, 1861, and was followed in a short time by the "Carondelet," "Cincinnati," "Louisville," "Mound City," "Cairo," and "Pittsburgh." Later, Eads built the "Benton" and the "Essex," powerful ironclads, the former of which was subsequently used as the flag-ship of the Western Flotilla.

The average capacity of these vessels was in excess of six hundred tons. They were one hundred seventy-five feet long, fifty-one and one-half feet beam, and drew six feet of water. The encased sides were built at an angle of thirty-five degrees from the water-line, which was increased to forty-five degrees for the bows and sterns. Wheels were at the stern and were protected by casements of iron, and like the "Monitor," which they preceded, these vessels carried pilot houses, also covered with iron. Of their service to the Union, Admiral

---

[250] U. S. War Department. War of the Rebellion, *Official Records*, ser. 3, vol. ii, 792; U. S. Naval War Records. *Official Records of the Union and Confederate Navies* (1894-1922), ser. 1, vols. xxii-xxiv.

David D. Porter later said: "Notwithstanding their defects and the vicissitudes they experienced, no vessels of the Navy engaged in so many successful battles or made such a record for their commanding officers."

By 1863, as a result of these and other building activities, the Union had a fighting fleet on the inland waters of more than fifty vessels, thirteen of which were, in whole or in part, ironclads. Among these were the vessels already named including the wooden gunboats, five additional wooden gunboats, two steam rams, and thirteen steam tugs designed for tenders. Together they made up the Western Flotilla which sometimes operated as a unit. Attended as these vessels were by thirty-eight mortar-boats, each equipped with a thirteen-inch sea-coast mortar, they constituted a large and formidable fleet, one of the largest, in fact, ever assembled under one officer, and "equal in number, though not in efficiency, to the vessels composing the navy of the United States when the rebellion broke out." Exclusive of the mortar-boats, the aggregate capacity of this inland fleet was in excess of twenty thousand tons, that of the ironclads ranging from five hundred to a thousand tons. Commanding officers were from the Navy, but crews for both the fleet and the mortar-boats were detailed from the Army.

But this did not comprise the entire fighting force then afloat on the western waters. Early in 1862, following the encounter between the "Monitor" and the "Merrimac," Secretary of War Stanton received information to the effect that the "rebels" were building river craft at New Orleans "clad in railroad iron like the "Merrimack" to be used on the upper Mississippi and even on the Ohio.[251] It was popularly and officially

---

[251] U. S. War Department. War of the Rebellion, *op. cit.*, ser. 3, vol. ii, 792; U. S. Naval War Records. *Official Records*, ser. 1, vol. xxiii, 315-386.

believed that such craft could ascend these rivers and sink or capture the Union fleet being assembled there, together with all the non-combatant tonnage afloat. As a result consternation reigned in these and other quarters, and Secretary Stanton called for suggestions for dealing with the situation. Various plans were proposed, but that for the use of floating rams received both official and popular approval.[252]

The tenseness of the situation was relieved somewhat when Captain Charles Ellet, engineer of the Wheeling suspension bridge, whose defiance of courts and whose professional ability had made that structure possible, was sent to the Ohio with authority to construct the proposed rams. His approval of the plan, he having been one of the first to suggest it, enabled him to put the best of his ability and energy into the undertaking. With the aid of local boatbuilders he was soon able to announce the completion of the proposed fleet.

The "ram fleet" consisted of a number of unarmed and unprotected steamboats rebuilt by the use of heavy inner timbers so as to enable them to strike heavy and rapid blows which, it was claimed, would be effective in anticipated encounters. It was expected that some, if not most, of these boats would be destroyed in any encounter with the enemy, but not before they had dealt destructive blows to the dreaded "Merrimacks." Commands were to be entrusted only to those willing to encounter extreme hazards. As long as he lived, Captain Ellet himself commanded them.

Already the river fleet had given a good account of itself. It was with its aid, under the command of Captain Foote, and the "many steamboats laid up at Cairo for the want of employment" that General Grant was

---
[252] — *Idem*, ser. 1, vol. xxii, 680.

able to move against Fort Henry and Fort Donelson and to effect their capture in such a manner as to cheer the Union and confound the Confederacy. Later, a part of this fleet, together with sixty steamboats acting as transports, made possible the success of the Union forces at Pittsburgh Landing.[253] The successful running of the Confederate batteries at Island no. 10 by the gunboats "Carondelet" and "Pittsburgh" of the river fleet was heralded throughout the West as "among the most venturesome enterprises" that ever made "immortal the navy of a nation." The fact "that in the capture of Fort Henry and Island no. 10 not a gun was fired by the Army" reflected much credit upon the inland navy.[254]

Official reports of some of the inland naval engagements of this time are not unlike those of modern naval battles. For example, that at Plumb Point bend, above Fort Pillow, was spectacular and thrilling. On this occasion five vessels from a Confederate squadron of eight ironclads attempted to seize a Union mortar-boat. First, one of the five attacked the "Cincinnati," covering the coveted prize, ramming her, and receiving and giving broadsides at close range. Disabled, the attacking gunboat drifted away, but not before a half dozen enemy craft had attacked her allies which were rushing to the rescue. Amid the clashing of rams and the explosion of boilers, broadsides were freely exchanged at close range, as a result of which each contestant sustained severe losses.

Meanwhile, Captain Ellet had used the ram fleet to

---

[253] Cincinnati *Commercial*, March 28, 1862.

[254] Grant, U. S. *Personal Memoirs* (New York, 1885-1886), vol. i, 288; Cincinnati *Commercial*, April 11, 1862; *Waterways Journal*, March 18, 1912; *idem*, October 12, 1918; *idem*, November 2, 1918; *idem*, November 30, 1918.

good effect. In the engagements about Memphis, in June, 1862, he passed the Confederate batteries at Fort Pillow without the loss of a man and, two days later, he was the determining factor in the capture of Memphis, also without the loss of a single life or vessel. Captain Ellet himself received a wound in the latter engagement from the effects of which he died, at Cairo, two weeks later.[255]

But for lack of coöperation the accomplishments of the fighting forces on the inland waters might have been even greater than they were. As already indicated the fleet was officered by the Navy and manned by details from the Army. Under these conditions, certainly before Admiral Porter took command, coöperation was not always what it could have been. From the beginning the ram fleet was attached to and under the command of the Army, its officers ignoring and at times defying requests and even commands from the Navy.

The achievements of the American navy, that part of it operating upon the inland waters as well as that upon the high seas, called for recognition. Against the greatest odds and difficulties it had won unforseen victories in unexpected places. More important still, it had conquered a place in the affections of the friends of the Union. Fitting recognition had therefore become imperative. Accordingly Congress, by an act of July 16, 1862, transferred complete control of the several fleets on the western waters from the Army to the Navy, the act being subsequently interpreted to include the ram fleet which became the Mississippi Marine Brigade, and, as such, continued to render valuable service.[256]

---
[255] U. S. Naval War Records. *Official Records*, ser. 1, vol. xxiii, 274.
[256] Blaine, James G. *Twenty Years of Congress* (Norwich, Conn., 1884-

The Navy was also completely reorganized. To this end three squadrons were created, the Atlantic, the Gulf, and the Mississippi, the latter two being placed under the respective commands of Admiral Farragut and Admiral Porter. The effect was a re-birth of the American navy. In transferring the western fleet Adjutant-general Lorenzo Thomas predicted that its former accomplishments would constitute "one of the brightest pages in the history of the war." [257]

It was after this reorganization, and while under the command of Admiral Porter, that the western fleet, now the Mississippi Squadron, achieved its greatest triumph. This consisted in successfully passing the Confederate batteries defending Vicksburg and thus enabling General Grant to establish a base of operations below, from which he was able to force the surrender of that strategic point. Under cover of darkness and a heavy sky it was not a difficult thing for one or two vessels to pass the batteries defending Vicksburg. This had, in fact, been done on one or two occasions, but, to take a whole squadron by, was considered well-nigh impossible under any conditions. However, Grant desired that the attempt be made, and Porter was willing to undertake it.[258] The result is well known.

Additional details of this feat may be worth while. To the surprise of the Confederates it was undertaken April 16, 1863, in the early part of a clear night, when some of those in command of the shore batteries were reported to be attending a ball in the city of Vicksburg. Silently the "Benton," Admiral Porter himself in command, led the way. Following at intervals of ten min-

---

1886), vol. i, 360; U. S. Naval War Records. *Official Records*, ser. 1, vol. xxiii, 388; *idem*, vol. xxiii, 428; *idem*, vol. xxiii, 469.

[257] — *Idem*, vol. xxiii, 389.

[258] — *Idem*, vol. xxiii, 410; Grant, *op. cit.*, vol. i, 460-462.

utes were the "Lafayette," "Louisville," "Mound City," "Pittsburgh," and "Carondelet," one of them carrying with her, on the protected side, the wooden transport, "Sterling Price." Next came the transports "Forest Queen," "Silver Wave," and "Henry Clay," each towing barges loaded with supplies. The "Tuscumbia" brought up the rear. The movement was not discovered until the "Benton" was directly opposite the main batteries which let loose at once with a shower of shot and shell, that was returned in kind. Simultaneously, as if by magic, burning houses and bonfires, prepared beforehand, made the scene almost as light as day and added to the accuracy of the aim of the defending batteries. As a result some of the gunboats were temporarily disconcerted; fourteen among the several gunboat and transport crews were wounded; the "Henry Clay" was consumed by flames; but her sister craft, under a canopy of their own smoke, pressed steadily forward.[259] As the last one passed out of range, some of the belated defenders reached their batteries. Like the revelers of Brussels before Waterloo, they came too late, and Vicksburg was practically lost. With it went the main hope of the Confederacy in the West.

Official and other statements regarding Porter's feat before Vicksburg attest its brilliancy, daring, and importance.[260] To General Sherman, who was present, it was "sublime"; General Grant, also an eye witness, thought it "magnificent but terrible"; and official reports pronounced it "a damper to the spirit of all rebel sympathizers along the Mississippi." Subsequently

---

[259] U. S. Naval War Records. *Official Records*, ser. 1, vol. xxiii, 408-410; Grant, *op. cit.*, vol. i, 462.

[260] Rhodes, *History of the United States*, vol. iv, 305; Grant, *op. cit.*, vol. i, 544; Mahan, Alfred T. *Farragut* (New York, 1904), 206; U. S. Naval War Records, *op. cit.*, ser. 1, vol. xxiii, 410.

General Grant spoke of it in these words: "The navy under Porter was all that it could be. . . . Without its assistance the campaign could not have been successfully made with twice the number of men engaged. It could not have been made at all, in the way it was, with any number of men without such assistance." Captain Alfred T. Mahan was unable to find in the history of combined movements "more hearty coöperation between the army and the navy than in the Vicksburg campaign of 1863, under the leadership of Grant and Porter."

Following the fall of Vicksburg the boatyards on the Ohio continued active with military preparations, those of Cincinnati being especially productive. By March, 1865, fifty-six gunboats had been built or equipped there, and others were then in process of construction.[261] Pittsburgh, however, attempted the unusual. In 1863 she launched from the famous Sligo mills of that place two ironclad monitors, the "Manayunk" and the "Umpqua," each of which was taken to the high seas by way of the Ohio and Mississippi rivers. Two years later these were followed by other monitors, among them being the "Marietta" and the "Sandusky." Meanwhile many other ports were contributing transports, most of which were privately owned but always available for public uses at the high price generally paid for such service.[262]

It was largely through the use of convoys and transports that the Union was able to push its military operations to a successful conclusion following victory at Vicksburg. Without them the later major military operations would have been practically impossible. For

---
[261] Cincinnati *Commercial*, March 18, 1865.
[262] Thurston, G. H., *Allegheny County's Hundred Years*, 118.

example, from January 21 to June 1, 1863, they "made, on an average, two trips a week to Nashville, taking never less than seven to eight steamers and barges, and sometimes fifty-five or six through at a trip," all of which were landed safely. As late as November, 1864, the gunboat "Fair Play" took a convoy of sixteen transports to Nashville.[263] Without the aid of these convoys and transports the Union victories around Chattanooga might have been defeats and Sherman might never have made his march to the sea.

In operation the Civil war convoys on the inland waters were not unlike those of the World war on the high seas. Usually one or more gunboats led the way and was followed by a line of transports, while other gunboats brought up the rear and still others flanked the procession. The guerrilla bands that infested the banks of the Ohio and the Mississippi played the rôle of submarines, picking off unaccompanied craft here and there but rarely attacking convoyed steamers.

Despite the success of gunboats in running down guerrillas and keeping navigation open, Ohio river packets plied their trades with difficulty. This was particularly true during the early years of the war. In passing the "pizen country," in 1861, a popular pilot felt like a solitary horseman on a mud road in western Virginia after a storm.[264] Everywhere "seceshes" infested that and the Kentucky country, it being a rare community of either that could not, on short notice, raise a raiding party ready and eager to capture a steamboat and rob it of its cargo. The experiences of the "Greenwood" were typical. In September, 1862,

---

[263] U. S. Naval War Records, *op. cit.*, ser. 1, vol. xxiii, 312; Cincinnati *Commercial*, November 15, 1864.

[264] Wheeling *Intelligencer*, June 17, 1861; *idem*, November 20, 1861.

she was hailed near Guyandot, Virginia, by about fifty Confederates. She refused to stop and was fired upon, several shots going through her cabin which was filled with women, children, and wounded soldiers. The following day she was again subjected to a shower of lead. Lawless bandits unattached to either army found steamboats easy and profitable prey. Nor were rivermen concerned alone with the enemy and the lawless. Union officers and soldiers were continually on the lookout for contraband, and all steamers that did not heed the eloquent voice of their six-pounders commanding the river, as in the case of the "Moses McClellan," were fired into, sometimes with fatal result to pilot-houses, machinery, and even persons.[265]

From the beginning to the close of the war many river towns on the Ohio were rallying points for Union soldiers. Among such were Pittsburgh, Bellaire, Parkersburg, Gallipolis, and Cincinnati, points where railroads were either tributary to or crossed the river. It was a great day in the life of any of these ports when soldiers came to town in large numbers. Small boys were kept busy selling pies, cakes, pop-corn, and lemonade, and mayors found employment in trying to keep bar-rooms closed. In the failure of the latter, commanding officers were sometime forced to declare martial law, close barrooms, and confiscate their contents which were usually poured into the street, thus affording an opportunity for such soldiers and others as had not already imbibed to their satisfaction. Frequent altercations took place between citizens and soldiers, resulting sometimes in fatalities. Any large movement of soldiers by way of any of the above-mentioned points was a summons for mothers, wives, sisters, and sweet-

---

[265] — *Idem*, September 27, 1862; *idem*, November 20, 1861.

hearts to gather at the wharf to bid adieu to their "soldier boys" as they passed onto the pontoon bridges across the Ohio.

The forerunner to the resumption of normal traffic on the Ohio, as well as on the Mississippi, was the trade in contraband cotton. This began on a large scale in June, 1862, immediately following the occupation of Memphis by Union forces. Already large quantities of tobacco had reached Cincinnati and other points in the North from Kentucky, but tobacco was not contraband. Under the lax policy by which it was planned to attach parts of the seceding states to the Union and incidentally to aid New England, numerous persons, among them enterprising Jews and self-seeking military officers, succeeded in shipping quantities of cotton with and without permits. Grant, Sherman, and other officers objected to any form of commercial intercourse with the enemy, insisting that it strengthened its resisting power; but one dollar and ninety cent cotton in Boston, 1864, for supplies that cost twenty cents per pound in the South, offered a tempting road to fortune. The possibilities for getting ready cash were such that deckhands, women, and children turned cotton thieves and robbed steamboats of their snowy treasures.[266]

Other effects of this traffic were numerous and far reaching. As early as 1862 Tennessee was urged to return to her place in the Union with the assurance that cotton would be to her what tobacco had been to Kentucky — "a veritable gold mine."[267] It was the lure of cotton that induced the Secretary of War to open the Mississippi to commerce immediately following the

---
[266] Cincinnati *Commercial*, May 23, 1862; *idem*, January 1, 1863; *idem*, February 18, 1864; Wheeling *Intelligencer*, January 3, 1863; Rhodes, *op. cit.*, vol. v, 275-295.
[267] Cincinnati *Commercial*, May 23, 1862.

fall of Vicksburg. In less than two months thereafter, through river traffic between New Orleans and Cincinnati was restored, the "Tempest," Captain "Dan" Parr, reaching the latter port from the former, August 23, 1863, "the first boat through."[268] In a short time the North was receiving more cotton than was then being sent to Great Britain,[269] and Georgia refugees were finding a route of escape by way of the Mississippi.[270] Moreover, they were able to pay their passage and other charges in the currency of the United States.

The coal trade was, however, a real factor in the success of the Union. The hundreds of references to coal in the official records both of the Army and of the Navy attest this fact. No successful commander in either ever reckoned beyond his coal supply which always determined the radius and duration of his striking power. Commanders quarreled about coal and threatened to resign when supplies were not to be had. In desperation some salvaged sunken coalboats, while others dredged river beds in search of coal.

At this time most of the coal used on the lower Ohio and the Mississippi was floated down stream from Pittsburgh in coalboats, but some shippers were already using towboats. Most large deliveries were made to the federal government, single transactions netting fabulous profits which became the basis for some of the large fortunes of modern Pittsburgh. Incidentally boat building was stimulated, and scores of persons again found employment in steamboating, among them being some of the later popular captains. Wages doubled and

---
[268] — *Idem*, August 24, 1863.

[269] Rhodes, *op. cit.*, vol. v, 275; Hammond, M. B. *The Cotton Industry* (Amer. Econ. Assoc., new ser., 1897), 263; Cincinnati *Commercial*, May 31, 1862; *idem*, May 23, 1863; *idem*, May 27, 1863.

[270] — *Idem*, December 6, 1864.

THE CIVIL WAR PERIOD 261

trebled, those of deckhands reaching the unprecedented figure of forty dollars per month, and the river press generally predicted a return of the "good old days."

A significant development was the use of "model barges" for the transportation of freight. It was at this time that Captain J. K. Booth, later known as the "Barge King," began to use the "Allegheny Belle" and the "Liberty" for the purpose of towing "model barges." At first they were used mainly between Baltimore and Ohio railroad terminals, Parkersburg and Wheeling, but later they made trips to the lower Mississippi and to Cumberland and Tennessee ports as well.[271]

As usual new packets were in keeping with the times and conditions. One such was the "Wild Wagoner," built at Cincinnati in 1864 for the Cincinnati and Wheeling trade.[272] She cost one hundred fifteen thousand dollars and had a capacity of seven hundred tons. Among her elegant finishings was a painting of the original "Wild Wagoner," her namesake and the hero of Thomas Buchanan Reed's poem bearing the same title. Reed, a resident of Cincinnati, and the author of "Sheridan's Ride," which had already been read and recited in hundreds of churches and school houses in the Ohio valley, was very popular. Hence the choice of one of his most popular titles as a suitable name for a local steamboat.

As in the country at large, readjustments following the Civil war brought reverses to the boating interests of the Ohio valley. As early as 1864 rivermen found themselves burdened with a surplus tonnage which was

---
[271] — *Idem*, September 15, 1863.
[272] — *Idem*, November 11, 1864; Goss, *Cincinnati, the Queen City*, vol. i, 272.

soon engaged in a ruinous competition. Strikes followed,[273] Irish and negro deckhands refusing to work for anything but war-time wages and some of the Irish refusing to work with negroes at any price. Pilots asked five hundred dollars per month, and other skilled workmen could not be had for money. At the same time railroads, by the use of bridges across the Ohio, completed through connections to the West, and towboats with their "model barges" ate into the profits of passenger packets.[274]

A great service remained, however, for the rivermen of the inland waters. Following the surrender of Lee at Appomattox more than a million Union soldiers were demobilized and returned to their homes, many of them by way of the Ohio. Among the grandest sights ever witnessed on that stream were the large number of steamboats crowding its banks at such ports as Parkersburg and Wheeling awaiting the arrival of soldiers on their way to the Middle West and the Northwest. These sights were surpassed only by the long lines of steamboats, miles in length, as they passed up and down the Ohio, at more or less regular intervals, with their burdens of homesick men.[275]

One of the greatest disasters incident to the Civil war, surpassing, if possible, either that of the "Titanic" or the "Lusitania," marred these preparations for peaceful living. It was the sinking of the "Sultana" near Memphis, April 27, 1865, by the explosion of her boilers. Immediately following the explosion fire broke out, sweeping the steamer from front to stern and precipitating a scene beyond the power of language to describe. Almost fifteen hundred of her two thousand

---
[273] Cincinnati *Commercial*, July 11, 1862; *idem*, June 20, 1866.
[274] — *Idem*, March 29, 1866.   [275] — *Idem*, June 8, 1865.

passengers, composed of paroled soldiers, officers, and their wives, lost their lives. For days following, the impoverished people of Memphis, laying aside sectional feelings and the memories of their own dead of a hundred battle fields, devoted themselves to the work of caring for the survivors.[276] Homes were thrown open, clothing provided, and medical attention given: all harbingers of a new era of peace and good will between the former warring sections.

---

[276] *Waterways Journal,* June 1, 1912; Memphis *Argus,* April 28, 1865.

Post-bellum Days to 1900

During the decades immediately following the Civil war the Ohio river was locally known as the "Poor Man's Highway." Although the new trend was toward industry and agriculture, local traditions were in the field of river transportation which now offered unusual opportunities. This was due to the fact that the Ohio continued to be the only practicable thoroughfare for large inland interests. As yet most of the railroads entering the Ohio valley crossed it at right angles to the river, leaving rich bottom lands, growing river towns and cities, and large hinterlands dependent upon water transportation. The mails, also, continued to be transported largely by water, government contracts therefor providing means for launching new river trades and maintaining old ones.

Even before the fall of the Confederacy active preparations were being made to take advantage of these conditions. To this end more steamboats were built along the Ohio in either 1864 or 1865 than in any one year before or since.[277] The preparations were for peace, but in the event that hostilities were prolonged, boatbuilders depended upon the national government to continue to use all surplus tonnage. All could see that it would be needed in the work of demobilization, and that too, as in war times, at high, sometimes fabulous, prices.

Generally things turned out as expected. A new

---
[277] U. S. *Census*, 1880, vol. iv, 671; Cincinnati *Commercial*, April 23, 1864.

period of river activity began. It embraced all inland America, assuming grand proportions in the early eighties and not spending its force before the closing years of the century. There were temporary setbacks, it is true. One of these came immediately following the cessation of hostilities; another followed the panic of 1873. The former was caused by the readjustments incident to Reconstruction, private owners finding difficulty in absorbing tonnage turned back to them from the national government. The causes of the latter are evident. Other periods of depression were short and only slightly interrupted river traffic.

As in the "olden days" Cincinnati again became the leading river town on the Ohio. Of her steamboat activities in 1867, James Parton, in the *Atlantic Monthly* for August of that year, said:

> The levee which now extends five or six miles around the large "bend" upon which the city stands, exhibits all the varieties of western steamboats. ... A traveler must indeed be difficult to please who cannot find upon the Cincinnati levee a steamboat bound to a place he would like to visit. From far back in the coal mines of the Youghiogheny to high up the Red river – from St. Paul to New Orleans, and all intermediate ports – we have but to pay our money and take our choice of the towns upon sixteen thousand miles of navigable water.

In the same issue of this publication Parton also mentioned a great number of other craft then to be found at Cincinnati, among them being merchantboats, floating theaters, circusboats, and houseboats.

Incidents in this "comeback" of the steamboat were sometimes spectacular. For example, the proposed return of the "Kenton," one of the first packets through direct from New Orleans, was announced weeks in advance. When she finally came, in February, 1867, her arrival was heralded with delight from port to port.

One reception, that at Wheeling, was typical. Scores of men, women, and children awaited her. At the first opportunity they went aboard; adults to greet old friends; youths, paddles in hand, to taste the sugar that dripped from the swollen hogsheads that covered the deck of the welcomed visitor. As she pushed into midstream, on her way to Pittsburgh, many of those left behind were heard to rejoice over the fact that the Union had been preserved and that old friends could and would be friends again.[278]

For the most part, however, the local "river news" of this period dealt with more prosaic, though scarcely less important, matters. Frequent mention was made of large shipments of salt from the Ohio and the Great Kanawha rivers to Mississippi ports, notably St. Louis which was now a chief distributing center for this monopoly-controlled necessity. There was also frequent mention of southward shipments of farming implements and plantation supplies and a new product called "oil" or petroleum.[279] Along with these were increased supplies of whiskey, dry goods, groceries, and other industrial products, some local towns and cities being designated according to their special contributions. For example, Wheeling became the "Nail City," because of the fact that it supplied most of the nails then used in the interior.

The river press noted a resumption of traffic from the South in molasses, sugar, cotton, tobacco, and subtropical products in general. However, the product from this source that did most to make steamboating profitable was iron ore which was transported in large quantities from Cumberland river ports and mines in

---

[278] — *Idem*, November 15, 1869; *idem*, August 20, 1870; *idem*, June 5, 1870. [279] Wheeling *Intelligencer* and other local newspapers.

Missouri to upper Ohio river industrial centers. Return cargoes consisted largely of railroad iron and railroad supplies, the construction of the Union Pacific, Chesapeake and Ohio, Texas and Pacific, and other railroad lines, then in progress, being a distinct stimulus to river traffic on the Ohio.[280]

Demands from the Mississippi and other streams for rivermen and craft were also a great stimulus to river activities along the Ohio, which continued to be the chief source of supply for boats and rivermen for the whole interior. In the absence of adequate rail transportation the region about the lower Mississippi was dependent upon its rivers, as was also, but to a less degree, the whole interior. To the former the Ohio now sent "cotton boats," some of which found their way to the rivers of Texas. It was at this time that Ohio rivermen developed trades on the upper Mississippi, some of which continued to be sources of profit until recent years. Meanwhile, other boats built on the Ohio were finding their way to the navigable waters of Florida, the Pacific coast, South America, Russia, and Africa.[281]

Despite the fact that the means of transportation of inland America have always been inadequate, the river craft of this period were creditable. Cotton boats were specially designed, as were packets, for particular river trades. For example, on the upper Ohio and its tributaries a type of light draught stern-wheeler came into more general use, while on its lower course and on the Mississippi the stately side-wheeler held its own.

Some packets built for these trades attracted atten-

---

[280] Cincinnati *Commercial*, February 18, 1865; *idem*, November 25, 1866; *idem*, February 13, 1867; Wheeling *Intelligencer*, August 3, 1868; *idem*, October 30, 1868; *idem*, November 29, 1869; Parkersburg (West Va.) *Daily Times*, March 20, 1866; *idem*, March 29, 1866.

[281] *American Shipbuilder* (New York, 1919), April 18, 1919.

tion throughout the whole interior. One such was the "Great Republic" built at Shousetown, Pennsylvania, in 1867, for use on the Mississippi. She was three hundred thirty-five feet long, fifty-one feet beam, and carried engines fifty-six inches in diameter and of ten-feet stroke. Her cabin was two hundred sixty-seven feet long and was surrounded by fifty-four state-rooms, each elegantly finished and furnished. Her launching and initial trip down the Ohio were topics of absorbing conversation among rivermen throughout the interior. When she passed Wheeling, the populace flocked to the levee in such numbers as to prevent her intended landing and forced her to "carry by" both freight and passengers.[282]

Like most boats of her day, the "Great Republic" carried modern equipment. For instance, she had a steam capstan, nigger, freight hoist, syphon pumps, steam fire engine, and running water for staterooms, steamboat construction having reached a high degree of perfection by mid-century. Although she was not a success financially, being too large and expensive to maintain, her size and elegance bespoke the hopes and ambitions of rivermen of this period. Before it ended their best packets carried electric lights and other modern equipment, the "Guiding Star," "Kate Adams" and "Scotia," packets of the early eighties, being among the first on the Ohio to be equipped with electricity.

A contemporary of the post-bellum period recently described the river business of Pittsburgh in the seventies in these words:

A great number of men depended upon the river for their daily

---

[282] Cincinnati *Commercial*, March 13, 1867; *idem*, March 19, 1867; Wheeling *Intelligencer*, March 9, 1867; *idem*, March 13, 1867; *idem*, March 18, 1867; *Waterways Journal*, March 22, 1919; *idem*, November 29, 1924.

labor. There was at that time eight boat-building companies who were building hulls, six cabin builders, six machine shops building engines for towboats, freight and packet boats, seven boiler firms building boilers for steamboats, four steamboat painters, three block makers, four steamboat tinners and coppersmiths, four steamboat pipe fitters, . . . six supply stores for supplying boats with groceries, meats, and vegetables, four firms doing outfitting and frame work outside of regular cabin building, and four firms catering to steamboat blacksmithing.[283]

Of practically every other important city on the Ohio at this time, a smilar story might be told. Wheeling, Marietta, Cincinnati, Evansville, Jeffersonville, and Louisville were especially active. Even small towns such as Wellsville, Steubenville, Clarington, Sistersville, St. Marys, Parkersburg, Murrayville, Ravenswood, and Point Pleasant had one or more boatyards and launched one or more packets, some of great size and elegance.

The barge was, however, the distinctive river craft of that day. As already indicated, John K. Booth used "model" barges as a connecting link between Baltimore and Ohio railroad terminals at Wheeling and Parkersburg. When his patron effected through connections with the Middle West, in 1871, by the use of a bridge across the Ohio at Parkersburg, the Wheeling terminus being already thus connected, Booth's favorite river trade was practically ruined, and he turned to other fields. For some time he found profits in the transportation of iron ore and other raw materials from St. Louis to upper Ohio river ports and in carrying return cargoes of railroad iron, railroad supplies, and other products of local industry. Later he was driven to the wall by the panic of 1873, but meanwhile Booth had

---
[283] — *Idem*, August 4, 1923.

taken a long step toward revolutionizing inland river transportation.[284]

Among the more successful barge owners and operators in the post-bellum days on the Ohio was John Porter of New Cumberland, a name inseparably connected with the rise and development of the brick and pottery industries of northern West Virginia and southeastern Ohio.[285] From humble beginnings, about 1832, these industries grew to large proportions, furnishing cargoes for boats in Ohio, Cumberland, and other river trades. From the Cumberland iron ore and other raw materials supplied profitable up-stream tows. When local iron industries began to draw raw materials from the region of the Great Lakes, Porter curtailed his towing operations on the Ohio, but he was able to carry on successfully into the present century.

During the seventies and far into the eighties barges were also used on the Ohio for the transportation of crude oil and its products. In the face of growing monopoly of the Standard Oil Company, that tended to control all phases of the oil industry, the "Poor Man's Highway" was the only avenue open to competing independents. A Congressional act of 1879, ostensibly in the interest of the traveling public, prohibited the transportation of "oil" and its products on board passenger packets. The effect was to increase the use of barges, much crude oil being transported thus both to Wheeling and to Huntington for re-shipment east over the Baltimore and Ohio and the Chesapeake and Ohio

---

[284] Cincinnati *Commercial*, January 5, 1867; *idem*, February 27, 1867; Wheeling *Intelligencer*, December 23, 1868; *idem*, September 24, 1869; *idem*, October 19, 1869; *idem*, December 3, 1869.

[285] Manuscripts. In possession of the Porter family, New Cumberland, West Virginia. See also Wheeling *Intellingencer*, March 12, 1879; *idem*, July 1, 1879.

railroads, respectively. A contemporary movement to parallel the Ohio river between these two points by a railroad track is said to have had its inception in plans to capture the local river traffic in oil, lumber, iron ore, and other products.[286]

The most successful barge owner and operator of this day, on the Ohio, was R. C. Gray of Pittsburgh. He entered the transportation business, on a large scale, on a rising tide of prosperity that followed the panic of 1873, and is said to have accumulated a fortune. For a long time he was head of the famous Iron line, consisting of scores of barges and several towboats. Among the latter were the "Iron Duke," "Ironsides," "Iron Age," and "Resolute." For years they plied regularly between the iron deposits of Missouri and upper Ohio river ports, carrying ore up-stream and its products down. Following rumors of plans to parallel the Ohio with a railroad and to draw ore supplies from the region of the Great Lakes, Gray shifted his boating activities to the upper Mississippi, where he became a factor in river transportation.

In the increasing use of barges on the inland waters some saw, even at this early period, the dawn of a future "Barge Age." The development was at least significant and gave rise to comment. For example, the Cincinnati *Commercial* for January 5, 1867, said: "It is clear that the barge system does not encourage the building of gorgeous steamers." About the same time W. Milnor Roberts, a famous engineer, expressed his belief that the time was near, when "a large portion of the steamers engaged in freighting would be towboats,

---

[286] Wheeling *Register*, May 3, 1876; *idem*, April 17, 1877; Wheeling *Intelligencer*, November 11, 1879; *idem*, April 13, 1881; *idem*, October 21, 1881; Tarbell, Ida M. *History of the Standard Oil Company* (New York, 1904), vol. i, 173-195.

running in connection with barges." [287] In this practice, a writer in the *Atlantic Monthly* for June, 1867, saw a "prodigious economy," for, continued he, "One of those large passenger boats on the Mississippi is run at an expense of a thousand dollars a day, and it wastes half of its time waiting for freight. A towboat capable of towing ten barges expends but two hundred dollars a day, and wastes fewer hours than a passenger boat wastes days." Still others believed that the time was near at hand when passengers would be transported in model barges arranged and operated after the fashion of modern Pullmans.

The conditions stimulating boat building on the Ohio gave rise to outstanding characters. Prominent among those on its upper course was James Rees of Pittsburgh. Like other boatbuilders of inland America, he was born in Wales and came to America at an early age to be educated in her workshops. Rees learned lessons of application, thrift, and economy in his youth and while working to support a widowed mother. Attracted by the unusual opportunities of the period he turned to boat building in the mid-sixties and was soon on an independent footing. Hence it was that he was able to finance the building of a number of steamboats for would-be owners on the Mississippi, among them ex-Confederates without money or credit. All received their boats, the debtors being told to "pay when you can." The fact that not a penny was lost in these transactions is a tribute to Captain Rees's knowledge of men, as well as to his patriotism. It may also have indicated unusually good times among steamboatmen. However that may be, the name Rees became a favorite along the Mississippi.

---

[287] *Journal of the Franklin Institute*, vol. xxxiv, 297.

In all his numerous activities Captain Rees employed the spirit and methods of the investigator. The results were many useful inventions and applications. Among these was the world's first steamboat of homogeneous steel-plate construction,[288] with water tight compartments. Other inventions and applications included the first iron railroad bridge, the first light steel angles of unequal legs, and the first all-steel-hull steamboat. Thus Rees became an international character. In the eighties his packets, especially his stern-wheelers, were in demand in Central America, South America, Canada, Alaska, Russia, and Africa. When he died, September 12, 1889, he was at the head of two boat building concerns, James Rees and Sons Company and James Thorn and Company, that have since combined and continue to operate under the firm name of James Rees and Sons Company and under the general direction of Captain Thomas M. Rees. This and the companies out of which it grew have built a total of more than six hundred steamboats, besides a number of other craft. At the present time Rees-built boats ply the waters of three continents.[289]

What James Rees and his stern-wheelers were to the upper Ohio, James Howard (familiarly known as "Uncle Jim") and his side-wheelers were to the lower Ohio and the Mississippi. Howard was born in England in 1814. At the age of six he emigrated to America living for a time in Cincinnati, where he learned the art of steamboat building. Later he established himself in Jeffersonville, Indiana, where he founded the Howard shipyards which are now operated by the Howard

---

[288] The "Montoya," built in 1878 for the Magdalena Steam Navigation Company of South America. See Thurston, *op. cit.*, 119.

[289] Pittsburgh *Times*, May 23, 1882; Pittsburgh *Gazette Times*, September 26, 1909.

family. Many things attested the popularity and worth of the elder Howard, but none more than the attendance at his funeral, which was estimated at fifty thousand persons.[290] He died in 1876.

Among other prominent contemporary boatbuilders on the Ohio M. G. Knox is deserving of mention. From his boatyard in West Marietta he launched more than one hundred steamboats, among them being the "Keystone State," "Emma Graham," and "Scotia," each famous in its day. At Wheeling, A. J. Sweeney and his son John M. Sweeney made a specialty of light draught stern-wheelers. They also built many cotton boats. At Elizabeth, Pennsylvania, the Larges and Wiegels maintained the reputation of the Walkers of an earlier day for the superior quality of their river craft. Meanwhile several prominent builders were using the Marine ways of Cincinnati, while others launched steamboats and barges from Louisville and Evansville.

Many of these packets were more famous than their builders. Outstanding among such were the "Robert E. Lee" and the "Natchez." The former was built by the Howards; the latter was a product of the Marine ways of Cincinnati, her cabin being the handiwork of a famous builder of that city, Elias Ealers, and her boilers the work of an equally famous artisan, C. T. Dumont. Both boats were built for use on the Mississippi, where they were rivals in the St. Louis-New Orleans trade in the seventies. Their race of July, 1870, is generally regarded as the greatest event of its kind in history. More than one million dollars is said to have been bet on the result which was never satisfactorily determined. Some objected because the "Natchez" took

---

[290] Gould, *Fifty Years on the Mississippi*, 638; *Waterways Journal*, November 27, 1909.

time out on account of fog. Others complained because the "Lee" used an auxiliary craft to supply her with fuel over a part of the course. Nevertheless, the friends of the "Lee" claimed the victory. Her time was three days, eighteen hours, and fourteen minutes.

Interest in this race was perhaps unusual, but it was, nevertheless, significant. A local print described it in these words: "The whole country watched with breathless interest, as it [the race] had been extensively advertised by the press, and the telegraph attended its progress along the river at every point. At all the principal cities people for many miles were present to see the racers pass, and the time of passing was cabled to Europe." [291] The captains, John W. Cannon of the "Lee" and T. P. Leathers of the "Natchez," were, temporarily, as much in the public eye, especially the sporting part of it, as are rival contenders of the prize fighter's ring and the baseball diamond today.

Scores of other Ohio river-built steamboats of this period attained a popularity that was more than local. Among them the "J. M. White," built by the Howards in 1878 after the model of the "J. M. White" of the forties, was outstanding. It was claimed that she embodied the last word in the art and utility of steamboat construction. To this day her record of seven hours and forty minutes between New Orleans and Baton Rouge is unbeaten. Then there was the "Kate Adams," which, with two other packets that bore the same name, plied the trade between Memphis and Helena for almost fifty years. The recent destruction of No. Three, known as the "Lovin' Kate," brought sadness to the hearts of

---

[291] Gould, *op. cit.*, 532-544. See also Mark Twain, *Life on the Mississippi*. The time of the "Natchez" in this race was 3 days, 20 hours, and 58 minutes. See *National Waterways*, July, 1930.

rivermen everywhere and called forth editorial expressions from the press of the entire country.[292] Another famous packet, the "Chesapeake," Captain Edwin F. Maddy, had to her credit a distinct achievement. Under her own power she made a continuous trip from Point Pleasant, West Virginia, to Jacksonville, Florida, a distance of thirty-one hundred miles, most of it on the high seas.

Most packets of this period operated in line arrangements after the manner of those of the forties and the fifties. For instance, on the lower Ohio there were the boats of the Louisville and Cincinnati Packet line, popularly known as the "Mail Line." Under the favorable conditions of the mid-sixties this line entered a period of prosperity that carried its capital stock to the million dollar mark and made it one of the most popular routes of travel in inland America. However, in a manner peculiar to the river, it encountered unforeseen reverses. In 1868 a collision between two of its choice packets, the "United States" and the "America" in which a number of lives were lost, brought successful actions for damages that turned it on the downward road financially. Then came the hard times of the seventies, forcing railroad reorganizations and temporarily curtailing river activities. To these adverse results the eighties added bad management and railroad competition. As a result the packets of this line were forced to pool their interests with those of the "White Collar Line," then operating between Cincinnati and Charleston, West Virginia, and Pomeroy, Ohio.

The "White Collar Line," a contemporary of another line by the same name in the trade between St. Louis

---
[292] See series of articles beginning in the *Waterways Journal*, October 4, 1924.

and New Orleans, was incorporated in 1866 as the Cincinnati, Portsmouth, Big Sandy, and Pomeroy line. Like others, it had its origin in the plans of a number of independent owners and operators to avoid the results of a ruinous competition.[293] During a decade or more following its formation a number of factors contributed to its success. Most important of these was the Chesapeake and Ohio railroad which reached the Ohio at Huntington in 1873 and for some time thereafter depended upon steamboats for shipping connections to the West. In the absence of a railroad closely paralleling the Ohio, local industries were dependent upon steamboats for transportation. Large quantities of salt and farm products were shipped by river, and it was no uncommon thing for "White Collar" packets to tarry hours at a time both at Hanging Rocks and at Ironton, taking aboard the products of local iron industries and unloading farm products and other raw materials. Moreover, these packets had splendid shipping connections both by river and by rail at Cincinnati, and their management was superior. From 1866 to well into the eighties they had only two superintendents, "Wash" Honshell and, following him, Chas. M. Hollaway.

Each of these rivermen deserves more than passing mention. Captain Honshell, the leading spirit in the organization of the "White Collar" line, was for a long time its mainstay. Like most successful steamboatmen, he was a strong and resourceful character in whom "way folks" imposed implicit confidence. Even with those who did not emulate his example, his popularity was enhanced by a reputation for total abstinence from the use of either intoxicants or tobacco.

---

[293] Cincinnati *Commercial*, September 23, 1866; *idem*, September 24, 1866.

Some of his more simple-minded admirers are said to have believed that the Ohio between the "Mouth of Sandy" and Cincinnati belonged to him. More than once raftsmen and washwomen asked his permission to use its waters.[294]

In his day, the eighties, Captain Hollaway was scarcely less prominent than was Captain Honshell in his. Among rivermen Captain Hollaway is still referred to as an example of the possibilities of their tribe, when opportunity comes their way. He is said to have commenced his career as a bar-tender on a small packet on the Great Kanawha. From this humble, even questionable, beginning, he became, in turn, manager of a large salt manufacturing and distributing concern, president of the Cincinnati Chamber of Commerce, and superintendent of the most important packet line then navigating the Ohio.

A contemporary, "Wash" Kerr, was equally popular and probably more widely known. Ten years before the Civil war he owned and operated the "Messenger," then the most popular packet on the Ohio river. With the "J. B. Ford" and other steamboats Captain Kerr rendered distinguished service in the transportation of troops in the Civil war, and later he became known as one of the most efficient and dependable rivermen on the western waters. So regular were his packets that farmers along the Ohio are said to have set their clocks by them. In the "Murphy Movement" for prohibition Captain Kerr was one of the first to banish the bar from his boat. This was done by placing a sign, bearing large letters, over the entrance. It read "This Bar is

---

[294] Wheeling *Intelligencer*, December 20, 1867; *idem*, October 2, 1869; *idem*, November 13, 1876; *idem*, January 28, 1883; *Waterways Journal*, October 16, 1909.

Closed Forever." His boats participated in no races, never ran ahead of time and rarely behind, and departed on schedule time, their commander refusing to tarry a minute beyond even for his wife who was thus left behind more than once.

Among other local rivermen equally popular were Charles Muhleman, previously mentioned,[295] and William and Charles List of Wheeling. The latter, known as the "Virginia Giant," was a power in the transportation world and this despite the fact that he weighed less than one hundred pounds. Still other popular rivermen of the upper Ohio were J. M. Gamble, and Thaddeus Thomas, both of Clarington, J. H. Roberts of Wheeling, E. P. Chancellor of Parkersburg, J. N. Williamson of Cincinnati, and E. F. Maddy of Gallipolis. During the nineties of the last century F. A. Laidley was easily the outstanding riverman operating packets to and from Cincinnati.

All these captains prided themselves on the efficiency and the regularity of their service. When the river was too low for the use of their "crack nags," low water boats were used to assure regularity and certainty in the transportation of the mail, always a first consideration. But local captains did not operate for the love of steamboating alone. They made money, net profits for some packets ranging around five hundred dollars weekly over long periods. When railroads made prorating arrangements, when local industries, particularly those engaged in the manufacture of iron and steel, shipped by water, and when boating stages could be depended upon, these boats always made profits for their owners.

Some of the packets of this period were among the

---

[295] See p. 147 of this work.

THE CHESAPEAKE AND OHIO RAILROAD PACKET, "FLEETWOOD"
Made regular trips between Huntington and Cincinnati in the eighties.

STEAMER "KATE ADAMS," THE "LOVIN KATE"
Built at Jeffersonville, Ind., 1899. For thirty years a favorite in the lower Mississippi trade out of Memphis.

most popular that ever plied the waters of the Ohio and made an impress upon the literature and song of the people whom they served. To this day their speed, elegance, and hospitality are among the proudest memories of local rivermen. Thus the names of some of them should be perpetuated. In the trade between Cincinnati and Pomeroy were the "Telegraph," the "St. James," the "Ohio no. 4," and the "Big Sandy," while the "Fleetwood"[296] and the "Bostona" ran between Cincinnati and Huntington. For a long time one of these boats reached Huntington daily in time for the morning train eastbound over the Chesapeake and Ohio railroad and the other landed in Cincinnati passengers received at Huntington the night before. To the north, with Wheeling and Parkersburg as their chief ports, were the "Courier," the "Diurnal," the "Rebecca," and the "Express," while the favorites to the south of Parkersburg were the "Emma Graham," the "Chesapeake," the "W. P. Thompson," and the "Katy Did." For a time the "Phil Sheridan," "Major Anderson," "Hudson," "R. R. Hudson," "St. Lawrence," and, after 1873, the "Andes," were popular in the trade between Wheeling and Cincinnati. Meanwhile smaller boats plied the river in scores of local trades, every port of importance being served by one or more favorite local packets. This was also true of tributary streams.

A significant development of this period was a through packet line between Pittsburgh and St. Louis, sometimes referred to as the Colson line or the "Big Seven." In 1880 it used seven packets of an average capacity in excess of a thousand tons, one of which left

---

[296] The "Fleetwood," probably the most popular of these boats, belonged to Captain J. M. Hollaway. She was two hundred fifty-seven feet long, thirty-nine and one-half feet beam, and carried engines of eight feet stroke.

each terminus daily. For a time these packets operated in conjunction with the Chesapeake and Ohio railroad carrying through freight from Huntington, West Virginia, to St. Louis, together with products of local industry and passengers from the upper Ohio. Return shipments consisted of agricultural products and other raw materials. The boats used in 1880 were the "Dacotah," "Montana," "Wyoming," "Carrier," "Pittsburgh," "Granite State," and "Bright Light,". the names of which tell something of the ambitions of their owners and the scope of their activities.[297]

Other factors, of a more general nature than those already mentioned, contributed to the success of the above named packets and their numerous contemporaries. Chief among these was the swelling tide of immigration that began to flow towards America following the Civil war and continued into the present century. Many considerations recommended steamboats to homeseekers as a means of transportation, especially when accompanied by their families and belongings, as most of them were. Then, too, about 1876, the Centennial year, Americans began to take time out from the grind of making a living, for travel. Many of them had gone west by way of the rivers and could think only in terms of steamboats, when they decided to visit their former homes, most of them for the first time. The hard times of the seventies and the numerous railroad strikes of that period and of the eighties also tended to encourage the cheaper and more dependable travel by steamboat.

But the strongest factors favoring steamboats, especially those on the Ohio, were low wages, good service, and small initial outlays of capital. In 1880 the aver-

---

[297] *Magazine of Western History*, vol. ii, 267; Wheeling *Intelligencer*, November 20, 1880; *idem*, December 6, 1880; *idem*, March 7, 1881.

age value of the 473 steamboats then employed on that stream was less than $12,000. At the same time it cost less than $2,500 per month to operate a packet of 500 tons burden, exclusive of fuel and upkeep, neither of which was ordinarily great. As a rule masters then received $125 per month, mates $60, clerks from $50 to $150, pilots $125, members of the cabin crew $15, and deckhands $25 each. Small boats paid less and were operated even more cheaply.[298]

It was under these conditions that the steamboats of the Ohio attained the heights of a second period of popularity and success surpassing in some features the palmy days of the forties and the fifties. In 1880 their aggregate capacity was more than 110,000 tons, and their total value exceeded $5,500,000.[299] At the same time they furnished employment for 9,000 persons, including 2,000 deckhands, and transported annually more than 1,000,000 regular passengers and 2,500,000 tons of freight. Their gross earnings for that year totaled $7,628,924 which represented 126 per cent on the capital invested. Through packets from New Orleans and other Mississippi river ports reached Pittsburgh more or less regularly, and local ports were served by scores of regular packets, those running to and from Cincinnati being in excess of forty. Of the conditions on the river the Wheeling *Intelligencer* for September 10, 1880, quoting the Cincinnati *Gazette*, said: "We have more boats than since the war."

A great change was impending, however. Characteristic of inland steamboating during the last century, a decline set in that might have been precipitous but for

---

[298] U. S. *Census*, 1880, vol. iv, 696.

[299] This includes boats engaged in the coal trade. See U. S. *Census*, 1880, vol. iv, 695.

the presence of modifying factors to be considered later. Suffice it to say that in 1882 the packets of the Big Seven line left the Ohio forever; about the same time the White Collar line entered a fatal decline; "independents" and "transients" became scarce; and many short trades were entirely abandoned. To save themselves rivermen resorted to "cut-throat" competition, and in a short time the river press everywhere noted the presence of hard times and spoke of the perfidy of Roscoe Conkling and other political leaders, both in the East and the West, whose consistent support of railroad and Standard Oil interests, in the halls of Congress and elsewhere, ran counter to the best interests of inland river transportation.[300]

As in the fifties, no single factor was responsible for this transition, but there is no denying that the railroads played a leading rôle. They built competing lines, manipulated rates and fares, and in other ways ran counter to river activities. For instance, in the eighties tracks paralleling the Ohio were constructed from Wheeling to Cincinnati. Soon thereafter, under the provisions of the Interstate Commerce act of 1887, railroads announced low freight and passenger charges to competing river ports, making good their losses by higher charges to non-competing inland points. Through connivance with and in some cases because of the ignorance of local municipal authorities, they were also permitted to obstruct local levees. About the same time floods came and the "ice demon" descended, entailing devas-

---

[300] Superintendent Sidney D. Maxwell's "The River Interests of the City of Cincinnati for the Commercial Year Ending August 31, 1883," in *Report to the Cincinnati Chamber of Commerce* (Cincinnati, 1884. Pamphlet); *idem, Report* (Cincinnati, 1888); Wheeling *Intelligencer*, June 1, 1881; *idem*, June 25, 1883; *idem*, November 19, 1883; *Waterways Journal*, August 21, 1920; *idem*, July 9, 1921.

tation and destruction to both railroad and river property, the floods of 1883 and 1884 being unprecedented for their destructiveness. Recovery therefrom challenged the resources of local railroads and was practically impossible for some river interests. Moreover, at this time, wherever possible, contracts for carrying the mails were given to the railroads instead of to the packets, as in the past. The country was growing speed mad and would brook no delays, certainly not in the matter of receiving and sending mail.

Nevertheless the passenger packets of the Ohio possessed great potentialities. As already indicated, their tonnage was great, and the interests involved were powerful and resourceful. Moreover, immigrants continued to arrive in large numbers and to show a preference for steamboats as a means of travel, and hundreds of local industries and businesses continued to use the Ohio largely as a matter of habit. And in the face of a common enemy, the railroad, competition among rivermen tended to give way to coöperation. As a result, river trades were extended in length and reduced in numbers, and out-of-date and worn craft gave place to the most up-to-date tonnage available. In 1888 a competent authority described the results in these words: "It has been a transition period in which . . . boating was characterized by expensive management and large returns for service performed, to a condition of things in which all great business interests, either from choice or constraint, find themselves occupying one [position] in which slender profits have to be acquiesced in, and very close economy practiced."[301]

Out of these conditions and with these modifications there were notable survivals. Outstanding among these

[301] Maxwell, *op. cit.*, 1884; *idem*, 1888, 4.

was the Louisville and Cincinnati Packet line which, with slight interruptions and under different names, has served the trade between Cincinnati and Louisville for more than a hundred years. About 1890 this line, together with what was left of the White Collar line, operating out of Cincinnati to and from Pomeroy, Ohio, and Charleston, West Virginia, passed under the management of Captain F. A. Laidley, an interested stockholder seeking to avert financial loss from himself and associates. Under his management the packet trade between Cincinnati and Louisville again earned profits, and for a time the White Collar line showed signs of returning vitality. During the years immediately following the Louisville and Cincinnati Packet line operated some of its best boats, among them being the "City of Cincinnati" and the "City of Louisville."

Everything considered, the successful operation of a packet line on the Ohio in the nineties was an achievement the secrets of which ought to be of general interest. Chief dependence was placed in the fact that boats in the Cincinnati and Louisville trade could carry freight in small quantities, of less than car load lots, quicker and cheaper than could competing railroads. Next in importance was the quality of the service rendered, all boats being dependable, well kept, and efficiently managed. Thus they were great favorites with the traveling public, particularly "traveling men" who after a hard day's work in one terminus, were able to "take a boat" and wake up the next morning in the other, fresh for a new day's business, baggage at hand. Moreover, in season, Sunday excursions were sources of profit. Attracted by a round trip fare of fifty cents, with good meals at the same price, hundreds of persons sometimes enjoyed these outings. Finally, these packets had

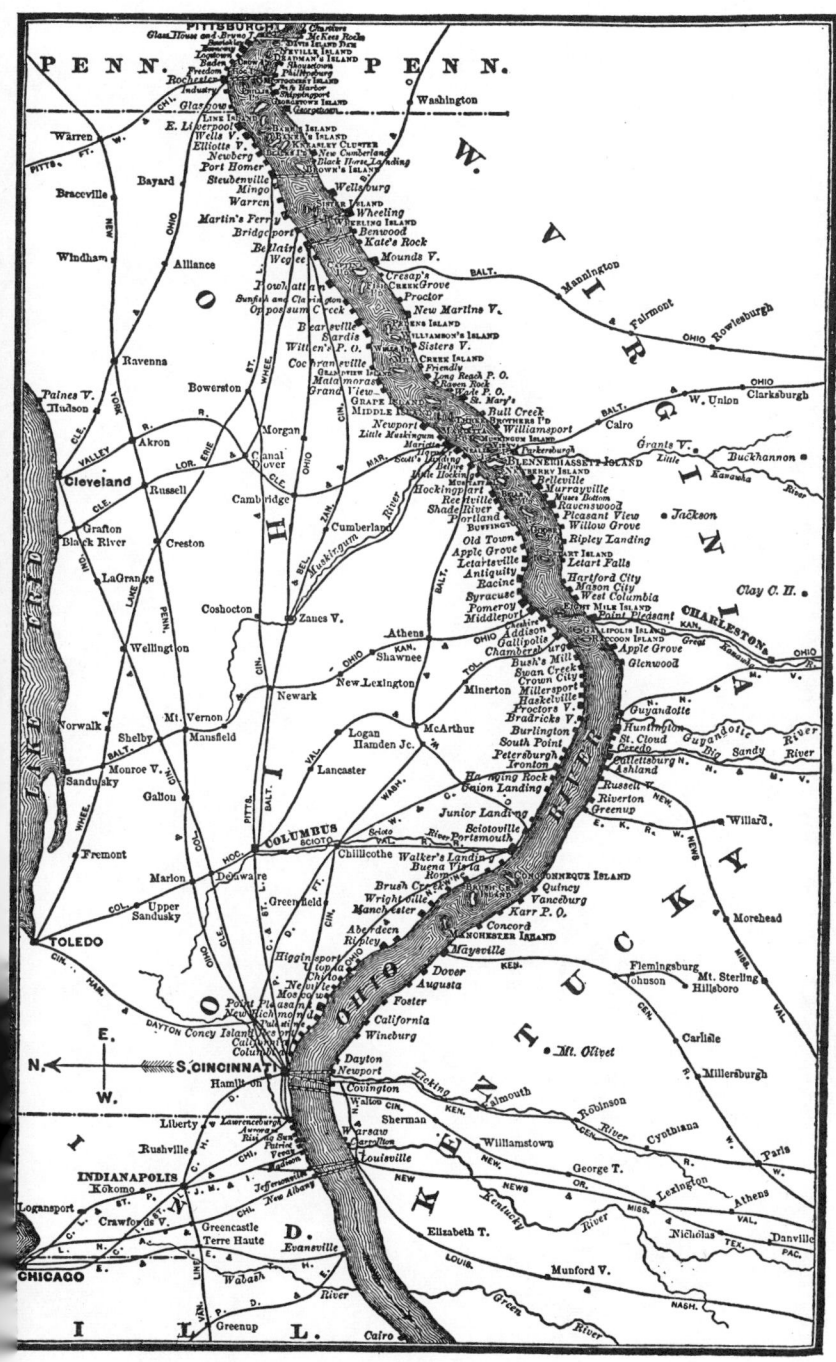

BOAT-LANDINGS ALONG THE OHIO, ABOUT 1900
Served by the packets of the second Pittsburgh and Cincinnati Packet line.

favorable shipping connections with packets of other lines, as well as with local railroads, which enabled them to give bills of lading to distant points.

While Captain Laidley was meeting with success in his favorite river trade, Captain Isaac T. Rhea and others organized the St. Louis and Tennessee Packet Company for the purpose of owning and operating packets and towboats in a long-distance trade between St. Louis and ports on the Tennessee river. The undertaking had the support of St. Louis interests which hoped to divert to their city the native products of the Tennessee valley, particularly lumber. After a period of competition with Captain Sweetser, who tried to keep the Tennessee valley tributary to Cincinnati, and with the Tennessee Navigation Company, operating a line of packets in the interest of the Louisville and Nashville railroad, the Rhea interests won and later built up a rich river trade which their successors maintained until recently.[302]

But the most significant development of this period on the Ohio was the restoration of a through and regular packet service between Pittsburgh and Cincinnati. In its initial stages this was primarily the work of Captain J. N. Williamson of Cincinnati and his favorite packet, the "Emma Graham." In the midst of the prosperous conditions of the late seventies Captain Williamson organized the Emma Graham Packet Company for the purpose of operating in a trade which he hoped to build up between Cincinnati and Pittsburgh. At first he used only two boats, the "Emma Graham" and the "Hudson." Contrary to common expectations they made money, and in a short time Captains "Wash" Honshell of Cincinnati, "Wash" Kerr and T. T. John-

---

[302] *Waterways Journal*, March 8, 1924; *idem*, October 29, 1927.

son, both of Ironton, and James Rees of Pittsburgh built the "Buckeye State" which was entered in the Pittsburgh and Cincinnati trade. Soon the latter and her sister packets were joined by the "Katie Stockdale," "Scotia," and "Granite State," giving the trade a daily packet for every day except Sunday.

Meanwhile the corporate control under which this trade was revived had been abandoned for a pooling arrangement directed by two managers or superintendents, one located in Pittsburgh, the other in Cincinnati. The first directors under this arrangement were Captain J. T. Stockdale, stationed in Pittsburgh, and Captain Williamson. Following the death of these captains, in the early eighties, Stockdale was succeeded by Captain James A. Henderson who was assisted by Captain Honshell in Cincinnati. Following the destruction of the "Buckeye State" on the Falls at Louisville, Captain Honshell retired and was succeeded by Captain J. F. Ellison. Under his direction and that of Captain Henderson these packets prospered as never before, and the "Katie Stockdale" and "Emma Graham" were replaced by the "Keystone State," and the "Andes," the former built for the trade.

As corporate ownership and control was becoming the general practice in river circles and as the future of the packets in the Pittsburgh and Cincinnati trade seemed assured, their owners decided to become incorporated. Accordingly, in 1893, the Pittsburgh and Cincinnati Packet line was formed. It had a charter from the state of West Virginia and a capital stock of two hundred thousand dollars, most of which was owned by interested officers and captains. The presidency was entrusted to Captain Henderson, George W. C. Johnston of Pittsburgh was secretary and treasurer, and Captain Ellison of Cincinnati was superintendent. Other interested stockholders were Captain Thomas S. Calhoon of Georgetown, Pennsylvania, and Captains Thomas M. Rees and John M. Phillips, both of Pittsburgh. The first boats in the new line were the "Keystone State," "Iron Queen," "Hudson," "Scotia," "C. W. Batchelor," and the "Andes." Later the "Virginia" and the "Queen City" were added to take the places of retiring packets.

In addition to the general conditions already mentioned in this chapter many factors of a more or less local nature contributed to the success of this line. Of first importance, probably, was a prorating arrangement with local railroads that enabled it to quote through rates and issue bills of lading for "fast freight" to "all points, south and west." Scarcely less important was the tonnage supplied by local industries, particularly those engaged in the manufacture of iron and steel. The passenger traffic was probably next in importance. A widely advertised fare of twelve dollars "from the Iron City to the Queen City and return; meals and berth included," attracted others than immigrants who continued, however, to arrive in large numbers and to go west by way of the Ohio. A scarcely less significant factor in the success of these packets was their corporate ownership and management, which offered an escape from individual liability and made possible needed efficiencies and economies. An item in a single cargo of the "Keystone State" will indicate something of the service rendered by this line to wayside farmers. It consisted of nine thousand cases of eggs of thirty dozen each. Finally the quality of the boats used and the efficient service rendered has never been excelled on the upper Ohio. To this day one needs only to mention the names Thomas S. Calhoon, J. F. Ellison, and Charles W. Knox, commanders of steamers in the "Second" Pittsburgh and Cincinnati Packet line, to revive the best river traditions of the Ohio. Incidentally these names also recall times and conditions, scarcely three decades removed, when steamboating on the Ohio was profitable. In 1898 the Pittsburgh and Cincinnati Packet line declared an annual dividend of nine per cent and added to its reserve, practically every trip made by its boats netting a profit.[303]

The steamboatmen of this period are the pride and boast of the inland waters. In courtesy they had few if any superiors; in efficiency and accomplishments they were surpassed, among rivermen, only by their contemporaries, the "coal barons." For a generation or more the richest river annals of America have been the stories of their deeds and achievements. Some of them still live, at ages well into the eighties and even nineties. From their biographies and those of their contemporaries who have passed on in the last generation could be written important chapters in the story of our national development. From simple beginnings as "boatmen" they in turn operated merchantboats, ran coal, transported troops, engaged in inland naval battles, built and operated barges and palatial steamers, and finally established themselves as farmers, bankers, railroad men, captains of industry, and wholesalers and retailers, few of them remaining on the river until the end of their careers.

---

[303] Manuscripts and Papers. (Office of James Rees and Sons Company, Pittsburgh).

The Coal Trade

For more than half a century following the Civil war a "coalboat stage" on the Ohio was a signal for great activity in the harbor of Pittsburgh. On the wharf and the streets immediately tributary thereto curious persons jostled one other, and "berth" seekers passed to and fro; heavy trucks drawn by large and well-groomed horses bumped and rattled over cobble stones; and, if the weather permitted, knots of pilots, in fine raiment, exchanged greetings, conjectured about the weather, and collected information about the conditions of navigation along "the River." Meanwhile, at the foot of the wharf, great towboats nosed one another for space, while they shipped crews and took aboard stores for proposed southern trips. In the harbor other large towboats, assisted by poolboats, puffed white waves of steam and emitted black clouds of smoke, as they made up their respective tows and prepared to "get away."

In more recent years long distance shipments of coal from Pittsburgh have practically ceased, the total local production being consumed by local industry. Nevertheless, the volume of the coal trade on the Ohio has increased. It moves steadily on the lower Monongahela and the upper Ohio south to Steubenville and, less regularly, to Wheeling. This is made possible by the use of stationary dams in the vicinity of Pittsburgh, which maintain permanent pools of navigable water, kept clear of ice by the constant use made of them by industry. Although New Orleans and other lower Mississippi points now receive their coal from the coal fields of Alabama, Cincinnati and Louisville continue to receive large supplies from West Virginia and Kentucky, thus maintaining an important river traffic between these points and the coal fields along the Great Kanawha and intermediate streams.

The rise and development of this traffic is inseparably connected with the growth of inland America. From the earliest days of white adventurers beyond the Alleghanies the presence of coal was known and commented upon. In his journal of 1750-1753 Christopher Gist recorded facts regarding coal deposits in the region of the upper Ohio and along rivers flowing westward through what is now a part of Kentucky. Later James Burd, George Croghan, and George Washington had something to say about coal deposits in the vicinity of Pittsburgh, but Dr. Schope, a German botanist and geologist, was among the first to point out their great possibilities, when, in 1783, he wrote: "The great supply will be uncommonly advantageous in the future settlement of this region, contributing, as it will, to the more general cultivation of the land, less wood having to be reserved." Even more in line with future developments was his prediction that "the use of the minerals here will be practicable, and these coals will form a considerable article of export." [304]

Shortly thereafter coal was being mined in the vicinity of Pittsburgh for both domestic and industrial purposes, but little was exported before the early days of the nineteenth century. What may have been the first shipment by water was made on the "Louisiana," which descended the Ohio in 1803 carrying coal for ballast.

---

[304] Pittsburgh *Gazette Times*, October 28, 1921; Thurston, *op. cit.*, 122.

This otherwise useless cargo was sold in Philadelphia at ten dollars per ton. Three years later John S. Giles and others were carrying coal in flatboats from mines in Meigs county, Ohio, to Cincinnati. In the same county, six years later, when on a trip of investigation to determine the practicability of steam navigation on the western waters, Nicholas J. Roosevelt mined and stored a supply of coal to be used by a proposed steamboat, the keel of which had not yet been laid.[305]

It was not until after the close of the War of 1812 that the coal traffic on the Ohio began to assume commercial importance. Even then the fuel supplies of the native forests greatly retarded the use of coal. Nevertheless, while the Treaty of Ghent was in process of negotiation, Zachariah Reno was floating coal from Pittsburgh to Louisville to be used in the foundries that were being established there, coal being better suited for such uses than wood. Three years later, when John C. Calhoun, Henry Clay, and Thomas Jefferson were in accord in demanding a tariff for the protection of American industries, "Pilot Tom" Jones began to carry coal down the Ohio from mines on French creek using as containers "French Creeks," flatboats named for the place of their origin and later used extensively for such shipments. By 1819, when David Bradshaw and others were making more or less regular shipments south from what is now Pomeroy, Ohio, the coal trade southward from Pittsburgh was increasing in volume and regularity.

Ten years intervened, however, before either the coalboats of the Ohio or their cargoes got far beyond its banks. Among the very first shipments to the Mis-

---

[305] — *Idem*, 121; Gould, *op. cit.*, 497; *Magazine of Western History*, vol. ii, 271.

sissippi was one made in 1829, when the owners of the Labranche plantation, located near Red Church, Louisiana, bought a small quantity to be used in making sugar. Other shipments in larger quantities soon followed.[306] Of even greater importance, in the development of the local coal traffic, were shipments made a few years later, by river and canal, from Pittsburgh and Pomeroy to cities in central and northern Ohio. It was thus that these cities, heretofore handicapped by an inadequate fuel supply, were permitted to grow into industrial centers, consuming annually ever-increasing quantities of coal.

Many factors contributed to this rather phenomenal development. First of all was the industrial and commercial awakening that followed the Treaty of Ghent. Soon thereafter the whole country about-faced to follow the lure of a "manifest destiny," and Henry Clay formulated the rules of the game in the principles of the American System. These factors stimulated the coal industry in two notable ways. First they gave it protection against possible competitors in Canada, and secondly they stimulated local industry, thus creating a demand for fuel. From 1824 to 1832 the duty on imported coal was one dollar and fifty cents per ton. In the latter year it was raised to one dollar and seventy-five cents where it remained until 1846, when it was lowered in response to the demands of the *laissez faire* teachings that were then gaining a temporary ascendency in the commercial affairs of the world. Meanwhile the local demand for coal increased annually. A second factor in the early development of the coal traffic on the Ohio was the growing scarcity of cord-

---

[306] Thurston, *op. cit.*, 122; Howe, H. *Historical Collections of Ohio*, vol. ii, 215; Wheeling *Intelligencer*, October 29, 1869.

wood. As the demand for fuel increased, local forests retreated before the woodman's ax to points where they could not profitably be pursued. The only alternative was a substitute which, fortunately, was at hand in coal.

It was under these conditions, in the forties of the last century, that coal became the "bread of industry" throughout the Ohio valley and neighboring sections. The annually increasing consumption tells a story all its own. That for Cleveland rose from 8,610 tons in 1840, to 97,960 tons in 1850; that for Cincinnati, for the same years, from 95,000 tons to more than 900,000 tons. The effect is evidenced in the increased output of local industry, that for Cincinnati advancing from $17,780,000 in 1840, to $54,550,000 in 1850.[307]

The local effect was gratifying and served to check a tendency to emigrate to California and to the Southwest, because many were beginning to look upon the Ohio valley as a veritable Eldorado, with minerals more useful than the gold of the Pacific coast and, in the long run, more valuable. Eastern capitalists continued to purchase lands, some of which their descendants still retain, and the local press could not share the fears then current in the East to the effect that California would drain the older sections of our country of their population and wealth, for said Cist, in his *Weekly Advertiser* (Cincinnati) for April 17, 1850: "The East has treasures that far surpass those of the West."

With the passing of the mid-century mark the coal traffic of the Ohio attained marvelous proportions. The greatest demand came from industry, the consumption

---

[307] *Hunt's Merchants' Magazine*, vol. xxi, 278; *idem*, vol. xi, 228; *idem*, vol. xx, 559; Wheeling *Times*, May 8, 1848, *Cist's Weekly Advertiser*, November 9, 1847; *idem*, April 11, 1848.

of Cincinnati increasing at the rate of one hundred thousand tons annually. The railroad was now penetrating the interior, facilitating the distribution and increasing the quantity of coal consumed, while steamboats were rapidly substituting it for wood. These demands forced the coal exports of Pittsburgh to one million tons annually and called into existence exporting mines at other points on the Ohio, notably Bellaire.

The inadequate craft used was no great handicap to the growth of the coal traffic. Greater difficulty came from the undependable navigation of the Ohio which could not float coalboats during periods in summer and autumn and was frozen over during shorter periods in winter. Under such conditions the plight of industry became desperate, urgent demands forcing the price of coal to fifty cents a bushel. It was to relieve such a situation that the railroads of the interior were first commissioned as coal carriers, the first through rail shipment reaching Cincinnati in 1852 by way of Zanesville.[308]

For several years thereafter the coalboat continued to be the favorite means of transporting coal on the Ohio.[309] This was a frail craft of only two gunwales, one on either side at the bottom, together supporting a frame that was boarded up, ends, sides, and bottom, with one and one-half inch lumber. Coalboats varied in length from one hundred sixty to one hundred seventy-five feet and were about twenty-four feet wide and eight feet deep. Their maximum capacity was about twenty-five thousand bushels, the bulk and weight of which was depended upon to keep containers in

---

[308] *Hunt's Merchants' Magazine*, vol. xxxi, passim.

[309] Thurston, *op. cit.*, 121; Gould, *op. cit.*; *Hunt's Merchants' Magazine*, vol. xxx, 440; Wheeling *Intelligencer*, November 30, 1858; U. S. House, *op. cit.*, 413.

shape. They were operated in pairs, being lashed together, side by side, and guided by long sweeps or oars. Each boat carried a large quantity of rope which was attached to large upright beams at the head, stern, and middle for the purpose of making "landings" and "tie-ups," real skill and much experience being required to accomplish these feats. If the ropes did not strengthen one another in tightening, they snapped, one after the other, as so much tow, and the boats were dashed to pieces and their contents destroyed. Each pair was provided with a shanty built on the bottom of one of the boats and in such a manner as to be almost completely covered by its contents when loaded. Thus protected from cold and storm the crew, of from twelve to twenty persons, "hands," pilots and cooks, rode to their destination, provided they did not "hit a snag." For use in making landings and meeting emergencies two skiffs of six oars each accompanied each pair of coalboats.

Most of the coalboats used at this time were built on the Allegheny, where timber was then cheap and abundant. They were floated thence to the Ohio and up the Monongahela, where they were loaded and assembled. They served for one trip only, being too frail and cheap to be towed up-stream. "Empties" were not, however, without value in the New Orleans and other southern markets. Here they were "knocked down" and sold, the best lumber for building purposes, the refuse for street paving material and for fuel. Sometimes the proceeds from such sales covered original costs, so that the only cash outlay in the transportation of coal in this manner was for labor which was cheap, pilots only being skilled.

Most coalboats were "run" only in the spring and late autumn. Then only could suitable boating stages be depended upon, nine feet being required to carry loaded boats in safety. When boating stages did not come with the usual regularity and followed long "freeze-ups" and "droughts" instead, industry throughout the interior was paralyzed, and thousands of men were out of employment. Under such conditions a resumption of traffic produced scenes in the harbor of Pittsburgh not unlike those of the later towboat days. The wharf became a veritable hive of activity, and hundreds of men vied with one another in placing themselves to advantage for "coal trips," the number finding employment at such times varying all the way from three hundred to two thousand persons.

The coalboatmen of the Ohio were a class to themselves, possessing many of the characteristics of the boatmen of the days of "Mike" Fink. Most of them followed coalboating as a business, but many young men, bent upon seeing New Orleans at small expense, looked upon a "trip" as an opportunity to get a great deal of adventure and frolic out of a little hard work. They joined coalboat crews as ordinary "hands" although they were in good circumstances and of best families. To them the usual wage of seventy-five dollars for the "trip" was a secondary consideration. Pilots were more professional and, as a rule, better paid. Returning from their "trips" they usually rode in the cabin as "cabin passengers" on the numerous steamboats then plying the Mississippi and Ohio rivers in increasing numbers, whereas "hands" returned as "deck passengers" and engaged, without restraint, in the usual deck amusements of fighting, gambling, and drinking.

The hazards of coalboating were great, and the losses were frequent and sometimes tragic. An example will suffice. In a storm between Pittsburgh and Wheeling, in January, 1854, seventy boats containing over sixteen hundred thousand bushels of coal were lost. Those reporting the event spoke with feeling of the cries of despair that went up from the helpless crews of these boats, as the angry waves of that dismal night dashed them upon Merriam's island and other dangerous points. When this storm had cleared, seventeen persons were found to have lost their lives; others were stranded; and dismay and alarm reigned throughout the ranks of the survivors. But these losses were only a small part of the toll exacted by a business whose profits depended upon the success of more or less inexperienced men in bringing frail and cumbrous craft safely to their destination after a voyage covering five hundred to sixteen hundred miles.[310]

Fortunately this primitive method of transportation was giving way to another, that of the towboat. For years steamboats had been towing barges and other auxiliary craft, the practice being either to drag them behind or to gather them about the boat at its sides and fore and aft somewhat after the fashion of a duck mothering her family. The "Condor" is said to have towed coal in this way from Pomeroy to Cincinnati in the early thirties, barges being used as containers. In this manner Daniel Bushnell, in 1845, used three small barges and a small stern-wheeler, the "Walter Forward," to tow coal from Pittsburgh to Cincinnati, while Thomas H. Baird was using the "Harlem," a side-wheeler, for the same purpose between Pittsburgh and Hanging Rocks.[311] As yet, however, few if any persons thought of towing coal and returning the con-

---

[310] Wheeling *Intelligencer*, February 27, 1854; Pittsburgh *Gazette*, January 25, 1854; *Hunt's Merchants' Magazine*, vol. xxx, 440.

[311] *Cist's Weekly Advertiser*, August 10, 1847; Thurston, *op. cit.*, 124; Howe, *op. cit.*, vol. ii, 215.

tainers to and from points below Louisville. Containers were too frail, and, with the devices in use, towing costs were too great.

Fortunately a radical change was at hand that was to revolutionize the transportation of coal in the interior. Coal was to be "pushed" instead of "towed." To this end one or two containers, either barges or coalboats, were lashed to each side of a steamboat for a distance of forty or fifty feet, leaving an open space between them and in front of the steamboat for the remaining length of the containers. Forward of these three or four additional containers were added, in tiers, the number in each and the number of tiers increasing as the method of assembling "fleets" became perfected and as the power of towboats increased.[312]

The first stage of this change was effected about 1850 and served at once to bring the stern-wheel steamboat into its own. First among local packets to be used in this way was the "Lake Erie," which pushed coal from Pittsburgh to Cincinnati and Louisville in the early fifties. She was followed in rapid succession by others that did the same thing, among them being the "James Guthrie," "Black Diamond," "Sea Gull," "Beaver," "Senator Lorimer," "Monongahela," and "Hercules." Soon these boats demonstrated the advantages of pushing coal instead of towing it. In fact, they developed great facility in the former, being able to back, flank, and otherwise maneuver in the narrow and sometimes obstructed channels of the Ohio. They could ascend the Monongahela, back down with an immense tow and up the Allegheny, right themselves without assistance, and set off for Cincinnati, Louisville, and New Orleans, rarely stopping *en route*. They also developed remark-

---

[312] Thurston, *op. cit.*, 121; *Waterways Journal*, January 14, 1911.

THE COAL TRADE

able dispatch, a round trip from Pittsburgh to Cincinnati and Louisville requiring from seven to ten days, while that from Pittsburgh to New Orleans was completed in from thirty-five to forty days.

The beginning of the towboat traffic in coal and coke between Pittsburgh and New Orleans was a noteworthy event. The newspaper press along the entire route commented with approval upon the achievements of the "Crescent City," the pioneer boat in the trade. Under the command of Captain Cochran she left Pittsburgh, January 19, 1854, in the wake of a terrible storm that had wrought destruction to scores of coalboats that had just preceded her on a coalboat stage. Of her departure the Pittsburgh *Gazette*, for that date, said: "The 'Crescent City,' a new towboat built expressly for the business by Geo. Ledlie and Co., will leave today for New Orleans with four coal boats in tow. This is the first adventure of the kind, and is noteworthy, on that account." Sixteen days later the New Orleans *Bulletin* announced the safe arrival of the "Crescent City" in New Orleans and predicted far-reaching results as a consequence of her achievements. Within forty days from her departure she was back in Pittsburgh ready for another trip, having netted her owners a profit of sixteen thousand dollars. Upon her safe return from her second venture the Cincinnati *Gazette* reported: "She towed up four barges of railroad iron and other freight, which will insure her quite as profitable a trip as the former one." [313]

Attracted by these profits and successes many other towboats soon engaged in the long distance coal traffic southward from Pittsburgh. Had they entered it ear-

---

[313] Pittsburgh *Gazette*, January 19, 1854; *idem*, February 14, 1854; *idem*, February 28, 1854; Gould, *op. cit.*, 499.

lier, their influences might have gone far to bind the North and the South by such unbreakable ties of interest as to have banished serious thought of secession on the part of the latter. As stated elsewhere, they were potent factors in the restoration of the Union in the sixties.

Some of the effects of the long-distance coal trade on the inland waters were immediate. Important among these was the substitution of barges for coalboats as containers. Although not complete this substitution did much to advance the coming of the "Barge Age" of inland transportation. In a short time thereafter barge building was almost as important an industry on the Ohio as was steamboat building or as had been flatboat building in the "Flatboat Age," and the practice of running coal from upper Ohio to lower Ohio and Mississippi markets practically ceased.

Of the more remote effects a writer in *Hunt's Merchants' Magazine* for April, 1854, said:

> The coal trade of Pittsburgh is yet in its infancy, but will evidently magnify every year. The fluctuations and the dangers of river navigation have hitherto rendered its delivery in the West uncertain and costly; but the practice now beginning to be adopted of carrying in barges, as also an improved navigation of the Ohio, will much diminish the price and augment the consumption. It will likewise have the effect of driving the small dealers out of the trade, as it requires more capital than in the present flatboat style. The Northwest, too, and the Lakes region, which have hitherto been shut out from all coal measures, will be supplied in part from Pittsburgh.

Similar possibilities had already been pointed out by such geologists as Richard Cowling Taylor and Sir Charles Lyell.

These predictions were not long in realization. At once the volume of the Ohio-river coal traffic increased in size; prices of coal were reduced; the Lake region and the Ohio valley were drawn closer together; and small dealers and shippers were either driven out of business or became members of firms and companies operating on a large scale. Of even greater significance, possibly, was a demand for the improved navigation of the Ohio river.

Improvements in transportation were reflected in the coal mining industry as well as in methods of disposing of the product. Here and there in the vicinity of Pittsburgh, the familiar coal mining village of today first made its appearance; boatyards for the construction and maintenance of towboats and barges took on new life and grew in size; scores of pilots, engineers, and captains found regular employment under yearly contracts and at fixed salaries; and thousands of additional laborers found employment in mines, in boatyards, and on the river. Although complete statistics of the coal produced in and about Pittsburgh in the fifties and the sixties are not available, a review, by decades, of the slackwater shipments from the Monongahela will tell a part of the story. From 230,260 tons in 1845 they grew to 1,111,700 tons in 1855 and to 1,979,235 tons in 1865, the value of the shipments to New Orleans alone for an intermediate year, 1859, amounting to more than $3,000,000.[314]

[314] U. S. House. *Executive Documents*, 50 cong., 1 sess., vol. xx, no. 6, pt. ii, 462; *Cist's Weekly Advertiser*, April 11, 1848. Except in 1856, when the Ohio river was frozen over for a long period, the coal trade on that stream tended to make consistent gains, as shown by the following statistics:

Year	Bushels	Year	Bushels
1845	2,660,340	1852	9,960,950
1846	5,236,500	1853	11,590,730
1847	7,200,450	1854	14,632,580
1848	7,150,355	1855	18,560,158
1849	7,145,150	1856	8,165,196
1850	8,560,180	1857	25,684,550
1851	8,250,120	1858	24,696,669

These large-scale operations and economies gave rise to large private fortunes in the Pittsburgh district and to the southward, their possessors being known locally as "coal barons." Prominent among them were Wm. H. Brown, Joseph B. Walton, John A. Wood, Wm. O'Neal, Joseph B. Williams, and Thomas Fawcett of Pittsburgh, Jacob Heatherington of Bellaire and Samuel Pomeroy and Valentine B. Horton of Pomeroy.

Although somewhat more successful than other coal barons, William Hughey Brown had a typical career. He was born January 15, 1815, in Westmoreland county, Pennsylvania. While in his teens he was alternately employed on farms and on canal boats, but when quite young he became a coal miner near Pittsburgh. With his first savings he purchased a horse and wagon with which he delivered coal to regular customers. Soon he was part owner in a mine and was supplying local industries with fuel on an increasingly large scale. After a time this partnership connection was dissolved, because, it is said, Brown's associates could not see possible profits in marketing surpluses on the lower waters, in engaging in the newly established coke industry, and in enlarging the scale of their operations generally. In 1848 Brown formed a new partnership and under the firm name of Lloyd, Black, and Brown, mined extensively both for local consumption and for shipment to lower river markets.

From the date of this new business alliance Brown's success was phenomenal. It is said to have had its impetus in the use of an improved coalboat, heavier and more durable than those then in use but lighter and less expensive than the standard barge of that day. First shipments were made only to Cincinnati and Louisville, but later they were extended to St. Louis and to New

Orleans. In the former city, where Brown's coal was extensively used for the manufacture of gas, his name became a synonym for the best quality of "black diamond." By 1860 his firm owned and operated many towboats and scores of coalboats. In the Civil war it received large contracts to supply coal for the use of the Army and the Navy on the Ohio and Mississippi rivers and is said to have accumulated millions. Brown, who had meanwhile acquired the controlling interest, was the chief beneficiary. Nevertheless, he retained his former friends in the South and was even accused of entertaining sympathies for the Confederacy. He died October 12, 1875, leaving an estate appraised at more than six million dollars. Many attributed his success to luck, but those who knew him best attributed it to a rare combination of brains, industry, and opportunity.[315]

Hundreds of official dispatches regarding the transportation, storage, and use of coal attested its importance to both the Army and the Navy of the Union in the interior during the Civil war.[316] What the enemy did not get of the available stores in the early stages of that conflict, rival Union commanders appropriated according to their opportunities and often in defiance of orders. All realized that military movements depended upon transportation which, in turn, depended upon fuel supplies. In 1862 Acting Rear-admiral Porter was using sixteen hundred tons of coal a month and asking for more. In a dispatch of December 21, 1862, he said: "Get me coal and send it to Vicksburg without delay." Under the same date he wrote: "There is not a pound of coal at Helena excepting what belongs to the army,

---

[315] Gould, *op. cit.*, 504; *Waterways Journal*, March 9, 1912.
[316] See p. 260 of this work.

who are sending it down in large quantities. Every boat of theirs is supplied, while we are helpless. Obtain tonnage and send me coal to Vicksburg at once, no matter what the cost may be. Do not stop to turn off coal barges. I must have coal." [317]

Unlike most other local enterprises the coal trade of the Ohio valley did not pass through a period of reorganization following the Civil war. For a time small scale operators in Kentucky and along the Great Kanawha river curtailed their outputs, but, except in the year 1861-1862, the shipments from Pittsburgh increased annually. In addition to large war demands, already mentioned, many local industries continued to flourish, and new ones came into existence. In 1865 Cincinnati was importing coal on a larger scale than ever before, her receipts by river for 1864-1865 being in excess of those of 1859-1860 by more than one hundred thousand tons.[318]

In 1868 the "great fact" about Pittsburgh was said to be coal. The Pittsburgh seam alone was estimated to cover eight and one-half million acres and to contain fifty-four billion tons. Locally this was valued at more than the estimated output of the California gold fields for one thousand years. Moreover, in some places there were two or more workable seams. The mines then in operation employed approximately seven thousand persons and produced two and one-half million tons annually, two-thirds of which was floated down the Ohio. By 1869 the Pittsburgh coal trade employed upwards of one hundred twenty steamboats, large and small, forty of which were used for towing down stream, the

---
[317] U. S. Naval War Records. *Official Records*, ser. 1, vol. xxiii, 644.
[318] U. S. House, *op. cit.*, 462.

THE COAL TRADE

others about the mines and in the slackwater pools on the Monongahela.[319]

Thus it was that proposals to construct additional bridges across the Ohio at this time met with bitter opposition from Pittsburgh coal shippers. Fearing that "railroad monopolies will ruin the commercial independence of the country at large, as they have been doing in state after state of the Union," [320] these shippers wished to preserve the free and unobstructed navigation of the Ohio river. This they urged not only as a natural right but also as a matter of sound public policy. To this end some would have dispensed with the use of bridges across that stream entirely, but others were willing to permit them where most needed, provided they were of five hundred feet span over the main channel and of such an elevation as not to interfere with navigation, even at flood stages.[321]

But other local and sectional interests combined to defeat the demands of the Pittsburgh coal shippers regarding the free navigation of the Ohio. "A creature of the Baltimore and Ohio railroad," West Virginia was not satisfied with her railroad facilities and sought additional trunklines. To this end she was not averse to bridges across the Ohio.[322] In this she was joined by Kentucky, also interested in railroads and bridges, one at Cincinnati, another at Louisville, and still another at Paducah. Except for Cincinnati and its immediate environs, the state of Ohio had lost interest in the free navigation of the Ohio river.

---

[319] — *Idem*, 414; *Atlantic Monthly*, January, 1868.

[320] U. S. *Congressional Globe*, 40 cong., 2 sess., pt. v, 4288 ff.; Manuscripts and Papers. James Rees and Sons Company, Pittsburgh.

[321] U. S. *Congressional Globe*, 44 cong., 2 sess., vol. v, pt. i, 522.

[322] — *Idem*, 40 cong., 2 sess., pt. v, 4288; Pittsburgh *Dispatch*, April 17, 1878.

As a result of these conditions, together with a growing indifference of the country at large towards its rivers, railroads were permitted to span the Ohio river by structures that interfered with its free navigation.[323] Most objectionable of these probably was the bridge at Bellaire, the main span of which was only two hundred twenty-two feet wide. At times it was such a hazard to navigation as to necessitate the breaking and re-assembling of coal fleets at that point. The bridge at Steubenville, built about the same time, was almost equally hazardous. An act of Congress of 1872 to prevent the erection of additional obstructions of this nature applied only to the lower Ohio below the mouth of the Big Sandy river.

The river coal trade, however, continued to increase in volume and in importance, a part of the losses due to artificial obstructions being canceled by the improved navigation made possible by the use of dikes and snag-boats. For the year ending 1886 Cincinnati received two million eight hundred seventy thousand tons of coal, only seven per cent of which was transported by rail. The chief sources, together with the amount supplied by each, were: Pittsburgh 1,293,835 tons; Kanawha river 649,447 tons; Ohio river, chiefly Pomeroy, 34,000 tons; and other sources, chiefly Kentucky, 100,000 tons. Meanwhile the coal traffic on the lower Mississippi continued to grow, that to New Orleans amounting to approximately 500,000 tons annually; sugar producers took about 250,000 tons more; and following the success of Captain Eads in deepening the channel of the Mississippi at its mouth, ocean-going vessels coaled at or near New Orleans in increasing numbers. As a result by 1890 the volume of the coal

---

[323] These bridges were built by Andrew Carnegie largely as experiments.

traffic on the Ohio, including that on the Monongahela and the Great Kanawha, first reached ten million tons annually.[324]

The last two decades of the nineteenth century witnessed the greatest success of the post-bellum coal companies and individual operators and shippers on the upper Ohio. On practically every boating stage they released from the slackwater pools about Pittsburgh a procession of towboats and coal containers almost a hundred miles long. As these craft descended the Ohio, at more or less regular intervals, the surrounding hills echoed and reëchoed with the blasts of their whistles, and, from a distance, spectators looked on with delight and admiration. Practically every large operator and shipper owned his own docks both for loading and unloading, as well as his own towboats and containers. All such property bore either the name of its owner or some other mark of identification. For example, the Wood boats carried between their smoke stacks an open star, the Walton boats a Maltese Cross, the Brown boats an anchor, and the Horner boats a shield. Prominent among other owners and operators, in addition to those already indicated, were Joseph B. Walton, Charles Jutte, Hugh Moren, Thomas Faucett, William Stone, J. C. Risher, I. D. Risher, and William B. Rogers who was subsequently president of the Pittsburgh Coal Exchange for more than twenty-five years. An average cargo for any one of their largest boats was about fifteen thousand tons which covered one and one-half acres of water surface, was worth about one hundred thousand dollars, and represented the product of from six to seven acres of coal strata.

To some, even at this early period, the depletion of

---

[324] See "Transportation on the Ohio River System," in U. S. War Department. *Bulletin*, 1927; U. S. House, *op. cit.*, 414.

Pittsburgh's coal reserves was a cause for alarm. They feared that their city would lose its place as "a chief commercial center." In the eighties their alarms were alleviated somewhat by the discovery and use of natural gas; but, when it was found that this only increased the amount of coal available for export, interested parties began to talk of conservation of natural resources. But suggestions to this end went unheeded, and the Pittsburgh district continued to ship coal in annually increasing volumes.

At the close of the century the outstanding fact in the coal situation on the upper Ohio was the Monongahela River Consolidated Coal and Coke Company, locally known as the "River Combine," or simply the "Combine." [325] This was formed in 1899 and included the holdings of all former independent owners and operators in the Pittsburgh district, except Charles Jutte and a few others who continued in the old way "in defiance of monopolies." Those entering the "Combine" received for their former holdings either stock or cash or both, as they themselves elected. All are said to have agreed not to reënter the local coal business in any form before the expiration of ten years and are said to have promised to do nothing meanwhile to further the interests of the local river over those of the local railroads. J. B. Finley was president of the new company which had an authorized capital stock of thirty million dollars.

This consolidation was the result of a general tendency towards industrial integration. The way to it had been paved by the destructive competition that had characterized the local coal business for decades. In the hard times of the early nineties the Grand Lakes

---

[325] Inland Waterways Commission, *Preliminary Report*, 1908, 115.

Company of Pittsburgh and other concerns were driven to the wall, and other producers and shippers curtailed operations. The surest way to avoid a repetition of such experiences seemed to be in pooling the interests of all. Local railroads were also a factor. As is shown elsewhere they were then tightening their growing monopoly of the coal carrying business.[326]

The first effects of the "Combine" were to stimulate the river coal traffic. Throughout the Pittsburgh district mining was stabilized, and inadequate and worn out craft gave place to new and up-to-date units, many of the former going to the Great Kanawha and lower Mississippi trades, while others remained idle. Among the new towboats that now appeared on the lower Ohio was the "Sprague," to this day the largest and the most powerful craft of its kind in the world. The construction of this "Titan of the inland waters" was commenced at Dubuque, Iowa, and completed at St. Louis. She was a stern-wheeler, three hundred and eighteen feet long and sixty-three feet wide with a wheel forty feet long and forty feet in diameter.

For a time the towing feats of the "Sprague" were the talk of the inland waters, that of February, 1907, being most frequently mentioned. On this trip her fleet consisted of sixty coalboats and barges containing an aggregate of seventy thousand tons. This "floating island" was nine hundred twenty-five feet long, three hundred twelve feet wide, and covered seven acres of water surface. Interested parties found amusement and information in calculating the number of railroad transportation units, then in use, necessary to move her cargo. Their researches revealed that it would have taken forty-nine engines each drawing thirty cars of

---
[326] See pp. 358-360 of this work.

forty-five tons capacity.[327] The fact that this and other towboats built at the same time and for the same purpose are yet in commission, although remodeled and even rebuilt to suit new trades, is proof of their superior qualities.

Thus facilitated, the volume of the coal traffic on the Ohio continued to increase by leaps and bounds. For 1907 including that on the Monongahela and the Great Kanawha, it was in excess of seventeen million tons, which was almost double the annual average for the five-year period immediately preceding the formation of the "Combine." In 1906 this concern alone owned and operated eighty towboats and steamers and about four thousand coalboats, barges, and other craft representing an aggregate capacity of two million seven hundred eighty-five thousand tons.[328]

Other coal fields than those of the Pittsburgh district augmented the volume of traffic on the Ohio.[329] In 1905 those along the Great Kanawha shipped one million four hundred sixty thousand tons by river, most of it to Cincinnati. Even Pittsburgh interests were then supplying down-river customers from the Great Kanawha region, a condition that led to the prediction that the "Smoky City will, in time, draw a large part of its coal supply from southern West Virginia," reversing the course of traffic, coal being towed up-stream instead of down. At the same time the United States

[327] *Waterways Journal*, June 1, 1907; *idem*, June 12, 1915; *idem*, October 12, 1918. Subsequently the "Joseph B. Williams" descended the whole course of the Ohio with a tow of coal, boats and barges together being one thousand nine feet long and one hundred twenty-two feet wide, the largest coal tow ever to descend the Ohio in the control of one boat. The "Sprague" assembled her tow on the lower Ohio.

[328] See "Transportation on the Ohio River System," U. S. War Department. *Bulletin*, 1927; *Waterways Journal*, October 19, 1907.

[329] Inland Waterways Commission, *op. cit.*, 113.

Coal and Oil Company of Holden, West Virginia, was shipping coal by the Ohio from its tipples near Huntington to elevators located a short distance below Cincinnati, whence reshipments were made to points inland.

In less than ten years, however, the long distance coal trade by way of the Ohio was ended. The entire output of the Pittsburgh district was needed at home, and New Orleans and other lower Mississippi points were drawing fuel supplies from Alabama. St. Louis secured her supplies from Illinois, Indiana, and Kentucky. As already indicated elsewhere, the local river traffic in coal continued to increase in volume, but new craft adapted to local needs were required for its transportation. For a time the great towboats formerly used, the "Sprague," "Joseph B. Williams," "Duquesne," "John A. Wood," "James Moren," and others, were tied up, but most of them later found employment with Standard Oil subsidiaries operating in the region of the lower Mississippi.

On the lower Ohio the coal traffic continued to increase in volume, but, as formerly, it was largely for consumption in and about Cincinnati and Louisville. Some years ago this traffic received a temporary setback from prorating practices favorable to local railroads, but in 1918 interested parties under the leadership of Colonel Lansing H. Beach of Pittsburgh, Albert Bettinger of Cincinnati, and J. T. Hatfield of Charleston, West Virginia, secured adjustments from the Interstate Commerce Commission that revived and have since sustained the river traffic in coal on the Great Kanawha.[330] Moreover, large quantities of coal continue to be carried from Huntington to lower Ohio-

---

[330] Cincinnati *Enquirer*, February 16, 1919.

river markets, and west Kentucky coal is now marketed in barges that are loaded at Caseyville.

Recent events in the coal traffic of the Ohio are interesting, possibly significant. For instance, February, 1927, two towboats arrived at New Orleans with twelve barges of West Virginia coal for reshipment to England. Three months later ten barges of coal reached New Orleans from Cincinnati, and meanwhile plans were being made for shipping West Virginia coal to St. Louis for commercial purposes.[331] Despite the abnormal conditions under which these events occurred, a coal strike in England, many thought that they heralded a possible resumption of the long distance coal traffic on the inland waters of America. Incidentally it was pointed out that the coal deposits along the Allegheny and in southern West Virginia were being made available and that they would be adequate to local demands for centuries.

---

[331] *Waterways Journal*, February 26, 1927; *idem*, March 3, 1927; *idem*, April 23, 1927; *idem*, May 21, 1927; *idem*, June 18, 1927; *idem*, July 30, 1927.

Life and Customs[332]

The events and conditions narrated and described in this chapter are, for the most part, those of the early eighties, the heyday of post-bellum steamboating on the Ohio and its tributaries. Moreover, reference is to that period when persons speak of the "good old days of steamboating after the War." In some respects these days were not unlike those of the forties and fifties.

On the Monongahela between Brownsville and Pittsburgh industry was then, as now, dominant. Throughout this entire stretch noisy, grimy, matter-of-fact industrial towns almost abutted one upon the other; the gruesome offals of mines and iron plants defiled the river; the air was heavy with smoke and soot discharged from hundreds of stacks; tipples of bituminous coal-shafts were everywhere; about these shafts were miners' hamlets of cottages, each cast in a common mold and painted red after the fashion of neighboring barns; and children, dogs, pigs, and chickens played and in some instances slept, together. To the sojourner the whirr, noise, and bang of revolving wheels and moving machinery were deafening. To this dynamic but otherwise forbidding situation, deserted mining villages, fallen tipples, and vacant, windowless cabins added an

---
[332] For additional information on life on the inland rivers see Mark Twain (Samuel L. Clemens). *Life on the Mississippi* (Boston, 1874); Quick, Edward, and Herbert Quick. *Mississippi Steamboatin'* (New York, 1926); Ferber, Edna. *Show Boat* (New York, 1927); Thwaites, R. G. *On the Storied Ohio* (Chicago, 1903); Habermehl, *Life on the Western Rivers*; Gould, *Fifty Years on the Mississippi*; Dunbar, *History of Travel in America*; Eskew, Garnett L. *The Pageant of the Packets* (New York, 1929).

appearance of desolation. Nevertheless, this was the heart of one of the world's greatest work-shops, giving rise to commerce in large volumes. Here Andrew Carnegie, H. C. Frick, and others had already made millions.

Obstructing bridges and unimproved navigation kept the Allegheny in a more primitive condition, its contributions to trade and commerce being largely restricted to petroleum, timber, farm products, and other raw materials; but the upper Ohio between Pittsburgh and Wheeling was not unlike the lower Monongahela. On the former some towns were rustic, shabby, and decadent, but New Cumberland, Steubenville, Mingo Junction, and Wheeling were industrial centers of importance. New Cumberland was the center of one of the greatest pottery industries in the world, and Wheeling was the source of most of the nails consumed in inland America. Interspersed between alternating hills, many of which were covered with small farms from base to summit, were semicircular bottom lands of great fertility. These were the sites of prosperous villages and fine farms. Here and there, in both villages and country were veritable palaces, the homes of captains of industry and landed nabobs who had sold their coal or "struck oil." Among these, however, were the third estate corresponding to the peasantry of Europe. These tilled fields, manned industry, and kept alive all the traditions of "poor white trash." As on the Monongahela, railroads paralleled one or both sides of the river. Tributary to these and the river were dirt roads extending into hinterlands that were the source of live stock, grain, fruits, timber, and other products, surpluses of which were hauled to "the River" by the use of horses, mules, and oxen.

Between Wheeling and Cairo and for miles inland on either side of the Ohio chief interest was in agriculture and grazing, but at such places as Parkersburg, Ironton, Hanging Rocks, Cincinnati, Louisville, and Evansville, industry had gained a foothold. The country around both Marietta and Parkersburg produced large quantities of crude oil. Hard wood lands, particularly those of West Virginia and Kentucky, were sources of seemingly inexhaustible supplies of timber which was being manufactured into cross-ties, lumber, and staves. But rich bottom lands produced grains of all kinds, while hilly lands supplied cattle, sheep, and fruit. As along the upper reaches of the Ohio, these products were transported to river markets over dirt roads and by the use of wagons. Arrived at their destination they supplied cargoes for boats, competing railroads being only in process of construction.

Throughout this vast area the extremes of life came face to face. There the highest culture came into constant contact with the basest ignorance; there were to be found the extremes of personal wealth and individual poverty. For example, the cultural traditions of both Cincinnati and Marietta were already well established, and here and there throughout the whole section were college bred men and others of the highest individual attainments; and, although not possessing the opulence of the "coal barons" of Pittsburgh, "oil magnates" were numerous in parts of this area, and successful merchants, bankers, and rivermen were everywhere. On the other hand was the proletariat, composed of all classes of beings from small farmers to poor whites. These resided in homes ranging all the way from modest cottages to the meanest log huts, and practiced an economy varying all the way from self-sufficiency to professional poverty. High schools were few and far between, and one section, as much as fifty miles in length and thirty miles wide, was churchless. As already indicated elsewhere, the whole area, but particularly that to the south of the Ohio, was one of comparatively arrested development.

Evidences of these facts and conditions are abundant, but only a few of those dealing with life on and near "the River" can be given here. Outstanding among these were numerous houseboats which, together with their more or less shiftless and nomadic inhabitants, were indicative of an unstable order. These boats were "scows" or "flats" varying in size, with low ceilinged cabins built upon them, sometimes of one room, sometimes of half a dozen, and varying in character from a mere shanty to a well-appointed cottage. Most of these craft floated on the river, moored to the bank, with a stage-plank running to the shore; but others were "beached," having found a comfortable nook in some high stage of water, and being fastened there, propped level with timbers and driftwood.

One who saw the inhabitants of these craft described them in these words:

Among the houseboat folk are young working couples starting out in life, and hoping ultimately to gain a foothold on land; unfortunate people, who are making a fresh start; men regularly employed in riverside factories and mills; invalids, who at small expense, are trying the fresh air cure; others, who drift up and down the Ohio, seeking casual work; and legitimate fishermen, who find it convenient to be near their nets, and to move about according to the needs of their calling. But a goodly portion of these boats are inhabited by the lowest class of the population, – poor "crackers" who have managed to scrape together enough money to buy, or enough energy and driftwood to build, such a craft; and, near or at the towns, many are occupied by gamblers, illicit liquor dealers, and others, who while plying nefarious trades, make a pretense of following the occupation of the Apostles.[333]

Both in town and country the houseboat element was in disfavor. It was not uncommon for these folk, beached or tied up, to remain unmolested in one spot for years, with their pigs, chickens, and little garden patch about them, and mayhap a swarm or two of bees and a cow and a horse. Occasionally, however, and as the result of spasmodic agitation, they were compelled to move on, for the majority of them were pilferers; farmers stood in awe of them and took precautions to protect chicken-roosts and vegetable gardens from their nocturnal visits. From fishing, shooting, collecting chance driftwood, and leading a desultory life along shore, they naturally fell into thieving habits. Having neither rent nor taxes to pay, and, for the most part, not voting and sharing in the political and social life of landsmen, they were a class unto themselves, in the state but not of it.

Interspersed among the houseboat denizens, but not of them, were many merchant peddlers, relics of a time and condition when transportation was wholly by water and dirt roads and when retail stores were few and far between. Their craft spent a day or two at each rustic landing, while their owners scoured the neighborhood for "junk" which they bought and collected in great heaps on the tops of their boats, giving therefor, at goodly prices, groceries, crockery, and "notions" which were also exchanged for eggs and dairy products that were, in turn, sold to passing steamers. There were, also, blacksmiths who moored their floating shops to a country beach or a village levee, wherever there was business; traveling "sawyers" with old steamboats made

[333] Thwaites, *op. cit.*, 52.

over into sawmills, who were employed by farmers to "work up" into lumber such saw-logs as they had been able to collect, the product usually being for local consumption; and a miscellaneous lot of craftsmen who lived and worked afloat; chairmakers, upholsterers, feather and mattress renovators, and photographers, who landed at villages, scattered their advertising matter abroad and remained only as long as patronage warranted.

In the autumn and winter seasons, numerous produce boats descended the Ohio. Like the craft mentioned above, they, too, were relics, but of a day when modern storage methods and refrigeration were practically unknown. They were great covered barges, quite of the fashion of ante-bellum barges, partitioned for the accommodation of passengers, freight, and live stock and propelled by long sweeps or oars, operated from the roof. Cargoes consisted chiefly of coarse vegetables and fruits and sometimes live stock, most of which was taken to Cincinnati and Louisville, but on occasional trips, to St. Louis and even to New Orleans. In this period many persons along the Ohio made a more or less regular business of this practice, and to this day their operators, locally known as "bargemen," constitute one of the closest river fraternities.

A form of amusement for this varied life was supplied by showboats, among them being the "Cotton Blossom," "French's Sensation," "Floating Palace," and "Water Queen." For the most part these boats specialized in theatricals, leaving to traveling circuses the menageries of the days of "Dan" Rice and P. T. Barnum, each of whom made his start on the Ohio. In fact, these boats were floating theatres towed from town to town by chartered steamboats, each of which, as a rule, carried a steam calliope whose "soul-stirring" music could be heard for miles inland. The annual return of this outfit, particularly the calliope, was almost an official proclamation of spring, being a more dependable sign of its coming than was the return of robins, the northward flight of wild geese, or the resumption of marble playing. Its summons was irresistible. Local church elders, Sunday school superintendents, and their families, usually denied such luxuries, found their way to its moorings, so that the children might have an opportunity to hear the "music." Sometimes these boats played a new town every night; sometimes, in regions that were populous and boasted a good back country, they remained a week, returning year after year.

Although of a somewhat earlier period than that described in this chapter, the following announcement, which was doubtless paid for in cash and invigorated by a liberal allowance of complimentary tickets, is indicative of the entertainment to be found on showboats in this period:

> The "Floating Palace," convoyed by the "James Raymond," will exhibit at the wharf at 2 o'clock P.M. and at 7. It carries one of the most splendid museums ever collected, embracing over 100,000 curiosities, among them being a live white bear. In the hall of the museum a series of performances will be given by Mr. Nellis, born without arms, and Madame Olinga, the beautiful and daring tight rope performer. In a fine concert room of the "James Raymond," Dave Reed's Minstrels discourse most eloquent music. These colored minstrels, led by Johnny Booker, are the best in the United States.[334]

Other sources of amusement were so-called pleasure-boats. These were found in greatest numbers on the Mississippi but were not unknown to the Ohio and its

---

[334] Wheeling *Intelligencer*, May 20, 1856.

tributaries. They were not self-propelled, the space generally used for boilers and engines being needed for other purposes. They were equipped with barrooms, dancing halls, dining rooms, state-rooms, and kitchens and were manned by women, many of whom were former "Cincinnati Janes" and "Louisville Belles" playing an unenviable rôle in the under world. In tow of a steamboat, or propelled by man power after the fashion of keelboats, these craft were usually on hand for sessions of local courts, and for church and political conventions, witnesses, jurors, justices, and delegates finding time to visit them in intervals between their efforts to mete out justice and uphold morals. To all external appearances pleasureboats were innocent, and, as they were generally owned by or operated in the interest of persons of means and influence, they did not come under the ban of the law, except in response to intermittent local demands which could be avoided by moving.

Incidentally reform movements had become regular institutions in all river towns, as elsewhere in the Ohio valley. Almost without exception they were inspired by local exhorters admonishing auditors to escape an everlasting torment by forsaking their sins, and were directed against pleasureboats, rum-shops, and other dens of iniquity. As a result, many towns became dry and spotless, and the reformed and awakened resolved to keep them thus. To this latter end pleasurcboats were driven away, and such packets as persisted in dispensing intoxicants in dry ports were boarded by singing and praying bands, some of which took bar-tenders in charge and entertained them in such a manner as to secure desired promises and, in some instances, professions of reform. As the result of such demonstrations and the general temperance wave that was then sweeping the country, many steamboat captains abolished barrooms, and some of them further commended themselves to "way folk" by earned reputations for total abstinence. As usual, such prohibition waves operated most directly and effectively upon the laboring element, negro rousters being among the first to appreciate this fact and to admonish the whites against the folly of attempts to reform the "nigger" and to make his money "no good no mo." [335]

These and other similar movements were, however, probable harbingers of a new and better order of things in the Ohio valley, where hard times had long made hard men. Local bullies were giving place to gentlemen; crudeness was gradually yielding a place to culture; and churches and school houses were becoming more plentiful, this being the period when local missionaries renewed their efforts to reclaim its churchless areas. Whereas many local persons of wealth continued to use their substance largely for personal and even sensual enjoyments, others turned to music, art, and literature. It was their interest and patronage that made the Cincinnati May Festival of the eighties a grand opera season for the whole Ohio valley, a veritable Mardi Gras, and caused Cincinnati to be referred to locally as the "Paris of America," whereas she had formerly been known as the Porkopolis of the West.[336] Moreover, local steamboat captains attended her classic functions and assured the traveling public that "accommodations to the next one will be better than to the last," and there are reasons to believe that they were actuated not alone by a love of Mammon.

The contributions of the Ohio continued, however,

---

[335] — *Idem,* November 29, 1883; Wheeling *Register,* February 10, 1874.
[336] Wheeling *Intelligencer,* May 1, 1882; *idem,* May 5, 1884.

to be largely economic. In many instances homes had been built out of materials salvaged from its waters, and farms along its banks had been paid for by proceeds from the sale of cordwood. For many people it was the only practicable road to market; for the capable it offered advancement, single families supplying as many as seven steamboat pilots; and for the small farmer and his squatter or poor white neighbors it provided employment. Fortunately the labor demands of the Ohio and the needs of those who lived along it supplemented each other. As a rule, the call of the former came after crops had been harvested, after children had started to school, after the zest for squirrel hunting had spent its force, and when money was needed for the payment of taxes and store bills. It mattered not that wages for deckhands and other laborers were rarely more than twenty-five dollars per month, with meals and lodging included, or that meals were served on deck in a tin pan, and lodging was provided by the use of a pine board. For many "the River" was the only dependable source of income. Along the upper Ohio, where negroes were as yet scarce and little used as laborers, the average small farmer could not afford to remain idle during the whole winter season. His wife and children could usually be depended upon to keep things going on the farm, even if at the sacrifice of the education and morals of the children. Therefore the farmer got a berth on the river, where he sometimes spent the whole boating season, unable and, in some instances, unwilling to go home, even for Christmas. When he indulged in the use of intoxicants and gambled, as many did, he returned poorer than he left, and in time was thrown back upon his family and society, a human derelict.

A cross section of the Ohio, as of the eighties, observed over a period of days from any point on its banks either one hundred miles below or above the "Mouth of Sandy," would have revealed a varied panorama of human effort and achievement, river life flowing and changing like the river itself. Lurking along the shore, either beached or moored, were houseboats, merchantboats, pleasureboats, and possibly a produceboat making ready for a trip to the lower Ohio and even to New Orleans. One would see, passing to and fro, majestic packets, locally referred to as "floating palaces," some of which could, by the use of electric lights, shoot a hole into the night a mile long, rendering the space covered as bright as day. If the period of observation happened to fall in a coalboat stage, coming down stream, at more or less regular intervals, could be seen numbers of low squatting, rustic towboats directing acres of barges loaded with coal. At the same time and in the same direction one might see passing rafts of logs and lumber floating to Cincinnati and Louisville, the songs of propelling raftsmen keeping time with oars and waves. Meanwhile, one might see slowly plodding towboats going up-stream pushing empties to be re-loaded with black diamond, and less frequently with bricks, cross-ties, lumber, crude oil, iron and steel, and the products of other industries. Finally, there might burst into sight an excursion boat or a showboat, the former bedecked with flags and banners and crowded to overflowing with hundreds of merry makers, and the latter, equipped with calliope, and calling the way folk to cease their toil for a temporary indulgence in pleasure.

But the most exciting incident in these views of river activity would be a boat-race, racing, despite the numerous efforts to regulate or suppress it, being the bane and the life of the Ohio. Although not within the range of the points indicated above, the effects of such an event may be gathered from a description of the famous races between the "Fleetwood" and the "New South" in the Cincinnati and Louisville trade, in 1890. The latter had just entered the trade as a competitor, reducing the fare for a round trip to one dollar and fifty cents, including meals and berth, whereupon the "Fleetwood," the regular packet, reduced its fare to fifty cents, including everything. As usual, the effect was to call forth numerous passengers, some of whom found it cheaper to travel than to stay at home. A contemporary has described the "war" that resulted in these words:

> The excitement on the boats was intense, as they ran side by side for miles, with their hundreds of passengers yelling for their boat and the crews taking every advantage to get the better of the race. The river banks would be crowded with lines of people shouting and waving their hats. Farmers drove to the river with their families in time to see these beautiful side-wheelers race by. At Madison, Indiana, where the only landing was made, the whole population would be on the levee cheering themselves hoarse.[337]

For the above and other local incidents and conditions river editors were both chroniclers and clearing-houses. Beginning with Professor J. A. Snodgrass of the Cincinnati *Enquirer* and James Locke of the Cincinnati *Gazette*, in the early post-bellum period, they included such popular and effective writers as Peter Lallance and his successor, George W. Budd, of the Cincinnati *Enquirer*, "Cons" Miller of the Cincinnati *Commerical*, and "Will" S. Hays of the Louisville *Courier Journal*. Popular correspondents for Pitts-

---

[337] *Waterways Journal*, October 22, 1927.

burgh newspapers were Captain William Evans for the *Times*, Robert Thornburgh for the *Commercial Gazette*, and Edward C. Sykes for the *Chronicle-Telegraph* which led in the fight for the freedom of the Monongahela river from toll charges, that resulted finally in the nationalization of its slackwater system. The names of all these writers became commonplace along the Ohio, and their productions set a high standard for their successors of today. Outstanding among these, together with their respective column headings, are Frank L. Sibley with his "Gallipolis Gossip," J. Mack Gamble with his "Upper Ohio," George A. Zerr and his "Pittsburgh News," Charles S. Henry and the "Missouri River," Parvin DeGaris and his "Evansville Events," A. Lee Patmore and the "Tennessee River," and Donald T. Wright, Fredrick Way, Jr., and other free lances.

In the post-bellum period the newspaper played an important rôle in the lives of those living on and near the Ohio river, particularly steamboatmen. Neither the telegraph nor the telephone was much used then, and all depended upon the newspaper to determine future weather conditions and stages of navigation. It, together with other articles of mail, mostly letters, was carried by local packets known as mailboats, among which there were many favorites. Mailboats ran on schedule time, low water boats being used, when necessary, to maintain regular deliveries. The sound of their whistles was as familiar as that of local church bells and town clocks. From a distance it summoned crowds to local levees, who, upon the arrival of their favorite packet, went aboard, some to greet friends, others to transact business, and still others to quench their thirst at the bar of the welcomed visitor. After the last bit of freight, which sometimes included a drove of cattle, sheep, or hogs, was safely aboard, and all had said goodby to the captain and the pilot, the crowd followed the postmaster to the postoffice to watch and share in the distribution of the mail. As yet private boxes were little used, for they were not necessary. The mail was emptied on the floor of the postoffice or, if the weather permitted, upon the ground, and was then distributed, item by item, by the postmaster after the fashion of an auctioneer disposing of goods at a fire sale.

Life on the Ohio proper was often best revealed in the songs and rhymes of those who followed and loved "the River." Like other rivers of the world, the Ohio bristles with romance, desperate adventure, mournful legend, and brilliant achievement, all of which have been fittingly commemorated in verse and song. In the following lines Uncle Henry Glenn, a former colored rouster, tells of the merits of the Ohio boats as compared with those he found on the Hudson:

> Dese steamboats on the Hudson,
> I guess dey's mighty fine,
> But de ain' got no paddle wheel!
> A-whirlin' roun' behine,
> Kickin' up de water
> An chawin' up de foam —
> De steamboats on de Hudson
> Ain' like de boats down home.
>
> De steamboats on de Hudson —
> Lord knows what makes 'em go —
> De ain' like de steam boats
> Dat I uster know,
> A-steamin' down Kanawhy
> An' de Ohio.
>
> I sho'ly miss de ole boats;
> I seem ter see 'em still;

City er Cincinnati,
And de City er Louisville,
De fine ole Annie Laury —
An' all dem was Queens —
An' der John K. Speed, a-speedin'
Clean down ter New Awleens!

Dem great white steamboats
Wid de smokestacks high,
Blowin' clouds er smoke out
On de wide blue sky;
Whistlin' in de mornin'
Way down roun' de ben'
An 'lawsy how I'd like ter see
De ole boats once ergain —

De schooners an' de liners,
An' de little tuggin' boats
A chuggin' through de water
Like bunch er frisky shoats,
Dey sho'ly goes a-bumpin'
But dis I wants ter know:
How come dem boats ain' got wheels
An' what makes 'em go?

I wuz fotch up on de ole boats
(No use fer me ter 'splain).
Git out de way an 'gimme room!
I's gwine home ergain.
I like de Hudson steamboats
But I jes got ter go
Back to de ole Kanawhy
An' de Ohio.

Of the many songs handed down from the boatmen to bargemen, raftsmen, and even to rousters the following is typical:

> The boatman is a lucky man,
> No one can do as the boatman can,
> The boatmen dance and the boatmen sing
> The boatman is up to everything.

Chorus

Hi O, the way we go
Floating down the O-h-i-o.

When the boatman goes on shore,
Look, old man, your sheep is gone,
He steals your sheep and steals your shote,
He puts 'em in a bag and tots 'em to the boat.

Chorus

When the boatman goes on shore,
He spends his money and works for more;
I never saw a girl in all my life
But that would be a boatman's wife.

Chorus

Of the difficulties in navigation at the narrow bend in the Ohio below Ravenswood, a Parkersburg lawyer of distinction, who had served time as a deckhand, used to sing:

Letart Falls and Graham Station:
The meanest places in all creation.
Little Amity between,
A meaner place I never have seen.

And a chorus used by colored rousters with most any combination of words ran:

Rango, Oh! Ho,
Rango, Rango.

Of the many stanzas inspired by the "rollicking" negro rouster, the following are among the best:

Ho, stevedore! Ho, roustabout!
The whistle's shriek has called you out.
You very interesting man,
Whose color grades from black to tan,
Whose hat is really nondescript,
Whose pants are patches, mostly ripped.
Come take your station on the bow,
We're going to make a landing now.

Haul in that line, haul, haul, I say;
Now swing the gangplank, more this way
Now ease 'er, stop 'er, let 'er go!
Pick up, pick up, you're far too slow.
Run out that hawser, up the bank,
You coal-black nigger, long and lank.
Lift up those sacks, get under, you!
You'll lift your wages, when they're due.
Up with that barrel, pick it up,
You long-legged, splay-foot, brown-eyed pup!

The rouster's a happy bird,
And human is, about one-third.
He aims to make of work a play,
He lives and plans for just to-day.
His work is heavy, hours are long.
He brightens both with grin and song.
Dame Fortune's knocks are simply "taps,"
If he can only win at craps.
His bed's the boat, on sack or plank.
He's wide awake at ship bell's clank.

O happy, care-free nigger man,
Perhaps yours is the better plan.
Why worry over things ahead?
Short, jovial life, a long time dead.[338]

Post-bellum steamboating in the interior inspired numerous other verses and rhymes of a more classical variety than the above, that were received favorably along the Ohio and tributary streams. First among these were stanzas from John Hay, a product of the Ohio valley, where his "Jim Bludso of the Prairie belle"[339] has long been a favorite, but scarcely less so than "Will" S. Hays's "Down in de Corn Fiel" and his "Roll out, Heave Dat Cotton." The publication of

---

[338] These lines were written by Dr. A. S. Greenwood of Chicago. See *Waterways Journal*, June 6, 1914.

[339] In writing this poem Colonel Hay is said to have selected the name of a boat to suit his rhymes. See *Waterways Journal*, December 7, 1918.

Songs and Poems by Hays (1886) marked the beginning of an epoch in the literary life of the Ohio that was closely related to that larger epoch that gave to the nation the Indiana school of poets and authors. Since, numerous other writers have memorialized the Ohio and its tributaries and such individual packets as the "Katie," "Kate Adams," "Natchez," and "Robert E. Lee" in lines that will live.[340]

The packets themselves, settled along lines of utility, comfort, and safety and, while representing the last word in speed, capacity, and accommodations, became worlds in miniature. The hold carried freight in quantities sufficient to equip and maintain a small army; the main deck held the boilers, engines, kitchens, accommodations for deck passengers, and room for as much more freight as could be piled aboard; the boiler deck contained the cabins, consisting of the boat's office, barroom, state-rooms in the waist, and the women's cabin aft. All these were reached by stairs leading up from the forward part of the main deck, called the fore-castle. A promenade ran around the boat between the state-rooms and the rail. The roof of the cabin was called the hurricane deck and held another row of cabins for the officers, called the "Texas" which was first added about the time of the annexation of the Lone Star State. On the lower deck and forward were the common folk – rousters, firemen, and deck pasengers, all full of noise and song, and too often of whiskey, whilst above, in the deck cabin, were all sorts of men and women, of all trades, from all parts of the world, and of all possible manners and habits. For all these the boat provided food in abundance, every boat being

---

[340] — *Idem*, July 20, 1907; *idem*, October 23, 1909; *idem*, January 29, 1921; *idem*, April 30, 1921; *idem*, May 21, 1921.

known by its table, or, in the more vulgar terminology of the deck, by its "grub."

Among all the officers of this little world state the pilot was the most potent. He has been fittingly described as a king. By experience and training and the use of a sort of sixth sense that enabled him to detect and avoid danger, he was a law unto himself, his direction of a boat being absolute. He could start or lay up when he chose; he could pass a landing regardless of the wishes of those ashore or others aboard; he could take a boat into what seemed certain destruction, if he had that mind, and the captain was obliged to stand by, helpless and silent, for the law was with the pilot in everything. Furthermore, the pilot was a gentleman. His work was clean and physically light. It ended the instant his boat tied to the landing, and it did not begin until it was ready to back into the water. Perched high in his glass enclosure, dressed in the height of fashion, and observed by all, he was a target for many smiles and greetings and was much sought by the women.

The captain was less fortunate. Knowing that commerce is a relentless master holding nothing in sacred remembrance that does not carry with it a golden reward, he had to be first of all a business man. But he was more. He, too, was a gentleman, and much of his success depended upon that fact. Not only did he provide for the comfort, accommodation, and entertainment of his passengers, but any real captain had to be a veritable encyclopedia, able to answer readily and accurately any question that might be propounded to him. On one short trip he might be asked questions about any, all, or more of such subjects as the depth, width, and length of the river; the geological, chronological, and agricultural statistics of the country;

population, wealth, and crops; leading and prominent characteristics of the people; their origin, average height, complexion, color of hair and eyes, nature of disposition, temperament, rate of increase and decrease; number of births, marriages, and deaths or serious attacks of illness; relative proportion of male and female progeny and why; causes of decline in prosperity and the different ways in which such disasters might have been avoided; the political, social, and religious peculiarities of the people, etc., etc. The ability to answer any and all such questions, with a knowing smile, was one of the tests of a good and successful captain, the curiosity of the traveling public, particularly the Yankee part of it, being as insatiable as was its appetite.

Of all the other employees of an Ohio river packet — engineers, clerks, stewards, mates, and chambermaids included — rousters were most important. On the upper Ohio many of them were white, but on its lower course they were mostly colored. Some of the former "followed the river" all their lives, while others came and went, as determined by financial necessities. Despite a fondness for "barrel-houses" and crap games and a memory that simply could not retain steamboat schedules, the negro rouster was fairly dependable. Recently an experienced steamboatman has proclaimed him "the noblest black man that God ever made."[341] A fine physical specimen, strong, cheerful, and ready to work at any hour of the day or night, or all day and all night, he was, while aboard, ready to stand by his favorite packet through thick and thin. He led the cheering at its races, composed the songs commemorating its achievements, and fought the maligners of its fair name. To-day some of his descendents are graduates of

---

[341] — *Idem*, December 9, 1911; *idem*, August 21, 1920.

THE MEMPHIS PACKET.
By George Willard Bonte

Waitin' on de landin'
  Fo' de Memphis Packet;
Dozin' in de shadow
  Ob de wa'house shed;
Green hides, tied up,
  Stinkin' in de sunshine;
Watahmelons piled up
  High ez yo' head.

De flies am a-bitin'
  An' de bees am a-hummin',
Sparrow birds a-rootin'
  In de dusty road,
Heah dat steamboat
  Coughin' up de ribber,
Eb'ry black niggah
  Gotta he'p unload.

See dem smokestacks
  A-comin' 'roun' de san' bar,
De pilot am a-pullin'
  On de big brown wheel.
Heah dat paddle
  A-churnin' up de watah—
Makes de pickaninny
  Clap his han's an' squeal.

De drays come a-crikin'
  Down de slantin' levy;
De hotel a-cookin'
  Up de po'k an' beans.

See dem white fo'ks
  A-leanin' on de railin',
Dey trabbled all de way heah
  F'um New O'leans.

De tackle am a-squeakin'
  An' de gangplank a-swingin',
De big buck niggahs
  Hol' de rope in han'.
De Capt'n am a-watchin'
  An' de mate am a-cussin',
De white fo'ks a-crowdin'
  'Cause dey wants to lan.

Push dat truck, coon,
  Jes' a li'l' quicker.
Grab dat calf
  By de ear an' tail.
Toss dem melons
  Jes' a li'l' faster,
If y' bus' a single one ob **dem**
  Yo'll lan' in jail.

De loadin' am finished
  An' de bell am a-ringin',
De gangplank a-standin'
  On his two hin' laigs.
Pay dis niggah
  Fo' his w'uk an' sweatin'—
Lemme git home
  To m' ham an' aigs.

Typical Rousters of the lower Ohio and Mississippi together with expressions of their sentiments

leading colleges and universities, but it is doubtful whether they are happier than were their fathers.

Except pilots, few river employees were organized. In 1826 steamboatmen of Pittsburgh organized the "Snag Marines" for social purposes, but near the Civil war, pilots' associations took the form of modern trade unions with "lodges" at Cincinnati, Louisville, St. Louis, and New Orleans. About the same time, also, a few engineers organized. In imitation of their employees, captains and other boat owners then talked of pooling their interests to the end that competition might be eliminated and profits shared in proportion to capital invested, but nothing was done. After a stubborn fight for existence, graphically depicted by Mark Twain in his *Life on the Mississippi*, pilots' associations were able to boost salaries to five hundred dollars per month in the Civil war period, but they themselves led in a movement for reduction in the period immediatly following, thus making possible their continued existence. Among their subsequent achievements, some of which were already in process of consummation, were: provisions for sickness and unemployment benefits for members; similar arrangements for their widows and orphans; a system of lights, maintained at national expense, for indicating navigable channels, as well as dangers to navigation on the inland rivers; and a system for the interchange, among members, of information regarding the conditions of navigation.[342]

Steamboat passengers found amusement in card games, even gambling. The average passenger did not object to a game "to pass the time away" and was not

---

[342] Cincinnati *Gazette*, September 24, 1853; Wheeling *Intelligencer*, September 24, 1853; *idem*, September 28, 1853; *idem*, January 19, 1859; *idem*, July 2, 1860; *idem*, September 26, 1860; Cincinnati *Commercial*, January 19, 1867; Pittsburgh *Dispatch*, April 10, 1879.

averse to betting enough to "make it interesting." Among them were always enough "suckers" to make a fair catch for the professional gamblers who then followed the river in large numbers, some of them clad in ministerial garb, others as pleasant amiable gentlemen, and still others as plain matter-of-fact business men. For all such gamblers, regardless of their attire or bearing, the passenger packet was a paradise. There was usually plenty of money aboard; time hung heavily on everyone; a holiday spirit permeated the whole situation; and victims came and went. Only a few captains attempted to protect passengers from their own foolishness, the severest punishment inflicted upon gamblers, as upon others, being to set them off into the willows. Thus protected by few restraints, professional gamblers, such as George H. Devol, "Dan" Kimball, and John Powell, plied their art almost continuously, relieving victims of money, watches, clothing, and in slavery days, of negroes, and even of plantations.

On the lower deck, gambling was a veritable mania. Deck passengers took a hand at cards as long as they could "make it interesting," and between landings colored rousters gathered in knots to shoot crap. Their familiar "seben come eleben" continued until some lucky fellow had won everything in sight, after which he usually sought the shore for a fling in its rum-shops and bawdy-houses.

When participants were intoxicated, and many of them were, games of chance frequently ended in free-for-all fights. In the upper cabins such encounters were usually adjusted without the use of weapons, but on deck they were more frequently negotiated by the use of pieces of wood, lumps of coal, knives and pistols, and other material arguments. Here and there on the

Ohio, as elsewhere in the interior, were a few hairy-breasted, muscle knotted, wiry giants, survivals of the boatmen and represented by Guyan Wright, who continued to fight for the love of it. When two such bullies met, either drunk or sober, a fight to the finish was in order; a ring was formed; and they entered for an encounter which sometimes lasted for hours, no quarter being asked or given by either contestant.

Passengers were not, however, always thrown upon their own resources for amusement.[343] In the early eighties practically every important Ohio river packet carried a colored orchestra, some of which were composed of members of the crew. Leaders of such aggregations were rather privileged, and some of them were very popular. Among these was "Ben" Coleman, a bass-violinist, who was much sought for his pleasing rendition of the "Mocking Bird" and "How Much Does the Baby Weigh." Still other celebrities were Alfred Smith and Charlie Robinson. During excursion seasons their services were regarded as indispensable.

Despite their resourcefulness and bravery most rivermen could not overcome their superstitions. For example, most of them believed that accidents came in triplicate; a white horse or cat aboard was an ill omen; rats were welcomed, as long as they did not desert the ship in considerable numbers; a worn sock tied around a sick man's neck was a sure cure for fevers of all kinds; horseshoes brought good luck; and the presence of a corpse aboard was insignificant, rousters and engineers using the container as a card table. Ghosts, however, were another matter, numerous places along the river, scenes of horrible accidents, being known to be haunted. Once in a while an "upstart" bobbed up among the

---

[343] *Waterways Journal*, December 12, 1914; *idem*, November 6, 1920.

younger generation of rivermen, who did not share these and numerous other superstitions, but he was laughed at by his fellows.

Such conditions kept officers, crews, and passengers, particularly passengers, in a state of suspense. Although navigation was greatly improved, and the art and science of steamboat construction had attained a high degree of perfection, and Congress required and regulated the licensing of pilots and engineers and the inspection of boilers, cautious passengers still slept near their life preservers. Some kept them hanging in their berth, inflated and ready for use at a moment's warning. To all such the least alarm or outcry was a signal for action, and scenes like the following, as told by an eye witness, were enacted: "In the midst of the hubbub, the door of the ladies' cabin flew wide open, and out burst a fat lady, dressed all in white, her face a map of terror and her waist surrounded by a life preserver, not inflated. Seizing this by the nipple with both hands, she rushed from one person to another exclaiming, in a voice of anguish, 'Blow me up! Blow me up! For God's sake blow me up!! Will nobody blow me up!!!"

The normal river life of the Ohio, as it existed in the early eighties, may be summarized by a review of a typical wharf scene preceding the departure of the "St. Lawrence," a packet in the Wheeling-Cincinnati trade.[344] The local newspaper press described her presence, either coming or going, as putting "the world on the warf." Bells were ringing; mates and draymen were swearing; negroes were singing; clerks were writing; and boxes, barrels, and bundles were rolling and tumbling. Thirty to forty rousters chased one another up and

---

[344] Wheeling *Register*, November 25, 1874; Wheeling *Intelligencer*, June 2, 1883; *idem*, November 12, 1883.

down the gang-plank, and above the monotony of it all could be heard the words "down below," as heavy articles of freight dropped into the hold. Now and then a barrel rolled off the gang-plank into the river and was chased by the rouster in charge, and the other rousters protested being pressed too closely. Otherwise all moved like clock work. From above, a hundred or more passengers gazed upon the scene and exchanged greetings with their companions and friends upon the shore, while the pilot surveyed it all from his throne on the "Texas." When darkness overtook the preparations, blazing Jacks were used to light up freight piles and gangways, and the scene continued.

Commercial Decadence

During the first and greater part of the opening decade of the present century signs pointed to continued prosperity for the river transportation interests of the Ohio valley. The years immediately preceding were record breakers in the amount of local tonnage carried, which increased during the first years of the period under consideration. The outstanding development was an increase in bulk traffic: coal, lumber, grain, sand, gravel, iron, and steel. Regular passenger packets, although reduced in number, were improved in quality and continued to hold their own generally. In 1905 those on the Ohio carried more than two million passengers, a larger number being ferried across its channel.[345]

In view of impending changes a more detailed account of traffic on the Ohio and its tributaries for the opening years of this decade is desirable. On its lower course, below Louisville, the St. Louis and Tennessee River Packet Company, with a capital of one hundred fifty thousand dollars, operated a fleet of six freight and passenger steamers between St. Louis and Waterloo, Alabama, carrying general merchandise south and forest products north; the Cumberland and Tennessee Transportation Company, with a capital of forty thousand dollars, operated two steamers and eighteen barges between Nashville, Tennessee, and Burkesville, Kentucky, and also, to Carthage, Tennessee, carrying staves,

[345] Inland Waterways Commission, *Preliminary Report* 1908, 118.

lumber, cross-ties, and coal; the Ryman line, with fifty-seven thousand dollars invested, operated a fleet of six packets between Nashville, Tennessee, and Evansville, Indiana, Paducah, Mills Springs, and Albany, Kentucky, carrying tobacco, live stock, grain of all kinds, pig iron, and general merchandise; and, with a capital of twenty-five thousand dollars, the Evansville, Paducah, and Cairo Packet line used two packets between Evansville and Paducah, carrying fluorspar, general merchandise, and farm products.[346]

On the middle Ohio, between Louisville and the Great Kanawha, there were a number of lines, most important of which was the Louisville and Cincinnati Packet Company, successor to the famous Mail line. With a capital stock of two hundred fifty thousand dollars it operated six steamers carrying passengers and all kinds of freight, other than bulk. Northward from Cincinnati was a remnant of the old White Collar line whose packets were giving way to those of the Cincinnati, Pomeroy, and Charleston Packet Company, later known as the Greene line. Under the direction of Captain Gordon C. Greene and his capable wife, Mary Becker Greene, who functioned equally well as captain or pilot, this line was operating packets between points indicated by its name, with occasional trips to Wheeling and Pittsburgh. Cargoes consisted of general merchandise going east, farm products going west, and passengers in each direction.[347]

On the upper Ohio the Pittsburgh and Cincinnati Packet line, with approximately two hundred thousand dollars invested, operated never less than three regular packets, carrying iron and steel manufactures, glass, and merchandise south and farm products, whiskey,

---

[346] — *Idem*, 109-110. [347] — *Idem*, 110.

furniture, and leather goods north. The Wheeling and Parkersburg Packet Company had reorganized as the Pittsburgh, Wheeling, and Parkersburg Packet line and was operating three steamers which carried, for the most part, the same kind of cargoes as did the packets in the Pittsburgh and Cincinnati trade. Moreover, the Muskingum, Great Kanawha, and Monongahela rivers each had their own packet lines with one or more regular packets.

Coal continued to be the largest single item transported by way of the Ohio. It was shipped in large quantities by the Monongahela Consolidated Coal and Coke Company. For this purpose this company owned eighty towboats and steamers and about four thousand coalboats, barges, and other craft. Its total river shipments for 1906 aggregated almost five million tons, one-half of which was consumed locally. At the same time a dozen other companies were transporting coal on the upper Ohio, some of them exclusively for local use, others to down river markets. Prominent among the latter were Charles Jutte and Company and the A. R. Budd Company.[348] Some of the operations of the above named firms were spectacular. For example, in October, 1907, the local press recorded the departure, from the pools about Pittsburgh, of sixteen hundred and eighty-five coal barges containing almost thirty-six million one hundred twenty-five thousand bushels.[349]

Meanwhile the volume of coal shipped south from mines in southern West Virginia was increasing annually. Most of this went to Cincinnati, where it was re-shipped by rail to points in the interior, more than twenty elevators being used there for re-shipping purposes. In 1905 mines on the Great Kanawha disposed

---

[348] —*Idem*, 112.   [349] *Waterways Journal*, October 19, 1907.

of one million four hundred sixty thousand tons in this way. At the same time shipments were being made by river from Huntington, West Virginia, to elevators at Sekidan, a few miles below Cincinnati, where coal was re-shipped by rail to points inland.[350] Some railroads terminating at Cincinnati had not formed through connections with other roads and welcomed river coal as a profitable inland-bound tonnage.

Next in importance to the coal traffic on the Ohio was that in timber and its products. In 1907 savings on this method of transportation aggregated three million dollars.[351] From its tributaries in West Virginia and Kentucky the Ohio then received great quantities of cross-ties and logs of poplar, oak, walnut, and other woods. Most of these came from points far inland, having been transported first over "tram-roads" and then by small streams to the Ohio. Here they were assembled, the cross-ties in barges and the logs in rafts, and towed and floated to market, lumber forming return cargoes. A familiar sight was the "boom" with its impounded "catch" of "ties" and logs aggregating, in some instances, millions of units. When the boom nearest the Ohio broke, as it sometimes did, the water below was literally covered with floating cross-ties and logs. On such occasions denizens of houseboats and others reaped small fortunes for their services in catching and holding logs and ties until claimed by their owners. In such cases identification was made possible by the use of "brands" imbedded in one or both ends of every log or tie by use of a steel-die hammer.

As already indicated, other leading items in the bulk traffic of the Ohio at this time were grain, sand, gravel,

---

[350] Inland Waterways Commission, *op. cit.*, 114.
[351] — *Idem*, 117.

COMMERCIAL DECADENCE 351

iron, and steel.[352] At Evansville and Henderson most of the corn grown in southern Illinois and Indiana was stored by local farmers in warehouses for shipment by river to Cumberland and Tennessee ports. On the upper Ohio the work of dredging and delivering sand and gravel had already commenced, both being used for building purposes and concrete work and the sand, also, for making steel and glass. Meanwhile, river shipments of iron and steel were increasing in volume. In 1905 the "River combine" alone shipped almost sixty thousand tons to Louisville and southern markets.

Although incomplete, statistics of Ohio river traffic for this period reveal its importance. For a period of years, 1900-1906 inclusive, the traffic aggregated annually more than twelve million tons, which was three million tons greater than the annual average for a similar period immediately preceding. In each instance these figures included coal but not the entire amount of other bulk freight, particularly grain and timber, statistics for traffic below Louisville being incomplete.[353]

The craft used tended to adapt themselves more and more to special needs and trades.[354] Everywhere there was a noticeable tendency on the part of passenger packets to reach out for bulk traffic and to use barges. The Louisville and Cincinnati Packet Company alone stuck to palatial packets and the transportation of passengers and small freight. On the other hand the Barrett line, with headquarters at Cincinnati, transported only bulk freight using towboats and barges. This was also true of the Ayer and Lord Barge Company with headquarters at Paducah. In 1907 this firm was the largest dealer in cross-ties in the world and operated a

---
[352] — *Idem*, 112-113. [353] U. S. War Department, *Interim Report*, 1927, 8.
[354] Inland Waterways Commission, *op. cit.*, 94, 131.

half dozen or more towboats and scores of barges which reached practically every important port in the Ohio valley and the Middle West. Meanwhile, the Bay line, with headquarters at Ironton and a continuous existence since the mid-sixties, used both packets and towboats.

Another significant development was that toward corporate ownership and management of river property. Formerly this property was owned and operated either by individuals or by partnerships. But by 1907 there were only sixteen individual owners and six partnerships to be found on the interior waters, whereas the corporations owning and operating river craft there had increased to fifty.[355]

More significant still was the zeal and enthusiasm of local rivermen and their friends over proposals for the improved navigation of the inland waters. About 1906 the Ohio Valley Improvement Association took on new life and developed an enthusiasm that became contagious. Soon every important tributary to the Ohio had its own internal improvement association, each organized, as had been the parent association, to promote local improvements and the interests of inland navigation generally. The combined efforts of these associations were determining influences with President Roosevelt in his action of March 14, 1907, appointing an inland waterways commission "to prepare and report a comprehensive plan for the improvement and control of the river systems of the United States."[356]

During the years immediately following 1907 enthusiasm for the Ohio and its interests found frequent

---

[355] —*Idem*, 99-108.

[356] Moulton, H. G. *Waterways versus Railways* (Boston, 1912), 5-9; *Waterways Journal*, 1907-1908, passim.

COMMERCIAL DECADENCE

expression locally, Pittsburgh vying with Cincinnati for leadership in such manifestations. Examples from the activities of Pittsburgh will suffice. On September 30, 1908, as a part of a sesqui-centennial celebration, she observed "Marine Day" in what was probably her greatest tribute to the Ohio. The outstanding feature of this day was a river pageant moving from Smithfield street to Davis island and return and passing in review outstanding incidents in the history of the Ohio river. Among these were Indians in canoes, La Salle and his companions in conformity to unfounded traditions, Celeron and his leaden plates, George Washington and Christopher Gist together on a raft, Nicholas J. Roosevelt and the "New Orleans," and towboats, dredges, and motorboats, in turn.[357]

Three years later Pittsburgh again took the initiative in celebrating the one hundredth anniversary of the introduction of steam navigation on the western waters.[357a] To this end she financed the construction of a replica of the original "New Orleans." The later "New Orleans" was launched with fitting ceremony, President Taft and numerous others participating. Under the command of Captain James A. Henderson, her builder, this craft, a side-wheeler, later descended the Ohio and the Mississippi, retracing as nearly as possible the course of her epoch making predecessor. Everywhere along the route she was an object of curiosity-inspiring reflections upon the achievements of a century – in the field of transportation, the greatest in the history of the world.

Meanwhile other forces and incidents were making

[357] King, Sidney. *The Story of the Sesqui-Centennial Celebration of Pittsburgh* (Pittsburgh, 1910).

[357a] For full account of proceedings see *Ohio Arch. and Hist. Quarterly*, vol. xxii, 1-125.

for what promised to be a new and great era in the history of inland transportation. Following a preliminary report of the Inland Waterways Commission, 1908, giving information regarding the extensive and profitable use then being made of the rivers of continental Europe and warning against the consequences of a threatened "commercial decadence" on our own,[358] public opinion became more intelligent and assertive in behalf of the improved navigation of our inland waters. As a result former "pork barrel" methods of using public funds for improving rivers and harbors were condemned; the preparation of a comprehensive plan for the improvement of the inland waters was demanded and provided; and, in a short time, a program was announced that called for the completion of a system of locks and dams to cover the whole course of the Ohio. Repeated failures of railroads to serve transportation needs in times of crises seemed to necessitate the immediate completion of this program, which was accordingly announced for the year 1922. The Monongahela river, then carrying the largest river traffic in the world, was an ever present reminder of the possibilities of slackwater on the Ohio.[359]

Nevertheless transportation on the Ohio river system again entered a decline. Unlike that of the preceding fifties this decline proved fatal to the old order of things. A remarkable vitality, sustained by large investments and resourceful leadership, prolonged the struggle, but the forces making for change were numerous, powerful, and in some instances unscrupulous, and in time prevailed. The appeal of local rivermen to corporate methods of owning and operating their prop-

[358] Inland Waterways Commission, *op. cit.*, 377-435.
[359] *Waterways Journal*, August 28, 1920.

erty, already mentioned, was an admission of their inability to carry on under existing conditions, as was also their appeal to President Roosevelt and their requests of this period that the whole matter of river rates and traffic be turned over to the Interstate Commerce Commission.[360]

Evidence of the commercial decadence that followed is abundant. A few typical examples relating to the Ohio will suffice. In 1908 both the Pittsburgh and Cincinnati Packet Company and the Louisville and Evansville Packet line were forced into receiverships, and their holdings were sold, those of the former bringing twenty-two thousand two hundred dollars, those of the latter eighteen thousand seven hundred dollars, in each case only one-fifth the appraised value.[361] Formerly the derelict and superfluous tonnage of the Ohio had found markets on the Mississippi and its lower tributaries, but these were now closed, the decadence of the rivers being general. In less than a decade after 1908 Pittsburgh ceased to send towboats to the South or even to the lower Ohio, her entire output of coal being consumed locally, and river shipments of coal on its lower course were temporarily curtailed. The local press described the situation in these words: "Never before has Ohio river tonnage been so worthless." Much of what was left was carried to destruction in the ice floes of 1918, the aggregate value of the tonnage, dredges, and terminals then destroyed in this manner reaching almost six million dollars.[362] For years before this event, however, one could travel along the upper Ohio below Wheeling for a whole day and never see a steamboat.

---

[360] — *Idem*, August 15, 1908; *idem*, November 9, 1907.
[361] — *Idem*, April 29, 1910; *idem*, August 20, 1910; *idem*, October 1, 1910.
[362] — *Idem*, January 18, 1919.

Worse still this decline affected the ardor of local rivermen and the "friends of the river" generally and was reflected in the local press which now gave serious consideration to suggestions looking to the abandonment of further efforts to improve the navigation of the Ohio and its tributaries. When the press did mention the rivers for other purposes, it was generally to laud a glorious past and to tell distressing stories of existing conditions. Even the game fish for which the Ohio had been famous disappeared, victims of or refugees from the acids with which industry was polluting its waters.

Here and there only did physical reminders of the former splendor of the river remain. About Pittsburgh, under conditions presented elsewhere, river traffic increased annually in volume, as did that southward from the Great Kanawha and Huntington. About Parkersburg local "oil booms" and industrial developments kept alive short packet trades, and Captain Greene and his wife continued to operate their packets in a trade between Cincinnati and Huntington and Charleston, West Virginia, and Gallipolis and Pomeroy, Ohio. In the trade between Cincinnati and Louisville conditions were favorable, and Captain Laidley carried on despite the failures of others. Meanwhile traffic in timber, grain, and other raw materials kept alive declining trades on the lower Ohio, Cumberland, and Tennessee rivers, sustaining packet lines in favor with railroads, and with the Barrett, Bay, and other packet lines. Otherwise the commercial decadence of the rivers was practically complete.

The causes of this decline were numerous, and the effects were varied and sometimes subtle. All causes were, however, contributory, no one of them singly being powerful enough to effect a destruction so complete.

Possibly first and most effective among them was a shortsighted policy that had neglected to improve inland navigation and had failed to provide adequate river terminal facilities. "Pork barrel" methods of administering federal funds were largely responsible for the former condition. Solution of the latter, where it was attempted at all, was left to private initiative. As a result snags, sandbars, shifting channels, and alternating high and low waters continued to make the navigation of the Ohio and its unimproved tributaries uncertain, and freight could not be handled with safety and dispatch at local levees. Under the complex and intricate economic conditions, the mainspring of which was competition, traffic shifted from rivers to railroads but not without considerable assistance, some of it of a questionable character, from the latter.

Some attributed this transition wholly to an alleged inadequacy of rivers to meet the transportation needs of a new age. Among these were most of those prophets who had for a long time predicted the final passing of the steamboat and the barge from our inland waters. The fact that the decline of river commerce was general, even where conditions were favorable, as on the Hudson and the lower Mississippi, was urged as a proof of their contentions which ignored the fact that European river traffic was increasing in volume to the benefit of railroads and of all parties concerned, and that, too, under less favorable natural conditions than in America.[363] Others regarded the fallen conditions

---

[363] Moulton, *Waterways versus Railways*, 77-96; Inland Waterways Commission, *op. cit.*, 375-435; F. H. Dixon's "Traffic History of the Mississippi River System," in *Report of National Waterways Commission* (Washington, 1909), document no. 11; Edgar A. Holt's "Missouri River Transportation in the Expansion of the West," in *Missouri Hist. Review*, vol. xx, 361-381.

of river traffic in America as a national calamity and fixed the responsibility therefor largely upon the railroads.

In their competitive warfare with river transportation interests railroads adhered to no common policy, methods varying to suit particular needs and conditions. Only the more important practices used in the Ohio valley are considered here. They are presented in the following order which, although open to some criticism, is meant to be suggestive of their relative importance: (1) consolidations resulting in advantages to the railroads in the transportation of first-class freight; (2) the more efficient organization of railroad service; (3) refusals of railroads to coöperate with water lines in prorating arrangements; (4) railroad control of river terminals and terminal facilities; and (5) railroad control of waterways and their carriers.[364]

The workings of the first two of these practices can best be understood in the light of historical developments making them possible. About 1897 the Baltimore and Ohio Railroad Company, which was then interested in rich West Virginia coal and timber lands contiguous to its lines, acquired a controlling interest in the Cincinnati, Washington, and Baltimore railroad, connecting Parkersburg and Cincinnati, which soon thereafter became the Baltimore and Ohio Southwestern railroad and acquired, in its own right, the Ohio and Mississippi railroad connecting Cincinnati and St. Louis. Meanwhile lateral lines were built, acquired, and leased, extending the Baltimore and Ohio system to St. Louis and paralleling the Ohio to the north by a network of tracks along most of its course. In 1889 the Chesapeake and Ohio railroad, which also passed

---
[364] Moulton, *op. cit.*, 78-96.

through rich coal and timber sections of West Virginia, extended its track from Huntington to Cincinnati and later effected through connections to Chicago, laterals being meanwhile extended to additional coal and timber fields in West Virginia and Kentucky. Moreover, about the same time the Louisville and Nashville railroad, over which large shipments of coal were accustomed to pass south from Louisville, became interested in coal mines in Tennessee and southern Kentucky and effected working arrangements with railroads to the north.[365]

Thus entrenched, the chief railroads of the Ohio valley proceeded to build a "fence" about the coal operators and shippers who were using the lower Ohio with Cincinnati as a chief base of operations. Materials for this obstructive fence were discriminating rates, control of car supplies, and inadequate re-shipping terminals. With each succeeding year this so-called fence came nearer Cincinnati and other re-shipping points and became so secure in other ways as to be in local terminology practically "bull high and hog tight."

Examples of typical methods used in its construction are informing. In the interest of the Baltimore and Ohio railroad freight rates and reshipping charges on river coal from Cincinnati were made so high that they could not compete in local markets with the price of coal produced about Fairmont, West Virginia, and Luhrig, Ohio, from mines in which railroads were interested. At the same time the Louisville and Nashville railroad charged more for carrying coal to points twenty-five and thirty miles inland from the Ohio than it did for carrying its own coal to the same points from

---

[365] Inland Waterways Commission, *op. cit.*, 375; Hungerford, *Story of the Baltimore and Ohio Railroad*, vol. ii, 227.

mines in Tennessee and southern Kentucky.[366] In the absence of court decisions on the commodities clause of the Hepburn act enacted 1906, forbidding railroads to transport freight which they themselves produced, and in the absence of control by the Interstate Commerce Commission these practices were ruinous to local river traffic in coal and were not helpful to that in other first-class freight. In despair some rivermen suggested the possibility of a remedy for their ills in anti-rebating laws of Congress.

In the second place railroad extensions and consolidations made possible systematic methods of handling traffic and advertising rail service. Already the great trunk lines crossing the Ohio at right angles were familiar with these devices. In 1885 the Cullom Committee of Congress found the "most effective cause of relative increase in railway tonnage" to be "administrative organization of the railway companies." The same committee noted, also, that the "inventive genius and the business talent of the country" were drifting to the railroads, "leaving waterways comparatively neglected."[367] After 1900 these tendencies became realities throughout the Ohio valley, particularly along the Ohio itself. Every important center had its railroad agent, one or more, in many cases former rivermen, actively engaged in soliciting traffic and boosting railroads, whereas the rivers got only such traffic as sought them.

The third of these practices, refusal to coöperate in prorating arrangements, was generally injurious but particularly so to passenger packets. In both the eighties and the nineties most Ohio river packets, as well as those on tributary streams, had such arrangements,

---

[366] Inland Waterways Commission, *op. cit.*, 111-116.
[367] Moulton, *op. cit.*, 86.

which after 1900 were practically all withdrawn. In 1907 only four lines enjoyed such benefits.[368] A few others like the Louisville and Cincinnati Packet Company which had close working relations with the Louisville and Nashville railroad, were able to continue without them, but, as has been shown, other packets went out of business. To this day scores of former steamboatmen trace their decisions to leave the river to the refusal of railroads to prorate freight receipts.[369]

In a letter to Major H. C. Newcomer of United States Army Engineers, August 19, 1909, Captain James A. Henderson, president of the second Pittsburgh and Cincinnati Packet line, summarized the effects upon packets of railroads refusing to coöperate, in these words:

> The first severe blow given to the packet lines occurred when the railroad lines withdrew and thereafter declined to renew traffic and equitable prorating arrangements on business that had always been interchangeable. The withdrawal was accomplished so nearly simultaneously, about 1900, as to force the conclusion that a "Community of Interest" existed among the rail lines to the hurt and detriment of the packet lines. From our own experience many instances can be cited where we were deprived of enormous tonnage through our inability to continue handling business to inland rail points and territories that we formerly reached regularly through prorating arrangements with rail lines. . . . Many reasons and excuses have been offered for this condition, one of the strong ones being the regulations of the Interstate Commerce Commission, but in our case, when we have always been willing to place our Line under the Commission's rules to connect with the rail lines, this willingness seldom accomplished the desired ends. It is one of the peculiarities of the workings of the Interstate Commerce Commission that rulings pertaining to rates and divisions applying to inland junction points, are not effective at river junction points. . . . In its operation the Interstate Commerce Com-

---
[368] Inland Waterways Commission, *op. cit.*, 375.
[369] *Waterways Journal*, January 15, 1910.

mission ignores river traffic and protects rail traffic by practically prohibiting the cooperation of the two.

It was in this period that the fourth of the above named practices became intolerable. To remedy a local situation, Cincinnati under the leadership of Albert Bettinger and others, staged an oldtime fight for the "freedom of the inland rivers." Their success is a memorable event in local river annals. A decision of the Supreme Court of the state of Ohio denied the local city council the power to authorize the obstruction of the local levee. Furthermore and of even greater importance, this decision said: "It is not in the power of the legislature, unless in the exercise of the power of eminent domain, to authorize property, dedicated to the public use for a specific purpose, to be used for a purpose inconsistent with the purpose for which it was dedicated." [370]

Finally, as already indicated, railroads were permitted to control waterways and their carriers. To this end they sometimes purchased tonnage. When to their interest, in meeting competition and making shipping connections, this tonnage was operated by the railroads. Otherwise it was sold and the trades in which it had been used were abandoned. In 1907 four packet lines, all on the lower Ohio below Cincinnati, showed traces of railroad influence.[371] The continued prosperity of the most important of these, for a number of years following, was probably due almost entirely to aid from friendly railroads.

Incidentally the effects of the two-cent railroad fare were injurious to transportation by the rivers. Al-

---

[370] Moulton, *op. cit.*, 81; Inland Waterways Commission, *Preliminary Report*, 1908, 139; *Waterways Journal*, June 6, 1914; *idem*, October 25, 1913.

[371] Inland Waterways Commission, *op. cit.*, 375.

though opposed by the railroads, these reduced fares benefited them in their competition with the rivers by diverting passenger traffic from the latter. Before mileage rates became legally compulsory, railroads made flat fares, rarely less than twenty-five cents each, however short the distance. Meanwhile local packets, where there were any, were charging fifty cents to one dollar for round trips covering twenty-five to fifty miles or more. But when it became cheaper to travel short distances by rail than by water, other things tending to favor the railroads, the traveling public deserted local packets.

The next, and possibly the most effective blow administered packets operating on the Ohio, particularly those running to and from Pittsburgh and Wheeling, was the formation of the United States Steel Corporation in 1901. Prior to this consolidation the subsidiary companies out of which it was formed "were large shippers by packets." Today they are again using the rivers, but they own and operate their own tonnage. Previously they depended upon privately owned tonnage which they supplied with large quantities of first-class freight that paid good rates and, as a rule, was carried over long distances. The policy of the consolidation was to ship by rail only and was adhered to so stringently that the river rates did not enter into the matter, as the Pittsburgh and Cincinnati Packet line demonstrated time and time again. Nor did the positive instructions of the purchaser of its products to ship by boat receive any attention or consideration, as this same line demonstrated by "bringing in orders specifically routed" by its boats.

Another contributing cause in the decline of river traffic, especially that on the Ohio, was the "cutting down of the mileage of the raw material," made possible by the westward march of industry, bringing industrial plants to and near raw materials and consumers. In the ante-bellum days steamboats bound west and south carried cargoes of industrial products, general merchandise, dry goods and groceries, while those returning north and east carried farm products and other raw materials, notably iron ore, in an exchange that was continued well into the palmy days of postbellum steamboating. But, when iron and steel industries of the Ohio valley began to shift their location towards the region of the Great Lakes, when the manufacture of agricultural machinery moved to the Middle West, when slaughtering and packing businesses were shifted to the same section, and when other industries tended to follow suit, local steamboats were robbed of first-class freight.[372] For the transportation of what was left, railroads were better suited than rivers with their uncertain stages and inadequate equipment.

A growing uncertainty regarding the type or types of boats best suited to future needs and conditions was almost equally depressing. Despite delays and uncertainties, slackwater had been promised for the Ohio and its chief tributaries. Under such conditions, plus the cheapness and durability of steel and the growing scarcity of timber, there was little choice between the all-steel-hull and the wooden hull steamer,[373] but there was less accord regarding the best methods of propulsion. The new Diesel engine, an internal-combustion oil-burning device, had its friends and its critics. The latter maintained that it would be hard to improve upon the

---

[372] *Waterways Journal*, October 29, 1927.

[373] The first all-steel hull steamboat for local uses, the "Chattahoochee," was built at Pittsburgh in 1881 under direction of Captain Thomas M. Rees. See *Waterways Journal*, September 16, 1916.

"improved steam engine," whereas the former insisted that their device, the Diesel engine, made possible necessary economies in both space and fuel and also in adjustments making for speed, dependability, and the use of double wheels.[874]

Chief discussion waged, however, over the comparative merits of paddle and screw-propelled boats,[875] the Diesel engine being used with either. Impressed with the further possibilities of the screw propeller, the essential principles of which had been understood and applied for more than half a century, Charles Ward of Charleston, West Virginia, produced a modified type of this device which he maintained would solve some of the navigation difficulties of inland America. First and most important of all, it was claimed that this device would assure greater power and dependability at less cost. The fact that an older type of the screw propeller had long been used successfully on the rivers of both Europe and Africa was thought to be indicative of its possibilities in America. With the courage of his convictions Ward began to manufacture screw propellers, and his friends, among them the W. C. Kelly Company of Charleston, West Virginia, began to use them. Soon engineers and others were advocating their general use, and, after a careful investigation, the national government decided to use them on its boats in the Federal Barge line on the Mississippi and Warrior rivers.

The paddle-wheel boat was not without its friends and defenders. Any craft that could accomplish the

---
[874] — *Idem*, January 2, 1926; *idem*, February 27, 1926.
[875] For the results of the government investigations see U. S. House. Document no. 857, March, 1914; U. S. House. Document no. 108, August, 1921. For typical articles on the discussion see *Waterways Journal*, February 25, 1911; *idem*, November 6, 1915; *idem*, November 13, 1915; *idem*, November 20, 1915; *idem*, January 15, 1916.

feats of the "Sprague" and the "Robert E. Lee" was not to be deserted by their builders and owners in the presence of innovators. In numerous articles the late Captain John M. Sweeney of Hollywood and Chicago, Captain Thomas M. Rees of Pittsburgh, and others, widely distributed but chiefly from the upper Ohio, established the superior advantages of paddle wheel propulsion for shallow and difficult navigation. They also showed that it is reasonably dependable.

The uncertainties aroused by these discussions temporarily depressed boat building on the inland waters and thus injured commerce, but they were wholesome signs of an otherwise deplorable condition. As in the past, the means of inland transportation were adjusting themselves to new needs. It was by discussion and agitation that the new order was able to preserve what was best in the old and make necessary changes.

Another contemporary force contributing to the decline of river traffic in the interior was low wages. After 1900 skilled river employees, pilots and engineers, received from seventy-five to one hundred dollars per month. At the same time mates were receiving from forty to fifty dollars per month and deckhands rarely more than twenty. Other employees were paid according to their traditional importance and with little reference to living costs. In practically every instance compensation was less than in the eighties, when the evil effects of low wages were offset by declining prices. In the latter period prices were rising, and river employment was more uncertain and irregular than in the former. As a consequence the condition of river employees became desperate; some were driven to the shore; and, when their place was filled at all, it was generally by those of comparatively inferior caliber.

COMMERCIAL DECADENCE

Naturally the change was reflected in the class of boats used and in the quality of service rendered.

Other factors of this transition were more local in their operation. Outstanding among these were "wharfage" and "agency," collectively known as "way charges." These were collected from steamboats by riparian municipalities, the former for the privilege of landing at local levees, the latter for the privilege of carrying freight and passengers across levees and for storing freight. Although levees were in bad repair and wharf masters and their assistants, in some places, received compensations greater than the total of all their collections, the practice of collecting these charges was fixed by custom which, like other customs, could not be abandoned despite the suicidal tendencies. Moreover, competition prevented packets from shifting them, and consequently they became burdensome, sometimes prohibitive. For example, during a two-year period, 1905-1907, a packet in the Pittsburgh-Charleston trade, making stops at many intermediate points, was assessed a total of approximately thirty-three hundred dollars in "way charges," which was more than one-fourth her net income.[376] Refusals to pay brought counter refusals of landing privileges. As a result some packets were taxed out of existence; others ceased to make unprofitable landings; and local packet accommodations were generally curtailed.

Among other local factors depressing river commerce were motorboats and motor-driven trucks. Their use to make quick deliveries of goods, in large quantities and over short radii, destroyed short packet trades and ate into the profits of long ones. An objectionable

---
[376] — *Idem*, January 15, 1910; Inland Waterways Com. *Preliminary Report*, 1908, 136-143.

feature of this situation was that packets were subjected to rigid governmental inspection and regulation, whereas motorboats of less than fifteen tons burden escaped inspection entirely and were subjected to few regulations. The situation called forth numerous protests.[377]

In addition to the more or less external forces operating to the detriment of river business, the Ohio itself contributed much to the undoing of its packets. In its natural state it was too low for navigation from three to five months annually, thus producing an uncertainty in deliveries made by it, that prevented shippers from accepting contracts based upon river rates. Moreover, the system of locks and dams, then in process of construction for the improvement of its navigation, did not temporarily remedy the situation. In some instances they made it worse. This was always true when locks were out of commission and when accumulated pools of water were used to create artificial waves below the mouth of the Great Kanawha for the use of towboats transporting coal from that stream to Cincinnati and other lower river ports.

Still other causes contributing to the commercial decadence of the Ohio might be enumerated, but enough have been given and described in their operations to show a divided responsibility. A reasonable inference is that the work of rehabilitation lies in coöperation. Like destructive forces, constructive ones are generally cumulative in their operation.

---

[377] — *Idem*, 98.

Floods and Disasters

Always rising or falling, the Ohio is a turbulent stream. A difference of thirty-five and one-half feet between low and high water marks at Pittsburgh, increasing to sixty-four feet at Cincinnati, is indicative of the range of its activities. Moreover, the coming of the white man seems to have accentuated its moodiness, recent floods and low waters occurring with greater frequency than in the distant past. But tradition holds stories of the shiftiness of the Ohio in the period in which nature alone held sway. It was from experience that friendly Indians were able to warn the white man against the consequences of building homes too near the banks of the "white foaming river." Nevertheless those who knew that stream best loved it most, having accepted it for better or for worse. Like the moodiness of a loving companion, its freaks were long regarded as natural phenomena, great floods being expected at more or less regular intervals of about seventeen years.[378]

While unable, as yet, to change this situation, science has thrown light upon the causes of floods in the Ohio valley. Briefly, they are due to "the accident of geographic location considered with respect to meteorological conditions."[379] Fortunately this explanation is explainable and that, too, from data supplied by the scientists themselves. First of all the Ohio valley is a vast area 203,900 square miles in extent, paralleling the

---
[378] Wheeling *Intelligencer*, June 30, 1865; *Cist's Weekly Advertiser*, January 11, 1848.

[379] See "Floods of 1913," in U. S. Department of Agriculture. *Bulletin Z,* 11.

western slope of the Appalachian Mountains for a distance of eight hundred miles and at an average width of two hundred fifty miles. Practically all this area lies within the range of the heavy winter and spring rainfalls that pass from Texas to New England directly over the axis of the Ohio basin, and the northern portion of this basin lies within the area of heavy rainfall produced by storms that pass over the continent from west to east along the region of the Great Lakes. Local storms of long duration and copious downpour may occur at the same time. Thus portions of the Ohio valley may be visited almost simultaneously by two or more downpours. As floods result primarily from rainfall, or melting snows, or a combination of the two, those of the Ohio valley are not mysterious in the light of the meteorological conditions under which they occur.

Physical features and natural conditions are also contributing factors. Chief among the former is the absence of surface storage in the form of lakes, either natural or artificial, and the steep slope of stream beds, the Ohio being four hundred thirty feet lower at its mouth than at its source. In proportion to their length the fall in its tributaries, particularly those flowing northward, is even greater. Moreover, when snow, in large quantities, collects on frozen ground about the headwaters of the Ohio and its tributaries, as it sometimes does, flood conditions are imminent. Any one of the meteorological conditions already described may then occur, melting collected snows even in winter. Fortunately all of them have never operated simultaneously; otherwise, the destruction wrought might have been complete.

The Ohio is said to be "flooded" when its waters

reach the danger line or the flood stage. These stages are points at which overflows first begin to damage property and are not necessarily the same for any two points, being determined in every case by the height of river banks. For example, flood stage at Pittsburgh is twenty-two, Parkersburg thirty-six, Cincinnati fifty, Louisville twenty-eight, Evansville thirty-five, and Cairo forty-five feet, respectively.[380]

The varying stages of the Ohio have been classified as: (1) technical floods or freshets, known locally as "rat row washes;" (2) severe floods, or stages from two to five feet above the danger line; and (3) great floods, or general inundations of the greatest recorded height.[380] Local conditions have given particular names to some of those of each of the first two classes. For instance, a freshet of 1864 was the oil flood, the upper Ohio being literally covered with floating oil barrels discharged from the Allegheny. Possibly still better known were two "pumpkin floods," one of which occurred in 1811, the other in 1861, when large portions of the Ohio were completely covered with floating pumpkins, squashes, and gourds.[382] Freshets and floods occur frequently, but great floods are fortunately rare, only those of 1884, 1907, and 1913 being thus designated in recent years.[383]

Because of their unusual size but otherwise typical features the flood of 1884 and the great flood of 1913 are given more than passing mention. The former was the greatest general inundation of the Ohio since records have been kept. It was caused by a short but heavy downpour upon a general snow of from four to five feet in depth. In hilly and mountainous sections this

---
[380] — *Idem*, 12.   [382] Wheeling *Intelligencer*, October 1, 1861.
[383] U. S. Department of Agriculture. *Bulletin Z.*

snow was even deeper, drifts remaining in many sections until late in the following spring. On the upper Ohio this flood reached peak stage on the eighth and ninth of February, when the main channel was literally covered with drift.

The great flood of 1913, thus called to distinguish it from another flood of the same year, reached its crest on the last day of March and the first day of April. Unlike most other great floods it was due entirely to excessive rainfall, the only other contributing factor, in addition to the natural conditions already described, being an open and rainy winter. The downpours immediately responsible for this flood were general but heaviest over the states of Ohio and Indiana, where total precipitations, for a four-day period, were in excess of ten inches. The result was a freak flood which raised the high water mark at Parkersburg to almost fifty-nine feet, which was five feet higher than any previous record. Thence both up and down stream few records were broken, the stage at Pittsburgh being five feet under high water mark.

Tributary streams may have floods of their own, that produce little or no effect upon the Ohio proper. For example, in July, 1888, the Monongahela established many new high records. At Fairmont it rose to thirty-five feet, at Brownsville to forty-four feet, and at Charleroi to forty-two, the resulting stage at Pittsburgh being little above normal. This was another freak flood following a local downpour and is mentioned, among other things, to show the possibilities of such phenomena in the mountainous sections of the Ohio valley.

As already indicated, this section was visited by floods before authentic records were kept and before its hills and mountains were stripped of their forests.

FLOODS AND DISASTERS

Indian traditions tell of great floods even before the coming of the white man. Up to 1866 floods occurred in the Ohio in the years 1786, 1792, 1806, 1810, 1832, 1847, 1852, 1860, 1861, and 1865, some of them being great, notably those of 1832 and 1847. Of all these, however, that of 1832 was probably greatest. Little is known of its causes, but its records, although unofficial, form a popular basis of comparison to this day. It was then that the high water mark for Pittsburgh was fixed at thirty-five feet, where it remained until 1884, when it climbed six inches higher.[384]

The flood of 1832 was probably more talked of and written about than any other that ever visited the Ohio valley. A diarist who witnessed it from a point about sixty miles below Wheeling counted one thousand houses floating down the Ohio at that time, together with "innumerable stacks of wheat, hay, oats, rye, etc., with shocks of corn, warehouses, mills, corn cribs, planks, barrels of flour, whiskey, apples, etc." His neighbor, a Mr. Riggs, lost "fifteen head of cattle and 2,000 bushels of Indian corn," and, continued the diarist: "It is said a man in Pittsburgh offered $500 for a skiff for an hour. The salt works up the Allegheny lost 41,000 barrels of salt. We do consider ourselves as lucky even at the worst. You may laugh, but it was no joke to see men come down in skiffs looking for a house, and to see another house tied to a tree, like a horse hitched by the bridle."[385]

Only those who have witnessed floods in the inland rivers can form an adequate idea of their scope and

---

[384] Wheeling *Intelligencer*, June 11, 1881; Wheeling *Register*, December 23, 1873; *Kanawha Banner* (Charleston, Va.), February 4, 1832; *idem*, February 18, 1832; *idem*, March 3, 1832.

[385] Manuscripts in possession of the family of the late Robert Henry Browse, Grape Island, West Virginia.

possibilities for destruction. Great floods swell river channels to many times their normal width; whole villages and large parts of cities are submerged; and the force of swollen currents sweeps everything before it. While yet a child the author of these chapters walked across the country, highways being impassable, to witness the flood of 1884 at its height. Surrounded by women and children who had taken refuge in the open on the river bank, he gazed upon that scene of desolation. Much of the village below was entirely submerged, a few projecting houses serving to indicate the location of streets over which skiffs and "Johnboats" were being used to rescue both persons and goods. Beyond, the main channel of the river was sweeping to destruction an unbroken and surging mass of drift that included boats, houses, fencing materials, hay stacks, and other objects too numerous to mention. Perched high on some of these were geese, ducks, chickens, and guineas, the defiant crows of passing cockerels alone adding life and zest to an otherwise gruesome and distressing panorama.

In a few days, however, the flood had subsided, and homes formerly submerged were cleared of mud and drift, aired, dried, and otherwise made ready for reoccupation. Meanwhile a government boat had administered to the relief of the sufferers, who in some instances came from miles inland. In a short time thereafter the whole event had passed into local tradition, incidents of which were preserved by suitable marks on the local railroad station and the post office and in the memories of local chroniclers. This experience was typical of that of many other cities and villages along the Ohio at that time. As of old, however, nothing was recorded against "the River," which, like the Nile, continued to be adored as an object of beauty and a source of profit.

Sometimes these floods effected freakish, even weird, things. For example, buildings were placed awry on their foundations and even carried to new locations, sustaining little or no injury in the operation. Large steamboats, too, were often left stranded high and dry. For example, the "Virginia," a famous packet of the Pittsburgh and Cincinnati Packet line, was left three quarters of a mile from the Ohio, in a cornfield near Ravenswood, West Virginia. Her re-launching was effected only after the lapse of considerable time and at great expense.

Flood damages of the Ohio valley are incalculable. Only recently have serious efforts been made to estimate them. The conflicting results are confusing and uninforming, it being next to impossible to determine, even approximately, the damage of high waters in such matters as injured buildings, interrupted trade, paralyzed utilities, sickness and death, and depreciated realty. Conservative estimates placed the direct damages of the flood of 1884 at more than $15,000,000, and similar damages for that of 1907 are thought to have reached $100,000,000, which did not include depreciation, "the most serious of all flood losses." In a period covering little more than one year, March 15, 1907 to March 20, 1908, the total flood losses for Pittsburgh aggregated $6,500,000, similar losses for a twenty year period immediately preceding being estimated at $17,000,000, whereas those for a similar period following were placed at from $25,000,000 to $40,000,000, the increase being due to an expected frequency and destructiveness.[886]

---
[886] Pittsburgh Flood Commission (Pittsburgh, 1912), *Report*, 66-71; Wheeling *Intelligencer*, March 6, 1884.

These losses have led to the conclusion that "Flood control is one of America's greatest peace time problems." Few, if any, contemplated the possibility of preventing such disasters, but numerous agencies wrestled with the problem of control. Among others the Inland Waterways Commission of 1907 was instructed to "take account of . . . the control of floods," and about the same time Pittsburgh appointed a flood commission for the purpose of ascertaining and reporting means of preventing flood losses to that city and vicinity. The former commission relied largely upon the researches and recommendations of M. O. Lighton of the United States Geological Survey and W. H. Bixby of the United States Army Engineers, which were published in reports,[387] whereas the latter commission relied upon Morris Knowles and other local experts whose findings and recommendations were printed in a volume of four hundred pages, not including accompanying maps and charts.[388] Incidentally, recent investigators of the problem of flood control have not ignored the findings and recommendations of those of an earlier period. Especially helpful were those of 1852 by Charles Ellet, those of 1857 by W. Milnor Roberts, and those of 1879 by Major W. E. Merrill.[389]

In all this voluminous literature two suggestions were outstanding, viz., flood control and flood prevention.[390] Under the former were included all those devices such

---

[387] Inland Waterways Commission, *Preliminary Report*, 1908, 451-491; Inland Waterways Commission, *Final Report* (Washington, 1912), 135-174; U. S. Senate. Document no. 325, 60 cong., 1 sess.

[388] Engineer's Society of Western Pennsylvania, *Proceedings*, July, 1907; *idem*, October, 1907.

[389] For a complete bibliography on the subject of flood control see Pittsburgh Flood Commission, *Report*, 416-419. See also U. S. House. *Executive Document*, 63 cong., 2 sess., no. 918.

[390] For typical articles on this subject see *Waterways Journal*, April 5,

as dredging, wall construction, widening and straightening of channels, and removal of obstructions, applied directly at points of overflow and damage. The possible benefits were generally conceded, but attention was called to the fact that they would be necessarily local, and that, whereas the destructiveness of great floods would not be lessened, those of lesser magnitude would be more injurious than formerly to those not thus protected.

These considerations led to more pretentious plans of control to be executed with a view to ultimate prevention. Outstanding among these was the plan for reforestation, the increasing frequency and destructiveness of floods, particularly those in the Ohio valley, being attributed to the destruction of native forests. It was claimed that a restored forest, if large enough, would act as a sponge from which the heaviest downpours would flow gradually to the great advantage of navigation, industry, and agriculture. Moreover, enthusiasts pointed to the fact that the work of reforestation had actually begun and insisted that the power of Congress to regulate commerce has removed possible legal difficulties to its completion.

Critics of this plan were numerous and insistent. They approved reforestation in a small way, largely as a means of providing a timber supply, but refused to see in it a panacea for floods. First of all, they insisted upon the impracticability of turning farm lands into forests of sufficient area to be effective. They also pointed to such baffling facts as these: the Indian traditions of great floods before the coming of the white man and

---

1913; *idem*, April 12, 1913; *idem*, April 19, 1913; *idem*, May 10, 1913; *idem*, April 25, 1914; *idem*, May 23, 1914; *idem*, August 22, 1914; *idem*, October 3, 1914; *idem*, April 8, 1916; *idem*, January 26, 1918; *idem*, February 2, 1918; *idem*, July 29, 1916.

that the high water marks along the Ohio were established in 1832, while those on the Great Lakes and the Mississippi were made in 1838 and 1841, respectively. The conclusion seemed inevitable: "The forest primeval did not prevent floods, neither will newly grown forests." Accordingly interested parties asked for a more certain and effective protection.[391]

For many the answer was a system of storage reservoirs, first proposed in 1852 by Charles Ellet and later dismissed before convincing objections from W. Milnor Roberts. This plan was based upon the assumption that "the logical way to control a river is to control the source of its water supply." Moreover, it was claimed that storage reservoirs could be used to develop electric power, for irrigation purposes, and to maintain navigable stages of water. Furthermore, the plan was said to be practicable both from a financial and from an engineering standpoint. Costs, however great, were to be distributed over a long period of years, thus reducing their burden to a minimum, whereas storage facilities were to be provided by a hundred or more dams instead of a few, as originally proposed by Mr. Ellet, thus reducing the dangers from impounded waters and making the plan more practicable from other viewpoints. To this latter end numerous surveys were made about the headwaters of the Ohio to determine possible locations for a sufficient number of dams to protect that section, and following a flood disaster in 1913 five dams were built on the Great Miami to protect Dayton and other cities.

Nevertheless, this system was open to serious criticism. Engineers were generally agreed as to its theo-

---

[391] Pittsburgh Flood Commission, *Report*, 73; National Waterways Commission, *Final Report*, 205-303; *Waterways Journal*, July 9, 1927.

retical possibilities but differed widely as to its practicability from legal, financial, and physical standpoints. They maintained that traditional notions and practices would not permit national encroachments upon state preserves, that the total cost would aggregate billions of dollars, which under existing conditions would be beyond the means of the states, or the national government, or both, and that it was practically impossible to secure sites of sufficient number and capacity to be effective. Those who remembered the Johnstown flood and other such disasters saw in the impounded waters of the reservoir plan a constant menace to life and property. Furthermore, it was said that such a system, designed as it would be primarily for flood control, would have to be used for that purpose, which would practically nullify its use for generating electric currents, for irrigation, or for improving navigation, impounded waters being, of necessity, so controlled as to prepare for floods rather than for other uses.

Other critics of the reservoir plan were those interested in internal improvement projects then in process of construction or contemplated and intended primarily to benefit navigation. They were unwilling to give up a bird in hand for two in the bush, whatever the possible benefits from the possession of the latter. All were agreed that neither the reservoir system nor reforestation could prevent a flood like the great flood of 1913, which had its origin in a section given over to agriculture on a large scale and not suited to the construction of dams, sites being unavailable. Meanwhile those in immediate danger continued to demand relief and to conduct themselves as if they did not expect to get it. To all such, the recent action of Congress providing for flood control on the Mississippi and its affluents on a grand scale brought new hope.

Discussions of and plans for flood control in the Ohio valley were, however, worth while. Among other things they kept in the foreground the importance of the subject as well as the difficulties and complexities involved, and they were potent factors with Congress in its recent decision to undertake flood control on a national scope. Henceforth informed persons did not think of this subject as separate from navigation, electrical power, irrigation, and other possible uses of water resources. Neither did they forget that any plan to be permanently successful must be not only legally and financially possible but scientifically correct. In fact the problem was primarily one for engineers and as such challenged the best talent of the nation, yes, of the world. A definite plan, scientifically determined, is needed not only as the basis of further congressional action but also as a means of directing and enlightening the public.

Disasters due to ice movements on the rivers of the Ohio valley have been almost as destructive as have been those due to floods. Fortunately the former have been rather infrequent. They occurred at irregular and indeterminate intervals after the manner of floods but not as their companions, ice years, as a rule, being somewhat removed from flood years. In the Ohio great ice floes occurred in the following of the last seventy-five years: 1856, 1857, 1867, 1873, 1879, and 1918 which were not, in any instance, dates of great floods.[392]

In each of the above years local rivers were frozen over for an unusually long time, the average period of

---

[392] Wheeling *Intelligencer*, March 7, 1856; *idem*, February 4, 1867; *idem*, February 7, 1857; Wheeling *Register*, January 5, 1873.

FLOODS AND DISASTERS 381

interrupted navigation because of ice, other years included, being only about ten days. As a result of these more severe "freeze-ups" the ice formed was sometimes of great thickness. When it broke and moved, it frequently gorged against obstructions and in narrow and crooked channels, a single gorge thus formed being miles in length and many feet high. When such a gorge moved, its force was irresistible, sweeping everything before it as if by magic.

Locally these movements or breakups were awaited with mingled feelings of joy, hope, and fear. The events were in fact among the most exciting and thrilling in local annals and were proclaimed by the use of bells and whistles. In March, 1856, between four and five thousand Pittsburghers were thus summoned to witness a long-awaited passing of an ice gorge.[393] The following year a Cincinnati newspaper described a local breakup in this characteristic language:

Soon after 12 o'clock, the ringing of bells and the scream of whistles proclaimed a third start of the ice. This time the start was in earnest, for only a few temporary stoppages occurred thereafter. Very soon the levee and the landings in Newport and Covington were crowded with thousands of spectators. The windows that commanded a view of the river were thronged with ladies, and many were driven down in buggies to view the exciting scene. As incidents occurred here and there, or boats were sunk, the multitude dashed through the mud to the spot with deafening shouts and yells.[394]

Of all the more recent ice floes in the Ohio that of January, 1918, was the most destructive and the most spectacular. As already indicated the total damages aggregated six million five hundred thousand dollars. It followed eight weeks of suspended navigation during most of which time ice continued to form. When it

[393] Wheeling *Intelligencer*, March 7, 1856.
[394] — *Idem*, February 9, 1857.

finally broke, many gorges formed, which in turn swept everything before them. Among the property thus carried to destruction were ferries, terminals, and steamboats, most of which floated beyond the reach of willing rescuers and were ground to pieces or dashed against dams, piers, and other obstructions. After the main floe had passed Cincinnati, the local levee was described as a "wreck." It was covered with splinters of boats and barges, and the harbor proper was strewn with sunken barges and steamboats, among the latter being two of the finest boats that ever plied the local waters, the "City of Cincinnati" and the "City of Louisville."

In the early days of steam navigation many disasters, most of them serious, were caused by exploding boilers. The safety-valve was unknown; experience with "corroding boilers" and "foaming waters" was limited; and racing was a mania. Excessive steam pressure and defective flues were the natural results which led as naturally to disasters. Horrid as these incidents generally were, the public loved to read about them. Accordingly, accounts thereof occupied a large place in the local press [395] and in such works as Lloyd's *Steamboat Directory and Disasters on the Western Waters* which, by the use of numerous illustrations, most of which were greatly exaggerated, went into the gruesome details of the most spectacular steamboat boiler explosions on the western waters before 1856, the date of its publication.

[395] For typical articles see *Kanawha Register* (Charleston, Va.), May 4, 1830; *idem*, June 4, 1830; *Kanawha Banner* (Charleston, Va.), September 23, 1831; *idem*, May 17, 1832; *Kanawha Republican* (Charleston, Va.), May 7, 1842; *idem*, October 30, 1844; Wheeling *Times*, January 4, 1848; Pittsburgh *Gazette*, January 8, 1853; Wheeling *Intelligencer*, May 4, 1855; *idem*, March 6, 1856; *idem*, March 16, 1856; *idem*, March 30, 1859.

The "City of Cincinnati"
Wrecked by the ice gorge of January, 1918, at Cincinnati.

A typical description of such a disaster is that of the sinking of the "Moselle," April 25, 1838:

> The "Moselle" was a fast boat, holding the record between St. Louis and Cincinnati (750 miles) at sixty-four hours. On the day mentioned she drew out of her pier at Cincinnati with a passenger list numbering over 250 men, women, and children. A landing in the suburbs of Cincinnati was made to take on a party of German emigrants. The boilers were being forced to their limit in anticipation of equalling or surpassing a previous record, and as the boat was leaving shore the four boilers exploded simultaneously. The entire end of the boat in front of the wheels was blown to kindling wood. . . . It is said that passengers were blown upon both the Ohio and the Kentucky shores, and the exaggeration may not be so great as it seems. Eighty-one persons were known to have been killed and fifty-five were missing.[396]

In a characteristic way this accident was denounced in public gatherings and elsewhere as unnecessary, even criminal. Nevertheless, it was followed by others, the number keeping close pace with the increasing use of steamboats. Finally, in 1852, as the result of two disasters, one on the Hudson and the other on Lake Erie, in which a total of more than four hundred lives were lost, Congress was forced to act, individual members having found from experience that it was more dangerous to use steamboats on the inland waters than to fight Indians on the frontier. The result was an act providing "for the better protection of human life on vessels propelled by steam." To this end pilots and engineers were first required to be licensed; hulls, engines, and boilers were to be inspected regularly; and the use of lifeboats, life-preservers and other safety devices was required. This law, together with subsequent discoveries tending to control corrosion and foaming, reduced

---
[396] Hulbert, *The Ohio River*, 344; Hall, *The West*, 179-184.

steamboat disasters from exploding boilers to a minimum.[397]

In the early days of inland navigation snags, sawyers, planters, and similar obstructions did much damage to steamboats and other craft. As already indicated sawyers and planters were veritable terrors to the early boatmen, but steamboatmen suffered also from these lurking foes, hundreds of boats, among them the "New Orleans," having been snagged and thus destroyed. This destruction continued until about 1830, when Captain Henry M. Shreve invented and began to use his famous snagboat. By its use most of these obstructions to navigation were in time removed, but artificial barriers, in the form of bridge piers, were allowed to take their place. Both the Steubenville and the Bellaire bridges have been referred to elsewhere as menaces to navigation, and that at Parkersburg was scarcely less objectionable. In 1869 the "Rebecca," Captain Thaddeus Thomas, of the Wheeling and Parkersburg Packet line, hit one of its piers and sank in a few minutes with great loss of life.[398]

Still other disasters came from head-on collisions. Outstanding among such was that of March 4, 1868, between the "United States" and the "America," packets of the Mail line operating between Cincinnati and Louisville, and that of July 4, 1882, between the "Scioto" and the "John Lomas," the former of the Wheeling and Parkersburg Packet Company. The first of these accidents occurred between Cincinnati and Louisville, the second about twenty miles above Wheeling. The first was probably due to a misunderstanding

---

[397] The use of zinc to control erosion in boilers was discovered accidentally by a French engineer. See Wheeling *Intelligencer*, August 26, 1875.

[398] — *Idem*, December 9, 1869.

FLOODS AND DISASTERS 387

regarding signals, the second to carelessness and possibly to the use of intoxicants.[399] In each instance interested packet lines were almost ruined through claims for damages instituted and prosecuted to successful conclusions by the friends and relatives of the scores of persons who lost their lives.

Windstorms have been a constant menace to rivermen of all classes. This was particularly true in the days of the boatmen and when steamboats were small and comparatively frail. Elsewhere mention was made of the destruction wrought by wind upon coalboat fleets in the fifties. Moreover, this experience was not exceptional. The following letter will speak for itself regarding similar accidents to steamboats:

VANCEBURGH, June 2, 1832.

I am under the painful necessity of communicating to you one of the most awful occurrences that ever happened on the Ohio River. On this day, about 3 o'clock, there came up a tremendous hurricane and, in a few moments after it commenced, our boat ["the Hornet"] was *bottom upwards*. The scene was dreadful beyond description and what made it more so, Captain Sullivan was lost, together with one of the pilots. A young lady from Greenup and the chambermaid were also lost. We suppose that between thirty and forty were drowned. We were crowded with both cabin and deck passengers. Our situation is dreadful indeed.[400]

Even more destructive than any of the causes already mentioned, except floods and ice, was fire. In the early days, when wood was used for fuel, a steamboat was as combustible as a theater; in its midst was a raging volcano spouting fire and smoke; and at the same time every available space on deck was strewn with combustibles. When fanned by prevailing river breezes, a stray spark, unobserved for a few minutes, became an

---
[399] — *Idem*, July 27, 1882; *idem*, November 8, 1882.
[400] *Kanawha Banner*, June 7, 1832.

unquenchable blaze that continued to rage until swallowed up by the river itself. River annals record such incidents in great numbers.

More destructive and spectacular still was the burning of a number of boats at one and the same time. This was always possible when several boats were tied up in close proximity to one another, motive power having meanwhile been temporarily dispensed with. Under such conditions, plus a heavy wind, a fire on one boat rapidly spread to all, effecting a destruction usually complete. Recently (1922), four steamboats and two wharfboats were destroyed in this manner at Cincinnati with a total loss in excess of two hundred fifty thousand dollars, but ever since the introduction of steam navigation such disasters have not been uncommon.

One of the most spectacular of these wholesale burnings was that at Cincinnati, May 17, 1869, when six steamboats, the "Melnetto," "Clifton," "May Irwin," "Darling," "Cheyenne," and "Westmoreland," were destroyed before "the largest crowd of people that ever witnessed a fire in that city after midnight."[401] Summoned by the ringing of bells and a "great light to the southward," thousands of men, women, and children rushed to the local levee. Before they reached it the burning boats were shrouded in sheets of flame and clouds of smoke. Soon thereafter their decks quivered and parted, and their tall chimneys toppled over and fell like forest trees, some upon the wharf, others into the water. About the same time oil burst from one of the uppermost boats, ignited, and flowed in a broad

---

[401] Cincinnati *Enquirer*, November 19, 1919; Wheeling *Intelligencer*, May 18, 1869. For different data and fuller description see Grayson, Frank Y. *Thrills of the Historic Ohio River* (Cincinnati, 1930?), 114.

FLOODS AND DISASTERS

stream far down on the surface of the river suggesting a separate rivulet of molten gold. Before fire engines could reach the scene a column of flame five hundred feet long and several hundred feet high was shooting serpentine tongues over the levee, making relief impossible.

One of the most gruesome misfortunes that could befall a steamboat, either a towboat or a packet, was an outbreak either of yellow fever or of cholera. Like a haunted house, a craft with such an experience was henceforth doomed. Both workmen and passengers avoided it, and municipalities refused it landing privileges. In 1878 the "John Porter," a towboat, was thus overtaken near Gallipolis. Her crew deserted; her barges were cut loose and allowed to float to destruction; and it was a long time before a pilot and other employees could be induced to board her and move her to other quarters. It mattered not that she later changed her name to the "Transporter"— like other boats with similar experiences, she was henceforth more or less of a castaway.

Another similarly gruesome experience was that of the "Annie Laurie," a favorite Great Kanawha river packet. In July, 1866, she left Cincinnati for Charleston, West Virginia, on a regular trip. When she reached Round Bottom, a deck passenger, a steersman of a saltboat from the Great Kanawha, developed a case of cholera. Before she reached Gallipolis he was dead, and the second engineer had contracted his malady, only to die before Point Pleasant was reached. Both were buried in a box and in such a manner as to create the least alarm. Soon, however, other cases developed, and passengers and crew began to seek the shore at every opportunity. Enough of the latter to man the boat were retained only by the use of force, the captain stationing himself on the gang-plank and threatening those who attempted to escape. Passing boats refused assistance; the dead remained unburied; and, when the ill-fated packet finally reached Charleston, her home port, she was met by a committee headed by a local minister, who informed her captain that she must not land. The tears and entreaties of homesick women and children were unavailing to secure landing privileges. After sleepless hours her intrepid captain fell upon the upper deck exhausted from overwork and exasperation. In a few hours he rallied and was able to read a newspaper account of his own death and of preparations for his burial.[402] Reference is to Captain F. A. Laidley of Covington, Kentucky, who is still living at an age well past eighty.

The above and other similar events and conditions have been a part of the development of the institutional, professional, and the industrial life of the Ohio valley. Plans for flood and ice control have already been mentioned. From still other contributions insurance has probably profited most. It will be recalled that the first important shipment of goods on the Ohio, that of 1765 by the British from Fort Pitt to the Northwest Territory, was insured, as were also the cargoes of the first packet line, that of 1794. Subsequent developments on that stream have contributed materially to the principles now governing insurance in general. Today some of the largest companies dealing in marine insurance are located on or near its waters. Here contributions were also made to admiralty law and to admiralty procedure, as well as to the principles governing riparian

---

[402] For an account of Captain Laidley's reported death see Cincinnati *Commercial*, August 15, 1866.

rights, local attorneys of distinction specializing in these subjects. On the industrial side the superior quality of Ohio-river built craft has long been admitted, and the Ohio valley has long been recognized as one of the "work shops of the world." Fortunately these benefits were national, even international.

Internal Improvements

George Washington, owner of large tracts of western lands, was among the first to suggest the improved navigation of the Ohio river and its tributaries. His purpose seems to have been to preserve the integrity of the United States and to protect his private interests. Scarcely had the Revolution ended before he again turned his attention to the Trans-alleghany. After a personal inspection of portages between its rivers and those flowing towards the East, he prepared a map showing routes of proposed roads and canals in a plan of improvement for connecting the eastern and western waters. It was at this time, also, that he expressed the wish that God might give his people wisdom to improve their waterways.

In all this, evidences of Washington's patriotic and farseeing purposes are abundant, but nowhere were they more evident than in a letter from him to his friend, Arthur Lee, in which he said: "There is nothing which binds one country to another but interest. Without this cement the western inhabitants, who more than probably will be composed in a large degree of foreigners, can have no predilection for us, and a commercial connection is the only tie we can have upon them." [403] Somewhat later, under Washington's leadership, Virginia and Maryland appointed commissioners to adjust differences between them regarding the navi-

---

[403] Washington, *Writings* (ed. Ford), vol. x, 488; Hulbert, A. B., *Washington and the West*, 32.

gation and the proposed improvement of the Potomac river. The meeting and the adjustment that followed led to another meeting and finally to the convention that framed the Constitution of the United States, setting up a government with ample powers to regulate commerce and its agencies among the several states of the Union.

About the same time a definite plan for the improvement of the Ohio and its chief tributaries was proposed by General Richard Butler.[404] This contemplated the use of dikes, or semicircular dams, so constructed and placed as to contract channels making them deeper and more continuously navigable. Streams with broad gravel beds, such as the Great Miami, for the improvement of which the dike was originally proposed, and with numerous islands dividing channels, as in the Ohio, seemed to invite this treatment. Moreover, it seemed adequate. Accordingly it found favor, and, like other makeshifts, it outlived its usefulness.

Following the purchase of Louisiana interest in internal improvements was revived largely with a view to the common defense. This brought forth Gallatin's report of 1808 proposing a system of roads and canals to be built at national expense and so located as to contribute "toward cementing the bonds of the Union." That part of this famous document relating to the Ohio valley proposed "artificial roads" to connect the navigable waters of the Allegheny, Monongahela, Kanawha, and Tennessee rivers with the nearest corresponding Atlantic streams: the Susquehanna or Juniata, Potomac, James, and either the Santee or the Savannah. It also suggested the future improved navigation of the above-named western rivers and the use of a

---
[404] Jones, R. R. *The Ohio River* (Washington, 1920), 148.

INTERNAL IMPROVEMENTS

canal to parallel the Falls in the Ohio at Louisville. Setting forth the possibilities of the western rivers this report also called attention to the fact that Brownsville on the Monongahela, two thousand miles by water from the sea, was elevated only about one hundred feet more than Cumberland on the Potomac.[405] Although nothing comprehensive, so far as the inland waters were concerned, came of this report, it was probably a determining factor in a decision of Congress to provide funds for an Atlantic coast survey and for the completion of the Cumberland road, already authorized, from Cumberland to Wheeling.

States bordering upon the Ohio had meanwhile been considering the matter of its improved navigation. In response to repeated overtures from Kentucky, first made in 1803, the state of Ohio, ten years later, asked neighboring states to join her in "exploring the rapids of the Ohio and considering the proper means of opening and improving the navigation of the same." Nothing came of this request and after the lapse of a short time, in which the steamboat became practicable, Ohio again asked her neighbors to aid in determining the probable cost of improving the river. Incidentally, a significant trend was indicated in a resolution of her legislature asking national aid for this, as yet, somewhat local enterprise. As expected nothing came from this request. Subsequently neighboring states were more interested, and a joint commission composed of representatives of Pennsylvania, Virginia, Ohio, and Kentucky recommended the construction of a canal around the Falls at Louisville, the cost of which was to be borne jointly by their respective states. Furthermore,

---

[405] Gallatin's "Report," in Inland Waterways Com., *Preliminary Report*, 1908.

this commission asked that each of the four states concerned contribute ten thousand dollars for the general improvement of the Ohio river.[406]

Following another period of delay and inaction, interested parties being unable to act concertedly, Ohio river improvement came into favor as a national enterprise. A congressional act of May 24, 1824, appropriated seventy-five thousand dollars to be used for the removal of planters, sawyers, and snags and served as an entering wedge. With the inauguration of the second Adams, federal appropriations for the improved navigation of the Ohio became more or less regular during a period of almost twenty years. As these appropriations were for a national purpose and never large, they weathered the Jackson regime with its Maysville veto and consistent opposition to things favored by Henry Clay, a popular favorite in the Ohio valley.

Once the Ohio river had found favor with Congress the local public would permit no reversal of policy, petitions requesting additional appropriations for its improved navigation becoming numerous and persistent. With one accord they urged their favorite enterprise as a national undertaking, one petition claiming a total loss to Ohio river craft and cargoes, for a period of ten years immediately preceding 1828, of one million four hundred forty-five thousand dollars, most of which, it was maintained, was sustained by immigrants and could have been prevented.[407]

Under this changed program the Ohio was put into usable condition for the great steamboat age that was approaching. Operating under a charter from Kentucky and with the aid of a subscription from the national government, in 1830, a joint-stock company com-

[406] Jones, *op. cit.*, 148.   [407] —*Idem*, 149.

pleted the Portland canal near Louisville. Meanwhile boulders were removed from the Grand Chain above Cairo. By 1837 some of the most dangerous bars had been reduced by the use of dikes, and more than three thousand snags had been removed from the main channel, thanks to the efficiency of Captain Henry M. Shreve and his invention, the snagboat. From 1837 to 1844 the work commenced by Shreve was continued by others who constructed dikes and removed snags, as conditions required.[408] Jackson had taught the public not to expect much in the way of internal improvements at the hands of the national government, and most interests along the Ohio were satisfied. The tolls collected for the use of the Portland canal were their chief source of complaint, the interested public insisting that inasmuch as this improvement had been made possible by subscriptions from the federal government, its use should be free.[409]

With the approach of mid-century, conditions in the Ohio valley changed rapidly, transportation facilities again becoming inadequate. Because of its contracted dimensions the Portland canal could no longer accommodate the large and fast steamers of the period, and delays on account of low water became frequent and expensive. The use of low water and other boats of special design did not overcome these disadvantages, because the demand was for through, rapid, and uninterrupted transportation. Moreover, inland industry was then calling for regular and adequate coal supplies.

The advent of the locomotive in the interior did

---

[408] — *Idem*, 148-150; Hulbert, *op. cit.*, 361; *Journal of the Franklin Institute* (Philadelphia, 1862-date), vol. xxxiv, 26.

[409] *Waterways Journal*, March 29, 1913; U. S. House. *Executive Documents*, 50 cong., 1 sess., vol. xx, no. 6, pt. ii, 488-550; "Internal Commerce in the United States," in U. S. Bureau of Statistics. *Report*, 1886.

much to quicken the mid-century movement for the improvement of its rivers, particularly the Ohio.[410] In 1852 the Baltimore and Ohio and the Pennsylvania railroads each established a terminus upon its course and was not long in discovering that the volume of railroad traffic fluctuated with that of the river. Accordingly, they both favored its improved navigation. It mattered not that they were each planning for through connections to the Middle West by the use of bridges spanning the Ohio. Rivers were the main thoroughfares of commerce and were generally expected to continue as such.

Accepting Lieutenant Maury's conclusion, that "The atmosphere pumps up our rivers from the sea, and transports them through the clouds, to their source amongst the hills," all agreed that the solution to the problem of improved rivers lay in the proper conservation of water supplies.[411] To this end plans varied all the way from the ridiculous to the admittedly practicable. For example, an eminent meteorologist proposed the use of fire for arresting the watery vapors and producing rainfall at will. Herman Haupt of Philadelphia would have used a succession of open dams from six to ten feet high, the pools thus formed being connected by an open channel two hundred feet wide and of sufficient length to equalize natural flows, the whole system to be operated in connection with a number of artificial reservoirs and without the use of locks. Alonzo Livermore favored the Haupt system with modifications eliminating reservoirs and contracting open channels to one hundred feet, by which latter device he thought that natural flows would be so retarded as to make them

---

[410] *Journal of the Franklin Institute*, vol. xxxiii, 1-24.
[411] —*Idem*, vol. xxxiii, 2.

adequate to all the existing needs of navigation. But the most popular of all these early suggestions for the improved navigation of the Ohio was that for the exclusive use of artificial reservoirs, first seriously proposed by Charles Ellet, a famous engineer, and later elaborated by Elwood Morris and others. In the spring of 1856 this plan was given wide publicity through the Cincinnati *Gazette* and the following year through the *Journal of the Franklin Institute*, published in Philadelphia.[412]

The Ellet plan was based upon observations made at Wheeling over a period of eleven years, 1838 to 1848, inclusive. These indicated a sufficient flow at that point in the Ohio, if equalized, to maintain a permanent depth of six feet, which was then considered adequate for all future needs. The problem was to collect the natural rainfall and equalize its distribution. To this end a small number of receiving reservoirs, "to be filled and emptied frequently during each year and controlled in their discharge by six regulating reservoirs each of sufficient capacity to hold the drainage of 600 square miles and located upon the larger affluents," were deemed sufficient. Moreover, this device was urged as sufficient within itself, dispensing with the use of locks and dams and thus leaving the main river channel free from obstructions. Furthermore, it was claimed that it would prevent floods and that it was both legally and financially possible. The cost of construction was estimated at twelve million dollars which was later increased by one-half, the number of major dams having been increased in the same proportion.

Fresh from the Monongahela, where he had com-

---

[412] U. S. House, *op. cit.*, 527-550; Inland Waterways Com., *op. cit.*, 452; Ellet, Charles. *The Mississippi and Ohio Rivers* (Philadelphia, 1853);

pleted a system of locks and dams providing slackwater navigation, six feet in depth, from Pittsburgh to Brownsville, W. Milnor Roberts, a distinguished engineer, so effectively disposed of all the above described plans for improving the Ohio that to this day one needs only to mention them to the informed to call forth the question "Have you read Milnor Roberts's Report?"

Admitting the correctness of the hypothesis upon which the plan for artificial reservoirs was based, Roberts, nevertheless, opposed their use. His chief objections were that initial costs and probable upkeep could not be definitely determined; that other costs to existing cities, towns, railroads, mines, and farm lands occupying proposed sites would be prohibitive; that the proposed storage was inadequate, insufficient allowance having been made for evaporation and extremely dry seasons; that the desired sites were physically impossible; that regular navigation and flood control through the use of reservoirs were incompatible, "one demanding that the reservoirs shall be allowed to fill to supply the river in drought, the other that they should be as nearly empty as possible, to be used in holding back floods;" and finally that the number of reservoirs proposed, even if increased to nine, would be inadequate.[418]

Instead, Roberts proposed to improve the Ohio by the use of a system of locks and dams such as he had installed on the Monongahela. Such a system had earlier been proposed by Edward F. Gay and others and was then in successful operation on the Muskin-

---

Morris, Elwood. *Treatise on the Improvement of the Ohio River* (Pottsville, Pa., 1857); Ellet, Charles. *Report on the Improvement of the Kanawha and Incidentally of the Ohio River* (Philadelphia, 1858).

[418] *Journal of the Franklin Institute*, vol. xxxiv, 23, 73, 146, 217, 289, 361; U. S. Engineer Department. *Report*, 1873, vol. i, 500; Roberts, Wm. Milnor. *Improvement of the Ohio River* (Pittsburgh, 1856).

gum, Kentucky, and Green rivers in America and on rivers in Europe. As originally proposed for the Ohio, the Roberts plan of improvement contemplated the use of about fifty dams, each with a lift of eight feet and at least one lock. For the free passage of arks, coalboats, flatboats, and rafts, which was demanded locally, each dam was to be provided with a chute. The use of reservoirs was not contemplated. The initial cost of the proposed lock and dam system was placed at twelve million dollars which, together with an estimated annual upkeep of one hundred ten thousand dollars, was to be raised through the collection of tolls.[414]

This plan was bitterly assailed by Elwood Morris and other proponents of the reservoir system. Without the use of reservoirs they attempted to show that the natural waterfall on the upper Ohio was inadequate to maintain a permanent stage of slackwater of the desired depth. Furthermore, they asserted that the use of locks and dams on the Ohio would increase the number and the destructiveness of floods; that ice floes would be more frequent and destructive than in the past; that slackwater pools would fill with sediment and become stale, thus entailing expense to keep them clear and endangering the health of local residents; that the existing river traffic in both lumber and coal would be destroyed; that initial costs and upkeep could not be determined with sufficient accuracy to warrant launching the enterprise; that the proposed tolls for meeting costs would be a source of dissatisfaction; that a thoroughfare of practically unlimited capacity, when usable, would be limited to the point of nullity by the time taken out for repairing locks and dams, the system, like a chain, being no stronger than its weakest link;

---

[414] *Journal of the Franklin Institute*, vol. xxxiv.

and finally that the arrangement for operating rafts and coalboats by the use of chutes was inadequate because of the hazards involved.[415]

To these objections, as already indicated, Roberts made convincing answers. Some of them were even prophetic. Among these were observations on the future of the coal traffic, in which he said:

> The old fashion of conducting the coal business, between the upper and lower Ohio, and the Mississippi valley, will, from choice, and from economical motives, be entirely abandoned. Barges will be substituted for *frail arks*, which now not only never return, but in too many instances never reach their destination. Consequent upon this change, the coal business will rapidly and largely increase, beyond the calculations of the most sanguine – to the advantage of the consumer as well as the producer; regulating the price to a nearly uniform rate throughout the season, and incidentally giving the coal operators more complete control over their mining hands; at the same time it will be better for the miners.[416]

Of still greater importance was Roberts's suggestion that the method of improving the Ohio be "investigated and reported upon in such a manner as *to command the respect and confidence of the country*," experience having taught the danger of legislative determination of such matters in the absence of scientific guidance and popular approval.[417] Had this suggestion been followed, when made, such a course might have kept subsequent internal improvement funds out of the orgy of "pork barrel" raids into which they fell. The consequent benefits to the country can scarcely be estimated.

The impending sectional conflict, together with other things, particularly a paucity of funds, prevented immediate and serious consideration of any of the above described plans for the improvement of the Ohio. Since

---

[415] — *Idem*, vol. xxxiii.   [416] — *Idem*, vol. xxxiv, 297.
[417] — *Idem*, vol. xxxiv, 299.

1844 appropriations to that end had practically ceased, and the Civil war temporarily put an end to all consideration of the matter and even to discussions regarding it. As a result the mid-sixties found this natural highway almost unusable, the report of a preliminary survey of 1866 revealing the location of one hundred forty sunken steamboats and barges and of one hundred sixty-six snags,[418] memorials of strife and neglect.

As the Ohio was yet the sole means of transportation for large inland areas and traffic thereon tended to become normal and to increase in volume, these conditions were intolerable. Accordingly, in 1866 and 1867, Congress appropriated a total of two hundred seventy-two thousand dollars for its improvement under a plan to provide a permanent stage of at least three feet by the use of dikes and the removal of obstructions. W. Milnor Roberts, supervising engineer of river improvements, was placed in charge. With the aid of a corps of engineers under the immediate direction of Sigismund Low and James E. Day and a snagboat under the command of Captain John Rogers of Civil war fame, Roberts cleared the Ohio of its most dangerous obstructions, constructed a number of dikes for deepening the channel over bars, and completed a survey covering its entire course from Pittsburgh to Cairo. Unable to find satisfaction in these makeshift devices and conscious of the future possibilities of the Ohio, in 1870 he renewed his proposal for a system of locks and dams for its permanent improvement.[419] At the same time he reiterated objections to other plans, adding little to the points already reviewed in this chapter.

[418] Jones, *op. cit.*, 150; Ohio River Commission, *Memorial to Congress* (Cincinnati, 1872); idem, *Memorial to Congress* (Cincinnati, 1878).
[419] *Journal of the Franklin Institute*, vol. xxxiv.

Meanwhile interest in the improved navigation of the Ohio bore still other fruit. A proposal to divert the waters of Lake Erie into its channel, in such quantities as to produce a stage permanently navigable, was revived along with some of the plans objected to by Roberts.[420] Of more consequence was the decision of certain pilots' associations using the lower Ohio to install beacon lights along the Grand Chain above Cairo to indicate the navigable channel, as well as dangers to navigation. Subsequently these were taken over by the national government and extended into a system covering the whole course of the Ohio and other navigable inland rivers. The work of enlarging the Portland canal, commenced in 1860, was carried to completion in 1874, when tolls were reduced from fifty to five cents per ton, to be abolished entirely six years later, when the improvement was nationalized.[421]

But plans for the radical improvement of the Ohio by a permanent stage of slackwater six feet deep, as desired by Roberts and others, fell into evil ways. Having effected through communications to the Middle West by extensions and consolidations and, as yet, ignorant of the fact that commerce tends to increase in proportion to the number and the character of the effective agencies for facilitating it, railroads lost interest in the improved navigation of the inland rivers and asserted their ability to provide for the transportation needs of the country. All they asked was to be let alone according to the teachings of a well-known school of econ-

---

[420] *National Inland Waterways*, September, 1919.

[421] Inland Waterways Com., *Preliminary Report*, 1908, 177; see "Transportation on the Ohio River System," in U. S. Board of Engineers for Rivers and Harbors, *Interim Report*, 1927, 2; Wheeling *Intelligencer*, October 28, 1869; Wheeling *Register*, May 24, 1875; *idem*, April 2, 1877; Gould, *Fifty Years on the Mississippi*, 509.

INTERNAL IMPROVEMENTS 405

omists of almost one hundred years standing. In return they promised to eliminate competition among themselves, to improve their efficiency, and to provide a service approximately universal.[422] As waterways had meanwhile declined comparatively, the case for the railroads seemed established. Moreover, in the absence of scientifically determined and popularly approved plans for the improvement of the Ohio, its friends in Congress and elsewhere were at sea. Under the circumstances it was not surprising that it, along with other inland rivers, fell a prey to "pork barrel" practices, annual appropriations of this character increasing from $1,374,688 in 1867 to $2,430,300 in 1872, $3,478,000 in 1875, $5,469,900 in 1878, and $12,676,900 in 1882, when the executive veto failed to arrest them.[423]

But for the Granger movement that found a counterpart in Germany and other European countries, where railroads were then being nationalized, rivers improved, and canals preserved and extended, the rivers of the United States would have fallen into a sorry plight in the seventies. Indeed, they might have been temporarily abandoned to be remembered only in songs and traditions. But the Grangers favored their use as an effective means of curbing the monopolistic tendencies and unfair practices of railroads. In Congress this gave rise to the famous Windom report of April, 1874, in which a select committee of the Senate tried to answer the self-propounded question: "By what means shall cheap and ample facilities be provided for the interchange of commodities between the different sections of our widely-extended country?" In addition to

---
[422] Wheeling *Intelligencer*, April 10, 1869.
[423] Inland Waterways Com., *Preliminary Report*, 1908; Wheeling *Intelligencer*, April 10, 1869.

the policy already indicated the answer to this question was "privately owned railroads must be made to compete," even at the expense of nationally owned and managed rival lines.

To the end that river traffic might be revived the Windom report proposed a comprehensive plan of river improvements that did not neglect the Ohio and its tributaries. In fact, their improvement was contemplated in two of its major projects: that for providing water communications between the Tidewater and the Mississippi by way of the James, Kanawha, and Ohio rivers and that for improving the transportation facilities between the Atlantic and the Mississippi to the southward by way of the Tennessee and Ohio rivers. Moreover, the Ohio was to be improved throughout its entire course by a slackwater navigation six feet deep. To this end sixty-six dams were planned at an estimated cost of approximately twenty-two million dollars. Construction would have commenced at Cairo instead of at Pittsburgh, as originally and later planned.[424]

When this program came before Congress in 1875, it went down to defeat before the prevailing piecemeal practices. A contributing factor was a proposal, of real merit, from Captain J. B. Eads of St. Louis, for deepening the mouth of the Mississippi by the use of jetties. Because of its strategic importance this improvement took priority over all others, and the recommendations of the Windom report were forgotten. Three hundred thousand dollars were, however, appropriated for the improvement of the Ohio river, one hundred thousand dollars of which were to be used for the construction of

---

[424] Inland Waterways Com., *op. cit.*, 180; U. S. *Congressional Record*, 45 cong., 2 sess., vol. vii, pt. iii, 2743.

a proposed "movable dam" to be located near Pittsburgh.

For some time thereafter the proposed "movable dam" was a local storm center. Some coal shippers desired it, the contracted dimensions of the slackwater pools on the Monongahela no longer serving their purposes, and certain packet and other boating interests favored it, as the initial step in a complete system of locks and dams embracing the whole course of the Ohio, as it proved to be. But there were others who opposed its construction, denouncing it as a "damnable move, most certainly movable by the floods of the Ohio." [425] Proposed sites were unsuitable, and when one was finally selected near Davis island, about five miles below Pittsburgh, the Pennsylvania legislature refused jurisdiction over the desired area. When this matter was finally adjusted to the satisfaction of the national government and the work of construction was scheduled to begin, August, 1878, opposition from certain other Pittsburgh interests became more pronounced than ever. Some of these did not wish slackwater near them because of its alleged pestilential effects; others saw ruin to local industry and even to the coal trade; and still others expressed a general disapproval by the use of torch light processions and other demonstrations. Moreover, after the work of construction began and all hope of preventing it and further delaying its progress had vanished, local politicians, after a fashion in which they later became more successful, would have controlled operations to their own

[425] — *Idem*, 43 cong., 2 sess., vol. iii, pt. iii, 2156; Wheeling *Intelligencer*, April 22, 1875; *idem*, December 13, 1875; *idem*, January 25, 1880; *idem*, August 30, 1882; Cincinnati *Commercial*, February 15, 1867; *Waterways Journal*, September 7, 1907.

advantage, thus delaying completion and augmenting costs. But for the firm opposition of Major Wm. E. Merrill, friend and successor of W. Milnor Roberts, they might have been successful.[426]

These delays and bickerings were not without their benefits. They permitted a thorough investigation of the lock and dam system, but, more important still, they permitted the use, on this particular dam, of an invention then coming into favor in France, by which it was possible to adjust wickets over wide spans thus reducing the number of piers in dams and lessening the dangers to navigation. The proposed use of this invention quieted the local opposition and paved the way for the subsequent canalization of the Ohio by similar devices, work on its first lock and dam being carried to completion in October, 1885, at a total cost slightly in excess of nine hundred thousand dollars.[427]

For a decade or more following the completion of the Davis Island dam neither local nor national conditions favored improved river navigation. The continent was being spanned by additional trunk lines; the Ohio river was being paralleled throughout its entire course by lines of steel; and lateral lines were reaching out to the smallest towns and cities making rail service almost universal. Moreover, in 1887, Congress, in the Interstate Commerce act of that date, declared its purpose to regulate and control railroads in the interest of the public. Under these conditions further investments in improved waterways seemed to be of doubtful expediency, and many were again ready to admit that the day might be near at hand when there would be no steamboats on the inland waters. Under the circum-

---

[426] See series of articles by Captain Thomas E. Clark in *Waterways Journal*, 1924 and 1925, passim. [427] Jones, *The Ohio River*, 150.

stances the usual appropriations for the construction of dikes, the removal of obstructions to navigation, and the maintenance of beacon lights, most of which had become a part of the regular dole to political spoilsmen, were considered ample for the needs of the Ohio and its tributaries.

But there were those who had not bowed the knee to Baal, and many of them resided in the Ohio valley. From experience they knew that river transportation, under favorable conditions, was cheaper and quicker for bulky commodities than that by rail. Many of them had read the Cullom report of 1886 setting forth the advantages of river transportation as a possible means of regulating railroad rates and services, and, more important still, their traditions were with the rivers. Furthermore, local conditions seemed to refute the claims being made for the railroads and to counsel the continued use of rivers. Outstanding among these was the Monongahela along which stream industry had continued to grow and railroads to prosper ever since it had been canalized in the forties. It was, also, generally conceded that the one thing doing most to prevent a similar development along the Allegheny and other tributaries to the Ohio was their unimproved navigation.[428]

Under these conditions the Ohio Valley Improvement Association was organized in 1895 for the purpose of "dealing with the transportation problems of the Ohio and its tributaries." Colonel John L. Vance of Gallipolis, Ohio, became its first president, receiving annual reëlections during a period of twenty-five years. During all this time his chief concern was for the improvement of the Ohio. To this end he received

---
[428] Moulton, *Waterways versus Railways*, chaps. 1-3.

the loyal and effective support of a committee of associates appointed for the express purpose of keeping Congress informed regarding the needs of the Ohio and the purposes of their organization.

Henceforth the river interests of the Ohio valley centered in this organization and in the smaller ones that grew up about it, and most that was done for the improvement of river navigation was directly attributable to their efforts. Their first accomplishment was to dispel the erroneous notions then gaining favor regarding the declining importance of local streams. To this end the first annual report of the parent organization went into details regarding the condition of traffic on the Ohio, revealing, among other things, that twenty thousand craft, large and small, with a total capacity of four million tons, then passed Davis Island dam annually and that almost one and a quarter million passengers continued to use the Ohio annually.

Following closely upon the heels of these revelations a program for the further improvement of the Ohio was launched. This called for slackwater, six feet deep, between Pittsburgh and Cincinnati, and, despite the decadent condition of rivers generally, Congress was asked for funds to carry it forward. As a result, in less than ten years, five additional locks and dams were built, extending slackwater from Pittsburgh to Beaver; plans were formed for extending this improvement to Marietta; and the locks and dams on the Monongahela were nationalized and extended to Fairmont. Probably more important was the fact that the public and those in authority came to look upon the improvement of the Ohio as a somewhat more meritorious undertaking than any of the improvements then being proposed for other river systems.

Incidentally the fight for the improved navigation of the Allegheny, championed, in its later stages, by Captain W. B. Rogers and other Pittsburghers, kept the subject of river improvement before the public and demonstrated some of the difficulties to be encountered, even in high places. This stream was obstructed by a number of bridges, most of them near its mouth. Fortunately for those interested in its improvement Congress, in the River and Harbor act of March 3, 1899, gave the Secretary of War full authority to deal with such conditions. Soon thereafter Secretary of War Root issued an order, later renewed by Secretary of War Taft, directing that the Union bridge over the Allegheny river, the most objectionable of those complained of crossing that stream, be raised, but saying nothing about others, some of which were almost as offensive. The official intimation that they might be permitted to stand as they were caused an appeal to Captain W. L. Sibert of Army Engineers and to counsel in the person of Albert Bettinger of Cincinnati. A technical and legal contest followed ending in 1917 in an order from Secretary of War Baker directing that all bridges on the lower Allegheny be raised to a height of forty-eight feet above pool levels. Following another period of delay and inaction, the objectionable bridges were either removed or altered, and the improvement of the Allegheny by a system of locks and dams is now (1930) being carried to completion.[429]

Meanwhile the United States entered world politics, changing somewhat the outlook and purposes of its people. At once they began to talk about the conservation

---

[429] Pittsburgh *Dispatch*, April 24, 1902; *idem*, October 1, 1905; *idem*, February 26, 1907; *idem*, March 7, 1907; Pittsburgh *Post*, August 5, 1904; Pittsburgh *Gazette*, August 6, 1904; Pittsburgh *Gazette-Times*, February 27, 1908; Pittsburgh *Times*, February 10, 1906.

of land, minerals, forests, and rivers; about an expected emporium of trade at the mouth of the Mississippi, following the completion of the Panama canal, then in process of construction; about prospective great inland ports to be located upon a proposed Lakes-to-Gulf waterway; and about connecting the Ohio and Lake Erie by means of a canal. Attention was also given to the transportation systems of France, Germany, and Belgium, where waterways and railroads were being built and maintained as complements one to the other.[430] In fact the effect of this national shift was to quicken the whole industrial, commercial, and agricultural life of the country, but nowhere more so than in the Mississippi valley.

As far as they affected water transportation the results of this awakening were numerous. Among other things in 1901 the first National Rivers and Harbors Congress met; two years later the state of New York voted one hundred and one million dollars for the enlargement and the improvement of the Erie canal; and in 1906 two historic meetings were held: the St. Louis Internal Improvement Convention and the Washington session of the Rivers and Harbors Congress. Out of the former grew the organization known as the Lakes-to-Gulf Waterways Association. In the early fall of 1907 members of the Inland Waterways Commission, accompanied by President Roosevelt, descended the Mississippi from Keokuk to Memphis, each of the intervening towns turning out more spectators to greet them "than its entire population; while day and night the air was rent with acclamations of voices, steam whistles, shrieking sirens, salvo of guns, and the roar and rattle

---

[430] Inland Waterways Com., *op. cit.*; Moulton, *op. cit.*, chaps. 1-2.

of fireworks." A veritable harvest of conventions and congresses followed culminating in the Deep Waterways Convention, held in New Orleans in October, 1909, with President Taft and Speaker Joseph G. Cannon as the guests of honor.

Already, in transmitting to Congress a preliminary report of the Inland Waterways Commission in 1908, President Roosevelt had ably summarized the sentiments of those favoring improved river navigation. In part he said: "Our river systems are better adapted to the needs of the people than those of any other country. In extent, distribution, navigability, and ease of use, they stand first. Yet the rivers of no other civilized country are so poorly developed, so little used, or play so small a part in the industrial life of the nation as those of the United States. In view of the use made of rivers elsewhere, the failure to use our own is astonishing, and no thoughtful man can believe that it will last. The accompanying report indicates clearly the reason for it and the way to end it.

"The Commission finds that it was unregulated railroad competition which prevented and destroyed the development of commerce on our inland waterways. The Mississippi, our greatest natural highway, is a case in point. At one time the traffic upon it was without a rival in any country. The report shows that commerce was driven from the Mississippi by the railroads. While production was limited, the railroads, with their convenient terminals, gave quicker and more satisfactory service than the waterways. Later they prevented the restoration of river traffic by keeping down their rates along the rivers, recouping themselves by higher charges elsewhere. They also acquired water fronts and terminals to an extent which made water competition impossible." [431]

In the midst of these developments friends of improved navigation in the Ohio valley were not mere interested spectators. In 1901, largely through their efforts, the National Rivers and Harbors Congress was revived from a rather comatose state of existence into an active and aggressive organization, and the next year the Ohio Valley Improvement Association, in convention at Parkersburg, West Virginia, resolved upon a new program for the improvement of the Ohio. This called for nine feet of slackwater from Pittsburgh to Cairo. Two years later Captain W. L. Sibert showed the advantages of such an improvement and pronounced it practicable, and soon thereafter a corps of government engineers worked out a program, together with estimates of costs, for carrying the work forward.

These developments increased the strategic advantages of the Ohio in the scramble for appropriations that followed. First of all, it had a scientifically determined program which appealed to those then tiring of the prevailing piecemeal methods of using public funds for the improvement of rivers and harbors. Thus the Ohio and its tributaries came to be spoken of, in Congress and elsewhere, as the "most important group of inland waterways in the country." [432] As a consequence, the further improvement of the Ohio was authorized in the River and Harbor act of June 25, 1910, and a liberal appropriation was made for that purpose.

The triumph of this pet enterprise brought joy and rejoicing throughout the Ohio valley. Proud of a vic-

---

[431] Inland Waterways Com., *op. cit.*, 111.

[432] *Waterways Journal*, October 1, 1910; *idem*, August 12, 1916; *idem*, October 27, 1923.

tory that was largely their own, its internal improvement associations expressed thanks to Congress and the President, as well as to former President Roosevelt. Articles appeared in local newspapers and elsewhere setting forth the possible advantages to be derived from the use of nine feet of slackwater in the Ohio from its source to its mouth. Cincinnati celebrated. At last she had found what promised to be a possible check upon the ravishments of those monsters, the railroads, that had ruined her river trade, thus making a mockery of her former proud position as "Queen of the West." In the days of their impotent infancy, in the interior, her leading citizen, Judge Alphonso Taft, had planned for the construction of railroads to and from Cincinnati, as the only means of preserving her greatness. Sixty years later his son, William Howard Taft, then president of the United States, welcomed the possible resumption of river navigation on the Ohio, as marking a "new epoch" in inland transportation.[433]

For some time following 1910 the work of improving the Ohio went forward according to schedule, but evil days were ahead for the enterprise. In the absence of plans for the improvement of other streams, scientifically determined and estimated, the "pork barrel" method of providing for all was continued, thus endangering the program of those of merit. For example, in 1914, Senator W. S. Kenyon of Iowa and the late Senator Theodore E. Burton of Ohio, both friends of improved rivers, maintained an all-night filibuster to prevent the approval of pending appropriations for that purpose. Meanwhile annual appropriations for the improvement of rivers and harbors had fallen from fifty-two million dollars in 1910, a high water mark, to

---

[433] — *Idem*, September 24, 1910.

twelve million dollars in 1914, the Ohio suffering with others. More alarming still were the effects of a commercial decadence that had practically stripped the Ohio of traffic. Heretofore the chief argument for its improved navigation had been the fact that the volume of traffic thereon was increasing annually. Now that it was gone, some said forever, there were those who were unwilling "to throw good money after bad" by building locks and dams along its course all the way from Pittsburgh to Cairo.

But the improvement of the Ohio had intrinsic merits. Some urged it as an experiment, and "in as much as millions had already been spent," others thought that its improvement should be carried to completion. While these and others debated, the World war came on, and railroads failed to meet the transportation needs of the country. As a result traffic again sought the Ohio in such quantities as again to renew demands for its improved navigation. It mattered not that the tonnage had shifted from coal, timber, and passengers to iron and steel.[434]

It was under these conditions that improved inland waterways again found favor with Congress. Accordingly, in 1922, a "waterways bloc," disregarding the recommendations of the federal budget, appropriated a total of forty-two million dollars for the improvement of rivers and harbors, which was increased to fifty-six millions the year following. To avoid the "pork barrel" Nemesis these amounts were turned over to the War Department to be allotted among individual projects according to their respective merits. Under this plan the belated improvement of the Ohio, formerly scheduled

---

[434] — *Idem*, November 19, 1921; *idem*, February 25, 1922; *idem*, January 27, 1923.

for completion in 1922, came in for liberal allowances, that for 1923 reaching five and one-half million dollars, and its boosters raised the slogan "On to Cairo by 1929." [435]

These anticipations were well founded. On schedule time, October 19-25, 1929, the Ohio Valley Improvement Association, together with numerous local chambers of commerce and other organizations, joined President Hoover, members of his cabinet, and other notables, among them the governors of Kentucky, Indiana, Ohio, and West Virginia, in the dedication of a system of locks and dams so constructed as to give the Ohio river, throughout its length and throughout the year, a uniform stage of slackwater of a minimum depth of nine feet. Although the total cost of this engineering feat aggregated almost one hundred twenty-five million dollars, or more than ten times the original estimate, all rejoiced in its completion, confident in its potentialities for manyfold returns.

A feature of these ceremonies was the "Dedication Cruise" that left Pittsburgh, October 18, the flagship "Cincinnati" and her sister steamers, the "Greater Pittsburgh" and the "Queen City," leading the way. With a passenger list totaling hundreds these and a score or more other craft set off from the Monongahela levee before a loyal throng of boosters said to have numbered almost two hundred thousand. On its way down the river these boats were joined by others and greeted by thousands of persons, some from gayly decorated wharves, others from autumn-tinted river banks, and still others from gayly illuminated bridges. At Cincinnati, October 22, they were joined by still other

[435] — *Idem*, October 10, 1923; *idem*, October 17, 1925; *idem*, October 24, 1925.

craft, among them the "Greenbrier," a government lighthouse tender that carried President and Mrs. Hoover. The President had just participated in the dedication of a monument, located in Eden Park, Cincinnati, to commemorate the completion of the canalization of the Ohio and the memory of some of those most instrumental in effecting it.[436] Thence the party proceeded to Louisville, where the President briefly outlined the history of internal improvements on the Ohio and the policy of his administration respecting inland waterways in general. Here he left the dedicatory pageant, a part of which continued to Cairo.[437]

The canalization of the Ohio was effected by the use of fifty locks and dams. Except the first structures at the head of the river, Emsworth dam at Emsworth, Pennsylvania, displacing Dams no. 1, and no. 2, and Dashield's dam, displacing Dam no. 3, all remaining dams on the Ohio are movable, of Chanoine or Bebout wicket type, with bear-trap regulating weirs.[438] At times of impending high waters the wickets forming these dams are lowered to the bed of the stream permitting vessels to pass over them through navigable passes instead of through locks as at other times. Wickets are three feet nine inches wide, from fifteen to eighteen feet long, depending upon the lift of the dam, and are supported in an inclined position, a maneuver boat being used to adjust them. Bear-trap weirs are used to make

---

[436] This monument bears two bronze tablets, one in memory of John L. Vance of Gallipolis, Ohio, first president of the Ohio Valley Improvement Association, the other in memory of Albert Bettinger of Cincinnati, a legal adviser and leader of that organization.

[437] *National Waterways*, November, 1929; *Waterways Journal*, October 19, 1929; idem, October 26, 1929; idem, November 2, 1929.

[438] See Jones, *The Ohio River* (ed. 1929), 4. In addition to the dams already mentioned, those on the Great Kanawha, completed towards the end of the last century, those on the Little Kanawha, completed in the

Dam number 1, Monongahela river
The first in the Pittsburgh district, built in 1840. The now obsolete comb type of timber construction

Locks and fixed dam, Emsworth, Pa.
Locks are 110 by 600 feet and 56 by 360 feet, with guide walls 600 feet long. Total length of dam 1746 feet

minor adjustments of pool levels and are operated by maneuver boats independently of wickets. The standard navigable pass is from six hundred to nine hundred feet wide and is the distinctive feature of the movable dam, at each of which there is one lock one hundred ten feet wide and six hundred feet long. At each of the two fixed dams, Emsworth and Dashield's, built to provide permanent pools of slackwater for the shipping inter-

early seventies of the last century, and others of the Ohio River System are stationary. The dams on the Ohio, together with number, distance from Pittsburgh, location, year commenced, and date of completion, follow:

Dam No.	Miles Below Pittsburgh	Location with reference to nearest town or other geographical location	Year Construction Commenced	Year Opened to Navigation
1	6.1	Emsworth, Pa. (replacing Nos. 1 and 2)	1919	1921
3	10.9	Glenosborne, Pa.	1899	1908
4	18.0	Legionville, Pa.	1898	1908
5	23.9	Freedom, Pa.	1898	1907
6	28.8	Beaver, Pa.	1892	1904
7	36.9	Midland, Pa.	1910	1914
8	46.1	Newell, W. Va.	1904	1911
9	55.6	New Cumberland, W. Va.	1910	1914
10	65.7	Steubenville, Ohio	1912	1915
11	76.3	2.3 miles below Wellsburg, W. Va.	1904	1911
12	87.0	2 miles above Wheeling, W. Va.	1911	1917
13	95.8	McMechen, W. Va.	1901	1911
14	113.8	Woodland, W. Va.	1911	1917
15	128.9	New Martinsville, W. Va.	1911	1916
16	146.4	Ben's Run, W. Va.	1913	1917
17	167.4	4 miles above Marietta, Ohio	1913	1918
18	179.3	4.5 miles above Parkersburg, W. Va.	1902	1910
19	191.4	Little Hocking, Ohio	1908	1916
20	201.7	Belleville, W. Va.	1911	1917
21	213.8	Portland, Ohio	1915	1919
22	220.1	Ravenswood, W. Va.	1915	1919
23	230.6	Milwood, W. Va.	1917	1921
24	242.0	Graham, W. Va.	1913	1919
25	260.0	5 miles above Pt. Pleasant, W. Va.	1917	1922
26	278.0	Hogsett, W. Va.	1908	1912

ests of Pittsburgh, there are two locks, one fifty-six feet wide by three hundred sixty feet long and the other one hundred ten feet wide by six hundred feet long.

Dam No.	Miles Below Pittsburgh	Location with reference to nearest town or other geographical location	Year Construction Commenced	Year Opened to Navigation
27	300.3	4 miles above Guyandot, W. Va.	1918	1923
28	310.9	Huntington, W. Va.	1911	1915
29	319.4	3 miles below Catlettsburg, Ky.	1911	1916
30	338.9	3 miles below Greenup, Ky.	1919	1923
31	358.4	3 miles below Portsmouth, Ohio	1912	1920
32	381.7	1 mile above Rome, Ohio	1919	1925
33	404.0	3 miles above Maysville, Ky.	1915	1921
34	432.8	Chilo, Ohio	1919	1925
35	449.7	1 mile below New Richmond, Ohio	1913	1919
36	459.2	10 miles above Cincinnati, Ohio	1920	1925
37	481.3	Fernbank, Ohio	1905	1911
38	501.3	McVille, Ky.	1920	1924
39	529.6	1 mile above Markland, Ind.	1914	1912
41	604.0	Louisville, Ky., New Power Navigation dam	1925	1927
43	630.2	3 miles below West Point, Ky.	1914	1921
44	660.3	Leavenworth, Ind.	1920	1926
45	699.7	Addison, Ky.	1923	1928
46	752.9	Owensboro, Ky.	1923	1928
47	772.5	Newburg, Ind.	1923	1927
48	804.1	6 miles below Henderson, Ky.	1912	1921
49	867.7	Ford's Ferry, Ky.	1924	1927
50	893.0	Golconda, Illinois	1925	1929
52	928.0	Brookport, Illinois	1924	1928
53	951.2	Foot of Grand Chain	1925	1929

Recent Years on the Rivers

When the United States entered the World war in 1917 river traffic in the Ohio valley, as elsewhere in the interior, was almost a thing of the past. Traffic on the Ohio had declined to four and one-half million tons annually, the lowest mark since 1890, and most of this was coal carried for short distances in the Pittsburgh district.[439] Conspicuous by their absence were the great coal fleets that had formerly descended from Pittsburgh to the lower Ohio and the Mississippi. Meanwhile, local packet departures from Pittsburgh had decreased from two hundred fourteen in 1915 to one hundred twenty-two in 1917, and, probably worse still, work on locks and dams for improved navigation had practically ceased. Practically completing the destruction, in 1918, most of the tonnage and terminals left on the Ohio were swept away in the ice floes of that year.

Only here and there were to be found traces of the former glory of the Ohio and its tributaries. On the lower Monongahela alone was traffic large and increasing, while on the lower Ohio coal was still being transported from the Great Kanawha to Cincinnati and Louisville. With headquarters at Cincinnati the Barrett line of towboats operated on the Ohio, Cumberland, and Tennessee rivers.[440] Packets were also maintaining themselves in trades between the former city and Charleston, West Virginia, and Pomeroy, Ohio.

Such was the local situation when our nation and associated powers turned to the Ohio valley, a great

---
[439] U. S. Army Engineers, *Interim Report*, 1927.   [440] —*Idem*, 11.

industrial center, for aid in a crisis involving the future of peoples and of governments. This section was asked to do its part in a mobilization of man power and of the products of industry. The final outcome of the struggle then waging seemed to hinge largely upon the ability of local interests to supply industrial products in such quantities and at such times as they were needed, but an inadequate transportation stood in the way of this accomplishment.

During a half century local railroads had boasted their ability to supply all transportation needs, only to fail the country in this crisis. In 1917 their breakdown was officially admitted, and both their officers and owners welcomed relief. Soon thereafter they were temporarily taken over by the national government which, at once, supplemented them by a nationally owned and controlled barge line on the Mississippi and Warrior rivers, leaving to private initiative the further solution of the transportation problem of the Ohio valley and of other sections.

Along the Ohio the response to this demand was immediate and effective. As in other crises, resort was to rivers, the first effort being to supply tonnage. To this end old and discarded steamboats were remodeled and recommissioned; new ones were built; and many local concerns entered the boat building business, some of them on a large scale. Chief activity was, however, directed to barge building, the total output of such craft for the Pittsburgh district reaching two hundred forty-five in 1918. The following year it fell to seventy-one but soon thereafter passed the 1918 mark and has tended to increase annually since.[441] The Barge Age of transportation, long promised, had at last arrived.

---
[441] — *Idem*, 11.

At once local barge building became the order of the day, almost a dozen companies participating in their construction.[442] The value of their products for the year 1920 was in excess of one million one hundred thousand dollars, and some of their craft, notably the boats built by James Rees and Sons Company, were for use on foreign waters. Meanwhile still other companies were building boatyards and otherwise preparing to supply the large and increasing demand for tonnage. In this one year the total expenditure for river craft in the Pittsburgh district alone reached five and one-half million dollars, while half as much more was spent by private individuals for terminals, docks, and other devices for improving navigation.

The restoration of boat building on the upper Ohio may be illustrated from facts in the history of a representative building concern, the Dravo Contracting Company. With headquarters at Coraopolis, Pennsylvania, this firm, first organized in 1891 under the name F. R. Dravo and Company, planned at first only to sell machinery and to maintain a general contracting business, the building of river craft, on a large scale, being scarcely contemplated. In 1906, under its present name, headquarters and a main plant were established on Neville Island, in the Ohio below Pittsburgh, but still comparatively little was attempted in the line of boat building. Following the entry of the United States into the World war this company, along with others, was driven into the boat building business, first to supply its own needs and later for commercial purposes. While hostilities lasted and for some time thereafter, it em-

---

[442] Pittsburgh *Post*, January 1, 1921. Prominent among local builders were the Dravo Contracting Company, the American Bridge Company, the Vesta Coal Company, the Hazelwood Dock Company, the Dravosburg Dock Company, the De Forest Barge Company, and the John Eichley, Jr. Company.

ployed fifteen hundred men daily, most of them in its boatyard, and at few times since has the number employed there fallen below five hundred daily. In 1925 it launched barges at the rate of ten to twelve monthly, together with an occasional steamboat, derrickboat, and dredgeboat. Meanwhile it maintained a general contracting business, building locks, dams, bridges, and houses, the total cost of which ran into millions annually.[443]

This revival was not confined to the Pittsburgh district. As in the forties and the eighties of the last century, boat building became an important industry in practically every important port of the Ohio valley. For example, near Charleston on the Great Kanawha, the Charles Ward Engineering works began to launch some of the finest boats and barges to be seen on the inland waters; at Jeffersonville, Indiana, the Howard ship-yards increased their output, maintaining meanwhile a reputation of long standing for the excellence of their products; at Paducah, Kentucky, the Ayer and Lord Marine ways were never idle; at Point Pleasant, West Virginia, the Marietta Manufacturing Company received more orders for new boats than it could fill; and at Nashville, on the Cumberland river, the Nashville Bridge Company began to build parts for sea-going vessels, that were assembled in Gulf ports and put into successful operation.

Incidentally the Ohio valley regained its place as a chief source of supply for boats and rivermen, not only for inland America but for other parts of the world as well. The Federal Barge line, already referred to as in successful operation on the Mississippi and Warrior rivers, drew most of its boats and barges from the Ohio,

---

[443] *Waterways Journal*, May 22, 1926.

as did also Standard Oil subsidiaries and sugar producers on the lower Mississippi, and self-propelled barges of the type of the famous "Inco no. 1," built in 1918 at the Carondolet Marine ways in St. Louis for use in France, were built on the Ohio and tributary streams.[444] Thus were the benefits and the achievements of the Barge Age of American inland transportation carried to the world, and that by a craft which unlike its forerunner of more than a century before, the inland built ship, was able to return to the place of its origin under its own power.

Present indications are that local production of river craft will be equal to all demands. In 1921 there was a temporary decline in the number of barges built, but this was due largely to a shift from the use of wood to steel as a building material and also to business depression and to uncertainties regarding the type, or types, of construction best suited to future needs.[445] Since that time however, as already indicated, the product of local boatyards has tended to increase annually, current river news being largely a chronicle of completions of boats and barges and of contracts for new ones. In 1928 the total value of the barges, boats, and terminals employed in the Ohio river system aggregated seventy-five million dollars of which sum forty million dollars was in river craft, and the capacity of the three hundred thirty-eight barges in process of construction aggregated almost one hundred and twenty-five thousand

---

[444] — *Idem*, January 18, 1919. The "Parana" and the "Mohawk Belle," self-propelled barges, were built on the Ohio before the Civil war. See *Waterways Journal*, September 16, 1916.

[445] U. S. House. Document no. 857, March, 1914; U. S. House. Document no. 108, August, 1921. For articles on various phases of these subjects see *Waterways Journal*, February 25, 1911; *idem*, November 6, 1915; *idem*, November 13, 1915; *idem*, November 20, 1915; *idem*, January 15, 1916.

tons.[446] At the same time more than two thousand vessels of all kinds were in use.

More significant still was the tendency to the exclusive use of steel for barge construction. The total number of wooden barges built on the Ohio since 1921 has not reached half of the total for 1920 alone. The same tendency prevailed in the construction of towboats and packets, most of those built recently being of all-steel construction. With the price of lumber tending to increase and the price of steel tending to decrease it is not probable, everything considered, particularly the greater durability of steel, that wood will again be used to any great extent for the construction of boats and barges anywhere in the Ohio valley.

Outstanding among the modern devices used is the Diesel internal combustion engine which uses oil for motive power and is displacing the old-time steamboat with its towering stacks and space consuming boilers and engines. The long drawn out fight between the devotees of the stern-wheel and the side-wheel boat continues with the odds in favor of the former, which now works in duplicate, thus increasing its effectiveness, but screw propellers are coming into general use. Everywhere the tendency is to the practical and the utilitarian at the sacrifice of the gingerbread embellishments of former days.

As yet, standardization is not a discernible feature of the locally built craft. For example, in the harbor of Pittsburgh one may now see, along-side of new all-steel hull paddle-wheel steamboats, of either stern-wheel or side-wheel construction, a wooden-hulled craft of the same general design and practically new. Here and

[446] — *Idem*, January 15, 1927; *idem*, December 17, 1927; *idem*, June 2, 1928.

there are also stern-wheelers of two sections, each independently controlled, together with screw-propelled boats and barges. At the same time one may see boats carrying Diesel internal-combustion engines, the whole, except for the sound of the exhaust of the oil-consuming devices, resembling more a lake tug than a steamboat. Together with old-time towboats these will be towing barges varying in size from eighty feet long, sixteen feet wide, and five feet deep to two hundred seventy-five feet long, fifty-two feet wide, and fourteen feet deep, the standard barge being one hundred seventy-five feet long, twenty-six feet beam, and eleven feet hold. Interspersed among these will be seen gasoline boats, dredges, derrickboats, and, in season showboats and excursion boats, the latter now plying the Ohio and tributary streams in increasing numbers. Twin screw turbo-electric towboats, the first on any inland waters, are now in process of construction for local uses.

The change in the character of the commodities carried has been as great as that in the craft used. Prior to 1922 the major portion of local river traffic consisted of coal and coke, the volume of which continues to increase. Logs and lumber, packet freight, and unclassified items of a miscellaneous variety were important prior to 1910, but since then they have been of declining importance. On the other hand the stone, sand, and gravel traffic increased from a nominal figure in 1920, until it now exceeds the volume of coal and coke transported. From a small volume in 1910 the iron and steel traffic on the inland waters showed little increase until 1925, since which date it has gone forward by leaps and bounds. Of all these products iron and steel have the longest haul.[447]

---

[447] *National Waterways*, October, 1929; U. S. Army Engineers, *Interim Report*, 1927.

Like the changes in the types of craft used on the inland waters, those in the character of the commodities carried did not come until well after the World war. In each the strikes and readjustments incident to the resumption of private control of railroads were possibly determining factors. All were trying to get back to normal conditions. In so doing it was discovered that production costs had declined greatly in the intervening years, and this despite the effects of war conditions. Moreover, the indications were that the greater efficiency of labor and machinery, together with a tendency to the elimination of waste everywhere, would cause production prices to go still lower. On the other hand transportation costs tended to increase, in some instances becoming practically prohibitive. Further progress had, in fact, become impossible in the absence of a cheaper and more dependable transportation.

It was under these conditions that the possibilities of water transportation for basic, heavy, and bulky commodities, such as iron and steel, fuels, forest products, building materials, and agricultural products were practically forced upon the country. Heavy freight was then being carried by rail on an average of twenty-four miles daily with only thirty miles promised as a maximum under the most favorable conditions, and the Transportation act of that year, guaranteeing profits to railroads and permitting them to combine, with the approval of the Interstate Commerce Commission, was not encouraging to agriculture and to other extractive occupations. The action of the "waterways bloc" of 1922 in overriding the wishes of the administration and demanding a resumption of the improved waterways program, on a large scale, was the answer of the country at large to the problem involved in the situation.

The "Iowa" of 2000 horse-power
With three barges containing 6000 tons of iron pipe at Lock number 2, Ohio river.

Already local Ohio valley interests had resolved upon the same solution. They, too, were suffering from the effects of an over production and of an inadequate transportation which, in some instances, was practically prohibitive because of uncertainties and delays. Moreover, demands were pouring into the Pittsburgh district for industrial products. Those from the South and the Southwest for casing, pipe, and oil well supplies were urgent. It was under these conditions that Pittsburgh and neighboring interests again thought of "Ole Man River," long deserted and by some practically forgotten.

But, in the absence of tonnage, rivers were practically useless. Except on the lower Monongahela, there were few private bottoms, and, as indicated elsewhere, common carriers were few and far between. In 1920 all of these that were available were called from the "bone yard," and a mosquito fleet of gasoline packets and towboats sprang into existence to help them. Through their use the usual movements of coal, coke, and raw materials were resumed, and finished products, sewer pipe, brick, tin plate, automobiles, steel, iron pipe, and machinery began to find markets, some of them in Mississippi ports.[448]

As conditions did not improve with the succeeding months, local industry was practically driven into the field of transportation. It mattered not that agriculture was thus deprived of the more or less exclusive benefits wont to be bestowed upon a time-honored handmaid. Orders for finished products increased in numbers and attractiveness. It was thus that local industries decided to market their own products by water and in their own bottoms, the initial trips of the "Transporter"

---

[448] Pittsburgh *Post*, January 1, 1921.

of the Wheeling Steel Company and the "Alliquippa" of the Jones and Laughlin Company, 1921, marking the beginning of a new era in the field of inland transportation, as well as in the field of industry. These boats carried steel products to Mississippi ports, the latter to a company-owned terminal at Memphis.[449]

In a short time other local corporations followed the example of these pioneers, each of which has since increased the scope of its activities. Beginning in 1922 the Carnegie Steel Company, in the same manner, has made scores of shipments of steel from Pittsburgh to southern markets. For this purpose and local uses it now (1930) operates a dozen or more towboats and more than three hundred barges representing a total value in excess of eleven million dollars, the largest and most valuable privately owned fleet on the inland waters. In October, 1927, the Jones and Laughlin Company of Pittsburgh made its fifty-sixth river shipment of steel from Pittsburgh to terminals on the Mississippi, the event being a feature of the program of the annual convention of the Ohio Valley Improvement Association of that year. Since then there has been scarcely an issue of the *Waterways Journal* (St. Louis, weekly) that has not recorded river shipments of steel and other industrial products from Pittsburgh.

In April, 1930, the "Century Tow" of the Jones and Laughlin Company passed down the Ohio to Memphis and New Orleans with a cargo which, together with the tonnage used to transport it, was valued at approximately one million dollars. The event was celebrated all along the route, and the owners issued an illustrated booklet to commemorate it. As this tow was somewhat

---

[449] *Waterways Journal*, January 1, 1921; *idem*, March 4, 1922; *idem*, June 30, 1923; *The Blast Furnace and Steel Plant*, January, 1923.

THE "SAM CRAIG," APRIL 16, 1930
This modern steamboat left Pittsburgh with a tow of 10,000 tons of steel.

typical of the others then descending the Ohio, it is described here somewhat at length. Ahead of the steamboat in charge, the "Sam Craig," were a dozen modern steel barges covering an acre or more of water surface, their contents being sufficient to fill several hundred freight cars. After all had been assembled a deep resonant whistle blew a long blast that was echoed and reëchoed from the surrounding hills. A bell was tapped, and a megaphone carried commands from the boat to men standing at the head of the tow several hundred feet forward. In response these cast off the ropes holding the boat and barges to the shore; bells tinkled in the engine room; the great high-riding paddle wheel began to thrash the water, lifting it into the air to glisten snow-white like a mountain cataract sparkling in the pale, early sunlight; and the huge mass swung slowly away from its terminal and was off for a voyage of two thousand miles of winding rivers.

A more accurate idea of the alliance thus formed between industry and commerce may, possibly, be gained from facts regarding the operations of another going concern. The Wheeling Steel Company is taken from among a dozen or more possibilities. This company operates many plants scattered along the Ohio all the way from Steubenville to Portsmouth. Company-owned steamers and barges supply all with fuel from company-owned and operated mines located at Harmersville, Pennsylvania. At the same time these craft maintain the closest inter-plant relations for the interchange of raw materials and finished products in varying stages of fabrication. Meanwhile other company-owned steamers, among them the "Conqueror," the "Transporter," and the "La Belle," carry finished products to Memphis for re-distribution from privately owned storehouses. A subsidiary, the La Belle Transportation Company, has charge of transportation.[450]

Facts from the history and activities of still another company of the same character, the American Steel and Wire Company of Pittsburgh, are informing. In 1900, in pursuance of a plan of eleven years standing, this company built and put into successful operation two towboats, the "Juniata" and the "Braddock," together with seventy wooden barges, the whole fleet being used to carry coal, billets, scrap, and rods. Its chief use, however, was for the transportation of coal which was carried from mines on the Monongahela to company-owned plants in Donora, Rankin, Braddock, and Pittsburgh. In 1905 this company began the use of steel barges as an experiment, its superintendent of transportation insisting that they would, in the long run, be more serviceable and durable than those of wooden construction, especially so since the company then contemplated the transportation of acids by water. In 1907 this experiment was put into successful operation, and soon thereafter all the barges used by this company were of steel construction. At present it owns and operates a number of towboats and about one hundred barges. Some of these are used for the transportation of fuel, others to maintain inter-plant relations, and still others to carry finished products to company-owned warehouses located in Louisville, Memphis, Baton Rouge, New Orleans, and St. Paul.[451]

As a result of these and still other activities the Ohio river system in 1930 carried the largest freight tonnage in its history. In 1928 the total for the Ohio alone reached almost twenty-one million tons which was two-

---

[450] *Waterways Journal*, August 14, 1926.
[451] — *Idem*, January 21, 1928.

thirds of the volume of traffic then passing through the Panama canal and surpassed that passing through the Suez canal. During the same period the gross traffic on the Ohio and its navigable tributaries increased from a little more than twenty-seven million tons in 1917 to almost sixty million tons in 1928, which included slight duplications.

For many streams this increase was phenomenal. This was certainly true of the Ohio, the traffic of which, in 1917, was less than five million tons. In the same year "20,000,000 tons annually for the Mon[ongahela]" was predicted as a possibility by the most sanguine river boosters,[452] but three years sufficed to carry the traffic for that stream well beyond the twenty-four-million-ton mark and to fix thirty million tons as the goal for the near future. Meanwhile the increase on still other streams was almost as rapid. For example, that on the Cumberland and the Tennessee rivers almost doubled, while that on the Allegheny increased from practically nothing to almost five million tons, the bulk of which was gravel.[453]

Another tendency in local river traffic is the increasing use of rivers for the transportation of crude oil and its products. Already many towns along the Ohio and its chief tributaries receive their supplies of these products by water, and the area thus served is gradually widening. By this method the Standard Oil Company of New Jersey, in 1927, made a single shipment of six hundred thousand gallons of gasoline from Parkersburg, West Virginia, to Fairmont in the same state.[454] Because of its success and its significance this feat was

---
[452] Pittsburgh *Post*, January 1, 1921.
[453] U. S. Army Engineers, *Interim Report*, 1927.
[454] *Waterways Journal*, April 2, 1927.

heralded throughout the Ohio valley, but it has been repeated several times since, the size of the shipments tending to increase.

Unlike the forties and the eighties of the last century, when bells and whistles were used to announce arrivals and departures of the one thousand or more steamboats that then plied the waters of the Mississippi and its chief tributaries and when hundreds of persons frequented important local levees daily, the present freight movements on the Ohio and its tributaries go on unobserved and even unsuspected. In the "good old days of steamboatin'" most boats were small but boisterous, whereas today a single tow, such as is sent forth on an average of one monthly by such corporations as the Carnegie Steel Company of Pittsburgh, consists of from fifteen to eighteen barges carrying a total of from ten to twelve thousand tons. Steamer and all, they are about nine hundred feet long by one hundred feet wide, and, like ships that pass in the night, they move quietly, unobserved, and unannounced, except for time taken out for "locking," uninterrupted, with not so much as a salute for the towns and cities passed in their course.

Fortunately the benefits of this new order, recently characterized by President Hoover as the "renaissance" of river navigation, are not local. With the recent passage of the Denison act which provides, among other things, for the establishment of rates and suitable division of revenue between the Federal Barge line and all railroads connected with its terminals, and the subsequent enlargement of its scope by the Interstate Commerce Commission, the outlook is most encouraging. As a result we may soon expect published combination rail and water rates, thus carrying the benefits of inland water transportation to forty million people residing between the Appalachian and the Rocky mountains.[455]

Already the enlarged local advantages are apparent. Within recent months Memphis has become the leading point in the South for the storage and distribution of steel products in that section and the Southwest. More than a half dozen large steel manufacturing companies own terminals there and distribute their products thence by rail and water. Moreover, following the extension of the services of the Federal Barge line from St. Louis to Minneapolis, in 1927, several Memphis firms went into the export business using barges and steamers, and the indications are that Memphis will become a great importing and exporting city.

Conditions following our entrance into the World war also stimulated the passenger packet trade on the Ohio, where patriotically inclined persons organized new packet lines and extended old ones. It was then that the Louisville and Cincinnati Packet Company temporarily extended its services to Pittsburgh and that the Liberty Transit Company came into existence. With a number of boats and an authorized capital stock of five hundred thousand dollars this company revived a regular packet service between Pittsburgh and Cincinnati. In a short time other packets entered local trades here and there, and a new company, the Independent Packet line, placed competing steamers in the Pittsburgh-Cincinnati trade.[456] Thus, about 1918, conditions and accomplishments indicated a possible come-back for the Ohio river packet.

---

[455] *National Waterways*, October, 1929; U. S. *Interstate Commerce Commission*. Ex Parte, no. 94 (November 12, 1928); *idem*, Ex Parte, no. 96 (November 9, 1929).

[456] *Waterways Journal*, February 2, 1918; *idem*, December 31, 1921; *idem*, February 11, 1922; *idem*, October 13, 1923.

As of old, however, this promised return met with reverses. First of all a decision of the Interstate Commerce Commission of 1918 permitting railroads to refuse to enter prorating agreements with steamboats proved almost fatal to the latter, putting them "out of commission over night."[457] In the years immediately following waters were low, dull times curtailed river activities, and, as already indicated, competition asserted its destructive influences. There was also the usual mismanagement. For example, instead of building new and modern tonnage, as the towing interests had learned to do, packet owners used old steamers, some of them mere derelicts, imported from Mississippi and other trades or resurrected from the "bone yard." As a result of these and other factors the Liberty Transit Company failed, surviving packet lines generally curtailed operations, and on the upper Ohio the packet service gravitated to the decadent condition of the years immediately preceeding.[458]

Fortunately counter forces prevented a complete reversion to pre-war conditions. Most significant of these, certainly in recent years, were decisions of packet owners to use only first-class tonnage. Assured of a permanent and dependable stage of slackwater from Pittsburgh to Cairo, they planned for better days. In anticipation of these, packets were generally of all-steel hull construction and were artistically designed and luxuriously equipped. Something of this vision brought to the Greene line, the creation of the late Gordon B. Greene, operating out of Cincinnati to the north, the "Chris Greene" and the "Tom Greene" and

---

[457] — *Idem*, December 7, 1918, quoting General Lansing H. Beach.

[458] — *Idem*, January 10, 1920; *idem*, January 6, 1923; *idem*, January 5, 1924; *idem*, January 12, 1925.

to the Louisville and Cincinnati Packet line, in the trade between Louisville and Cincinnati, the "Cincinnati," one of the most modern and best equipped steamers that ever stirred the waters of the Ohio. On the upper Ohio efforts have been less successful, but the persistence of interested captains, among them Fredrick Way, Jr. and William S. Pollock, was commendable, if not profitable.

Although not wholly devoid of advertising features, the race between the "Betsy Ann," Captain Way, and the "Chris Greene," Captain Greene, July 24, 1928 repeated in 1929 and again in 1930, was heralded as marking the beginning of a new day in the history of Ohio river packet service. It certainly revived memories of an old and glorious past. It was run over a twenty mile course between Cincinnati and New Richmond and was won by the "Greene" which nosed out her rival by two boat lengths. The time was two hours and twenty-five minutes and was the talk of the year in river packet circles. Approximately one hundred thousand persons saw it, and it inspired editorial comments throughout the country.

In 1928 ninety-five per cent of the freight traffic on the Ohio was carried in privately owned and operated bottoms,[459] but many would have welcomed a common carrier service for that stream such as that provided by the Federal Barge line on the Mississippi and Warrior rivers. It mattered not that this line was being operated with a view to its ultimate private ownership. Unlike the steel companies and other concerns previously mentioned, some local interests were unable to own and operate their own tonnage and would have welcomed any means, however temporary, that would

---
[459] U. S. Army Engineers, *Interim Report*, 1927.

have enabled them to use river transportation. A survey, made with a view to the possible extension of the government's Mississippi service to the Ohio, disclosed more than three hundred fifty prospective shippers representing seventy-four different localities and promising freight aggregating almost three million tons annually.[460]

It is not likely, however, that such a service will be provided for the Ohio river in the near future. In submitting the report made with a view to its possible extension Wilmer M. Jacoby of the Inland Waterways Corporation, acting under directions from the Secretary of War, recommended it only in the event that privately owned tonnage, under proper encouragement from the national government, failed to build up and maintain an adequate river transportation service.[461] Thus far government officials and others have acted on the assumption that the best way to encourage private initiative in this matter is by assuring it a free field from the beginning. Developments described elsewhere in this chapter would seem to justify this course. Moreover, local traditions and business interests are opposed to government ownership and control in any form, their sentiments being well expressed in these words from a local Pittsburgh editor:

> This city, keenly interested in waterways development, has never been excited over government operation of barge lines. It has believed, and still believes, that when the government completes its project for a dependable stage to Cairo, the boats will come to Pittsburgh without further government aid or subsidy. Just as motor cars fill highways as fast as state and local governments can build

---

[460] *Waterways Journal*, August 4, 1928.

[461] Wilmer M. Jacoby's "Freight Traffic Studies on the Ohio," in manuscript.

them, so boats ply rivers as fast as the government makes them navigable. Private initiative needs no further stimulus.[462]

Recent events have justified these predictions. Although other similar enterprises have failed in the recent past, the Inland Waterways Corporation of Louisville, organized in 1920, maintained itself as a common carrier on the Ohio and tributary streams, as did also, for a brief period, the Kelley Barge line of Charleston, West Virginia, organized somewhat later. The consolidation of these two companies in 1928 under the name of the American Barge line of Louisville, with a combined capital stock of one and one-half million dollars, provided Ohio river shippers with a dependable and reasonably adequate common carrier service that promised to be permanent.[463] Since then other concerns have considered the possibilities of this field, but all of them now (1930) restrict their activities to contract towing. When conditions warrant, it is fair to presume that they will enter the common carrier service.

The most assuring thing about the inauguration of a common carrier river service on the Ohio was the character of the initial equipment used to maintain it. For the propulsion of the fifty or more barges of the American Barge line, of all-steel construction, three of the Diesel propelled steamers were used. These were the "Duncan Bruce," a twin stern-wheeler, the "W. A. Shepherd," and the "George T. Price," each twin-screw propelled. In 1928 these were among the largest and most powerful boats afloat on the inland waters, their aggregate capacity, boats and barges, being in excess of thirty thousand tons. Among other towboats

[462] *Waterways Journal*, October 15, 1927.
[463] —*Idem*, October 16, 1926; *idem*, November 13, 1926; *idem*, November 20, 1926.

since added to this fleet were the "Dorothy Barrett" and the "Plymouth," which carried the first set of under flow engines ever installed for river or marine propulsion.

It is for the accommodation of such craft that local river interests are now directing attention to the construction of standard terminals. Without such aid to navigation it has long been agreed that expenditures for locks and dams would be somewhat prodigal. That is why November 1, 1926, was a memorable day in the history of the Ohio river. On that day the Wierton Steel Company of Wierton, West Virginia, put into operation, at its local plant, the first modern terminal on that stream.[464] It cost approximately one million dollars and had a maximum capacity of more than four hundred tons per hour. Although it was constructed for private uses, its completion was regarded as the initial step in a movement that is expected to bring similar accommodations to all the chief ports of the Ohio valley. Since that date several such terminals have been built.

Apropos to river terminals, "Steel," a statue seventy feet high by Frank Vittor of Pittsburgh, memorializing the part of iron and steel in our national development, was significant. This work was a present from the Jones and Laughlin Steel Company of Pittsburgh to the Sesqui-centennial Exposition at Philadelphia, 1926, commemorating one hundred fifty years of American independence. But it was more than a memorial – it was a prophet. Its pedestal carried in relief a modern railroad terminal in full operation in conjunction with a modern river levee. On a track above the latter were a railroad engine and a train of cars which were being

---

[464] — *Idem*, January 22, 1927.

loaded from barges by the use of a revolving crane. All seemed to suggest the possibility of an improved and enlarged transportation system in which railroads and rivers would supplement each other.

In anticipation of such a consummation a recent decision of the United States Supreme Court was heralded locally as the "most momentous good news affecting river transportation ever printed." [465] This decision grew out of a controversy between the New York Central railroad and the New York State Barge canal and conferred upon the Interstate Commerce Commission authority to require railroad companies to establish physical connections with waterways and to provide means for the interchange of freight. Inasmuch as this decision applied generally, it was predicted that its effects would be revolutionary.

Other recent developments were not without significance. Among these was a device for the use of pulverized coal as fuel, long experimented with but first successfully installed in 1927 on the stern-wheel towboat "Illinois" of the Mississippi Federal Barge line. From this one device great economies were predicted. Meanwhile successful experiments were being made with barges designed for combined river and ocean uses and with "car-floats" for combined river and land service. It was claimed that the use of such devices would tend to break down the barriers to a perfected transportation system to embrace the world.[466] To this possible end, as well as to facilitate local transportation, persons of vision urged a greater standardization of the locks and dams in use in the Ohio valley.

In anticipation of the possibilities of inland transportation numerous persons have tried to forecast the

[465] — *Idem*, February 5, 1927.   [466] — *Idem*, April 2, 1927.

future. Among other things they have predicted a commercial rivalry between Pittsburgh and Chicago in which each of these cities will be frequented at will by ocean-going vessels. With the completion of the proposed deep waterways between Lake Erie and Pittsburgh and between Lake Michigan and the Mississippi river their prophecies seemed assured. Inspired by their enthusiasm local prints have, for some time, carried illustrations of "Pittsburgh a Seaport," together with editorials on the impending commercial warfare between the "Smoky City" of the upper Ohio and the "Windy City" of the Middle West.[467]

Strange and impossible as these things may seem, the potentialities of improved river navigation are far reaching. As already shown in this chapter, it is transforming the life and industry of the Ohio and the Mississippi valleys. The extent of this metamorphosis will be determined, of course, by the extent of the improvements and the subsequent use of rivers. In the event that Lake Michigan and the Mississippi river are united by a canal, there are those who say that the entire Mississippi valley, including the Ohio valley, will be placed in an advantageous relationship, from a transportation standpoint, with the West coast and the Orient. The differential that developed in favor of the Atlantic coast states with the completion of the Panama canal will then, it is claimed, be neutralized. With conditions thus equalized central western producers will be able to enter into competition with eastern industry. The political, financial, and other results of such a change must remain, for the present, a matter of speculation.

---

[467] Pittsburgh *Press*, February 5, 1928. See also Pittsburgh *Post-Gazette*, December 9, 1927; *Waterways Journal*, April 3, 1926.

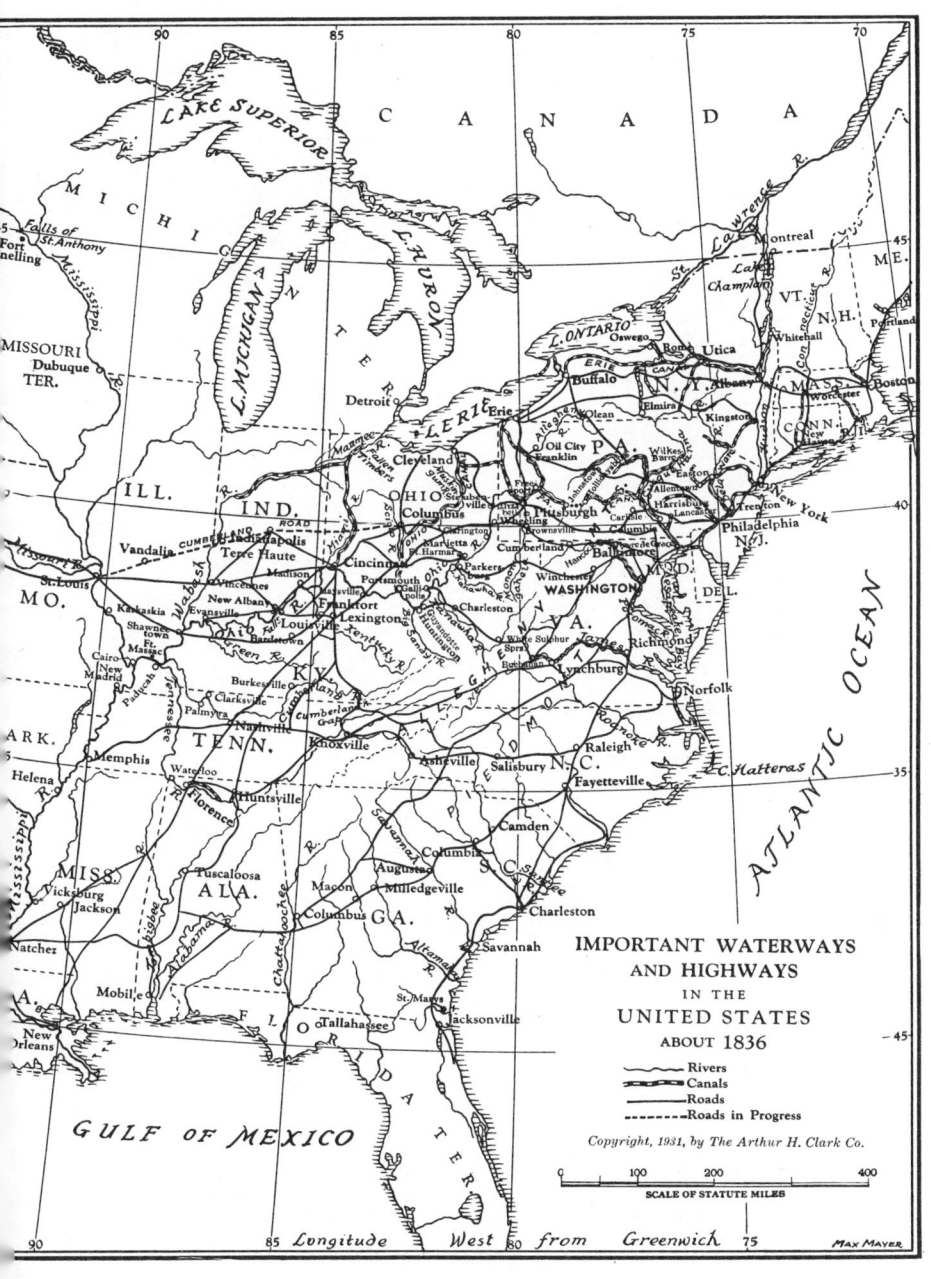

Index

Index

"Aetna": 124-125
Allegheny river: caste-bound population, 320; conquest by steamboats, 152; growth of exports, 165-166; ice, 22; too low, 49
"Allegheny": 152
"Alliquippa": see Jones and Laughlin Company
"America": 103, 386
American Barge line: 445-446; see also Kelley Barge line; Inland Waterways Corporation (Louisville)
American Steel and Wire Company: 438
"Amity": 88
"Annie Laurie": 389-390
"Ann Jane": 87-88
"A. O. Taylor": 242, 248
Arks: structure, 43-44
Atlantic Monthly: 266, 273
Ayer and Lord Barge Company: 351-352, 426

Baltimore and Ohio railroad: 142, 167, 358-359; connects with river traffic, 207-208; effects, 194; fight with Wheeling, 230; opening, 185-186; refuses to subsidize, 202-203
Barges: "barge age" arrives, 424-425, discussed, 272; "model," 208-209; structure, 43; substituted for coalboats, 306; use in iron and coal trade, 270-271; see also Booth (John K.); Coal; Gray (R. C.); Porter (John); Oil
Barnum, P. T: 324
"Baron De Kalb": 249
Barrett line: 351, 356, 423

Bay line: 352, 356
Baynton, Wharton, and Morgan Company: 32
Bedford-Lancaster pike: 140
"Belle Riviere, La": see Ohio river
Belle Transportation Company, La: see Wheeling Steel Company
"Ben Franklin": 159, 173
"Benton": 249
"Big Seven" line: see Colson line
Bixby, Horace: 196
Bixby, W. H: 376
Blennerhassett, Harman: 78
Boatmen: Allegheny crews, 166; Civil war secession attitude, 245, readjustments, 261-262, value in war, 248; coalboatmen, 302; crew of "New Orleans," 120; demands for on Ohio, 268; effects of river traffic decline, 199-201; effects of steamboats, 158; famous captains, 280; high quality, 294; life and social importance, 76-77; low wages change type, 366-367; packet crews, 45, 338-341, captains, 337-338, pilots, 337; precautions, 47-48; rivermen, 33; superstitions, 344; transform Ohio, 73; types of men, 49-58; see also Honshell (Captain); Kerr (Wash); Labor; Labor unions; Muhleman (Charles); Wages
Booth, John K: 270-271
"Braddock": see American Steel and Wire Company
Broad-horns: 49
Brown, William Hughey: 308-309
"Buckeye State": 174, 197
Budd (A. R.) Company: 349

"Buffalo": 125
Burr, Aaron: 77-79
Butler, General Richard: 394
Butler, William O: *The Boatman's Horn*, 52

"CAIRO": 249
Canals: dikes, 397; feeders to Ohio river from Atlantic, 147; Great Lakes-Mississippi canal plan, 103-104; Ohio to Lake Erie project, 141; routes, 148-149; Virginia interest, 68; Washington's proposals, 67-68; see also "George Abner Leacock"; "Hit and Miss"; Muskingum canal; Ohio and Lake Erie canal; Ohio canal; Pennsylvania canal; Portland canal
Canoes: age, 25; discarded, 29, 31; types and construction, 25-26; uses and users, 26-27
Cargoes: 153, 349-350; Civil war possibilities, 247-248, post-war trade, 259, southern necessities, 243; comparison of early and later, 106; early, 34; during 1787, 70; during 1854, 193; during panic of 1857, 208; effects of river traffic decline, 199; increase in bulk, 347; noted by "River Press," 267-268; of "Monongahela Farmer," 87; of new regions, 154; of Pittsburgh and Cincinnati Packet lines, 293; of "St. Clair," 86; of "White Collar" packets, 278; Ohio trade during 1786-1787, 65-66; Ohio-South trade, 240; on Allegheny, 165-166; on Mississippi during 1812, 79; on Ohio during 1845-1855, 172-173; Pittsburgh-Cumberland trade, 153; Pittsburgh to Philadelphia, 149; possibilities, 62; recent changes in commodities, 416, 429-430; storage, 47; supplied by wagon, 38; see also "Ann Jane"; "Amity"; Coal; Flour; Grain; Iron and steel; "John Farnum"; "Louisiana"; "Nanina"; Oil; "Pittsburgh"; Salt; Sand and gravel; Shipping lines; Trade and commerce; Traffic; "Western Trader"

Carnegie, Andrew: 320
Carnegie Steel Company: 434, 440
"Carondelet": 249
Carondolet Marine ways: 427
Carpenter and Talbott: 54
Central Ohio railroad: 203
"Century Tow," the: see Jones and Laughlin Company
Charleston (W. Va.): newspaper files, 13
"Chesapeake": 277
"Cheyenne": 388
Chicago: railroad center, 230; rivalry with Pittsburgh forecast, 448
"Chris Greene": see Greene line
Cincinnati: 64, 70, 249; attitude toward secession, 241; last river center, 196; municipal railroad, 235-238; "New Orleans" visits, 121; newspapers, 13; "Porkopolis" of west, 130; "Queen City," 172-173; railroad projects, 191-192; resumes river traffic lead, 266; rivalry with Louisville, 230-238; steamboat fire, 388; strategic position, 207
"Cincinnati": see Louisville and Cincinnati Packet line
Cincinnati *Commercial*: 49, 173, 204, 241, 243, 248, 272, 330
Cincinnati *Daily Enquirer*: 241
Cincinnati *Gazette*: 241, 246, 285, 305, 330, 390
Cincinnati *Enquirer*: 330
Cincinnati, Lexington, and East Tennessee railroad: 233
Cincinnati, Pomeroy, and Charleston Packet Company: 348
Cincinnati, Portsmouth, Big Sandy, and Pomeroy line: 277-278
Cincinnati *Railroad Record*: 192
Cincinnati Southern: 236

INDEX 453

Cist's Weekly Advertiser (Cincinnati): 104, 299
Civil war: 239-265; impending struggle hurts river trade, 201
Clark, George Rogers: 64
Clarksville: 64
Clement, Captain: 124
"Clermont": 110
Cleveland *Plain Dealer*: 174
"Clifton": 388
Clipper ships: 101
Coal: barges used, 306; Civil war trade, 310, effect on Union, 260, post-bellum trade, 313; Cincinnati receipts, 310; conservation, 314; decline of river traffic, 423; development during 1812, 297; discovery, 296; early transportation, 297-298; expansion, 299-300; factors causing growth, 298-299; first shipments, 296-297; fortunes made, 308; importance to navy, 309-310; increases in trade, 312; influence on cities, 295-296; long-distance trade, 306; mining industry improvements, 307; minor coal areas, 316; monopoly effects, 315; navigation restrictions, 311-312; Pittsburgh ceases to supply south, 317; Pittsburgh-New Orleans traffic, 305; prices cause river traffic decline, 205; prices reduced, 306; production figures, 299; production statistics, 1840-1860, 307; pulverized as fuel, 447; reasons for monopolies, 314-315; receipt records for 1886, 312; recent coal traffic, 318; Roosevelt opens mines on Ohio, 113; stimulates shipping, 260-261; traffic, 1906-1907, 316; value to Pittsburgh, 310-311; volume increases, 306; see also Brown (William Hughey); Coalboats; Cochran (Captain); "Crescent City"; Great Kanawha region; Monongahela River Consolidated Coal and Coke Company;

"Sprague"; Towboats; United States Coal and Oil Company
Coalboats: coalboatmen, 302; hazards, 302; structure, 300-301; use, 301-302; see also Towboats
Cochran, Captain: 305
Colson line: 283-284
"Comet": 125
"Conestoga": 248
Conestoga wagon: 34; construction, 37; contributions, 37-38; origin of name, 36
Confederacy tariff act of 1861: 242
Congressional Globe: 206
Cotton: contraband trade, 259; opens Mississippi, 259-260
"Crescent City": 305
Croghan, George: 31-32
Cramer, Zadok: 214-215; *Navigator*, 100, 115
Cullom report of 1886: 409
Cumberland and Tennessee Transportation Company: condition, 347
Cumberland Gap turnpike: 139
Cumberland (National) road: 134-137
Customs and life: Allegheny river inhabitants, 320-321; amusements, 324-327, on steamboats, 341-343; arrival of mail packet, 331-332; boat racing, 330; coalboatmen, 302; condition of packet employees, 337-341; cross section of Ohio river life, 329; Dickens's description of Ohio, 169; educational facilities, 322; extremes of wealth and culture, 321; gambling, 342; houseboat life, 322-323; in 1806, 73-76; in 1812, 79-80; merchant pedlers, 323-324; Monongahela river environment, 319; Ohio river during Civil war, 258-259; packet accommodations, 336; Pittsburgh in 1758, 28; reform movements, 326-327; river press and writers, 330-331; river songs and poets, 332-336; river superstitions, 343-

344; river supplies employment, 328; river towns, 58; shipbuilding broadens outlook, 98-99; steamboats as educational forces, 182-184; typical family travel, 144-147; wharf scene, 344-345; see also Boatmen; Showboats
Cutler, Manasseh: see Ohio Company

"Darling": 388
Davis Island dam: 408
"Dean": 97
Deep Waterways Convention: 413
De Hart, Captain: 124
Denison act: 440
Devol, Captain Jonathan: 86-87
Devol, Stephen: 85-86
Dickens, Charles: 168-169
Disasters: bridge piers, 386; construction of "New Orleans," 114-115; exploding boilers, 382-386; fire, 387-389; head-on collisions, 386-387; "New Orleans" maiden voyage, 123; "snags," "sawyers," "planters" and uncharted rivers, 46-47, 386; windstorms, 387; see also "America"; "Cheyenne"; "Clifton"; Coalboats; "Darling"; Disease; Floods; Ice; "John Lomas"; "Louisiana"; "May Irwin"; "Melnetto"; "Monongahela Farmer"; "Moselle"; "Rebecca"; "S c i o t o"; "Sultana"; "United States"; "Westmoreland"
Disease: 133; causes river traffic decline, 205; yellow fever and cholera, 389-390; see also "Annie Laurie"; "John Porter"; Laidley (Captain F. A.)
"Dispatch": 127
"Dorothy Barrett": see American Barge line
Dravo Contracting Company: 425-426
"Duncan Bruce," the: see American Barge line

Eads, James B: 249
"Eclipse": 177
Economic influences: after War of 1812, 101; banking systems, 94; causes of traffic decline, 201-208; causes of final river failure, 356-368; causes of 1882 river decline, 286-287; early Ohio detractions and attractions, 66-67; educational aspects of steamboats, 182-184; effects of canals, 143; effects of packet lines, 277-278; effects of river traffic decline, 198-201; effects of steam navigation on settlers, 129-131; effects of turnpikes, 139; exceptional conditions prevent Ohio decadence, 207-209; factors aiding remaining packet lines, 288; factors aiding steamboats, 284-285; factors delaying steamboating, 133; factors futhering shipbuilding, 85; forces unite to defeat steamboats, 209; Fulton's Ohio steamboat construction, 114; in 1805, 78-79; industries created by steamboats, 164; industries fostered by shipping, 103-104; influences causing decline of shipping, 106; Louisiana Purchase unites Ohio, 94; New Orleans Embargo of 1802, 93; opposition to canals, 151; panic of 1819, 133; steamboats aid exploration, 154, dominate Ohio life, 181-182
Elizabeth (Penn.): 34, 181; first ship-yard, 83
Ellet, Captain Charles: 399; flood control of 1852, 376; see also Ram fleet
Ellis, Captain Ira: 101
England: discovers Ohio river, 24; plans for Ohio, 28; takes Ohio valley, 31-32; Treaty of 1794, 71
"Enterprise": 125
"Eruktor Amphibolis": 109
"Essex": 249
Evans, Oliver: 109

INDEX   455

Evansville, Paducah, and Cairo Packet line: 348
Everett, Edward: 244
Express: 162

"FAIR PLAY": 257
"Falls City": 195
Father Abraham's Almanac: 81
Federal Barge line: 365, 426, 440, 443
Finance: Bank of Pennsylvania, 94; banking system spreads, 94
Fink, Mike: 53-58
Finley, J. B: see Monongahela River Consolidated Coal and Coke Company
Fitch, John: 108-109
Flatboats: 31; structure, 41-42; unique devices, 38; unique services, 74
Floods: control and prevention, 376-380, reforestation, 377-378, storage reservoirs, 378-380; damages, 375; Ohio flood causes, 369-370, dates, 373, impressions of 1884 disaster, 374, kinds, 371, 20, records of 1832, 373, records of 1884 and 1913, 371-372, stages, 371
Flour: 199
Fluger, Colonel: 54
Fort Stanwix, Treaty: 33
France: claims Ohio river, 27; Ohio experiments, 63
"Francis": 97
Franklin Institute *Journal*: 399
Franks (David) and Company: 32
Franquelin (geographer): 24
French, John: 109
Frick, H. C: 320
Fulton, Robert: 109-110; Ohio operations, 111-112

GALLATIN: *Preliminary Report*, 99, 394-395
Galley bateaux: 29, 32; structure, 44
"George Abner Leacock": 149
"George M. Bibb": 182

"George T. Price": see American Barge line
Good Intent: 162
Government aid: 395; Allegheny river improvements, 411; Cincinnati municipal railroad asks, 237; dam structures, *footnote*, 421-422; Erie canal improvement by New York, 412; federal barge line possibilities, 444-446; flood control and prevention, 379-380; Granger movement, 405; Lincoln's southern railroad plans, 234; locks and dams, 151; Memphis convention proposals, 171; moveable dam, 406-408; neutrality enforced, 247; Ohio congressional appropriations, 403, 410, improvements, 156, 396-397, 416-422, national project, 396-397, state project, 395-396, locks and dams, 354, plans, 141-142, "pork barrel" policies, 405; petitions for, 71-72; Pittsburgh roads and canals, 212; Portland canal enlargement, 404; vessels armed, 84; Wheeling bridge, 214-217; see also Canals; Cumberland road; Davis Island dam; Improvements; *Interstate Commerce Act of 1887*; Regulations; *River and Harbor act of 1910; Windom report*
"Grace Darling": 103
Graham (Emma) Packet Company: 291-292
Grain: 350
Granger movement: 405
Gray, R. C: 272
Great Kanawha region: 316; importance to Ohio river, 151-152
Great Miami: 64
"Great Republic": 269
Greene, Gordon B: see Greene line
Greene line: 348, 356, 442
"Greenwood": 257-258
Gunboats: advocated on Ohio, 248; inland fleet lacks cooperation, 253; purchased by Union, 248; struc-

ture, 249; Union fleet and Western Flotilla, 250; see also "A. O. Taylor"; "Baron De Kalb"; "Benton"; "Cairo"; "Carondelet"; "Cincinnati"; "Conestoga"; "Essex"; "Fair Play"; "Lexington"; "Louisville"; "Manayunk"; "Marietta"; "Merrimac"; "Monitor"; "Mound City"; Navy; "Pittsburgh"; Porter (Admiral David D.); Ram fleet; "Sandusky"; "St. Louis"; "Umpqua"

"G. Washington": 127, 129

"G. W. Kendall": 173

HEPBURN ACT: 360
"Hit and Miss": 149
Holmes, Captain W. L: 199-201
Honshell, Captain: 278-279
Howard, James: 274-275
Howard, John: 26
Howard ship-yards: 426
Hunt's Merchants' Magazine: 193, 244, 306

ICE: 21-22; cause of river traffic decline, 204; dates of Ohio ice floes, 380; destroys remaining Ohio shipping, 355; effects of ice floes, 381; Ohio ice floe of 1918, 381-382
Immigration: aids packets and steamboats, 173, 284; effect of coal, 299; lull during 1855, 201; routes of entrance, 65; stimulated by steamboats, 130; suffers losses on Ohio, 396; Trans-alleghany, 59; westward sweep, 166-168; see also Settlers
Improvements: Allegheny, 411; beacon-lights, 404; conflicting theories, 401-403; dam structures, *footnote*, 421-422; delays in river improvement, 415-416; Erie canal improved by New York, 412; international interest, 411-412; *Interstate Commerce act of 1887* stops river improvement, 408-409; Lake Erie drainage, 404; moveable dam, 406-408; national interest, 412-415; navigation of inland waters, 352; Ohio river appropriation from congress, 403, 410, improvements, 156, 395-397, 416, 422; Ohio Valley Improvement Association continues, 409-410; Pittsburgh centennial celebration and "Marine Day," 353; plans abandoned, 356, fail, 404-405, of Butler (General Richard), 394, of Ellet (Charles), 399, of Gay (Edward F.), 400-401, of Haupt (Herman), 398, of Livermore (Alonzo), 398-399, of Roberts (W. Milnor), 400, of Washington (George), 393-394; Portland canal enlargement, 404; see also Davis Island dam; Gallatin's *report*; Government aid; Granger movement; Inland Waterways Commission; Ohio Valley Improvement Association; *River and Harbor act of June 25, 1910*; *Windom report*

"Illinois": 177-178
Illinois State Journal: 244
Independent Packet line: 441
"Indian Country": opened by congress, 69
Indians: 28, 32; attack boats, 46
Inland Waterways Commission: 354, 376, 413
Inland Waterways Corporation (Louisville): 444-445
Insurance: 390; packets, 45
Interstate Commerce act of 1887: 286; government to regulate railroads for public, 408
Interstate Commerce Commission: 317, 440, 442
Inventors: see Evans (Oliver); Fitch (John); French (John); Fulton (Robert); Livingston (Robert); Longstreet (William); Mowry (Captain Samuel); Ormsbee (Elijah); Ramsey (William);

INDEX 457

Reed (Nathan); Rees (James); Roosevelt (Nicholas J.); Rumsey (James); Starr (Jehosephat); Stevens (John); West (Edward)
Iron and steel: 153, 173, 351; building material, 158; important cargo, 208
Iron line: 272

JACOBY, Wilmer M: 444
James river and Kanawha turnpike: 138-139
"Jefferson": 182
"J. M. White": 178; Howards' craft, 276
Johnboats: 44
"John Farnum": 103
"John Lomas": 386
"John Porter": 389
"John Simonds": 178
"John Swasey": 104
Jones and Laughlin Company: 434-437, 446
"Juniata": see American Steel and Wire Company
Jutte, Charles: 314
Jutte (Charles) and Company: 349

"KATE Adams": 276
Keelboats: decline of, 162; navigation, 43; number used, 48; structure, 42
Kelley Barge line: 445
Kelly (W. C.) Company: 365
"Kenton": 266-267
Kentucky: 65, 231; see also Regulations
Kentucky Central railroad: 233, 238
Kerr, Wash: 279
King, William: 178-179
Knowles, Morris: 376
Knox, M. G: 275

LABOR: coal relieves unemployment, 307; employees in 1880 on steamboats, 285; recent barge construction, 425-426; see Boatmen; Customs and life; Labor unions; Wages
Labor unions: pilot organizations, 341, 404
Laidley, Captain F. A: 390
Lake Erie canal: 141-142
Lakes-to-Gulf Waterways Association: 412
Larges and Wiegels: 275
La Salle, René, Robert Cavalier, *Sieur* de: 24
Ledlie (Geo.) and Co: 305
"Lexington": 248
Liberty Transit Company: 441, 442
Licenses: 205
Lightning line: 196
Lighton, M. O: 376
Lincoln, Abraham: 234
Little Miami: 189
Liverpool *Saturday Advertiser*: 97
Livingston, Robert: 109
Lloyd: *Steamboat Directory and Disasters on the Western Waters*, 206, 382
Lloyd, Black, and Brown: see William Hughey Brown
Logan, Lineas: 170
London *Times*: 102
Longstreet, William: 109
"Louisa": 104
"Louisiana" (Louisiana of Marietta): 89-90
Louisiana Purchase: 93-94; need of, 72
Louisville: 64; busiest Ohio city during Civil war, 246; lines to Pittsburgh, 162; "New Orleans" honored, 122; population increase, 156; rivalry with Cincinnati, 230-238; strategic position, 207
"Louisville": 249
Louisville and Cincinnati Packet Company: 348, 441, 443; sole palatial packets, 351; lines, 159, 163, 277, 288
Louisville and Nashville railroad: 232, 235, 359

458 TRANSPORTATION IN THE OHIO VALLEY

Louisville *Courier*: 195
Louisville *Courier Journal*: 330
"Lovin' Kate": 276

MAIL LINE: see Louisville and Cincinnati Packet line
Mail lines: continue by water, 265; during Indian wars, 71; early packet lines, 45; importance, 331; on Ohio, 139; pass over Cumberland road, 138; postmaster endorces Wheeling bridge proposal, 216; postoffices, 332; see also Ohio and Mississippi Mail line; Shipping lines and owners; United States Mail
"Manayunk": 256
Marietta: 70, 101-103; leading shipbuilder, 85
"Marietta": 102, 256
Marietta Manufacturing Company: 426
Marietta Ship Company: 101
Marine ways (Cincinnati): 275
"Mary Belle Roberts": 105
May, Captain: 46
"Mayflower": 70
"May Irwin": 388
"Melnetto": 388
Memphis Convention: 171
Merrill, Major W. E: 376
"Merrimac": 250
"Messenger": 174
Miami canal: 142
Miami Exporting Company: 93
Michaux: *Travels*, 90
"Michigan": 182
"Midas": 173
"Minnesota": 105
Mississippi Marine Brigade: 253
Missouri: conquest by steamboat, 154-155
"Monitor": 249
Monongahela Consolidated Coal and Coke Company: 314-315, 349
"Monongahela Farmer": 87
Monongahela river: boatbuilding, 34; ice, 22; industrial territory, 319
Monopolies: Fulton-Roosevelt Ohio steamboat plans, 112; independents obtain rights, 125, 128; line rivalry stimulates enterprise, 177; Pittsburgh interest in free passage, 218; pooling arrangements, 277, 292; railroad consolidation damages packets, 362; see also Fitch (John); Jutte (Charles); Monongahela Consolidated Coal and Coke Company; Ohio and Mississippi Mail line; Shipping lines and owners; Standard Oil Company
"Moselle": 385
"Mound City": 249
Mowry, Captain Samuel: 109
Muhleman, Charles: 144-147
Municipal rivalry: 149, 189, 201, 211-239; Cincinnati-Louisville rivalry, 230-238, 246-247; history, 211; Pittsburgh-Wheeling rivalry, 150, 212-230
"Muskingum": 102
Muskingum canal: 142

NASHVILLE Bridge Company: 426
"Natchez": 275; boats, 180
National Rivers and Harbors Congress: 412, 414
National Waterways: 15
Navy: 83; given control of inland fleet, 253; importance of coal, 309-310; importance of transports, 256-257; reorganized, 254; siege of Vicksburgh, 254-256; success during Civil war, 253-254; use of convoys, 257; see also Gunboats
Negroes: cause strikes, 262
Neville, Morgan: 54
New Orleans: 84; coal trade with Pittsburgh, 305; port of entry, 167
"New Orleans": 353; launching and maiden voyage, 116-124
New Orleans *Bulletin*: 305
New Orleans Embargo: 99-100

INDEX 459

New York *Courier*: 228
Northwestern turnpike: 138
Northwest Territory: 69

OGDEN, Captain: 124
"Ohio": 97, 103
Ohio and Mississippi Mail line: 163; maintains steamboat connections, 207; railroad, 203
Ohio canal: 142
Ohio Company: 70, 92, 94
Ohio Pilot: 162
Ohio river: "Beautiful River," 17; beauty, 19; "coalboat stage," 295; discovery, 23-24; early appearance, 24-25; fear loss through Civil war, 244; losses due to dangers, 396; low and high water marks, 369; merits of Pittsburgh and Wheeling locations, 213; navigation improved, 156; origin of name, 21; physical facts, 19-20; "Poor Man's Highway," 265; poor navigation causes river failure, 368; possibilities, 62; secession attitude, 241-242; thoroughfare east and west, 17; tributaries, 19, 22; valley, 22-23, in 1780, 64, loyal to Union, 243-244; see also Croghan (George); Floods; Ice; Improvements
Ohio Steam Navigation Company: 114
Ohio Valley Improvement Association: 352, 409-410, 414
Oil: 439-440; barges used, 271
Ordinance of 1787: 69
Ormsbee, Elijah: 109
Overland traffic: volume on turnpikes in 1817, 140-141; see also Conestoga wagon; Cumberland road; Pack-trains; Railroads; Stage-coaches; Traffic; Turnpikes

PACKETS: schedule, 44-45; structure, 44; see also Shipbuilding; Shipping lines and owners

Pack-trains: business, 35; progress, 36; reach upper Ohio, 28; routes, 35
Panic of 1857: 207
Parkersburg: 207
Passengers: change to railroads, 197; first railroad, 185; immigrant travel, 173; influence on packets, 166; "New Orleans," 124; of 1787, 70; Ohio 1787 average, 65-66; packet lines, 45; Pittsburgh-Cumberland route, 153; stage-coaches, 137; statistics for 1905, 347; see also Shipping lines and owners; Traffic
Passports: 84
Pennsylvania: 63
"Pennsylvania": 194
Pennsylvania canal: 147-148
Pirates: attack boats, 46; half-breed renegades of Cave-in-Rock (Ill.), 46
Pittsburgh: 64, 84; assumes new life, 149; celebrates steam navigation, 353; coal navigation freedom demanded, 311-312, output used locally, 317, shipments, 296-297, trade influences, 295, value as industry, 310-311; customs, 28; English fail, 29; lines to Louisville, 162; lines to St. Louis, 162; named by English, 28; "New Orleans" leaves, 120-121; newspapers, 13; population, 28; port survey for 1840, 168; railroad construction, 192; rivalry with Chicago forecast, 448; rivalry with Wheeling, 212-230; shipbuilding center, 32, 34, 88; see also Municipal rivalry
"Pittsburgh": 88, 249
Pittsburgh *Advocate and Advertiser*: 167
Pittsburgh and Cincinnati Packet line: 170-171, 197, 292-293, 348; famous ships and captains, 194; greatest success, 194; reasons for success, 293-294; see also "Buckeye

State"; "Messenger"; Shipping lines and owners
Pittsburgh *Chronicle-Telegraph*: 331
Pittsburgh *Gazette*: 126, 150, 153, 305, 331
Pittsburgh *Times*: 331
Pittsburgh *Tree of Liberty*: 90
Pittsburgh, Wheeling, and Parkersburg Packet line: 349
Pleasureboats: see showboats
"Plymouth": see American Barge line
Pollock, William S: 443
"Polly": 84
Population: 80; by 1800, 73; in 1775, 63; in Kentucky, 65; Louisville growth, 156; Pittsburgh in 1760, 28
Portage Railroad: 185
Porter, Admiral David D: 249-250
Porter, John: 271
Portland canal: 156, 397
Prentiss, David: 126
"President Adams": 84
Putnam, Rufus: see Ohio Company

QUEEN and Crescent: see Cincinnati Southern

RAILROADS: advertise, 360; break down under World war stress, 424; cause river improvement failure, 404-405; cause river traffic decline, 202-204, 358-363; cause shipping decline since 1882, 286; Cincinnati-Louisville rivalry, 231-238; consolidate, 360; early projects, 189-193; effects on packets, 277-278; first rail reaches Pittsburgh, 185; obstacles, 191-192; Ohio "railroad mania," 186-189; Pittsburgh-Wheeling rivalry, 228-230; replace river traffic during Civil war, 246; supersede river traffic completely, 197-201; tributaries to river traffic, 161, 193; Virginia refuses charter, 229; see also Baltimore and Ohio; Central Ohio; Cincinnati, Lexington, and East Tennessee; Cincinnati Southern; Kentucky Central; Little Miami; Louisville and Nashville; Ohio and Mississippi; Municipal rivalry; Portage Railroad; Rates; Regulations; Strader (Jacob); Taft (Alphonso); Traffic
Ram fleet: 251-253
Ramsey, William: 38
Rates: cut by monopolies, 163-164; decline, 158; excursions on packets, 288; increase, 193-194; lines regulate, 162; "New Orleans," 124; passenger fares on Pittsburgh and Cincinnati Packet line, 293; Pittsburgh to Cumberland, 153; prorating, 360-361, 442; railroads, 359, 362-363, compete with steamboats, 286; reduced during panic of 1857, 207; see also Economic influences; *Interstate Commerce act of 1887*; Interstate Commerce Commission
"Rebecca": 386
Redstone (Brownsville): 64
Reed, Nathan: 109
Rees, James: 273-274
Rees (James) and Sons Company: 274, 425
Regulations: cotton causes free-trade, 259-260; debt limit of Ohio, 232; early international treaties, 71; Fulton patents, 113, tested by Shreve as monopolies, 126; inspection of packets, 368, 385; Kentucky charters railroads, 231-232, challenges Cincinnati, 238; lack of railroad rate regulations, 360; licenses, 385; New Orleans embargoes, 84, 93; New York Central-New York State Barge canal decision, 447; Ohio navigation restrictions, 311-312; oil transportation limited, 271; Pennsylvania refuses railroad extension, 185; ports of entry, 70-71; river-railroad traffic in coal regulated, 317; seces-

sion threatens free navigation, 239; shipping regulations during Civil war, 247; "St. Clair" avoids, 86; Virginia railroad interests, 213, 229; west refuses railroad charters, 190; see also *Hepburn act*; Interstate Commerce Commission; Licenses; Passports
Revolutionary war: inland boat services, 64; Ohio privateers, 64
Rhea, Captain Isaac T: 291
Rice, Dan: 324
Richmond *Enquirer*: 196
River and Harbor act of 1910: 414
River Combine (Combine): see Monongahela River Consolidated Coal and Coke Company
River press: causes river traffic decline, 206; comments on post-war conditions, 267-268; importance of newspapers to river life, 331; writers and publications, 330-331
"Robert E. Lee": 275
"Robert Hall": 97
Roberts, W. Milnor: 376
Roosevelt, Nicholas J: 109; surveys western rivers, 113
Roosevelt, Mrs. Nicholas J: 120
Roosevelt, Theodore: attitude toward river navigation, 413-414
Rumsey, James: 68, 108-109
Ryman line: 348

"SALEM": 104
Salt: 151; pack-train cargo, 36
Sand and gravel: 350
"Sandusky": 256
"Scioto": 386
"Senator Ross": 84
Settlers: enter Ohio in 1765, 29-31; move westward, 33-34; see also Immigration; Population
Shipbuilding: 33, 38-41, 64, 152; adapt craft to trade, 351; barge construction recently, 425-429; best types uncertain, 364-366; builders, 103, from New England, 83; clip-

per use, 101; coal-pushing packets, 304-305; comparison of building periods, 106; competition with coast builders, 104; construction improvements, 179-180; designs improved, 166; during Civil war, 256; economic influences, 85; effects of barges, 272-273; factors killing, 100; first sea-going vessels, 83-84; first ship-yard, 83; "floating palaces," 194; Franklin's suggestion, 82; Fulton's Ohio plan, 112; gradual decline, 105; inadequate, 81; increase during 1864-1865, 265; iron hulls and ships, 158-159, 182; landing improvements, 157; luxuries, 193; maintained at Wheeling, 208; materials in Ohio, 83; modern improvements, 269-270, 428-429; "New Orleans" construction controversy, 118-119; number of boats from 1830-1840, 161-162; packet accommodations, 336; profitable industry, 90; pulverized coal as fuel, 447; retarded by Spain, 84; river vessels unsatisfactory, 90-91; second high period, 103; services, 61; shipbuilding centers, 97; showboat construction, 326; steamboats adapted to cargoes, 170-171, earliest, 108, European influence, 110, first Ohio-built, 114-116, improvements, 156-157, increase, 161, type change by coal towing, 304, trans-Atlantic, 161; trade designs, 268; value on Ohio during 1800-1808, 98; waning interest, 100; see also "Aetna"; "Allegheny"; "America"; "Amity"; "Ann Jane"; Arks; Ayer and Lord Marine ways; Barges; Baynton, Wharton, and Morgan; Broad-horns; "Buffalo"; Canoes; Carondolet Marine ways; "Clermont"; Coal; Coalboats; "Comet"; "Dean"; Devol (Stephen); "Dispatch"; Dravo Contracting Company; Eads (James B.); "Eclipse"; Elizabeth (Penn.); Ellis (Captain Ira); "Enterprise"; "Eruktor Amphibolis"; "Falls City"; Flatboats; "Francis"; Gallatin; Galley bateaux; "George M. Bibb"; "Grace Darling"; "Great Republic"; Gunboats; "G. Washington"; Howard (James); Howard ship-yards; "Illinois"; Inventors; "Jefferson"; "J. M. White"; Johnboats; "John Farnum"; "John Simonds"; "John Swasey"; Keelboats; Kelly (W. C.); King (William); Knox (M. G.); Larges and Wiegels; Ledlie (Geo.) and Co.; "Louisa"; "Louisiana"; "Marietta"; Marietta Manufacturing Company; Marine ways; "Michigan"; "Minnesota"; "Monongahela Farmer"; Monongahela river; "Muskingum"; "Nanina"; Nashville Bridge Company; "Natchez"; "New Orleans"; "Ohio"; Ohio Steam Navigation Company; Packets; "Pennsylvania"; Pittsburgh; "Pittsburgh"; "Polly"; Prentiss (David); "President Adams"; Rees (James); Rees (James); Rees (James) and Sons Company; Redstone; Regulations; "Robert E. Lee"; "Robert Hall"; "Salem"; "Senator Ross"; Shipping lines and owners; Shreve (Captain Henry M.); Skiffs; Sligo mills; "Sprague"; "St. Clair"; Steamboats; Swasey (John); Sweeney (A. J. and J. M.); Tarascon Brothers, Berthoud and Company; Thorn and Company; Towboats; "Valley Forge"; "Vesuvius"; "Walhoning"; Walker (John); Ward (Charles); Ward (Charles) Engineering works; "Western Trader"; White (George); "Wild Wagoner"; "Wm. D. Duncan"; "Zebulon M. Pike"

Shipping lines and owners: attitude of executives, 174; captains, 280; coal lines and operators, 313; corporate ownership, 352; damage prosecutions, 387; decline since 1882, 286; first-class tonnage, 442-443; Fulton-Roosevelt interests, 112-127; line agreements, 162; scarcity, 433-434, survivors, 356; packet lines, 138, names, 283; races revived, 443, records, 276-277; pooling arrangements, 292; private fleet values, 434; profits until 1840, 159-160; rivalry, 174; shipping-industry alliance, 434-438; smaller lines, 159; Smith (Samuel) independent interests, 125-126; steamship lines fail, 355; survivors of decline, 288; traffic created by railroads, 194-195; transition to railroads, 197-201; "way charges" exorbitant, 367; see also Ayer and Lord Barge Company; Barrett line; Bay line; Budd (A. R.) Company; Carnegie Steel Company; Cincinnati, Pomeroy, and Charleston Packet Company; Cincinnati, Portsmouth, Big Sandy, and Pomeroy line; Colson line; Cumberland and Tennessee Transportation Company; Evansville, Paducah, and Cairo Packet line; Express; Federal Barge line; Good Intent; Graham (Emma) Packet Company; Gray (R. C.); Greene (Captain Gordon C.); Greene line; Honshell (Captain); Independent Packet line; Inland Waterways Corporation (Louisville); Insurance; Iron line; Jones and Laughlin Company; Jutte (Charles) and Company; Kelley Barge line; Kerr (Wash); Liberty Transit Company; Lightning line; Logan (Lineas); Louisville and

INDEX

Cincinnati Packet line; Marietta Ship Company; Miami Exporting Company; Monongahela Consolidated Coal and Coke Company; Monopolies; "Natchez" boats; Ohio Company; Ohio Pilot; Pittsburgh and Cincinnati Packet line; Pittsburgh, Wheeling, and Parkersburg Packet line; Rhea (Captain Isaac T.); Ryman line; Shipbuilding; Standard Oil Company; Steamboats; St. Louis and Tennessee River Packet Company; Strader (P. Wilson); Tennessee Navigation Company; Traffic; Tupper (E. W.); Union line; United States Mail; Wheeling Steel Company; White Collar line

Showboats: 183, 324-327
Shreve, Captain Henry M: 125
Skiffs: structure, 44
Slavery: 102-103; related to packet lines, 196; uneconomic in Ohio, 243
Sligo mills: 256
Smith, Samuel: 125
Spain: Treaty of 1795, 71
"Sprague": 315-316
Stage-coaches: lines, vehicles, drivers, 137
Standard Oil Company: 271, 427, 439; employs coalboats, 317
Starr, Jehosaphat: 109
"St. Clair"; 86
Steamboats: "comeback" after Civil war, 266-267; conquest of Allegheny, 152, Cumberland, 153, Missouri, 154; descend Mississippi, 107; difficulties during Civil war, 257-258; European influence, 110; Ohio-built steamboats, 114-116; start in 1811, 48; Tidewater navigation, 110; upstream navigation, 61; use in demobilization, 262; vessels plying on Great Kanawha and Ohio, 152; see also "Greenwood"; "Kenton"
"Steel": 446-447

Stevens, John: 109
St. Louis: lines to Pittsburgh, 162; steamboat center, 230
"St. Louis": 249
St. Louis and Tennessee River Packet Company: 291, 347
St. Louis Internal Improvement Convention: 412
Strader, Jacob: 189
Strader, P. Wilson: 170
"Sultana": 262-263
Swasey, John: 104
Sweeney, A. J. and John M: 275
Symmes, John Cleves: 70

Taft, Judge Alphonso: 415; projects proposed, 189-191
Taft, William Howard: 415
Tarascon Brothers, Berthoud and Company: 88
Tariff: free-trade policy of secessionists, 242; south forgets free-trade promise, 242-243; see also "A. O. Taylor"; Regulations
Tennessee Navigation Company: 291
Thorn (James) and Company: 274
Tobacco: 259
"Tom Greene": see Greene line
Totten, Colonel Joseph G: 247
Towboats: "pushed" instead of "towed," 304; replace coalboats, 303; see also Coalboats
Trade and commerce: 33; Allegheny river outputs, 320; canals and railroads revolutionize, 239; competition from motorboats, 367-368; contraband cotton running, 259; credit lacking, 91; declining interest in navigation freedom, 312; decrease in steamboat traffic, 198-201; difficulties during Civil war, 243-244; effects on secession, 240-241; foreign demand for goods, 103; freight by rail congested, 234; international success, 82; Monongahela river outputs, 319; New Orleans freight receipts, 130; Ohio

freight shipments during 1850-1860, 181-182; Ohio-South traffic revives, 240; Ohio transportation decline, 354; passing of passenger packets, 196-197; post-war conditions, 262; profit from steamboat lines until 1840, 159-160; river transportation revives, 265-294; river combine shipments, 351; steamboat on lower Ohio, 196; time of navigation shortened, 158; typical voyage of "Louisiana," 89-90; unusual trade methods, 92; volume of Wheeling freight in 1822, 138; world plans, 62-63; see also Cargoes; Economic influences; Traffic

Traffic: advantages of renewed shipping, 441; amount and value on Ohio during 1880, 285, on water from 1800-1807, 73; changed character of shipping, 440; coal traffic from 1906-1907, 316; counter forces, 442-443; "cut-throat" competition since 1882, 286; decline of river traffic, 198; during 1788, 70; early river increases, 29; fluctuates with river condition, 398; government traffic possibilities, 444; Ohio river averages for 1785-1787, 65, between 1900-1906, 351, canal effects, 143-144, during Civil war, 247-248, failure, 355, increase between 1845-1855, 172-173, increase on upper, 164; Pennsylvania canal, 148; Pittsburgh port survey of 1840, 168; Portland canal, 162; private traffic amount, 443-444; river by 1917, 423, regulated, 317, relieves railroads during World war, 424, reverses, 442, suited to changed commodities, 433, unites north and south, 239-240; shipping-industry combination, 438-439; steamboats on Ohio in 1835, 159; suspended during Civil war, 245; terminals, 446-447; tributary traffic during 1840, 164-165; volume in early years, 97; western possibilities, 448; see also Cargoes; *Denison act*; Economic influences; Passengers; Railroads; Regulations; Shipping lines and owners; "Steel"; Trade and commerce

Trans-alleghany: sale of lands, 65
"Transporter": see Wheeling Steel Company
Tupper, E. W: see "Louisiana"
Turnpikes: 138-140
Twain, Mark: *Life on the Mississippi*, 196, 341

"UMPQUA": 256
Union line: 194-195; appeals to south, 196
"United States": 386
United States Coal and Oil Company (Holden, W. Va.): 317
United States Constitution: commercial significance, 68; ratification, 69
United States Mail: 162
United States Steel Corporation: 363

"VALLEY FORGE": 182
Vance, Colonel John L: 409-410
Vandalia: 62
"Vesuvius": 124
Virginia: 65-68; refuses railroad charter, 229
Vittor, Frank: 446

WAGES: coalboat crews, 260-261; deckhands, 328; low in interior river trade, 366; low pay favors packet lines, 284; pack-train drivers, 35; pilots' associations' work, 341; salaries of crews, 285; strikes, 262; see also Boatmen; Labor; Labor unions
"Walhoning": 103
Walker, John: 83, 84, 87, 92; see also Elizabeth (Penn.)

INDEX

Ward, Charles: 365
Ward (Charles) Engineering works: 426
"W. A. Shepherd": see American Barge line
Washington, George: 67, 393-394
Waterways Journal (St. Louis): 13, 434
Way, Frederick Jr: 443
Wells, Captain William R: 102
West, Edward: 108-109
"Western Trader": 89
"Westmoreland": 388
West Virginia: 62
Wheeling: 64; entrance of railroad, 185-186; newspaper files, 13; rivalry with Pittsburgh, 212-230; river center, 138
Wheeling and Belmont Bridge Company: 219; see also Wheeling Bridge Company
Wheeling bridge: Congress rider to Post Office Appropriation bill, 227; construction by private company, 219; destroyed by storm, 228; opening, 220-221; opinions concerning, 223; rebuilt, 228; supreme court decision, 223-226; see also Government aid; Improvements; Pittsburgh; Wheeling; Wheeling Bridge Company
Wheeling Bridge Company: 214
Wheeling *Intelligencer*: 197, 228, 230, 285
Wheeling Steel Company: 434, 437
Whipple, Commodore Abraham: 86
White Collar line: 180, 288, 348; packets, 278-279; see also Cincinnati, Portsmouth, Big Sandy, and Pomeroy line
White, George: 127
Wierton Steel Company: 446
"Wild Wagoner": 261
Williamson, Captain J. N: 291
"Willing" (galley bateau): 64
Windom report: 405-407
"Wm. D. Duncan": 152
Wood, Abraham: 24

ZANE, Ebenezer: see Ohio Company
"Zebulon M. Pike": 126-127